Aristotle's Ethics as First Philosophy

In *Aristotle's Ethics as First Philosophy,* Claudia Baracchi demonstrates the indissoluble links between practical and theoretical wisdom in Aristotle's thinking. Referring to a broad range of texts from the Aristotelian corpus, Baracchi shows how the theoretical is always informed by a set of practices and, specifically, how one's encounter with phenomena, the world, or nature in the broadest sense is always a matter of *ethos.* Such a "modern" intimation is shown to be found at the heart of Greek thought. Baracchi's book opens the way for a comprehensively reconfigured approach to classical Greek philosophy.

Claudia Baracchi is Professor of Moral Philosophy at the Università di Milano-Bicocca, Italy. The author of *Of Myth, Life, and War in Plato's* Republic, she is the co-founder of the Ancient Philosophy Society.

Aristotle's Ethics as First Philosophy

CLAUDIA BARACCHI
New School for Social Research

CAMBRIDGE UNIVERSITY PRESS
Cambridge, New York, Melbourne, Madrid, Cape Town,
Singapore, São Paulo, Delhi, Tokyo, Mexico City

Cambridge University Press
32 Avenue of the Americas, New York, NY 10013-2473, USA

www.cambridge.org
Information on this title: www.cambridge.org/9781107400511

First published 2008
Reprinted 2009
First paperback edition 2011

A catalog record for this publication is available from the British Library.

Library of Congress Cataloging in Publication Data

Baracchi, Claudia, 1962–
Aristotle's ethics as first philosophy / Claudia Baracchi.
p. cm.
Includes bibliographical references and index.
ISBN 978-0-521-86658-3 (hardback)
1. Aristotle. 2. Ethics. 3. First philosophy. I. Title.
b491.e7b37 2007
185–dc22 2007013966

ISBN 978-0-521-86658-3 hardback
ISBN 978-1-107-40051-1 Paperback

Le vicende trovano la soluzione
le ipotesi tagliano il traguardo
le strategie rilanciano la luce
i meccanismi conservano le ali
i secoli sono vivi

–Roberto Alperoli

Contents

Acknowledgments

I began writing this work during the academic year 2003/4. The project was generously supported by an American Council of the Learned Societies/Andrew W. Mellon Fellowship.

I wish to thank wholeheartedly my colleagues and students at the New School for Social Research for their trust, enthusiastic support, and tireless inspiration. In particular, I am grateful to Ben Grazzini, Fanny Söderbäck, and Chris Roberts for their careful assistance at various stages of the elaboration of the manuscript.

My gratitude goes also to Beatrice Rehl, at Cambridge University Press, for believing in this work from the start, and to Stephanie Sakson for her editorial contribution.

Dulcis in fundo, thanks to Michael Schober, for his fantastic friendship.

Castelvetro (Modena, Italy)
January 2007

Introduction

1. ON ETHICS AS FIRST PHILOSOPHY

By reference to the ethical treatises and the *Politics*, but also to other texts of the Aristotelian *corpus* (most notably, the *Metaphysics* and the treatises of the *Organon*), the present study undertakes to demonstrate the indissoluble intertwinement of practical and theoretical wisdom (*phronēsis* and *sophia* as well as, concomitantly, *praxis* and *theōria*) in Aristotle's thinking. In this manner, I propose that *sophia*, theoretical wisdom, far from an autonomous and separate pursuit, should be acknowledged as integrally involved in becoming, sensibility, experience, and, hence, action. Of course, this line of inquiry cannot but address critically the established view of the separation, indeed the opposition of the two modes of reason. Such a dichotomous logic is retained even by those who, like Arendt and Gadamer, variously emphasize the practical over against the theoretical and do so by merely inverting the order of the hierarchy. However, the point is not to respond to the traditional privilege of theoretical wisdom by privileging practice or "rehabilitating" practical thinking instead. Rather, the aim here is to understand these modes of human endeavor in their irreducibility, to be sure, and yet, simultaneously, in their inseparability. More precisely, the investigation should cast light on the way in which practical considerations decisively mark the beginning or condition of all contemplation as well as discursive investigation.

Ultimately, it is a matter of showing how the theoretical is always informed by a set of practices, by the modality of comportment toward phenomena – of showing, that is, how encountering phenomena, the world, or nature in the broadest sense is always a matter of *ēthos*. As will be expounded in the present work, *this apparently "modern" intimation is to be found at the heart of Greek thought.*

Implicated in an investigation thus oriented is the demonstration that Aristotle thinks ethics as first philosophy, that is, sees the philosophical articulation of scientific-theoretical knowledge, even of ontology, as resting on living-in-action, that is, as phenomenologically, experientially, sensibly grounded. Indeed, if it is the case that all manner of theoretical investigation comes to be through the primordial involvement in sensibility and action, then ethics, the structural study of such ineludible conditions, is the discipline crucially (if not exclusively) disclosing the origins, principles, and assumptions of knowledge, even of wisdom.[1] Ethics as first philosophy means that first philosophy is that reflection informed by *ēthos* (that reflection constituted in the experience of being traversed by life and living in a certain way) and aware of this ground that it cannot possess but only acknowledge.

Of course "ethics as first philosophy" here cannot mean a normative or prescriptive compilation. Nor can it signify a self-founding, all-encompassing, and rationally self-contained discourse. Understood as ethics, first philosophy may not retain such privileges, which would be the privileges of rational autonomy. Rather, the phrase "ethics as first philosophy" indicates that ethics is characterized by a certain comprehensiveness vis-à-vis all manner of human endeavor. At the same time, precisely qua ethics, the discourse coming first exhibits the consciousness of its own openness vis-à-vis that which exceeds it, that is, vis-à-vis that which is not discursive and in which all discourse as such belongs. This *logos* cannot fully account for its "differing and wandering" subject matter, nor can it itself bring about that which it strives to clarify, namely, the good or happiness. In other words, the *logos* of ethics is manifestly aware of its own incapacity for self-enclosure and remains open to that which can neither be discursively exhausted nor simply formalized. Such a *logos* understands itself in its openness to the infinite. Once again, central to this investigation will be tracing the limits of reason – or, more precisely, acknowledging how Aristotle draws such a delimitation.

Thus, despite the obvious Levinasian reference, "first philosophy" should be understood in an altogether Aristotelian sense, as the structural

[1] As al-Farabi puts it, the "science" and "inquiry" of ethics "investigates these intellectual principles [which are in the human being] and the acts and states of character with which man labors toward this perfection" (*Alfarabi's Philosophy of Plato and Aristotle*, trans. Muhsin Mahdi [New York: Free Press of Glencoe, 1962], 23).

study of conditions and of the principles arising from them.[2] After all, the phrase *philosophia prōtē* is exquisitely Aristotelian in its use and elaboration. Granted, in the treatises gathered under the title of *Metaphysics* Aristotle often calls first philosophy *epistēmē*. However, the point will be to see what *epistēmē* could possibly mean and be like, if understood as "science of principles." For principles, on Aristotle's own terms, are not the subject matter of science, but rather constitute science's very premises and presuppositions.

2. ON INTERPRETING ARISTOTLE: *EPISTĒMĒ* AS FIRST PHILOSOPHY?

It is almost universally agreed on that first philosophy, the intellectual pursuit in its highest and grounding (ground-laying) function, is identified by Aristotle with *epistēmē*, science, knowledge, or scientific knowledge. I say "almost universally" because such "universal agreement" does in fact pertain to a rather exiguous region of the world and to its determined, however self-confidently hegemonic, cultural formation(s) – a region and cultural lineage that we usually qualify as "Western." Within the philosophical "debates" taking place in the Western district, however, general consensus has made this understanding of Aristotle axiomatic. Indeed, with very few exceptions since Patristic-Scholastic (con)versions of the Aristotelian *corpus*, Aristotle's thought has been expounded particularly in its logico-systematic and "proto-scientific" vocation.[3] In this context, the concern with cognition remains the genuine ground back to which all other reflective modes are referred – the principal task of philosophy, the task revealing philosophy as first philosophy. Even when a certain emphasis on *praxis* is acknowledged in Aristotle (as is the case,

[2] While the concern with the infinitely, indeterminately pre-originary (pre-logical and prediscursive) may be common to both Aristotle and Levinas, the Levinasian interpretation of infinite priority in terms of injunction is clearly remote from Aristotle's horizon.

[3] On the mode of inheritance and transmission of the Aristotelian discourse in the exemplary case of St. Thomas, see the excellent text by Mark D. Jordan, *The Alleged Aristotelianism of Thomas Aquinas* (Toronto: Pontifical Institute of Mediaeval Studies, 1992). See also, to mention but a few titles, Charles B. Schmitt, *The Aristotelian Tradition and Renaissance Universities* (London: Variorum Reprints, 1984); F. van Steenberghen, *Aristote en Occident. Les origines de l'aristotélisme parisien* (Louvain: Éditions de l'Institut Supérieur de Philosophie, 1946); P. O. Kristeller, *The Classics and Renaissance Thought* (Cambridge, Mass.: Harvard UP, 1955); Lorenzo Minio-Paluello, *Opuscula: The Latin Aristotle* (Amsterdam: Hakkert, 1972); F. Bottin, *La scienza degli occamisti. La scienza tardo-medievale dalle origini del paradigma nominalista alla rivoluzione scientifica* (Rimini: Maggioli, 1982); and H. Blumenthal and H. Robinson, eds., *Aristotle and the Later Tradition* (Oxford: Oxford UP, 1991).

inevitably, with the ethical treatises and the *Politics*), the all-encompassing primordiality of *praxis* is not. The discourses of the practical as well as the study of the physical-phenomenal (such discourses and study share a common destiny) are understood in stark distinction from, and at once in subordination to, the scientific or "theoretical" endeavor.

Thus, approaches illuminating the centrality of the "practical" over against the "theoretical," of *phronēsis* over against *sophia*, of *vita activa* over against *vita contemplativa*, end up merely inverting the hierarchical order while preserving intact the separation of the "purely contemplative" from worldly engagement. Even when allegedly eclipsed, *epistēmē* (discursive and demonstrative knowledge, i.e., the exercise of *logos*) is in effect still sanctioned as *philosophia prōtē* – the operation of "reason" detached from the movements of desire as well as embodiment. Attributed to Aristotle, such an understanding of reason already inaugurates or promises a certain emancipation from the involvement with what-is – an emancipation from the commitment to phenomena in their glow and guiding truth, the "commitment to being" that modern "formal" logic will have assumed finally and with profit to have left behind. (Parenthetically, here one sees adumbrated the convergence and deep unity of Christian-theological and modern scientific discourses.) Such would be the axiom of Aristotelian exegesis in the "universe" of the West, certainly in its universities.[4]

2.1. Difficulties of Knowledge

Yet, as the Aristotelian reflection itself reminds us, axioms and principles (the beginning and ultimate foundation of demonstrable and hence demonstrated knowledge) are not themselves demonstrable, that is to say, are not themselves objects of knowledge. First principles neither pertain to nor result from the operation of knowledge, which finds in them its inception. They present themselves in and as perceptions exhibiting a cogency, a self-evidence that persuades and compels assent. Such is the character and extent of their force. These statements will receive further

[4] One finds, no doubt, exceptions and countermovements to this prevalent trend. Among them, it is necessary at least to mention Rémi Brague's *Aristote et la question du monde. Essay sur le contexte cosmologique et anthropologique de l'ontologie* (Paris: Presses Universitaires de France, 1988), which undertakes to recover the Aristotelian meditation as a whole in its unfolding out of the phenomenological datum of the world. Two indispensable works by Pierre Aubenque should also be recalled, namely, *La prudence chez Aristote* (Paris: Presses Universitaires de France, 1963) and *Le problème de l'être chez Aristote* (Paris: Presses Universitaires de France, 1962).

argumentation in the study that is to follow, mostly focusing on Aristotle's ethical discourses. They are, however, corroborated by numerous Aristotelian observations on the complexity of the question of knowledge (its *genesis* and foundation), most notably in the "logical" treatises. Let us merely recall here the opening of the *Posterior Analytics*, in which it is said that "[a]ll teaching and learning through discourse [διανοητική] proceed [γίγνεται] from previous knowledge [ἐκ προϋπαρχούσης γνώσεως]" (71a1–2).[5] It is *gnōsis* (or *progignōskein*) that provides the conditions for the discursive procedures of demonstrated knowledge. But *gnōsis*, this knowledge that is prior or precedent in the sense that it rules by lying under, as an underlying governing principle, is a rather inclusive designation. It ranges from belief or conviction to the comprehension of what is necessarily true, from understanding in the sense of *eidenai* as well as *xunienai* to perception through sensation (*aisthēsis*).[6]

However, the indemonstrability of principles is not the only difficulty. As the "experimental" sciences make especially clear, axioms and principles may not be immutable. An entire axiomatic configuration can be overturned and overcome by the results of the demonstrative procedures it grounds (and hence, at once, un-grounds). This is the case, for instance, whenever hypotheses axiomatically assumed are either not confirmed or explicitly negated by the end of the trial, whether such a trial be epistemic-syllogistical or empirical – and one *must* wonder whether these different dimensions of demonstration can ever *simply* be dissociated. The competing conjectures of the pre-Socratics concerning the elemental composition of the cosmos, or the very broaching of the question of the cosmos in elemental terms, or, even more broadly, the Aristotelian understanding of the cosmos in terms of regions uniquely characterized, as distinct from the Galilean mathematical model, from the Cartesian notion of space as

5 Here and throughout this study, I have fruitfully consulted, whenever available, Hippocrates G. Apostle's translations of the Aristotelian texts – even though my own rendition often diverges from his. The following translations by Apostle were published by the Peripatetic Press (Grinnell, Iowa) in the year indicated in parenthesis: *Metaphysics* (1979), *Physics* (1969), *Nicomachean Ethics* (1975), *Categories* and *Propositions* (1980), *Posterior Analytics* (1981), *On the Soul* (1982), *Politics* (with Lloyd P. Gerson, 1986). I have translated the passages from further treatises by Aristotle here cited. All other translations of ancient Greek texts quoted in the course of the present work are likewise my own. As regards the Aristotelian corpus, I have utilized W. Jaeger's edition of the *Metaphysics* (Oxford: Oxford UP, 1957) and all the dual editions in the Loeb Classical Series (Cambridge, Mass.: Harvard UP, various years).

6 Of interest in this regard is also the passage at *Topics* 100a18ff. (esp. 101a30–31), where Aristotle speaks of first principles as compelling belief and agreement, while being established on the basis of commonly held views.

homogeneous extension along rectilinear coordinates, from the curved space of relativity or of non-Euclidean geometries – the juxtaposition of these axiomatic pronouncements concerning the same (the "universe") bespeaks the elusiveness and fragility of that which is articulated in and through them. It calls attention to the role of the interpretation of "the same," that is, to the role of interpretation in the constitution of what is spoken of as "the same." What will have been called a "paradigm shift" fundamentally gives itself as a shift in axiomatics or axiomatic reconfiguration.

It could perhaps be objected that, for Aristotle, (1) premises or principles that are *held* to be true (definitions, theses, experimental hypotheses) do not have the same status as premises that are both true and necessary (axioms in the strict sense); (2) experiential or experimental evidence is not strictly but only derivatively apodictic; (3) subsequently, investigations resting on such "demonstrations" do not qualify as *epistēmē stricto sensu,* that is, necessary and unqualified knowledge. But the question is exceptionally intricate, and, while Aristotle consistently distinguishes between qualified and unqualified (hence immutable) knowledge, the instability of this distinction is also often intimated in the course of his reflections. A passage may be recalled from the *Posterior Analytics,* which is indicative of the problems involved in the definition of unqualified knowledge and its proper realm. It is said here that unqualified knowledge is restricted to the domains of the single disciplines and that, in demonstrating in an unqualified way, one cannot "prove something in one genus by passing over from another genus" (75a38–b21). Unqualified knowledge would seem to be granted by the restriction of its scope: it appears to be unqualified precisely because it is not formal, not abstractly comprehensive, in fact uniquely adhering to the matter at stake in each kind of investigation. Yet, Aristotle adds, because unqualified demonstration (if indeed its conclusion is to be universal and eternal) necessitates universal premises, "there can be no unqualified demonstration and no unqualified knowledge of destructible things, but there may be as if in an accidental way, namely, not universally but at a certain time or in a qualified manner" (75b24–27). But if there cannot be unqualified knowledge of what is destructible, of what is mortal, one wonders *of what* unqualified knowledge would be, *to what* it would properly pertain, and how such a scientific knowledge (if it were in fact to come to be) of the indestructible and immortal could constitute just a discipline among others.

Largely devoted as it is to the analysis of logico-apodictic procedures, Aristotle's meditation nevertheless appears to be crucially attuned to the obscure, difficult origin of knowledge – to the unfolding of the discourses (*logoi*) of knowledge out of an agreement that, precisely because axiomatic, is less a matter of "epistemic certainty," let alone of "objectivity" (all anachronistic terms in the Aristotelian context) than of shared belief or conviction. The *Organon* itself exemplarily displays the scope of his reflection, ranging from the painstaking interrogation and formalization of scientific method in the two *Analytics* to the emphasis on the dialectical, ultimately doxico-political ground of knowledge in the *Topics*.[7] Indeed, the doxic and dialectical dimension of the beginning of *epistēmē* is explored in the "analytical" treatises as well, as the following statement from the *Posterior Analytics* shows:

> All sciences share together [ἐπικοινωνοῦσι] some common [axioms, principles] [κατὰ τὰ κοινά] (I call "common" those which the sciences use [as axioms, principles] from which they demonstrate conclusions; and those [axioms, principles] are not that about which they prove something, nor that which they prove [as belonging to something]); dialectics too is common to all sciences; and so is any other discipline which tries to prove universally the common [axioms, principles], e.g., that everything must be either affirmed or denied. . . . But dialectics is not concerned with anything definite or with any one genus, for it would not be asking questions; for the one who demonstrates would not ask questions because he cannot prove the same conclusion from opposite things. (77a27–34)

The exploration of both sides of a contradiction pertains to dialectics (see also *Prior Analytics* 24a21–b12). Aristotle later on will repeatedly underline how difficult it is to distinguish clearly the work of those who demonstrate, and therefore posit premises as true (i.e., begin with that part of the contradiction *given* as immediately true), from the procedure of the dialectician, who cannot start from a given premise and must therefore ask for assent (i.e., mediate) in order to grant the truth of his or her beginning (see, e.g., 77a36–40).

2.2. Other Readers

It is perhaps in virtue of this posture, of this alertness to the problematic origin of scientific knowledge, that in other cultural districts, most notably in the circles of the mediaeval Judeo-Islamic commentators, the reception of Aristotle (and, for that matter, of Plato as well) has taken a

7 On the possibility of reading an *Ur-Ethik* in the *Topics*, see Hans von Arnim, "Das Ethische in Aristoteles *Topik*," *Sitzungsberichte der Akademie der Wissenschaften in Wien*, 205, no. 4 (Vienna, 1927).

direction significantly divergent from the Western privileging of *epistēmē* as the primary, purest philosophical mode.[8] In the Persian-Arabic context the noetic, psychological, and "metaphysical" strands of the Aristotelian inquiry have been understood not so much, or not exclusively, in terms of the priority of cognitive concerns, but rather in their ethical and political relevance – in light of a certain ethical primacy. In this connection it becomes evident that *logos* rests on *dia-logos* – that dialogue (the *logos* open to infinity, taking place as communing and communication) grounds the quest for knowledge and, most significantly, constitutes the condition for the possibility of being human.

The bare fact *that* the "same" texts *can* be (and have been) heard in such considerably different, if not irreconcilable ways corroborates Aristotle's insight into the doxic provenance and labile, even paradoxical status of knowledge – that is, of *logical*, discursive articulations, of "argument," or, which is the same, of reason (*logos*).[9] For the agreement out of which knowledge becomes and on which it rests is achieved thanks to less than essential reasons, and remains exposed to rather imponderable, fleeting, in fact, dialectical circumstances. Such an agreement is not inevitable, not automatically compelled by necessity, but critically obtained thanks to the plausibility and power of rhetorical presentation – thanks to *logos* less in the sense of logical articulation than in that of conversation. Because of this, knowledge (in general, and in a most perspicuous fashion the knowledge explicitly articulated through interpretive practices) comes to be revealed in its ethico-political valence, indeed, as a *basically* ethical issue always involving questions of discursive, dia-logical,

8 To mention only a few fundamental contributions on this theme: Philip Merlan, "Aristoteles, Averroes, und die beiden Eckharts," in *Kleine Philosophische Schriften* (Hildescheim-New York: Olms, 1976); A. Badawi, *La transmission de la philosophie grecque au monde arabe* (Paris: J. Vrin, 1968); F. E. Peters, *Aristoteles Arabus: The Oriental Translations and Commentaries on the Aristotelian* Corpus (Leiden: E. J. Brill, 1968); F. E. Peters, *Aristotle and the Arabs: The Aristotelian Tradition in Islam* (New York: NYU Press, 1968); P. Merlan, *Monopsychism, Mysticism, Metaconsciousness: Problems of the Soul in the Neoaristotelian and Neoplatonic Tradition* (The Hague: Martinus Nijhoff, 1963); and R. Sorabji, ed., *Aristotle Transformed. The Ancient Commentators and Their Influence* (Ithaca, N.Y.: Cornell UP, 1990). See also the especially noteworthy text by E. Booth, *Aristotelian Aporetic Ontology in Islamic and Christian Thinkers* (Cambridge: Cambridge UP, 1983).

9 Let this be underlined again: *logos* means, simultaneously, word, language, saying, discourse, story, argument, speech, reason, rationality (*ratio*), and logical structure (in the sense of informing law). Its relation with the verb *legein* illuminates its further, perhaps most embracing meaning as "gathering." As in the case of other essentially untranslatable terms, such as *nous*, the various semantic facets and nuances of *logos*, in particular its discursive and rational dimensions, should be held in play simultaneously.

argumentative comportment, and the ensuing responsibilities and communal configurations. After all, as Aristotle observes in *Metaphysics* Alpha Elatton, "[t]he way we receive a lecture depends on our custom [κατὰ τὰ ἔθη]; for we expect [a lecturer to use] the language [λέγεσθαι] we are accustomed to, and any other [language] appears not agreeable [ὅμοια] but rather unknown and strange because we are not accustomed to it [ἀσυνήθειαν ἀγνωστότερα καὶ ξενικώτερα]; for the customary is more known [σύνηθες γνώριμον]" (994b32–995a3). Rigorously following from this remark is the intimation that all inquiry, including the genuinely scientific one, presupposes a range of rhetorical conditions, a certain "how" of *logos*. Such conditions constitute the axiomatic structure of the inquiry, its "way or turn," *tropos*: "Therefore, one should already be trained in how to accept statements, for it is absurd to be seeking science and at the same time [ἅμα] the way [τρόπον] of [acquiring] science; and neither of them can be acquired easily" (995a12–14).

It is because of such problems that one finds in the Jewish and Persian-Arabic approaches to Aristotle a pervasive preoccupation with language, an awareness of the rhetorical dimension of "metaphysical" discussions, of the simultaneously obscuring and illuminating operations of *logos* and, consequently, of its limits.[10] Finally, what is thus intimated is a certain impossibility of metaphysics understood as emancipation from *phusis* and, *mutatis mutandis*, of *theōria* understood as transcendence of *praxis*. Metaphysics *as such* would indeed be the study of what is beyond nature – but in the wake of a semantic stipulation leaving nothing unturned. For that which is "beyond nature" would not be construed as that which without further qualification transcends nature, but rather as that which, though

10 Maimonides' case is exemplary in this respect. On this subject, see Idit Dobbs-Weinstein, *Maimonides and St. Thomas on the Limits of Reason* (Albany: SUNY Press, 1995). For an approach to Aristotle's *Metaphysics* focusing on the "many ways" in which being can be said and the relation between language and metaphysical or theological inquiries, see al-Farabi, *Book of Letters*, ed. M. Mahdi (Beirut: Dar el-Mashreq, 1969), and the following related studies: Shukri B. Abed, *Aristotelian Logic and the Arabic Language in Alfarabi* (Albany: SUNY Press, 1991); Fuad Said Haddad, *Alfarabi's Theory of Communication* (Beirut: American University of Beirut, 1989); and Joep Lameer, *Al-Farabi and Aristotelian Syllogistics: Greek Theory and Islamic Practice* (Leiden: Brill, 1994), esp. chap. 9, 259–89. Consider also the systematization of the disciplines in Avicenna, according to which rhetoric, in its psychological stratum, is a part of logic. See, e.g. (particularly concerning the relation of Avicenna's brief text "Character Traits and Passions of the Soul" to the Logic of the *Hikma*), L. Massignon, D. Remondon, and G. Vajda, *Miscellanea* (Caire: Institut Français D'Archéologie Orientale, 1954), 19ff. See also the Logic of the *Danesh-Name Alai* (*Avicenna's Treatise on Logic*, ed. and trans. Farhang Zabeeh [The Hague: Nijhoff, 1971]), esp. 40ff.

belonging in nature, is *not by nature* and cannot be accounted for by reference to nature. It is in this peculiar, highly qualified sense that one can here speak of transcendence.[11] Such is the character of ethical and political matters, in fact, of human undertakings as a whole – and, thus understood, this would be the properly metaphysical concern.[12] The perception of the unity of action and contemplation calls for a semantic shift according to which transcendence can only mean that which eludes and surpasses the scientific grasp; separation comes to indicate that which is shared in common and impossible, unthinkable aside from community (Averroes); metaphysics comes to mean ethics (politics); and ethics signifies first philosophy, in which science belongs and properly positions itself.

2.3. Phenomenal Wisdom

Not only, thus, is knowledge (the articulation of reason) shown in its dependence on *phusis* and *praxis*, hence as belonging in the domain of ethical considerations, but metaphysics itself turns out to be irreducible to the discourse of *epistēmē*, to reason *tout court*. In Aristotle this is most explicitly the case in those moments of the investigation broaching the inevitable problem of the *theos*, of the ultimate source of all that is, lives, and moves. In engaging the ultimate question of the divine (i.e., *nous*), the metaphysical discourse exceeds the bounds of knowledge (reason) and exposes itself in its wondering thrust toward the unmoved, that of which there is or can be no science.[13] Whether focusing on first principles

[11] The simultaneity of belonging and excess with respect to nature makes it clear that at stake is neither a kind of naïve naturalism nor the logic of the transcendental in its rational-practical implications.

[12] See, e.g., al-Farabi, *The Philosophy of Plato and Aristotle*, esp. the programmatic concluding remarks (130). See also how Avicenna's Metaphysics of the *Shifa'* (*Healing*), after culminating with a discourse on god (Books 8–10), is brought to its proper end by political considerations ranging from cultic forms to civic institutions and law-making (Avicenna, *La métaphysique du* Shifa', trans. G. Anawati [Paris: Vrin, 1978], 2 vols.).

[13] One will recall the mythical turn in *Metaphysics* Lambda, which represents a most unusual development in Aristotle. At this crucial stage, immediately after declaring that "there is only one heaven" and before examining the question of *nous*, Aristotle puts forth a remarkable reflection that deserves to be quoted in full. "The ancients of very early times [παρὰ τῶν ἀρχαίων καὶ παμπαλαίων]," he says, "bequeathed to posterity in the form of a myth [ἐν μύθου σχήματι] a tradition that the heavenly bodies are gods and that the divinity encompasses the whole of nature [περιέχει τὸ θεῖον τὴν ὅλην φύσιν]. The rest of the tradition has been added later as a means of persuading the masses and as something useful for the laws and for matters of expediency; for they say that these gods are like

or on the ultimate non-objectifiable object of contemplation (a mover as unknown as it may be unmoved), in its intuitive, non-discursive, non-logical (*a-logon*) trait philosophy is revealed as, *first of all*, philosophical conduct – *ēthos* without the unqualified and absolutely necessitating guidance of reason, without fully rational (or, for that matter, doctrinal) prescription.[14]

The theoretical, thus, emerges as essentially implicated in phenomenality and always informed by one's comportment to phenomena. As becomes apparent in the *Nicomachean Ethics*, theoretical wisdom does indeed extend beyond the domain of human concerns – but not in the sense that human concerns are left behind, let alone that the realm of sensibility, of phenomenality and practice, is transcended. As it contemplates that which exceeds the human, theoretical wisdom remains grounded in the human. Indeed, it originally discloses the situatedness of humans in what is not human and, thus, broaches the question of human finitude, of the proper place and function of humans in the cosmos. Says Aristotle:

> And if one were to say that the human being is the best of the animals, this too would make no difference; for there are also other things much more divine in their nature than the human being, like the most visible objects of which the universe is composed. (*Nicomachean Ethics* 1141a35–b2)

On the basis of similar statements, it would not be inappropriate to say that, through the analysis of *sophia*, theoretical wisdom, Aristotle is outlining a kind of critique of anthropocentrism. To be sure, theoretical wisdom entails the realization that human good is not the good without

humans in form and like some of the other animals, and also other things which follow from or are similar to those stated. But if one were to separate from the later additions the first point and attend to this alone (namely, that they thought the first substances to be gods), one might realize that this was divinely spoken and that, while probably every art and every philosophy has often reached a stage of development as far as it could and then again has perished, these opinions [δόξας] about the gods were saved like relics up to the present day. Anyway, the opinion of our forefathers and of the earliest thinkers is evident to us only to this extent" (1074b1–14). With this reflection on knowledge disappearing (the problem of the evanescent lighting up of knowledge was addressed by Diotima in the *Symposium* and will return to haunt Maimonides), Aristotle effects a discursive shift decisively preparing and orienting the discussion of *nous*. Notice how, in this passage, the motif of myth is intertwined with the dialectical strand of Aristotle's argumentation and with his alertness to hermeneutic-archeological difficulties.

14 In *The Therapy of Desire: Theory and Practice in Hellenistic Ethics* (Princeton: Princeton UP, 1994), Martha Nussbaum underlines the pragmatic or "medical" character of the ethical discourse (22). However, she adds, "[e]ven Aristotelian truth in science may not be . . . altogether independent of human theories and conceptions," let alone desires (23).

qualification – that what is good for humans is not necessarily *the* good. *Sophia* would, then, have to do with the good *as such.* And yet, it is of the utmost importance to emphasize that, far from entailing what will have been called a "purely theoretical" posture, in stretching out beyond matters of human utility *sophia* remains bound to phenomena and orients reflection toward the glowing sky, the non-human in which the human belongs – as a reminder of the irreducibility of the cosmos to the order of the human. *Sophia,* then, names a reorientation of the gaze, from the horizontal order of human togetherness to the encompassing connection with what exceeds the human – a reorientation transcending the human (indeed, showing the human precisely as such a movement stretching out beyond itself) but not phenomenality and sensibility themselves.

2.4. Hodos

But these interpretive hypotheses, which are relatively extravagant in our *milieu,* need to be confirmed by a closer textual analysis. On the basis of Aristotle's suggestions and of the resonance they have received in certain interpretive traditions, in what follows I undertake to show how ethics in the Aristotelian texts (particularly in the *Nicomachean Ethics*) is disclosed as *philosophia prōtē* – ethics, in its "praxical," intuitive, indeterminately a-logical or pre-logical features, as first philosophy, out of which (meta)physical, epistemological, and psychological reflections unfold in intimate connection with each other. It will be necessary to proceed with great caution, moving through the *Nicomachean Ethics* preeminently in the mode of commentary and without neglecting the first Books, in which the mode and structure of the ethical investigation are laid down. In this systematic traversal of our main text, there will be numerous occasions calling for references to related discussions, especially in the ethico-political treatises. The investigation culminates with the discussion of the intellectual virtues (Book Zeta), undertaking to set *nous* into relief in its essential character, as both sensible-intuitive and non-rational (literally, not related to *logos*). These are clearly the most noteworthy features of the *aretē* that constitutes the basis of knowledge (of reason) and, even more importantly, of wisdom. This "excellence" pertains to intellectual seizing as well as sensuous perception, to what is first as well as what is ultimate or particular, and hence indicates at once the bond with the "divine" and the "natural." Exhibiting the nature of reason (*logos*), thus, should be understood according to the double (subjective and objective) genitive. It simultaneously means displaying reason in *its nature* (viz., its finitude, dependence) and to recognize reason as *of nature,* encompassed by nature, taking place within nature, and having to position itself there (however irreducible to nature, in fact supplementary with respect to it).

Though I will focus on the ethical treatises, it is important again to underline that Aristotle's "ethical" and "metaphysical" writings should be regarded not as separate and somewhat autonomous regions of the corpus, but as dynamically related and forming an organic whole. For the corpus is not simply the compilation of scattered texts plausibly by the same author, but rather what remains (the traces) of the living, embodied engagement in inquiry, in the manifold of reflection. While, indeed, one finds in Nicomachus cogent remarks supporting the hypotheses here put forth, it is crucial minimally to delineate a development of the same position drawing on the *Metaphysics* and "logical" treatises. In fact, even in the treatises gathered under the title *Metaphysics,* so paradigmatically discussing first philosophy in terms of science, one finds numerous provisos – most remarkably, the emphasis on dialectic as the ground legitimizing knowledge. It is precisely in the course of his "metaphysical" meditations, after all, that Aristotle repeatedly calls attention to philosophy as a communal enterprise – as a matter simultaneously of politics and history, of community seen both as the present political organism and as lineage, entailing transmission as well as loss.[15]

At the end of this work, it will be appropriate to draw a few consequences out of the analyses carried out, which might assist us as we attempt to think through urgent issues such as the function of dialogue (the *logos* infinitely split open) in furthering skillful manners of co-existence, the meaning of politics in a global perspective, the place of the human in the non-human cosmos, and our relation to the "other," whether human

15 Among Aristotle's striking remarks in this text, let us recall the following: "The contemplation [θεωρία] of truth is in one sense difficult, in another easy. A sign of this is the fact that neither can one attain it adequately, nor do all fail, but each says something about the nature [of things]; and while each of us contributes nothing or little to the truth, a considerable amount of it results from all our contributions" (993a30–b4). Aristotle continues with the statement that the predecessors should be honored, however irrelevant their contribution may have been – for they handed down the "habit" of thinking (thinking is thus indicated as a political-temporal formation, and not as unqualified prerogative of humans). And again: "some of them handed down to us certain doctrines, but there were others before who *caused* them to be what they were" (993b18–19, emphasis added). The passage previously quoted, at the pivotal juncture in Book Lambda, also adumbrates the boundless difficulties inherent in *dia-logos* – especially in "diachronic dialogue," that is, in the relation to the past and the status of inheritance.

or otherwise (and, hence, to the environment, animality, and, broadly speaking, nature and the divine).

Particularly suggestive in this regard is Aristotle's emphasis on dialectical negotiation, that is, on the dialogical stipulations necessary in order to arrive at a consensus regarding principles or beginnings whose evidence is neither immediate nor uncontroversial. For essential reasons, Aristotle does not speak of dialogue in "universalistic" terms, that is, of a "universality" of values and consensus. Indeed, dialectic as he conceives of it is a matter of ongoing engagement, of the continuing effort and arduous work of mediation taking place within a given *polis*, community, or cultural context. Yet, precisely because the ethico-political labor of dialectic is sensibly or phenomenologically informed, we must wonder about the possibility of extending such a thought beyond "locality." That is to say, we must wonder about the possibility of envisioning something like a "planetary," indeed "cosmic" dialogue on Aristotelian grounds, long before the conception of the *kosmopolis* in the Epicurean and Stoic developments.[16] At stake here are the issues of dialogue as structuring the togetherness of the different (of the diverging, even) and of the ethical as well as physical framework embracing all human enterprises, whether theoretical or more genuinely political. In other words, at issue is the possibility of understanding politics beyond the *polis* as well as beyond humanism or anthropocentrism. Indeed, a certain strand of Aristotelian thinking seems to intimate a concern with the belonging together of differing forms of living within the fabric of the cosmos – with a bond among humans and beyond the human, gathering the human to its beyond, to the other than human in the direction both of nature and of the divine.

The work is structured as follows:

- Introduction
- Prelude: On *Metaphysics* and *Posterior Analytics* (in which I situate the reading of the ethico-political treatises in the broader context of the

[16] Of "political science," al-Farabi states: "It consists of knowing the things by which the citizens of cities attain happiness through political association in the measure that innate disposition equips each of them for it. It will become evident to him that political association and the totality that results from the association of citizens in cities correspond to the association of the bodies that constitute the totality of the world. He will come to see in what are included in the totality constituted by the city and the nation the likenesses of what are included in the total world." It is in such a seeing that human perfection would be attained: "This, then, is theoretical perfection" (*Alfarabi's Philosophy of Plato and Aristotle*, 24–5).

Aristotelian corpus and show the essential cohesiveness of Aristotle's reflection)

- Main Section (on the *Nicomachean Ethics* and related treatises): Commentary on *Nicomachean Ethics* Alpha to Eta (in which, through a close reading of the text in its diverse articulations, I draw out the emphasis on the intuitive, experiential, and therefore practical conditions of the theoretical stance; such an emphasis pervades the preparatory methodological considerations as well as the analysis of justice and, most notably, of the intellectual virtues)
- Interlude: On *Metaphysics* Gamma (in which I consider Aristotle's thoroughly practical argumentation regarding noetic axioms such as the "law of non-contradiction")
- Concluding Section (on the *Nicomachean Ethics* and related treatises): Commentary on *Nicomachean Ethics* Theta to Kappa, on friendship and the good (in which, focusing on the question of community, human and beyond, I analyze Aristotle's vision of the bond among humans and of the human bond with nature and the divine).

The work that is to follow develops out of a close exegetic engagement with a broad range of Aristotelian texts. References to so-called secondary literature are rigorously limited to footnotes and, even there, kept to the barest indications. The texts providing the background of the present study are listed in the Selected Bibliography. While the relevant literature is virtually limitless and any claim to exhaustiveness seems to be out of the question, the Bibliography includes diverse works I have encountered in different contexts and traditions.

1

Prelude: Before Ethics

Metaphysics A and *Posterior Analytics* B.19

Aristotle opens *Metaphysics* A with a reflection that points to the emergence of ethics, as an explicit discursive articulation, after a long trajectory of human endeavors and inquiries – in fact, as the culmination of the unfolding of human seeking. In the order of knowing, the discourse of ethics will have come onto the scene *after* those other discussions, including the so-called metaphysical treatises: that which is closest to us, indeed most immediately crucial in and for us, reveals itself last, can be glimpsed at only toward the end of an exploration variously oriented outward, taking us far from ourselves, away from the beginning that we provide and are. The trajectory of such an exploration, thus, in the end leads one back to the previously unquestioned beginning, in order to unravel, to make explicit what was implicit, implied, and implicated in the beginning. In this trajectory the exploration ends up turning upon itself, catching a glimpse of its source and informing principles. It ends up somehow reflecting upon itself.[1]

Thus, out of the "logical," "physical," and "metaphysical" texts would emerge the questions of cognition, of the manifold forms of life, of the

[1] The arrangement of the *corpus aristotelicum* as we know it today, beginning from the "logical" treatises and culminating with the ethico-political ones and the discussions on rhetoric and poetry, can ultimately be ascribed to Andronicus Rhodius (1st Century B.C.), who proceeded to organize the "esoteric" writings systematically, in a precise design based on their thematic focus and on the hypothetical order in which they should have been read. It is usually accepted that Andronicus formulated his "editorial plan" on the ground of didactic schemes attributable to the early Peripatos or even to Aristotle himself. See Paul Moraux, *Les listes anciennes des ouvrages d'Aristote* (Louvain: Éditions Universitaires, 1951).

relation between knowledge and comportment, eventually of the distinctively human. But of course, albeit in an implicit, unthematized fashion, the human would have been in play since the beginning of such investigations, as their very possibility – as the condition silently underlying their discourses. The question of the human, encompassing and grounding all research and undertaking, is liminally illuminated at the inception of the *Metaphysics*, but even here remains essentially unaddressed. It presents itself at this threshold, begins to become thinkable on the margins of the main discussion, but will not receive its formulation and sustained elaboration in this context. Only within the meditation on ethics will the heretofore undisclosed ground of human endeavor come to be developed. It may be opportune briefly to recall the prodromes of Aristotle's thematization of the human, particularly in the *Metaphysics*. Here we witness a discourse on the verge of wondering about itself, of interrogating itself concerning its own conditions and presuppositions – a discourse inceptively opening onto that self-reflective exercise that will have been the ethical investigation proper.

1. *METAPHYSICS* A: ON "METAPHYSICS" AND DESIRE

As is well known, the *Metaphysics*'[2] inaugural statement immediately poses the question of desire at the heart of the human quest for knowledge: "All human beings by nature desire having seen [τοῦ εἰδέναι ὀρέγονται]" (980a21). The motive force underlying human striving for understanding is identified as desire, *orexis*. It is by nature that human beings pursue knowledge. It has even been said that, in pursuing knowledge, human beings in a way pursue themselves, their own nature, their own fulfillment

[2] Throughout this study, my approach to the *Metaphysics* is informed by the structural analyses put forth by Giovanni Reale in his *Il concetto di filosofia prima e l'unità della* Metafisica *di Aristotele* (Milan: Società Editrice Vita e Pensiero, 1961). Contra the view of the fragmentary and essentially heterogeneous character of the treatises gathered under the heading of *ta meta ta phusika*, a view first articulated by Werner Jäger (*Studien zur Entstehungsgeschichte der Metaphysik des Aristoteles* [Berlin: Weidmann, 1912], *Aristoteles. Grundlegung einer Geschichte seiner Entwicklung* [Berlin: Weidmann, 1923]), Reale proposes an interpretation of the *Metaphysics* in its unity and integrity. More broadly, he calls for a genuinely philosophical approach to Aristotelian thought, irreducible to (if integrated by) philological research. In this connection, see Enrico Berti's remarks in *Aristotele nel Novecento* (Rome: Laterza, 1992), 260–3. See also Joseph Owens, *The Doctrine of Being in the Aristotelian Metaphysics: A Study in the Greek Background of Medieval Thought* (Toronto: Pontifical Institute of Medieval Studies, 1978), and Pierre Aubenque, "Sense et structure de la métaphysique aristotélicienne," *Bulletin de la Société Française de Philosophie* 57 (1964): 1–56.

and perfection – that in this way they become what they are to be and realize the plenitude of their being.[3] But what must be underlined here is that human beings *are drawn* to such a realization, that their becoming themselves occurs in the mode of desire and not, say, in the mode of self-determination. The movement toward completion must be understood as originating in an impulsion, in fact, as the stretching out of a lover toward the beloved, toward that which imposes itself as eminently lovable or desirable. Thus, knowing and, broadly speaking, comprehending come to pass in virtue of a certain *pathos*. For the human being will always already have striven for having seen. In capturing with laconic precision the human longing for having seen, this opening peremptorily reveals a basic passivity at the heart of the manifold phenomenon of the human. The feature of passivity, then, receives further magnification through the reference to another human passion, namely, the liking of *aisthēsis*, the affection for the undergoing and taking in of what gives itself perceptually. Aristotle proceeds to substantiate his inceptive statement as follows:

> A sign of this is their liking of sensations; for even apart from the need of these for other things, they are liked for their own sake, and of all sensations those received by means of the eyes are liked most. For, not only for the sake of doing something else, but even if we are not going to do anything else, we prefer, as one might say, seeing to the other sensations. The cause of this is the fact that, of all the sensations, seeing makes us know in the highest degree and makes clear many differences. (980a21–27)

Both the desire for "having seen" as well as the draw toward "taking in" point to the passion and passivity marking in a manifold fashion the human condition. Human beings will have undergone the drive to pursue insight. In turn, the pursuit of insight will have been taken up in virtue of another undergoing of the soul, the undergoing that occurs in and as perceptual apprehension. Understood in light of the fundamental trace of passivity, the human being already emerges in its openness and receptiveness vis-à-vis what it is not. In its hospitality toward what it is not, in its being inhabited (if not invaded) by that which exceeds it, the human being is inceptively manifest as a strange ontological structure defined through alterity, that structure whose definition involves alterity and, therefore, a certain infinity, a certain lack of determinacy and of delimitation.

[3] Alexander of Aphrodisias, *In Aristotelis Metaphysica commentaria*, ed. Michael Hayduck (Berlin: G. Reimer, 1891), I, 4–10.

Two main issues need to be emphasized already, which will subsequently receive further resonance. In the first place, the originary character of desire vis-à-vis what will have been called "metaphysical investigation" cannot but radically qualify the whole enterprise of first philosophy understood as *epistēmē*. Indeed, this inception seems to dictate that the nature of the investigation will hardly have been metaphysical – that, rather, the pursuit of science in the inquiry of first philosophy will have been stirred up, animated, and sustained from a condition, that of humans, essentially marked by a desirous motility. It is in light of such an altogether "physical" dynamism, of this striving both embodied and never quite beyond or past (*meta*) nature (*phusis*), that the actualization, the coming to be of science should be understood. Already from these first lines it could be said not only that the language of "metaphysics" and related terms is literally not available to Aristotle (this terminology arises from the later Peripatetic systematization of the Aristotelian corpus), but also, more importantly, that metaphysics as the beyond of *phusis* remains essentially unthinkable for Aristotle and that the Aristotelian reflection rather develops on the hither side of nature. Turning to Aristotle in such a way as to illuminate the implications of this, notwithstanding a long history of Aristotelian interpretation that has read Aristotle reductively and anachronistically, according to an unproblematic notion of science and a naïvely dualistic construction of the relation between physics and metaphysics, is precisely what imposes itself on us as a problem, maybe even *the* problem. This is what we take up here as our task.

The second issue to be put into relief is the broad gesture by which Aristotle draws together the desire for knowing as "having seen" and the love of sensation, most notably of visual perception. This provides a most synthetic anticipation of the indissoluble cluster of sensible perception and perception of the universal, to which Aristotle will return time and again. As a "having seen," understanding, *eidenai*, comes to be in the repetition of the experience of seeing. The *pathos* of vision, whose exemplarity rests with its surpassing and intensifying the other perceptual modes, lets beings light up in their differences and, therefore, in their distinctness and unique perspicuity. However, in its recurrence, visual perception also brings about a certain ordering of the teeming differences it takes in. Far from being the bare exposure to a proliferation without either scansion or structure, seeing (knowing as having seen) entails realizing the iterative character of the articulation of what is: in experiencing beings I also experience their return, their reappearance after an interval, whether spatial or temporal. Indeed, (1) in virtue of what could be called "a structured spaciousness of the gaze," I seize the similarities compelling me to gather certain beings together at a glance, to acknowledge their belonging together, that is, in a sense, their being the same, and, (2) in virtue of mnemonic retention, I seize the similarities that turn the *perception* of a being into the *recognition* of a being, that is, the recognition of a being as the same, as a being that comes back after having been seen already, however altered in its returning or self-reproduction. In returning, reappearing, or being replicated, beings come somehow to abide. Thus, the "many differences" that vision makes "clear" receive their vividness and definition in virtue of the power to discern them as well as in virtue of the sameness and constancy organizing them. It is in this sense that vision, or more generally sensation (*aisthēsis*), "makes" (*poiei*) me "know" (*gnōrizein*).[4]

1.1. "Physiology" of Intellection

To elaborate on this, Aristotle proceeds right away to develop a genetic account of the emergence of intellection, that is, the perception of universals. The formation and apprehension of universals is illuminated as a simultaneously sensible and noetic matter: the universal arises from sensation, from the passivity that sensation bespeaks. Let this be foreshadowed: it is this simultaneity and indissolubility, if not identity, of sensibility (*aisthēsis*) and intellectual perception (*noēsis*) that will entail the most far-reaching consequences. For the moment, Aristotle lays out the genealogy of noetic perception and surfacing of universals in broad strokes. The root of such a development lies deep within the most primordial folds of life:

> By nature animals [τὰ ζῷα] are born having sensation, and from sensation [ἐκ δὲ ταύτης] memory [μνήμη] comes into being in some of them but not in others. Because of this, animals which can remember [δυναμένων μνημονεύειν] are more

[4] The suggestion here is that, in the specific human experience, sensation already may present an inherently iterative and hence mnemonic constitution, i.e., that memory, *mnēmē*, may not simply be a somehow subsequent addition to the bare fact of sensing. This suggestion is to an extent obscured by the discussion in Alpha 1, which focuses on a genealogy of intellection whose horizon is life, the animal domain at large, and not the properly human experience. It is, however, corroborated by a remark in *De anima*. Here, while surmising that each organ of sense receives the sensible being proper to it, but without the matter, Aristotle adds a statement assimilating sensation to imagination and pointing to a kind of "memory of the senses": "It is in view of this that sensations [αἰσθήσεις] and imaginings [φαντασίαι] [of the sensed beings] are in the sense organs even when those [sensed beings] are gone" (425b24–5).

prudent [φρονιμώτερα] or more teachable [μαθητικώτερα] than animals which cannot remember. Of the former, those which cannot hear sounds are prudent but cannot be taught [ἄνευ τοῦ μανθάνειν], such as the bee or any other species of animals like it, but those which can hear can also be taught [μανθάνει]. (980a27–b25)

The capacity for being taught, that is, for learning, at a most basic level presupposes the power of sensing. For from sensation arises in certain cases memory, and this development already in and of itself makes possible a degree of prudence (*phronēsis*) and learning (*manthanein*). There is no such thing as teaching and learning without the ability to retain mnemonically. Yet, with respect to learning the power of recollection is not simply a more proximate condition than sensation: indeed, the fact that, as prerequisites, sensation and memory must be complemented by the possession of the specific sense of hearing shows that the power of recollection is folded back into sensation so as to be determined in its implications and outcome by the specific configuration of sensibility. Two further issues are also worth noting, at least in a preliminary fashion, concerning the crucial Aristotelian term usually translated as "prudence." In the first place, it is remarkable that the term is employed in reference to manners of life other than human. For reasons that will become clear only later on in the course of our study of the ethical treatises, this cannot be set aside as a mere episode of terminological looseness. Second, "prudence" is here disclosed as somewhat independent from learning. The discriminating sense of hearing sets the two apart in such a way as to show that prudence would belong to living beings prior to and aside from their being teachable. But even before the specification concerning hearing, when "prudence" and "learning" are mentioned coextensively, it is clear that prudence, in fact learning itself, cannot be explained by reference to learning alone, that is, simply on their own terms. Rather, they must be understood in their altogether physiological preconditions and seen as arising from the dimly lit intertwinement of sensation and memory.

Aristotle continues to unfold his "physiology" of noetic perception by further associating the term "imagination" (*phantasia*) to the cluster of sensation, memory, and prudence and by introducing the language of "experience" (*empeiria*).[5] Here he comes to unfold in more detail the previous intimation of apprehension as linked to repetition:

5 Concerning the connection between imagination, *phantasia*, and memory, *mnēmē*, I recall Aristotle's definition of memory as "the having or habit [ἕξις] of a phantasm [φάντασμα]

All animals [except human beings] live with the aid of imaginations [φαντασίαις] and memories [μνήμαις], and they participate but little in experience; but the race of human beings lives also by art [τέχνῃ] and judgment [λογισμοῖς]. In human beings experience comes into being from memory; for many memories of the same thing result in the capacity [δύναμιν] for one experience. And experience seems to be almost similar to science and art, but science and art come to human beings through experience [διὰ τῆς ἐμπειρίας], for, as Polus rightly says, "experience made art, but inexperience, luck." (980b25–981a5)

Experience, then, finds the condition for its possibility in memory, that is, in the ability to recognize the recurrence of the same as such. Because of this, we may say that experience somehow bespeaks knowledge as "having seen," the fruit of an iteration leading to a progressively sharper definition of what is perceived, such that the perceived is brought into an outline, into a limit, and stabilized therein. It could then be said that experience, *empeiria*, signifies the knowledge of limit, *peras* – a knowledge at once resting on the limit of the perceived and seizing the perceived in its limit, and hence a knowledge that, far from "conceptual" abstraction (of which there is no sign here), adheres to the things themselves, remains in their proximity and, thanks to this intimacy with them, delimits them, draws them out in their definiteness. Conversely, inexperience (*apeiria*) would designate a lack and ignorance of limit, a certain indefiniteness or indeterminacy. Such a lack would even seem to disconfirm the relevance of more formal knowledge (*logos*), because it would betray the missing link between such a knowledge and the world of which it would speak: "in fact," says Aristotle, "we observe that human beings who are experienced succeed more than those who, without experience, have *logos*" (981a14–15). To be inexperienced, then, would signify to live in a world without clear boundaries, to find oneself in underdetermined circumstances, positioning oneself in the world, relating to the world in confused ways.

1.2. Experiencing and Knowing

However, before considering this latter issue more closely, it is important to examine further the connection between experience and knowledge. Aristotle qualifies and refines their relationship so that, far from positing their identity, he illuminates the manifoldness of knowledge and the

regarded as a likeness [εἰκόνος] of that of which it is a phantasm" (*On Memory and Recollection*, 451a15).

irreducibility of certain modes of knowing to the peculiar kind of knowledge that experience names. At the same time, experience is nevertheless said to harbor a genuinely noetic content:

> Now art comes into being when out of many notions [ἐννοημάτων] from experience we form one universal [καθόλου] belief [ὑπόληψις] concerning similar facts. For, to have a belief that when Callias was having this disease this benefited him, and similarly with Socrates and many other individuals, is a matter of experience; but to have a belief that this benefited all persons of a certain kind who were having this sickness, such as the phlegmatic or the bilious or those burning with high fever, is a matter of art. (981a5–12)

The perception at the heart of experience, then, possesses an intellectual character; it is indeed an *ennoēma.* Yet the knowledge that is enacted in and as "art" (τέχνη) seems to surpass experience in articulateness and degree of complexity: as "universal knowledge [γνῶσις τῶν καθόλου]," the knowledge that presides over production arises out of numerous episodes of "knowledge of individuals [γνῶσις τῶν καθ' ἕκαστόν]" (981a16), that is, out of various *ennoēmata* formed through experience. Universal knowledge in the broadest and most proper sense, thus, seems to come to be through the mediation of experience, indeed, of a multiplicity of experiences having analogous content. In the example given, through the various experiences of individual human beings suffering from certain illnesses and reacting to certain cures, an intuition may light up concerning the extendibility of such observations to all cases presenting similar features. The immediacy of the moment of intuitive luminosity yielding the universal must be understood by reference to the mediation of experiential, and therefore temporal, conditions. Thus, while experience yields insight into a configuration of individuals stabilized in their concatenation (e.g., the patient, the symptoms of the sickness, the cure), the insight into the universal captures what, in each singular situation, holds "according to the whole," that is, not only according to the cases experienced but according to all possible such cases.

What is remarkable here, in the first place, is that Aristotle should refer to *tekhnē* as the paradigm for the knowledge of universals. That such a knowledge, which is nothing less than the fundamental and primordial knowledge sought in the inquiry of first philosophy, would be best (or even only) illustrated by reference to the knowledge inhering in the "technical," poietic process, should put us on the alert already at this stage – especially if we consider Aristotle's contrasting insistence on the fact that first philosophy, "the science of wisdom," will have exceeded in worth and accomplishment the sciences devoted to production. We will have more than one occasion to return to this crucial issue and consider its farthest implications. For the moment we should emphasize, second, that the perception of the universal is addressed as "belief" and, therefore, has the same status as the apprehension from experience. Of course, this will raise the question concerning the character and authority of the "science" at stake in first philosophy. For not only is this science concerned not with demonstration but with universals as principles of demonstration, which are indemonstrable, but, furthermore, knowing universals will have meant acquiring them through belief, however firm. Again, we will have numerous occasions to come back to this.

1.3. Knowing Why

Aristotle now continues by surmising once more that, in contexts where the focus is on action (*praxis*), there seems to be no discernible difference between experience and art. However, he will conclude, if we consider them for themselves, aside from practical involvements, we will have to acknowledge the superiority of art. The ensuing contrast between manual worker and master-artist (the one who not only executes but also possesses the understanding of the reason *why* he is proceeding in that way, i.e., the understanding of *how* to proceed in order to obtain *what*) is meant to cast further light on the difference between knowledge of individuals and knowledge of universals. Again, it is quite outstanding that the knowledge animating production should provide an explanatory reference for universal knowledge:

> Experience does not seem to differ from art where something is to be done; in fact, we observe that those who are experienced succeed more than those who have the theory [λόγον ἐχόντων] but are inexperienced. The cause of this is that experience is knowledge of individuals but art is universal knowledge, and all actions and generations [πράξεις καὶ αἱ γενέσεις] deal with individuals. The doctor does not cure a human being [universally taken], except accidentally, but Callias or Socrates or someone else to whom also it is said that "human being" happens to belong. If, then, someone without experience has the theory [λόγον] and knows the universal but is ignorant of the individual included under this universal, he will often fail to cure; for it is rather the individual that is curable. Nevertheless we regard understanding [εἰδέναι] and comprehension [ἐπαΐειν] as belonging to art more than to experience, and we believe that artists [τοὺς τεχνίτας] are wiser than those who have experience; and this indicates that wisdom [σοφίαν]

> is attributed to human beings according to their understanding [εἰδέναι] rather than their experience, inasmuch as those who have understanding know the cause but those who have experience do not. For those who have experience know the "that" [τὸ ὅτι] but not the why [διότι]; but those who have the art know the why of it or the cause. It is because of this that we regard also the master-artists [τοὺς ἀρχιτέκτονας] of a given craft as more honorable, as possessing understanding [εἰδέναι] to a higher degree, and as wiser than the manual workers [τῶν χειροτεχνῶν], since the former know the causes of the things produced, but the latter are like certain inanimate things [ἀψύχων] which act but do so without understanding that action, as in the case of fire that burns. (981a12–b3)

Two complementary aspects must be drawn out of this reflection. On the one hand, Aristotle dwells on the fundamental role of experience. While it may be the case that universal knowledge is irreducible to knowledge of individuals, still the latter is acknowledged as the ground and ineliminable condition of the former. This is so, not only because science and art are said to come to humans "through experience," but most notably because, without experience, art or in general the knowledge of universals remains empty and formal. It is experience that endows universal knowledge with meaning and relevance: without it, those possessing abstract cognition alone (the *logos*) would be at a loss as to what they are speaking of. As though their knowledge would lack content, they would not know how it might relate to the worldly circumstances, indeed, they would move in the world without being able to make connections between their formal cognition and their surroundings: they would be unable to recognize individuals in the world, to encounter them in their delimitation and definiteness, as belonging together in a given universal. *Logos*, the knowledge of universals, whose work is the discursive organization of the universals in their configurations, constitutes a potential factor of alienation. If emancipated from its intuitive inception, severed from its connection with the individual, *logos* says literally nothing. It abstracts the one who knows or speaks in this fashion from action and, more broadly, from life. Here we hear anticipated the prescription of the adherence of *logos* to experience, on which Aristotle copiously insists in the ethical treatises. But also, to remain within the compass of the *Metaphysics*, this foreshadows the numerous remarks on the one-sidedness of mathematics as well as the analysis of the principle of non-contradiction in Book Gamma, crucially based on the critique of contentious arguments that are self-destructive to the extent that they go against the experience of the speakers themselves.

On the other hand, however, by emphasizing the living ground of experience Aristotle by no means ends up privileging blind practice, the automatism of habit not illuminated by discrimination, by the awareness of causes, of the why. Understanding (*eidenai*), and therefore wisdom (*sophia*), are attributed to those who have art rather than to those who have experience alone, and, among artists, to those who know the principles according to which they operate rather than to those who merely execute various kinds of manual labor without fully comprehending what they are doing and why. In fact, the latter provide an extreme illustration of the limits pertaining to those who lack understanding. For not only do they not know the cause (the "why"), despite the fact that they act as artists, but also they carry out their task without displaying the most elementary signs of reflection or awareness, as though by nature. They are like inanimate things, determined in their motions by their nature and the insurmountable necessity it carries. Thus, not knowing the cause bespeaks in a way acting outside life, having fallen off from life: being inanimate, tool-like. The phenomenon of the alienation from life seems to be characteristic of both *logos* without experience and exercise without insight.

Finally, it should be observed that, however much said to be dissociated from practical or productive endeavors, wisdom, *sophia*, is nevertheless manifested through concrete actions, for example, the ability to teach. There appears to be no other, non-practical access to or symptom of it: "in general, a sign [σημεῖον] of someone who understands is the power [τὸ δύνασθαι] to teach, and because of this we regard art more than experience to be science" (981b7–9). In the exercise of art I make the experience my own in such a way that I no longer merely undergo what presents itself and recurs: rather, I frequent the perceived, cultivate an intimacy with it, comprehend it and am shaped by this apprehension, in such a way that I can share this with others. I gain a degree of familiarity with the matter at stake and am able to guide others in that proximity. Aside from these altogether concrete involvements, wisdom would remain undetectable. Understanding wisdom first of all by reference to skilled craftsmanship, as Aristotle himself does in the *Nicomachean Ethics* (1141a10ff.), is not merely a matter of acknowledging the archaic usage. Even as that which is pursued in first philosophy and hence transcends every manner of insight pertaining to specific fields, wisdom makes itself manifest as such *in deed.* It becomes recognizable through the way one is, acts, and lives.

1.4. Practical Genealogy of Wisdom

Aristotle draws to the conclusion of the discussion in Alpha 1 by restating the notion of science sketched so far. Again he outlines the practical genealogy of the knowledge of universals, showing the awakening of reason and noetic insight through and as art, production, creative engagement within the world. Again, Aristotle surmises that the arts transcending matters of usefulness, necessity, and the resolution into an object brought forth, arts practiced more for their own sake and resulting in a kind of "activity" (διαγωγήν, 981b18), "were always believed to be wiser . . . because their sciences were not oriented toward use [μὴ πρὸς χρῆσιν]" (981b18–20). It is in this self-overcoming of the arts as essentially productive that the sciences proper "were discovered" (981b22), specifically there where human beings could experience a certain leisure, and therefore a freedom from the necessities of life. At this point, as if to make more explicit the ethical conditions of the inquiry to be undertaken here, Aristotle refers to the *Ethics*, where, he says, a more sustained discussion is developed concerning art and science in their difference. This reference is hardly casual, since in closing he points out again that the inquiry called first philosophy, that is, the inquiry pursuing wisdom and the intuition of first principles, must be framed in terms of belief and appearances. Such is the ground of the determination of wisdom and of the progression toward it:

> [A]ll human beings believe [ὑπολαμβάνουσι] that what is called "wisdom" is concerned with the first causes and principles; so that, as stated before, someone of experience seems [δοκεῖ] to be wiser than someone who has any of the sensations, someone who has art wiser than someone experienced, a master-artist wiser than a manual worker, and theoretical inquiries [θεωρητικαὶ] to be wisdom to a higher degree than the productive ones [ποιητικῶν]. Clearly, then, wisdom is a science of certain causes and principles. (981b28–982a2)

In the end, a certain ineffability or elusiveness of wisdom seems to emerge from this consideration. Even the theoretical inquiries, those not motivated by utility but oriented to contemplation, do not coincide with wisdom. They approximate wisdom. They strive, desire to seize it, but do so only "to a higher degree." To conclude by anticipating analyses that will be carried out later in the course of this work, we might add that, qua "science of certain causes and principles," and hence science of the indemonstrable ground of demonstration, wisdom will prove to be a strange science indeed. For wisdom will name an apprehension that lies beside and beyond demonstration, an apprehension that is in fact defined by belief and is itself a matter of belief – which again marks the belonging of wisdom in the order of appearance and of the practical. The "science of wisdom" is, thus, not quite and not simply a science. It will be said in the *Ethics* that wisdom is science perfected, science accompanied by its leader, as it were: science, that is, demonstrated knowledge, supplemented by the intuitive perception (*nous*) of its own ground and principles. But science perfected by *nous* means science perfected nonscientifically, for *nous* presents itself as excessive with respect to the syllogistic procedures that science designates, in fact, as excessive to the order of discourse, of *logos* itself.

2. *POSTERIOR ANALYTICS*: ON *NOUS* AND *AISTHĒSIS*

The above considerations are echoed and amplified in the *Posterior Analytics*, where, at various stages, we find the intimation of the indissoluble concomitance (if not the sameness) of noetic and sensible perception, *nous* and *aisthēsis.* Here Aristotle gestures toward *aisthēsis* as informed by *nous* and deepens his examination of the structure of the intertwinement of the two.[6]

The treatise begins by elaborating the thesis that scientific knowledge rests on premises that are better known than the conclusions to which scientific demonstration leads: better known by their nature, without qualification, or *simply*, and not relative to us.[7] Premises, principles, or causes are prior in the order of what is, and hence eminently knowable, although they may be posterior in the order of human coming to know. The priority here at stake, however, may not simply be said to be ontological without qualification, just as the meaning of the knowledge pertaining to it requires further clarification. Priority in the order of being designates a priority indeterminately exceeding ontology as the distinctively human philosophical discourse. It designates the priority inhering in nature itself, in that which imposes itself on the human prior to any attempt at discursive systematization – the priority of what is and, in virtue of this, compels assent. Knowledge here indicates

[6] Segments of the following discussion on *Posterior Analytics* and of the elaboration of *nous* in the Main Section below appear in my "Ethics as First Philosophy: Aristotelian Reflections on Intelligence, Sensibility, and Transcendence," in Silvia Benso and Brian Schroeder eds., *Levinas and the Ancients* (Bloomington: Indiana UP, 2007).

[7] The reverse is the case with induction (*epagōgē*), which moves from what is clearer and more known to us (72b29f.). See also 71b35–72a6.

precisely the compelling, inevitable character of that which can only be affirmed.

The premises of demonstration are more known, that is, compel assent to *begin with*. Yet, as beginnings, *arkhai*, they exhibit a certain elusiveness, an excess vis-à-vis the procedures of demonstrated knowledge which they initiate. They are knowable above all, and yet, not according to the demonstrative/scientific practices. This irreducible distinction and discontinuity, in Aristotle, between knowing demonstratively and knowing otherwise, that is, the perception of principles, is of incalculable consequence. At stake is the unbridgeable rift between *logos* and *nous*, even though, at this juncture, Aristotle is not explicitly casting the discussion in these terms.

In the context of discursive or apodictic knowledge, the principles or premises appear as given. Within the procedures of knowledge, the question concerning principles can at most be formulated, but not addressed. Indeed, the principles remain radically extraneous to the demonstrative practices: the latter base themselves on principles, but cannot examine, assess, or clarify them. The principles remain liminal, and therefore ungraspable, vis-à-vis the discourses they make possible. And yet, if the sciences must *begin* with and from principles that have always already elicited conviction, knowledge of the principles, in the mode of intuitive belief and reliance must be experienced *primordially and decisively*. In this sense, ontological and noetic priority, or priority in the order of being and priority in the order of human knowing as intuition, would coincide – precisely in virtue of the irreducibility of human knowing to syllogistic knowledge. Indeed, ontological and noetic priority would converge in a primacy altogether excessive to the order of apodictic knowledge. Says Aristotle:

> [Demonstrated knowledge, ἐπίστασθαι ὧν ἀπόδειξις, must be acquired] from [premises which are] first and indemonstrable.... [The premises] should be the causes, more known [γνωριμώτερα], and prior [to the conclusion]. They must be the causes [of the conclusion] since we know [ἐπιστάμεθα] a thing when we know [εἰδῶμεν] a cause of it; they must be prior [πρότερα] [by nature to the conclusion], if they, as such, are its causes; and they must be previously known [προγιγνωσκόμενα], not only in the other manner, i.e., by being understood [ξυνιέναι], but also by being known that they are [εἰδέναι ὅτι ἔστιν]. (71b27–33)

It is telling that, in order to point to the intuitive apprehension of principles, Aristotle repeatedly switches from the language of *epistēmē* to that of "having seen," *eidenai*. It is this indeterminately prior vision that grounds the syllogistic procedures of scientific knowledge in the proper sense. It is this perception that constitutes the principle and beginning, the *arkhē*, of discursive articulation and analysis. And such a beginning is first simply and absolutely. It is origin, and as such its priority is less a matter of chronology than a matter of the always already of immediacy, of that which is immediate and has no middle, no beyond, no further reference. Aristotle says: "a principle of demonstration is an immediate [ἄμεσος] premise and a premise is said to be immediate if there is no other premise prior" (72a7–8).

Not only, then, are the principles acquired through intuitive perception and ultimately a matter of belief, but they moreover enjoy a higher status than demonstrated knowledge. The latter, after all, is *derived* from the premises intuitively acquired and is therefore marked by a certain secondariness with respect to them. What comes to the fore is, thus, the irreducibility of knowledge, even of *epistēmē* itself, to the order of demonstration. On this point Aristotle could not be more explicit:

> We on the other hand say that (1) not all knowledge [ἐπιστήμην] is demonstrable but that (2) knowledge of immediate premises is indemonstrable. And it is evident that this is necessary; for if it is necessary to know [ἐπίστασθαι] the prior [premises] from which a demonstration proceeds, and if these [premises] eventually stop [ἵσταται] when they are immediate, they are of necessity indemonstrable. Such then is our position, and we also say that there is not only knowledge [ἐπιστήμην], but also a principle of knowledge [ἀρχὴν ἐπιστήμης] by which we know [γνωρίζομεν] the limits [ὅρους] [of that knowledge]. (72b19–25)

It is noteworthy that Aristotle, on the one hand, preserves a certain distinction between the modes of *epistēmē* and of *gnōsis*, reserving the latter for knowledge in the comprehensive sense, which includes but exceeds demonstration. On the other hand, however, he also proposes a loose usage of the language of *epistēmē* in order to signal a kind of overflowing of scientific knowledge with respect to itself: science seems to be characterized by a centrifugal movement according to which it finds its boundaries and stability only in its other, in the non-scientific, non-demonstrable beginnings. It founds itself on principles it cannot found, and this means that it is neither self-sufficient nor self-enclosed. In this sense, the principle appears in a way as an end: as that which brings to an end the concatenation of causes, as that which stands secure and past which no further movement can be thought. It is only thus that the field and scope of science can be delimited.

2.1. *Epagōgē*, or, What Introduces Itself into Me

First principles, then, whether axioms or principles pertaining to the particular sciences, are known not by demonstration but through noetic intuition. As we shall see, this will receive further elaboration in the course of the ethical discussion. But what is crucial in this context is Aristotle's insistence on the connection between noetic apprehension and induction, *epagōgē* – on the belonging of the phenomenon of intuitive perception in the broader experience of the physical, sensible surroundings.[8] From the point of view of the human condition, *noēsis* gives itself in and through the perceptual acknowledgment and ensuing investigation of the environment, whether we should call this *phusis* or *kosmos*. The final section of the *Posterior Analytics* (Beta 19) is devoted to this issue, but this articulation is variously foreshadowed at earlier stages, most notably at Alpha 18, which deserves to be quoted extensively:

> It is also evident that, if a [power of] sensation is lacking, some corresponding science must be lacking, for a science cannot be acquired if indeed we learn either by induction or by demonstration. Now a demonstration proceeds from universals [ἐκ τῶν καθόλου], whereas an induction proceeds from particulars [ἐκ τῶν κατὰ μέρος]. But universals cannot be contemplated [θεωρῆσαι] except through induction (and even the so-called things from abstraction [τὰ ἐξ ἀφαιρέσεως], although not separable, are made known by induction, since some of them belong to each genus insofar as each is such-and-such), and it is impossible to learn by induction without having the [power of] sensation. For of individuals [τῶν γὰρ καθ' ἕκαστον] [there can be only] sensation, and no knowledge of them can be acquired; and neither can we [demonstrate conclusions] from universals without induction, nor can we [acquire universals] through induction without sensation. (81a38–b9)

While sensing may pertain to the perception of individuals, of which there can be no knowledge strictly speaking, it is also the case that possessing the manifold power of sensation is a necessary condition for the development of scientific knowledge. For sensation is the ground of inductive investigation, and it is through such an investigation that the universals are obtained. Indeed, Aristotle emphasizes, even universals that appear to be abstracted from the sensory datum, those which appear to be removed from the sensible and are thematized separately, as though autonomous,

[8] For paradigmatic ("traditional") discussion of *nous* and inductive apprehension in *Posterior Analytics*, see, e.g., C. H. Kahn, "The Role of *Nous* in the Cognition of First Principles in *Posterior Analytics* ii 19," in Enrico Berti, ed., *Aristotle on Science: The* Posterior Analytics (Padua: Editrice Antenore, 1981), 385–414.

are indeed taken in thanks to the experience of the sensible surrounding. As laid out in *Metaphysics* Mu and Nu, the mathematical objects, such as numbers, are not separate from the sensible beings, though they can be separated in thinking or discourse, *logos.* This, however, crucially extends the claim with which the section opens. To be sure, if a specific power of sensation is lacking, the corresponding science also will be lacking: for instance, in the absence of the power of hearing, the scientific investigation of acoustic phenomena will be unthinkable. But saying that even universals arrived at through discursive abstraction are ultimately acquired in virtue of induction means that science as such could not develop aside from the basic involvement in sensibility.

Induction, *epagōgē,* then, is the operation whereby I take in (*epagō*) the surrounding and, in so doing, make possible the lighting up of an intuition that is no longer limited to the contingent particular or configuration I am sensing, but rather embraces all possible analogous cases and illuminates something *katholou,* "according to the whole" – universally, so to speak. More precisely still, induction refers to that *possibility* that introduces (*epagō*) itself into me with the sensory experience. Indeed, sensation brings (*agō*) into and upon (*epi*) me the possibility of an insight exceeding the scope of my immediate sensing or observing – the possibility of revealing and actualizing the capacity for such an insight, the power of *nous.* Strictly speaking, sensation pertains to being affected by individuals, and yet, it implies the possibility of grasping that which cannot be reduced to individuals and, rather, gathers and configures them. The interpenetration of affection and formative involvement should be noted in this regard.

As though implicated in, folded into sensibility, the possibility of contemplating universals is led into me as I sense. Apprehending by induction means, therefore, realizing the possibility that is imported into one by the very fact that one is alive and sensitive, that one is stirred up by what comes in and responsive to it. But, of course, to speak of realizing the possibility implicit in sensing (the potential of sensation) also raises the question whether sensation may always already be ordered, structured, and informed – whether, that is, instead of attempting to isolate the moment of sensation as the mere report of raw and chaotic data, we should see in the articulate differentiation yielded by the senses the intersection of *aisthēsis* and *nous.* While we are not in the position of elaborating on this question further at this point, we can minimally say that induction presents itself as a certain conjunction or intersection of sensation and noetic perception, as the advent of noetic insight out of the undergoing of the sensible. It is striking that Aristotle refers to the inductive grasp of universals in terms of *theōrein,* properly contemplative or theoretical understanding: in my exposure to the sensible, I come to see, to discern what is not itself sensible, not a thing among things, but belongs in the sensible and imparts to it its shapes and rhythm.

2.2. Thinking by Sensing

Later in section 31 of Book Alpha, Aristotle underlines again that knowledge (*epistēmē*) is not through sensation, for sensation is of the "this," which "of necessity is somewhere and now," while "that which is universal and belongs to all cannot be sensed" (87b30–31). Accordingly, sensation is found to be less honorable than the knowledge of the universals, which (1) reveals the cause and (2) enables demonstrated knowledge. Nevertheless, here once more the bond between sensation and intuition of universals is restated. It is indeed formulated in terms of dependence of the latter on the former:

> It is evident, then, that it is impossible for one to know something demonstrable by sensing it, unless by "sensing" one means having knowledge through demonstration. In some problems, however, reference may be made to lack of sensation; for we might not have inquired if we could see [ἑωρῶμεν], not that we would understand [εἰδότες] by seeing [τῷ ὁρᾶν], but that from seeing [ἐκ τοῦ ὁρᾶν] we would have the universal. For example, if we would see [ἑωρῶμεν] that the burning glass had holes in it and the light passing through them, by seeing [τῷ ὁρᾶν] each instance separately it would also be clear why it burns and simultaneously [ἅμα] the thought [νοῆσαι] that such is the case in every instance. (88a10–17)

Witnessing various instances of a certain phenomenon reveals its cause, as though, by repeated experience, the intimate structure of what is experienced would be laid bare. This immediately entails the intuition that what has been revealed holds in all analogous cases, according to the whole. In this sense, cause and universal are simultaneous, or even identical. Here Aristotle's effort seems especially acute, to convey in the linear unfolding of discourse the simultaneity or coincidence (*hama*) of thinking and sensing, the interpolation of the immediate into the temporal, unmediated intuition at once breaking through repeated perceptual exposure.

2.3. Singularity Making a Stand

But it is in Beta 19 that we find the decisive statement concerning the arising of universals or first principles out of repeated sensible perception.

The way in which Aristotle here pursues the issue of "the principles, how they become known and what is the knowing habit [γνωρίζουσα ἕξις] of them" (99b18–19), parallels the analysis in *Metaphysics* Alpha 1, situating the preconditions and development of intellectual perception in the field of life broadly understood. It does, however, introduce a few points of decisive importance that are not illuminated in the "metaphysical" discourse.

Sensation, the innate (*sumphuton*) power (*dunamis*) that all animals possess and is less honorable than knowledge in accuracy, is in and of itself said to be "discriminating" (κριτικήν) (99b36). In certain living beings, however, the sensation presents an abiding character (*monē*): it is retained in the soul. Here, unlike in the discourse of the *Metaphysics*, Aristotle elaborates on the mnemonic power (*mnēmē*) in terms of the ability to "draw out a *logos* from the retention of such [sensations]" (100a3f.). For certain animals, the formation and formulation of *logos* seems to occur out of (*ek*) the constancy of sensation harbored in the soul and constituting memory. Thanks to the persistence of the impression, they can divine, out of the phenomenon, the *logos* at the heart of the phenomenon. Again, as is said in the *Metaphysics*, many memories of the same lead to one experience. Here, however, experience seems to be equated with the formation of the universal: the latter seems to give itself immediately alongside the former, out of the memory of sense impressions – out of that abiding that also lets the *logos* transpire and be grasped. From this level of experiential seizing of the universal would proceed the principles of science and of art:

> Again, from experience[s] or from every universal which has come to rest [ἠρεμήσαντος] in the soul and which, being one besides the many, would be one and the same in all of them, [there arises] a principle [ἀρχή] of art and of science, of art if it is a principle about generation [γένεσιν], but of science if it is a principle about being [τὸ ὄν]. (100a6–9)

At this point Aristotle distinguishes the universals from the principles properly understood, suggesting that it is from the distinctness and fixity of the universal that a principle would issue. What is important to note, however, is the characterization of the formation of universals as a halt, a stabilization. Out of the indefinite flow of sensations, the universal names the endurance of an all-embracing insight, of an intuition that, because according to the whole, does not simply pass away:

> So neither are these [knowing] habits present in the soul [from the start] in any determinate way, nor do they come into being from other more known habits, but

from sensation [ἀπὸ αἰσθήσεως], like a reversal (τροπῆς) in battle brought about when one makes a stand [στάντος], then another, then another, till a principle [ἀρχὴν] is reached; and the soul is of such a nature as to be able to be affected in this way. (100a10–14)

The disposition to know universals issues from sensation in a way similar to the countermovement that arrests a retreat in the course of a battle. As the flux of men fleeing is countered by one of them halting, others similarly take position in succession: in this way, an order is established and fixated. As in the passage previously quoted concerning immediate and indemonstrable premises (premises "of necessity indemonstrable," which "eventually stop, ἵσταται, when they are immediate," 72b19–22), seizing universals appears to be not simply a matter of resting in the soul but, more precisely, a matter of stopping and standing upright. Knowing, most clearly in the mode of *epistamai*, is illuminated in terms of setting up, over, and steadfastly (*histēmi, ephistamai*). It is such a crystallization, such a steady posture bespeaking reliability, which allows for discernment. Aristotle elucidates further, this time making it clear that universals broadly understood and first principles alike stem in the end from the exposure to the sensible:

When one of those without differences [ἀδιαφόρων] has made a stand [στάντος], [there is formed] in the soul the first universal (for though one senses an individual [τὸ καθ' ἕκαστον], sensation is of the universal, e.g., of a man, not of the man Callias), and then again another among these makes a stand [ἵσταται], till a universal that has no parts [ἀμερῆ] makes a stand [στῇ]; for example, "such and such an animal," and this proceeds till "animal," and in the latter case similarly. Clearly, then, of necessity we come to know the first [principles] [τὰ πρῶτα] by induction; for it is in this way that sensation, too, produces in us [ἐμποιεῖ] the universal. (100a15–b5)

As Aristotle also specifies at 97b29–31, by "those without differences" (τοῖς ἀδιαφόροις) we should understand the particular individual.[9] Mnemonically retained and erected, the sensory impression of the individual gives rise to the intuition of a universal. This occurs as though immediately, for, as Aristotle underlines, "sensation is of the universal," it literally "produces the universal in us," makes it actual in our soul. Indeed, let this be said in passing, the intimation here is that there can be no sensation

9 "It is also easier to define the particular (τὸ καθ' ἕκαστον) than the universal, so one should proceed from particulars (ἀπὸ τῶν καθ' ἕκαστα) to universals; for equivocations, too, escape detection (λανθάνουσι) in universals more than in those without differences (ἐν τοῖς ἀδιαφόροις)." The "therapeutic" tenor of this remark, aiming at preserving any inquiry from straying too far from experience, i.e., from particulars, is noteworthy as well.

of an absolutely unique individual, which would not belong in a broader class and through which a universal could not be discernible. The fixation of a multiplicity of universals makes it possible for human beings to perceive more comprehensive ones, under which the universals brought forth by sensation may be gathered – just as, for example, the definitions of various animals may belong together under the genus "animal."

2.4. The Truth of the Things Themselves

Once the intimate implication of noetic intuition in sensation has been thus articulated, the remarks concluding the *Posterior Analytics* sound all the more peremptory in their pointing to the experiential, and hence thoroughly practical, presuppositions in virtue of which scientific inquiry may at all take place. Such is the life of scientific practices:

> Since of the thinking habits [τῶν περὶ τὴν διάνοιαν ἕξεων] by which we think truly [ἀληθεύομεν] some are always true while others (e.g., opinion and calculation [δόξα καὶ λογισμός]) may also be false; since scientific knowledge (ἐπιστήμη) and intuition [νοῦς] are always true and there is no genus [of knowledge] that is more accurate [ἀκριβέστερον] than scientific knowledge except intuition; since the principles of demonstration are [by nature] more known [than what is demonstrated], and all scientific knowledge is knowledge with *logos* [μετὰ λόγου] whereas there could be no scientific knowledge of the principles; and since nothing can be more true [ἀληθέστερον] than scientific knowledge except intuition; it follows from the examination of these [facts] that intuition would be [the habit or faculty] of principles [ἀρχῶν], and that a principle of a demonstration could not be a demonstration and so [the principles] of scientific knowledge could not be scientific knowledge. Accordingly, if we have no genus of a true [habit] other than scientific knowledge, intuition would be the principle [beginning, origin] of scientific knowledge. Moreover, a principle would be of a principle, and every [other kind of knowledge] is similarly related to a pertinent fact [πρᾶγμα]. (100b5–17)

Of the dispositions to know, only noetic intuition and science are always true, disclose the true (*alētheuein*), and pertain to that which is necessarily and always. But, again, noetic intuition appears as more honorable: intuition itself is said to be "more true" than science and to surpass it in accuracy, while the principles intuition yields are found to be in themselves more known. It could be said that the *alētheuein* that intuition names releases truth to a higher degree than *epistēmē*. But these two modes of knowledge are not compared as though their difference were merely a matter of degree in exactness. They are, instead, essentially heterogeneous. The knowing of intuition does not take place with and through *logos*: it is not discursive, does not share in the demonstrative and inferential procedures constituting scientific knowledge. Intuition of principles is non-discursive, not mediated by the articulation in and of *logos.* While scientific knowledge is established and firmed up by its apodictic strategies, the contemplation of principles involves another kind of certainty, namely, the unshakeable conviction immediately compelled by the evidence of the phenomena themselves. Without proof or syllogism, what is experienced induces assent. In Aristotle's words, "[in the case of induction,] the universal is proved through the being clear of the particular [διὰ τοῦ δῆλον εἶναι τὸ καθ' ἕκαστον]" (71a8–9). Accordingly, it is far from accidental that in the *Metaphysics* the "science of wisdom," the strange science endowed with an awareness of itself and of its own intuitive "ground," is said to be necessitated and guided by the truth itself (*autē hē alētheia*) (984b10), that is to say, by the things themselves (*auto to pragma*) (984a18) or phenomena (986b31).

Noetic perception, then, concerns the non-mediated perception of principles. It provides the origin of scientific inquiry and, at the same time, is radically discontinuous, indeed, disruptive vis-à-vis the linear unfolding of such an inquiry. The apprehension of principles is not knowledge *meta logou,* accomplished through *logos,* although it grounds *logos* and discerns it in the phenomena perceived and ordered according to the whole. Awareness of the noetic stratum by nature prior to scientific investigation may, alone, grant *logos* its proper positioning. It alone may acknowledge *logos* as emerging out of phenomena (100a3–4) and anchor *logos,* the discursive elaboration of scientific demonstration, to experience. The possibility, always inherent in *logos,* of an emancipation from experience and the corresponding need to prevent such an alienation, such a drifting away that makes *logos* abstract, indeed formal, are central concerns for Aristotle. As already announced, they constitute a leading thread not only of the ethical discourse but of the meditation in the *Metaphysics* as well. Again, we will have ample opportunity to return to this.

2.5. Lateness of Discursive Knowing

Let us merely note, to conclude this brief excursus through the *Posterior Analytics,* that the remarks on science and intuition in the final section of the treatise only magnify what was already stated at the very beginning. The inquiry opens with a proposition both laconic and pregnant with consequences: "All teaching and learning through discourse [διανοητική] come to be from previous [ἐκ προϋπαρχούσης] knowledge [γνώσεως]" (71a1–2). All transmission and reception of knowledge that move across (*dia*) intuition or thinking (*noēsis*) in order to articulate themselves discursively presuppose a knowledge that must always already be there in order for any exchange to take place at all. Since the first sentence, with the reference to preceding knowledge we witness a bifurcation in the language of knowing. We notice, concomitantly, the intimation that knowledge of principles, of that from (*ek*) which discursive knowledge begins, cannot be taught or learned – not, anyway, conveyed according to the way of human dialogue. The apprehension of principles emerges out of the silent unfolding of life itself: it is inscribed in my own constitution, or, rather, inscribes my constitution as never simply my own. I never subsist aside from the apprehending, but am constituted in this exposure to and undergoing of that which arrives, in this permanent openness.

The problem of prior and unmediated knowledge, adumbrated in the beginning of the treatise, is retained as such, as a problem, in its disquieting, unsettling potential. For such a knowledge is a prerequisite for all human mediation, communication, and scientific practices, yet is not humanly established and remains, as a matter of fact, only dimly illuminated. Discursive knowing is, in a sense, always already late: always already requires and finds a ground that exceeds it in worth and originary force. This does not, however, pose the problem of infinite regress. As we shall see in addressing the ethical texts, such a problem is implicit (though remarkably left unaddressed) in Aristotle's statement that the formation of habits always rests on a previous having, on previous habituations – for, he maintains, in matters of human custom and construction, actuality comes to be out of actuality. However, in the examination of the origin of scientific discourse, the prior knowledge always already required does provide an absolute beginning. As we saw above, first principles as such constitute a halt, the term beyond which no causal concatenation may continue. And yet, we already observed and will, no doubt, notice again that such an unqualified priority remains by definition impervious to analysis. In virtue of itself, it poses difficulties that, for the scientific endeavor, are hardly less severe than the abyss of infinite regress.

3. ARCHITECTURE AS FIRST PHILOSOPHY

From the preceding observations, we should become aware, in the first place, of the originary problems that the practice of scientific investigation and concomitant demonstrative operations entail and cannot themselves properly grasp. Second, and even beyond the disquietudes of science as such, we should notice the strangeness of the "science of wisdom." Aristotle elaborates on the tasks taken up in the *Metaphysics* as follows:

> Further, to understand [εἰδέναι] things or to know [ἐπίστασθαι] them for their own sake belongs in the highest degree to the science of that which is known or knowable [ἐπιστητοῦ ἐπιστήμῃ] in the highest degree; for he who pursues [αἱρούμενος] knowing [ἐπίστασθαι] for its own sake will pursue [αἱρήσεται] most of all the science [ἐπιστήμην] taken in the highest degree, and such is the science of that which is known or knowable [ἐπιστητοῦ] in the highest degree; and those which are known or knowable [ἐπιστητὰ] in the highest degree are first or the causes, for it is because of these and from these that the other things are known [γνωρίζεται], and not these because of the underlying subjects [ὑποκειμένων]. (982a30–b4)

The science unfolding in the treatises that will have received the title of *Metaphysics*, thus, presents itself as a science proceeding in unfamiliar ways, beyond science as demonstrability. For it concerns first principles, which ground demonstrative procedures but are themselves indemonstrable. What, in the *Metaphysics*, is termed science (*epistēmē*) or first philosophy (*philosophia prōtē*) falls outside demonstration. It deserves, therefore, to be addressed as "science," with quotation marks signaling its eccentricity. Despite the insistent claims (paradigmatically in Alpha 2) that first philosophy is "free" because "not productive," it remains the case that this very peculiar "science" is essentially implicated in sensibility – and this means, at once, in human action (*praxis*). After all, as is said in the *Posterior Analytics*, the inductive operation by which one gains noetic insight into principles out of sensing lies at the heart of dialectical and rhetorical stipulations as well.[10] This, as we shall see, is examined further in the *Topics*.

The twofold claim put forth in this study, subsequently, is (1) that the science articulated in the *Metaphysics* remains essentially "architectonic," that is to say, involved in human action and even human construction, and (2) that, conversely, the domain of ethics must be considered in its originary character, that is to say, in its ontological priority as well as systematic comprehensiveness. Besides what has been highlighted so far, at this point let us also add that Aristotle's language itself offers innumerable occasions to call into question the rigid distinction between, on the one hand, the designation of practical discourse as "architectonic"

[10] "Rhetorical discourses, too, produce persuasion (συμπείθουσιν) in the same way; for they do so either through examples (διὰ παραδειγμάτων), in which case there is an induction, or through enthymemes, [each of] which, as such, is a syllogism" (71a9–11).

(*arkhitektonikos*) and, on the other hand, that of first philosophy as "commanding" (*arkhikos*) or "most commanding" (*arkhikōtatos*). The fluidity of the Aristotelian terminology deserves, in this connection, close scrutiny.

3.1. Terminology

3.1.1. The Discipline "Architectonic" and "Authoritative" in the Highest Degree

Granted, Aristotle does indeed characterize ethical or political analysis as pertaining to the order of making and to the operation of the master artist (*arkhitektōn*). In *Nicomachean Ethics,* however, ethics or politics is said to be "architectonic" in the sense of encompassing: "in every case the end of the architectonic [science] is more choice-worthy than all the ends of the [sciences] subordinate to it [τῶν ὑπ' αὐτά], for the latter ends are pursued for the sake of the former end" (1094a14–16). Aristotle spells out more fully the implications of this:

> [The highest end] would seem to belong to the [science or faculty] that is most authoritative [κυριωτάτης] and architectonic in the highest degree [μάλιστα ἀρχιτεκτονικῆς]. Now politics appears to be such; for it is this which regulates [διατάσσει] what sciences [ἐπιστημῶν] are needed in a state and which of the sciences should be learned by each [kind of individuals] and to what extent.... And since this faculty uses the rest of the sciences and also legislates what they should do [πράττειν] and what they should abstain from doing, its end would include [περιέχοι ἂν] the ends of the others. (1094a27–b6)

It is ethical considerations that shape the very domain within which the sciences may, then, take place and operate. In their very subsistence, features, and practices, the sciences are arranged according to the exigencies of the *polis* and the negotiations informing communal life. Because of this, ethics (politics) is said to be most architectonic and authoritative. This is also emphatically stated in the *Politics,* where Aristotle again insists on the inherently ethical dimension of the search for the highest good: "In every science and every art the end aimed at is a good; and the supreme good and the good in the highest degree [μέγιστον δὲ καὶ μάλιστα] depends on the most authoritative [κυριωτάτῃ] faculty [δύναμις], which is politics" (1282b14–16). That the primacy of ethics or politics is indicated in terms of its "architectonic," that is, constructive character, may seem to set it apart from the unqualified eminence of first philosophy. And yet, it is remarkable that the architectonic power and function of ethics or politics is said to underlie and comprehend all other activities, most notably those pertaining to the sciences. It could be said that the ethical reflection is "architectonic" precisely because "most authoritative," that its power to shape, configure, and build is at once the manifestation of its overarching rule.

3.1.2. "Authoritativeness" of First Principles or Being

The fact that the "architectonic" investigation into *praxis* should be elucidated by reference to "authoritativeness" (*kuriotēs*) claims our attention also because Aristotle consistently utilizes the language of "authoritativeness" in order to designate the unparalleled dignity of first principles or being. Let us mention only a couple of moments from the *Metaphysics* providing evidence in this regard. The first one attributes the trait of authoritativeness to being itself:

> But since combining [συμπλοκή] and dividing [διαίρεσις] are in thought [διανοίᾳ] and not in things [πράγμασι], and being in this sense is distinct from being in the authoritative [κυρίως] sense (for thought attaches [to] [συνάπτει] or detaches [ἀφαιρεῖ] [from the subject matter] either a what-it-is or a quality or a quantity or something else), we must leave aside being as attribute and being as the true.... And so, leaving these aside, we should examine the causes and principles of being itself qua being [τοῦ ὄντος αὐτοῦ τά αἴτια καὶ τὰς ἀρχὰς ᾗ ὄν]. (1027b29–1028a4)

Again, in the context of yet another remarkable meditation on what would distinguish the "science of wisdom," Aristotle attributes superlative authoritativeness to the highest principle. This takes place as late as treatise Kappa and is worth quoting:

> Since there is a science of being qua being [τοῦ ὄντος ᾗ ὄν] and separable [χωριστόν], we must inquire whether we should posit this to be the same as physics or other than it in the highest degree. Physics is concerned with things having in themselves a principle of motion, while mathematics is a theoretical science and one concerned with things that remain the same but are not separable [χωριστά]. Thus, there is a science distinct from these which is concerned with separable [χωριστὸν] and immovable being [ὄν], if indeed there is such a beingness [οὐσία], that is, one which is separable [χωριστὴ] and immovable, as we shall try to show [δεικνύναι]. And if indeed there is such a nature [φύσις] in beings [ἐν τοῖς οὖσιν], the divine [τὸ θεῖον], too, would be in them [ἐνταῦθ'] if anywhere [που], and this nature would be the primary and most authoritative principle [πρώτη καὶ κυριωτάτη ἀρχή]. (1064a28–b1)

What is so noteworthy here is that, despite the insistence on the requirement of separability and the apparent distance asserted with respect to physics, being itself, "being qua being," is elaborated on in terms of nature: a nature, *phusis*, separable and unmoved, which, *if it could indeed be shown*, would have to be seen *in beings*, as belonging in them. Aristotle is here asking us to think together, however unbearable the tension in such a thinking may be, unmoved separability *and* inherence in that which is – and to think being itself in and as such a togetherness. And *if* nature thus understood were to be, that is to say, to be in and as beings, what would thereby be indicated would be being in its magnificence, being as "most authoritative principle." It is in this way that Aristotle evokes the divine and intimates the closeness, intimacy, indeed, the inherence of the divine with respect to beings. And this inherence would be irreducible to the immanence defined by contraposition to transcendence: for it would name a belonging, a dwelling-in precisely of that which remains transcendent, in the sense that it transcends the order of demonstrative knowing and even marks the limits or borders of such a knowing. Of course, given the semantic range of the language of *kuriotēs*, the designation of ethics as "architectonic" and "most authoritative" (*kuriōtatē*) is hardly restrictive. In addition to this, and conversely, passages such as the one just quoted emphatically disclose the study of first principles as altogether involved in the physical, the phenomenal, and, hence, the practical.

Thus, the "architectonic" characterization of ethical discourses must be understood in light of the noblest authoritativeness, which more fully conveys the sense of ethics as all-encompassing. Indeed, it cannot be overemphasized that the language of authoritativeness is drawn on in order to characterize the discourses of ethics and first philosophy alike. Authoritativeness appears, then, as the common thread linking ethics and what will have been called "metaphysics" – the "architectonic" and the "most commanding" modes of inquiry. First philosophy, the "science" of wisdom studying the most authoritative first principles, is itself most authoritative, *kuriōtatē*. In *Metaphysics* 997a11ff., Aristotle posits that the science examining the principles of demonstration eminently possesses authoritativeness and priority, thus complementing the previous description of first philosophy as "most commanding" (ἀρχικωτάτη) (982b4).[11]

[11] Incidentally, in the context of the latter passage Aristotle remarkably exposes the inquiry of first philosophy (the "most commanding" study of first principles and causes) as the discipline "which knows [γνωρίζουσα] that for the sake of which each action is done, and this is the good in each case [τἀγαθὸν ἑκάστου], and, comprehensively, the highest good [τὸ ἄριστον] in the whole of nature" (982b5–7). Just as authoritativeness constitutes the common thread of ethics and first philosophy, so the "most commanding" investigation concerns at once first principles and ethical directives – indeed, in a vigorous synthetic gesture first and ethical principle(s) are indicated as virtually indiscernible.

3.1.3. "Authoritativeness" of Choice or Desire

The terminology pertaining to *kuriotēs* is also employed to relate the authoritatively decisive function of choice (*hairesis, proairesis*). Take, for example, the discussion on "potency according to *logos*" (δυνάμεις αὐτῶν μετὰ λόγου) in *Metaphysics* at 1047b31ff. Here it is pointed out that such a potentiality, unlike that without *logos*, *can* produce contrary effects: while a body is subject to only one law of gravity, in virtue of the knowledge of her art a doctor can either heal or kill. Aristotle then proceeds to affirm that, because it is impossible that the two contraries should be brought about at the same time (*hama*), "there must be something else which decides [something that is eminently decisive, authoritative] [κύριον], and by this I mean desire [ὄρεξιν] or choice [προαίρεσιν]. For whichever of two things an animal desires decisively [authoritatively] [κυρίως], this it will bring about [ποιήσει] when it has the potency to do so and approaches that which can be acted upon" (1048a10–13). This consideration, of course, brings to our attention the peculiar fact of powers indifferently producing opposite outcomes: abilities acquired through practice or discursive teaching, as is exemplarily the case with the arts (*tekhnai*), may be exercised in opposite directions. They may allow for saving as well as annihilating, building as well as destroying. What is decisive, what ultimately has authority in the employment, deployment, and guidance of such resources is choice – and the movement, motion, and motivation concomitant with it. Without the desirous movement of choice, "technical" ability and in general all abilities accompanied by *logos* remain indifferent, or even unmoved, inert – in fact, they do not reach actual articulation. In this perspective, yet again, the primordiality of the question of *ēthos* becomes perspicuous.

Choice, then, is a certain principle of movement. Indeed, one of the definitions of "principle" or "beginning" (ἀρχή) in *Metaphysics* Delta reads:

> that in accordance with whose choice [προαίρεσιν] that which is in motion moves or that which is changing changes; for example, the magistracies in the cities and the dynasties [δυναστεῖαι] and kingships and tyrannies are called "principles," and so are the arts [τέχναι], and of these the architectonic ones [the master arts] [ἀρχιτεκτονικαὶ] in the highest degree. (1013a10–14)

But what should be underscored, again, is the way in which *kuriotēs* and related terms, besides designating the authoritativeness of being itself and the highest principle(s), signify the authoritativeness that orients – the decisive factor or motive force determining a course of action or actualization, that is to say, the course of coming to be. Or, perhaps, the authoritativeness of being might precisely be specified in terms of its power to steer and direct, and, in this way, the reference to the orienting power might simply constitute an incisive explication of what is implied in the authority of being. At any rate, as *kuriōtatē* first philosophy comes to be situated back into the very heart of ethical concerns. After all, it should not have gone unobserved that, in a passage quoted already, the pursuit of first philosophy is disclosed precisely as a matter of choice and striving, of *hairesis,* which once more points to the non-scientific ground of the sciences, and above all of that peculiar "science" said to be "of wisdom": "he who pursues [αἱρούμενος] knowing [ἐπίστασθαι] for its own sake will pursue in the highest degree [μάλιστα αἱρήσεται] the science taken in the highest degree [μάλιστα ἐπιστήμην], and such is the science of that which is known or knowable in the highest degree [μάλιστα ἐπιστητοῦ]," that is, that which is first or the causes (982a32–b2).

3.2. First Philosophy and the Life Chosen

Beyond strictly terminological considerations, Aristotle is even more explicit, in presenting first philosophy in its exquisitely "architectonic" or ethico-political implications, when he attempts to set it apart from the apparently indiscernible practices of sophistry and dialectic. In *Metaphysics* Gamma, after noting that the examination of being qua being constitutes the proper task of the philosopher, he continues:

> Now sophistry and dialectic busy themselves with the same genus of things as philosophy, but philosophy differs from dialectic in the turn of its capacity [δυνάμεως], and from sophistry in the life chosen [τοῦ βίου τῇ προαιρέσει]. Dialectic is tentative concerning that which philosophy knows, sophistry makes the appearance of knowing without knowing. (1004b22–26)

Leaving aside the distinction between philosophy and dialectic – a distinction in and of itself elusive and gesturing toward the greater power or ability of philosophy to contemplate *at once* both sides in a dialectical engagement, while as such the exercise of dialectic would lack such a power of bringing together[12] – it should be underlined that the decisive

[12] In *Metaphysics* Beta, while considering how the recognition, formulation, and elaboration of various manners of *aporia* are essential to the exercise of the "science of wisdom," even to its delimitation and teleological clarification, Aristotle adds a further feature distinctive of first philosophy, namely, the ability to take into consideration, or even assume, diverse and conflicting positions. As he puts it, "with regard to judging [πρὸς τὸ κρῖναι], one is necessarily better off having heard all the arguments [λόγων ἀκηκοότα πάντων], like one who has heard both parties in a lawsuit or both sides in a dispute" (995b2–4).

feature distinguishing philosophy from sophistry is the decision concerning one's life. The way in which life is pursued, the choice orienting one toward life or, in fact, *in life*, is precisely that which, prior to all searching involvement, has always already determined a posture either as philosophical or as sophistical. Most importantly, the motive force sustaining the philosophical endeavor seems to be marked by a genuine concern with being, a concern that is least of all appeased by the spectacle of apparent wisdom and concomitant repute. This reveals choice, most notably the choice of the philosophical endeavor, as least of all a matter of rational (self-)determination, let alone of willfulness. Choice emerges, rather, as a matter of compulsion, of being drawn to that which is perceived as desirable. It is such an irreducibly pre-scientific commitment, such a choice preceding and animating all seeking, such an indeterminately prior having said yes to the provocation of wonder (982b11ff.), which ultimately defines the "science of wisdom" and sets it above – or beneath – all other manners of human undertaking.

It is because of its being "science in the highest degree" that the "science" of wisdom involves premises as well as a manner of proceeding that exceed scientific methodology and, most decisively, attempts to be mindful of this – for that which, by nature and by its own nature, is first and knowable in the highest degree is not the subject matter of science in the main and ordinary sense. The highest "science" is precisely that manner of reflection that begins to cultivate the awareness of the excessive character of its own beginnings and developments – that manner of reflection in which the consciousness of its dependence on that which exceeds it remains active, wakeful. It is far from accidental, then, that Aristotle should often turn to the language of belief and opinion in connection with the premises of the sciences or even the "supreme" (*arkhikōtatē*) science itself. In *Metaphysics* Alpha, while observing how this science is "for its own sake" and therefore "free," yet also becomes possible only once "almost all the necessities [of life]" are supplied, "both for comfort and activity [διαγωγὴν]" (982b22–23), he delineates such a pursuit in its altogether human but simultaneously divine aspects:

> For the most divine science is the most honorable, and a science would be most divine in only two ways: if god in the highest degree would have it, or if it were a science of the divine [things]. This science alone happens to be divine in both ways; for the god seems to all [δοκεῖ τῶν αἰτίων πᾶσιν] to be one of the causes and a certain principle, and god alone or in the highest degree would possess such a science. (983a5–10)

It is by reference to that which is commonly (indeed, unanimously) held, what "seems to all," that the priority and divinity of this science is confirmed. Within the human community that which imposes itself on everyone and compels assent in virtue of its evidence, literally of its visibility, becomes founding. Of course, let us notice in passing, it is remarkable that, even according to the shared view, the god would not be the cause and principle without any further qualification, and may not be the sole repository of knowledge.

3.3. Ethics as Fulfillment of First Philosophy

"Metaphysics," then, which in the order of inquiry comes before ethics, finds in ethics its ground, explication, and self-awareness – finds in ethics that which is prior in the order of being, that is to say, by nature. In the *Metaphysics,* presumably referring to first philosophy, Aristotle affirms that "the most commanding [ἀρχικωτάτη] science, and in command of any subordinate science [ὑπηρετούσης], is the one that knows [γνωρίζουσα] that for the sake of which each thing is done [ἐστι πρακτέον ἕκαστον], and this is the good in each case, and, in general, the highest good [ἄριστον] in the whole of nature [ἐν τῇ φύσει πάσῃ]" (982b4–7). This statement is usually read as announcing that the ethical discussion, regarding "the good in each case," would start once the good "in the whole of nature" would be established through the investigation of the "science of wisdom" – and that the good at stake in ethics would be the exclusively human good, which, with its limits and partiality, should be situated within the compass of the good without qualification. In other words, the passage would yet again underscore the secondary and dependent role of ethics vis-à-vis "metaphysics." Yet, broadly speaking, it could be replied that, in its very character and possibility, wisdom rests on essentially ethical conditions. More specifically, at certain crucial junctures in the ethico-political works Aristotle refuses to relegate ethics (politics) to the ancillary function of a science focusing on the strictly human good and reclaims this discourse in its all-embracing dignity. In the above quoted passage in the *Politics,* Aristotle notes: "In every science and every art the end aimed at is a good; and the supreme good and the good in the highest degree [is aimed at] in the most authoritative faculty [μέγιστον δὲ καὶ μάλιστα ἐν τῇ κυριωτάτῃ πασῶν], which is politics" (1282b15–16). In the *Nicomachean Ethics,* just before the designation of ethics as "architectonic," he makes it clear that it is the task of this investigation to study the good as such, in the highest sense:

> Now if of things we do there is an end which we wish [βουλόμεθα] for its own sake whereas the other things we wish for the sake of this end, and if we do not choose [αἱρούμεθα] everything for the sake of something else (for in this manner the process will go on to infinity and our desire [ὄρεξιν] will be empty and vain), then clearly this end would be the good and the highest good [ἄριστον]. Will not the knowledge [γνῶσις] of it, then, have a great influence on our way of life, and would we not [therefore] be more likely to attain that which is needed [δέοντος], like archers who have a mark to aim at? If so, we should try to grasp, in outline at least [πειρατέον τύπῳ], what that end is and to which of the faculties or sciences it belongs. It would seem to belong to the one that is most authoritative and most architectonic. Now politics appears to be such. (1094a19–28)

Here it becomes perspicuous that glimpsing at the good itself, the good without qualification (*to ariston*), far from being a purely contemplative act and exceeding ethical considerations, remains an essentially ethical matter: the ability not only to grasp the good for and of human beings, but also to situate it in the context of that which may exceed human concerns, seems to be all the more ethically relevant, indeed, to carry genuinely ethical implications and guide human *ēthos* most pertinently. For only in the attempt to catch a glimpse of the good constituting the *ultimate end*, the good embracing all partial ends and delimiting the sphere of finality, may human comportment find its measure and direction, however tentative. And, conversely, it is only through the human involvements and operations always already under way that an inquiry into "the good itself" finds its structure. Thus, on the basis of these observations, we come to wonder whether there may indeed be a purely contemplative act, or even whether the theoretical gesture, contemplation as such, might perhaps demand to be thought least of all in terms of separation from worldly, human affairs. We will, no doubt, have to return to this.

3.4. The Perfection of Imprecision

For the moment, let us, in passing and to conclude, call attention to the two following points. In the first place, by reference to the passage just quoted (1094a19ff.), we should be mindful of the role of desirous striving (*hairesis, boulēsis, orexis*) in the movement toward and determination of the good. Desire is so decisive, indeed, that here Aristotle anchors to its logic the argumentation concerning infinite regress: the process of referring a final and moving cause to a prior and more comprehensive one cannot go on to infinity, for, we are told, desire would become "empty and vain." In other words, what desire desires, however scarcely definite and remote, cannot and must not be altogether elusive, unreachable, let alone impossible. In the lack of a limit and delimitation of its pursuit, desire would be paralyzed by a sense of futility. It is, therefore, the very *fact* of desire, the experience of desire as we know it, which in and of itself exposes the impossibility and even the inconceivability of infinite regress: in light of human evidence infinite regress makes no sense.[13]

In the second place, we note that Aristotle says that, through the ethico-political investigation, we should aim at seizing the highest end at least "in outline," *tupoi.* After the statement just quoted, he further corroborates this sense of tentativeness and approximation by warning that it is not appropriate nor, for that matter, "the mark of someone educated" (1094b23) to expect absolute clarity and "precision" (1094b24) from the ethical inquiry. It is all-important here to avoid reading these cautious remarks as the exclusive qualification of the ethical discourse and contrasting the latter to the allegedly exhaustive and unproblematically adequate discourse of the "science of wisdom." It is not the case that we should perceive the ethical investigation as in and of itself imprecise and the articulation of first philosophy as paradigmatically precise. If the former is not geometrically or demonstratively argued, this is because of the overflowing complexity of its theme, for "beautiful and just things, with which politics is concerned," present "many fluctuations and differences" (1094b14–16). Thus, far from being imprecise in the sense of partial and imperfect, ethics is presented "roughly and in outline" (1094b20), in fact, in the register of dialectic and persuasion, *precisely because it undertakes to comprehend a domain of unparalleled vastness.* Its non-mathematical tenor is therefore the ultimate mark of propriety and appropriateness to the subject matter, to the nature and comprehensiveness of the task undertaken. Mathematical precision seems to be an inappropriate, even

[13] Compare the argumentation concerning infinite regress in *Metaphysics* Alpha Elatton. Even if the pressing concern in this context seems to be preserving the possibility of knowledge, Aristotle's statement that infinite regress would "eliminate knowing [ἐπίστασθαι], for it is not possible for us to understand [εἰδέναι] unless we come to the indivisibles [ἄτομα]" (994b20–21), comes as an afterthought. What precedes and frames it is a reflection altogether ethically inflected, that is, oriented to and by considerations regarding action and motivation: "Those who introduce an infinite series are unaware [λανθάνουσιν] of the fact that they are eliminating the nature of the good, although no one would try to do anything if he did not intend to come to a limit [πέρας]. Nor would there be intellect [νοῦς] in beings; for, at any rate, he who has an intellect always acts [πράττει] for the sake of something and this is a limit, for the end is a limit [τὸ γὰρ τέλος πέρας ἐστίν]" (994b12–16).

unsophisticated criterion vis-à-vis the infinitely subtle, wandering, and self-differing unraveling of life.

3.5. "Physical" Character of First Philosophy and "Metaphysical" Character of Ethics

Nor may the discourse of the "science of wisdom" lay claim to adequacy and mathematical exactness. We already variously discussed the non-scientific character of the principles of the sciences in general and considered in particular the non-scientific character of the "science of wisdom." Let us simply underscore, at this point, that the motif and motive of desire lies at the heart of the research taken up in the *Metaphysics* – a research rather infelicitously understood as "metaphysical," since its questions are exposed and developed in terms that do not appear to point "beyond" the physical, the embodied, or the phenomenal, in brief, beyond the broad problematic of life. Here we simply recall that in Book Alpha of this work, in the course of his survey of the predecessors, Aristotle reserves a rather unusual treatment for Hesiod and Parmenides. While, without noticeable hesitations, he assesses and shows the one-sidedness of the meditations of most forefathers, in the case of these two figures he seems to vacillate and postpones a final word. Hesiod and Parmenides' hypothesis of love, *erōs*, as a principle "of beings" (984b21) or "in beings" (984b24), that is, as "cause of what is beautiful" and that in virtue of which "motion belongs to beings" (984b21–22), is never quite refuted. It is in fact explicitly left suspended, but eventually finds an echo, or even a magnification, in Lambda, where Aristotle unfolds his understanding of *erōs* as mover. This will be the culminating discourse on intellect, *nous*, as that which moves through desire (*orexis*), indeed, as that which moves qua beloved, *erōmenos*. This trajectory is anticipated in the suspension of judgment accorded to the ancient poet and thinker in the opening Book:

> One might suspect that Hesiod was the first to seek such a cause, or someone else who posited love [ἔρωτα] or desire [ἐπιθυμίαν] as a principle in things, as Parmenides does also; for the latter, in describing the generation of the all [τοῦ παντὸς], says:
>
> > love first of all the gods she planned.
>
> And Hesiod says,
>
> > first of all chaos came to be,
> > and then broad breasted earth . . .
> > and love amid all the immortals supreme.

And these suggest that there must be in beings some cause that will move them and bring them together. As to how we are to assign priority to these thinkers concerning these beliefs, let this await later judgment [κρίνειν]. (984b23–32)

In lack of a thematic assessment of these sayings, the resurfacing of the language of desire and *erōs* in the discourse on the unmoved mover appears as an implicit confirmation, or at least as a gesture toward the archaic hypothesis, vigorously assimilated and rearticulated in Aristotle's discourse. Understood as "that which is desired [ὀρεκτὸν]" (1072a26) and as the "beloved [ἐρώμενον]" (1072b3), the final cause and unmoved mover is remarkably illuminated in terms of beauty, that is, of phenomenality, for "the desired [ἐπιθυμητὸν] is that which appears beautiful [φαινόμενον καλόν]" (1072a28), that which shines forth with ennobling glow. And it is because of such an appearing that we desire, that we are moved and compelled to pursue it: "we desire [ὀρεγόμεθα] because it seems [δοκεῖ], rather than it seems because we desire" (1072a29). Accordingly, that which moves (*nous*, the god, the good, indeed the best) is intuited by reference to life, that is, to energy in its utmost plenitude: as a matter of being so fully activated and actualized, at work in such an unmitigated way that no decay may be conceived of it. In Aristotle's words, "life belongs [to the god], for the actuality [ἐνέργεια] of the intellect is life [ζωή] and [the intellect] is actuality" (1072b27).[14]

Life, then, however "wondrous" and "eternal" (1072b25–30), defines the domain within which the inquiry of first philosophy unfolds. Hardly "metaphysical," such an inquiry would not so much entail a redirection of the inquiring gaze "beyond" the "physical," but rather realize the irreducibility of life to human life, of the cosmos to human architecture, of *phusis* to human construction. It would thereby situate the human within that which cannot be brought back to the human, while preserving in view the phenomenal character of the whole: that which exceeds the order of the human may not automatically be conceived as a matter of transcendence, let alone of transcendence of the sensible or phenomenal. As we shall see in the course of our analysis of the *Nicomachean Ethics*, the inquiry of first philosophy is such that it distinctively redirects the gaze from human interactions to that which encompasses all: but it remains a

[14] In *De caelo* Aristotle develops the plenitude of energy, the full actuality of the divine in terms of unending life, and therefore motion: "The actuality [ἐνέργεια] of the god is immortality, which is eternal life [ζωὴ ἀΐδιος]. Hence, of necessity, to the divine belongs eternal motion [κίνησιν ἀΐδιον]" (286a9–11). In the *Cratylus*, by reference to the heavenly bodies (sun, moon, earth, stars), Plato derives the etymology of the word *theos*, god, from *thein*, moving or rushing (397d).

gaze gazing at altogether visible beings – indeed, at those most shining bodies (*phanerōtata*) in the sky (1141b2).[15]

Conversely, it could be said that it is ethics that presents properly metaphysical traits, although saying this already entails a semantic reconfiguration of the term "metaphysics." It could be suggested that the ethical reflection is "beyond *phusis*" in the sense that it concerns what is not *by* nature, not simply and automatically determined by nature, although neither separate from it nor against it. Or, which is the same, it could be said that ethics is "beyond *phusis*" in the sense that it concerns what may still be *according* to nature but, to us, illegibly so. Accordingly, ethics would address the possible harbored in *phusis*, hidden within it, that is, that which would reveal and unravel nature in its mutability, in its indeterminate margins, availability to interaction, and openness to transformation. Ethics would concern what, by our lights, is not necessitated by nature but remains within the compass of nature as its complement or, better, supplement. Ethics would thus indicate that which, in and of nature, remains out-law with respect to nature, in the sense that it is either not ruled by or not intelligibly ruled by nature. It would pertain to human reflection on ethical matters to order that which nature hands over to human beings with a certain indifference and only partial directives. It is in the context of such an abandonment on part of nature that what has been called "human freedom" becomes necessary.

In this peculiar sense, then, ethics would be metaphysics. And it would be first philosophy, because it would concern that which is first in the orders of being and of intuitive knowing – that which, precisely as unexamined or even unconscious, will always already have grounded all other inquiries, most notably that of the "science of wisdom." Indeed, in the order of discursive knowing, of human inquiry, ethical awareness and ethical inquiry may well have appeared as the last, crowning step. Before ethics, will have taken place the various investigations outwardly directed, the sciences, even the meditation on the formal ("logical") structures of inquiry as such. And yet, all manners of study taking place before ethics will have been late with respect to the always already of the ethical framing. This fact, which is incipiently addressed in certain discourses of the "science of wisdom," is made perspicuous through the ethical analysis. Ethics,

[15] In the *Metaphysics*, too, Aristotle employs the language of appearance in order to characterize the intelligible objects. In considering the difficulty pertaining to the attainment of truth, he observes: "Perhaps the cause of this difficulty . . . is in us and not in the facts. For as the eyes of bats are to the light of day, so is the intellect of our soul to those which in their nature are most evident [φανερώτατα] of all" (993b9–11).

thus, comes to appear also as the sustained engagement with the ineffable, with that which, silently, operates from the beginning and informs all speaking and other pursuits – as the commitment to articulate the silence within, to interrogate the beliefs and practices from which alone any discourse, whether scientific or theological, receives its authority.

The study that follows, closely examining the text of the *Nicomachean Ethics* and supplementing it with references to relevant moments in the other ethical and political treatises, will therefore put into focus what could be called an "implied ethics." Far from ethics understood derivatively or reductively, let alone as "applied," the present analysis undertakes to let the ethical reflection emerge in its "firstness," in its primordiality, as that reflection that uncovers what is first *in itself*, harbored *within* what is always already first *for us*, that is, within our actions, endeavors, and involvements.

2

Main Section

Ēthikōn Nikomakheiōn Alpha to Eta

The Aristotelian treatise transmitted under the title *Ēthikōn Nikomakheiōn* presents itself as a comprehensive reflection on the problem of human behavior. The word *ēthos* signifies precisely disposition, character in the sense of psychological configuration, and hence comportment, the way in which one bears oneself. However, the semantic range of the term exceeds this determination and signals that it must be situated in the broader context of custom, of shared usage, and even understood in the archaic but abiding sense of the accustomed place where the living (animals, plants, or otherwise) find their haunt or abode.

When describing Paris in shining armor rushing through the Trojan citadel in order to reach Hector, the poet of the *Iliad* resorts to the image of a well-fed horse breaking free from captivity, glorious in its splendor as it gallops "to the haunts and pastures of mares [μετά τ᾽ ἤθεα καὶ νομὸν ἵππων]" (VI.511). *Ēthos* is here the place in which a particular animal belongs, where others of the same kind gather and thrive. Belonging somewhere, then, means to find there the possibility of flourishing, of finding the most appropriate conditions to unfold and become whatever a being happens to be. The free horse at once moves in the direction of the haunts of horses, not unlike the way in which earth moves downward, in the direction of earth, and fire upward, in the direction of fire. A similar use of the term *ēthos* is to be found in a passage from Hesiod magnificently rendering the grimness of winter. Here Hesiod, after a stark evocation of the roar of Boreas through the immense forest, contrasts the sense of protection enjoyed by the young girl at home with her mother to the misery of the beasts pierced by the northern wind blowing, and in particular to the "boneless one," the octopus, "in its fireless house and wretched haunts [ἔν τ' ἀπύρῳ οἴκῳ καὶ ἤθεσι λευγαλέοισιν]" (*Works* 525).

But *ēthos* may also indicate the place or environment where properly belong forms of life understood in a broader sense. In the *Phaedrus*, Plato develops his vision of the "grammatical garden" and articulates the analogy between sowing seeds in the earth and disseminating words (*logoi*) in the soul. In this context, the word *ēthos* designates the place where plants abide, that is, the soil out of which they grow, to which corresponds the "psychological place" where the *logoi* abide and multiply. Indeed, Socrates says, dialectic entails sowing (*speirein*) and planting (*phuteuein*) "in a fitting soul words with knowledge... which are not fruitless, but harbor seed from which there grow [φυόμενοι] in other places [ἐν ἄλλοις ἤθεσι] other [words] sufficient to grant this [ongoing generation] forever immortal, and which make the one who has them happy to the highest degree humanly possible" (276e–277a). Simultaneously soil and character, a matter of *phusis* and of *psukhē*, habitat and habituation, *ēthos* names the manifold of fecundity sustaining plant and *logos* alike.

In a remarkable passage reporting the records of the Egyptians, through the sign *ēthos* Herodotus conveys the regularity of the sun's daily trajectory, the sameness, stability, and hence familiarity of the sun's motion in its repeated returns. In this sense, the language of *ēthos* designates the "customary place" (or, in fact, places) of the sun's course, the dwelling of the moving sun: "Four times in this period, they said, the sun rose away from its usual places [ἐξ ἠθέων]; twice it came up where it now goes down, and twice went down where it now comes up. And nothing in Egypt changed as a consequence, either in the produce from the earth and the river, or in matters concerning sickness and death" (*Historia* II.142).

Finally, *ēthos* names the exquisitely human abode – most basically, but not only, in the sense of the land in which a people settles, the geo-political space in which a community is as such constituted and lives. Hesiod, for instance, after recalling that many of the divine race of heroes found death in war, whether at Thebes or Troy, tells that Zeus gave to those remaining "a living and an abode [ἤθε'] apart from human beings... at the limits of earth. And they dwell without sorrow in the islands of the blessed along the shore of deep-swirling Ocean, happy heroes for whom the wheat-giving earth bears honey-sweet fruit sprouting thrice a year" (*Works* 167ff.). In turn, Herodotus recounts that the Cimmerians had to move into Asia because "driven away from their abodes [ἐξ ἐθέων] by the nomad Scythians" (*Historia* I.15).

On the ground of its manifold signification, then, and limiting ourselves to human preoccupations, we could say that *ēthos* designates the manner of action and psychological conformation wherein an individual as well as a community find their home. Aristotle's treatise focuses on that which pertains to *ēthos*, on *ta ēthika*, those aspects of demeanor revealing character and the presence (or absence) of a sense of appropriateness, adequacy, precision, or even tactfulness with respect to any given circumstance. It could be said already, in an anticipatory fashion, that the central concern of the ethical investigation will be the response to the requirements inherent in any situation. That is to say, the ethical inquiry acknowledges and formulates the task of harmonizing (1) the needs and inclinations leading one to act and (2) the structure of the place and time of the action. The attunement of action and circumstance for the sake of thriving, that is, the building or configuring of action and circumstance in their unity is, thus, the ultimate, if elusive, task toward which ethics projects itself. But "circumstance" means the ever-unraveling surroundings, the unfolding of time in its locally singular stances. *Ēthos* comes to name the form of the moment, the shape of each moment, of this moment in which one dwells, lives. The dwelling is the moment.

1. HUMAN INITIATIVE AND ITS ORIENTATION TO THE GOOD

The treatise opens with the statement: "Every art and every inquiry, every action and every intention is thought to aim at a certain good; hence human beings have expressed themselves well in declaring the good to be that at which all things aim" (1094a1–3). Any and all activities oriented to bringing forth (*tekhnē*), as well as all manners of pursuing an investigation (*methodos*), action in the broadest sense (*praxis*), and the blend of inclination and discerning choice that sustains action (*proairesis*) appear to human beings to tend to the good, however this should be understood. Indeed, human beings recognize the good as that which orients everything. The Platonic reminiscence could not be more explicit in this inception: transcending not only practical endeavors, but the pursuit of knowledge as well, whether "technical" or properly scientific, the good is intuitively assumed as that which, alone, may determine the course of development of every human enterprise (one thinks here of the "divided line" in *Republic* VI). The good names that for the sake of which everything is ultimately choice-worthy and, qua ultimate end of action, decides with regard to that which, from within the horizons of a single science, productive project, or practice, would remain undecidable.

What is here brought to our attention is the peculiar and disquieting resourcefulness allotted to human beings. Their multifarious entrepreneurship includes investigative initiatives as well as interventions that can drastically reshape the human environment. The human ability radically to alter the world between earth and sky, to harness or intervene in *phusis*, ultimately to bring forth from non-being into being bespeaks a resourcefulness arresting in its terribleness, because potentially both fecund and destructive, yet in itself utterly indifferent to its orientation toward realization or affliction (*Antigone* 365–75). From within the single disciplines or practices one cannot retrieve directions regarding how to guide human ventures. Only a concern with that which exceeds the single discipline and constitutes the common aim can provide such a direction.

Through the four terms in the opening statement, *tekhnē, methodos, praxis,* and *proairesis,* is suggested the unity of reflective, productive, evaluative, and overall practical modes of comportment. The whole range of human enactment, of human modes of self-manifestation, seems to "aim at a certain good." Nothing is left out, let alone any allegedly separate, "purely theoretical" activity, which would not participate in the orientation toward the highest good, the good *tout court.* Or, in other words, nothing is left out that would not relate to, strive for, desire the good. Remarkably enough, this opening, which sets the tone for the rest of the discussion, presents doxical or dialectical qualifications. It is based on consensus, on views that are common and agreed upon – if not uncritically accepted. The gathering of all proximate finality under the supreme end that the good names is what human beings somewhat immediately acknowledge. The discussion starts with an acknowledgment of such a shared acknowledgment. It starts by making the sharing explicit and thematic, by bringing it to consciousness. Ethical reflection will largely have to do with the analysis of such a starting point in its innumerable facets: it will have to do with the attempt to take apart the beginning, to analyze it and own it at a deeper level.

1.1. Theme and Performance of the Ethical Discourse: "Implied Ethics"

It should also be pointed out that the discussion unfolds simultaneously on two levels, one that could be called thematic and another that presents itself as genuinely self-reflective. Indeed, alongside the thematization of human practice, we detect a constant meta-theoretical or meta-thematic concern. The investigation opens and develops displaying a sustained awareness regarding its own status precisely as an investigation, a preoccupation with questions of *methodos.* The investigation watches itself as it proceeds, remains mindful of its *how,* of its manner of proceeding, no less than of its *what,* its subject matter. The inquiry is not simply *about praxis,* but reveals itself in its practical dimension, in its performative character, that is, in its comportment. For instance, the ethical discussion will raise the question concerning the degree of precision that it is fitting and "educated" to expect of itself, or consider its own impotence vis-à-vis listeners who are inexperienced and did not enjoy an appropriate upbringing. Or it will repeatedly underscore its own awareness of its dialectical ground. Discourse (*logos*) and the thought it articulates are not extraneous to the domain of *ēthos*: on the contrary, they consciously expose themselves from the start in their self-interrogation, in their concern with how to proceed and become. Above all, they expose themselves as resting on and stemming from human practices, from what human beings have shared, thought in common, and thus formulated. The treatise, then, takes shape in its newness and tentativeness: this is a first, original attempt at a systematic reflection on *ēthos*, a reflection explicating the implicit, exposing it and making it thematic. While doing so, however, the discourse keeps an eye on itself, as it were, reflects on itself, practices on itself the same degree of attention brought to the phenomena of human comportment. It is at once a path traced for the first time, *hodos,* and a path looked upon with awareness, *as though* already traced and followed again – a *methodos.*

Already announcing itself, thus, is what could be called an "implied ethics": ethics implied in the unraveling of the discourse on ethics and, indeed, of any discourse as such. Aristotle's ethics lets such an "implication" become visible, explicit. In this way, ethics presents itself as a discourse recognizing itself not as autonomous but, in fact, always already belonging in the fabric of our actions and endeavors; a discourse uncovering what is first, however mostly unseen, within itself.

In the order of human knowledge, ethics will have come after even metaphysics. Only at the culminating moment of the investigations taking the human being outside and away from itself, will the human being wonder about the conditions of human undertaking, about the human being itself. Ethics is the only science that appears as genuinely self-conscious, aware, self-reflective concerning its own proceeding, the science for which proceeding itself, and the course traced, become an issue. The way of proceeding of discourse becomes an issue, and an especially problematic one, because ethics recognizes its own first principles as non-demonstrative and its ground as constitutively dialectical, that is, resulting from communal stipulations. This is the "science" that most forcefully circles back to its beginning as non-scientific, and hence cannot close the circle. In this sense, it could be said that ethics provides a sort of "critique of reason," in the sense of an analysis and delimitation thereof. With ethics, philosophy, first philosophy, is brought to open up to what exceeds it, to its own excessive conditions: in the impossibility of including and enclosing its own conditions in a gesture of perfect self-possession, first philosophy ruptures itself, presents itself in a kind of dehiscence, of readiness for its own self-transcendence. Paradoxically, this is precisely what signals a certain completion of the philosophical inquiry: completion not in the sense of coming to rest in the end, let alone in the full accomplishment of the philosophical task, but rather in the sense of the philosophical awareness of belonging and being situated in that which is not under philosophical mastery, completion in the sense of an opening up to the phenomenon and experience of life. In such an awareness, the end, far from being attained, remains a task and requires the utmost adhesion and alertness.

1.2. Ethics as Politics

Ethics is said to be an "architectonic" "science" or "power" (1094a27), for it embraces all manners of human initiative in their "theoretical" as well as productive, practical as well as psychological dimensions. The oscillation between the language of science and that of power or faculty, *epistēmē* and *dunamis*, is not unusual in Aristotle and signals a certain terminological fluidity maintained even as the establishment of a specialized vocabulary and rigorous precision in usage are sought after. The identification of ethics with politics and its characterization as "architectonic" rests, as already anticipated, on its recognition of the good as that into which all proximate and partial ends converge. The following passage was already variously cited above, yet deserves to be considered again and more extensively, as it may occasion further considerations:

> Now if of things we do there is an end which we wish for its own sake whereas the other things we wish for the sake of this end, and if we do not choose everything for the sake of something else (for in this manner the process will go on to infinity and our desire will be empty and vain), then clearly this end would be the good and the highest good. Will not the knowledge of it, then, have a great influence on our way of life, and would we not [as a consequence] be more likely to attain the desired end, like archers who have a mark to aim at? If so, then we should try to grasp, in outline at least, what that end is and to which of the

> sciences or faculties it belongs. It would seem to belong to the one which is most authoritative and most architectonic. Now politics appears to be such; for it is this which regulates what sciences are needed in a state and what kind of sciences should be learned by each [kind of individuals] and to what extent. The most honored faculties, too, e.g., strategy and economics and rhetoric, are observed to come under this [faculty]. And since this faculty uses the rest of the [practical][1] sciences and also legislates what human beings should do and what they should abstain from doing, its end would include the ends of the other faculties; hence this is the end which would be the good for humankind. For even if this end be the same for an individual as for the *polis*, nevertheless the end of the *polis* appears to be greater and more complete to attain and to preserve; for though this end is dear also to a single individual, it appears to be more beautiful and more divine to a race of human beings or to a *polis*. (1094a19–b10)

The ethical reflection, in the first place, recognizes the good in which the multifarious activities of humans are gathered and, second, is committed to explore that which is indicated as "the good." It is also in virtue of this recognition and this commitment that the ethical reflection is "architectonic," in the sense that it is involved in *building* human comportment, in shaping and structuring the ways of humans living together. As a mode of *tekhnē*, indeed, as *tekhnē* in its most originary sense, proceeding in a certain rarefaction of natural prescriptions, ethical reflection envisions and brings forth human shapes and shapes of human community. The relation between this "science" or "faculty" that is architectonic, primordially formative and creative, and the other arts or sciences is analogous to that between the architect, that is, the master artist, the one who designs and devises, and the other builders or workmen, those who execute the ideation of the architect. Indeed, in configuring the human, whether in terms of character, *ēthos*, or in terms of the outward shape of a *polis*, politics also rules over the domain of scientific practices, determining its very structures, priorities, and propriety. The single sciences, then, do not enjoy some kind of autonomous status. They are ultimately not ends in themselves, but are evaluated according to the exigencies of the community, that is, subjected to a more overarching order of finality.

In its "architectonic," all-comprehensive character, ethics is politics.[2] Of course, the decisive assumption of the unity of ethical and political discourses cannot not problematize the distinction between private and

[1] *Praktikais* elided in Aristotle, *Ethica Nicomachea*, ed. Ingram Bywater (Oxford: Oxford UP, 1891). Needless to say, much is at stake in the decision concerning this addition.

[2] On the question of the architectonic vis-à-vis the relation between ethics and politics, see Pierre Rodrigo, *Aristote. Une philosophie pratique: praxis, politique et bonheur* (Paris: Vrin, 2006), esp. chap. 1.

public with which "we moderns" are so familiar, at least in its most facile and automatic versions. Ethics, then, understood in its essential traits, at once concerns and rests on the political space. For, on the one hand, there is no such thing as an analysis of human comportment severed from the domain of human community, the *polis*, whether this be understood as a particular nation, group, political organism, or as the community of humankind as such. As emphatically pointed out in the opening of the *Politics*, the human being is essentially communal, that is to say, political – and this means that the human individual is unthinkable aside from the complex relational web of the community. It is through the political gathering that the human *as such* emerges. On the margins of the political spectrum, we can envision only brutes and human beings resembling deities. Outside it, beasts and gods. On the other hand, all genuine modifications in the orientation and values of a community rest on the ways in which an individual, each individual, is shaped and comes to shape him- or herself. It is through exigencies and aspirations nascent in each, rather than by decree, that a community is determined in its character. Politics, then, both constitutes the horizon of ethics and begins with ethics. As the writer of *Magna moralia* stresses in the very opening of his discussion: "if one is to be effective [πρακτικὸς] in political matters, no doubt his or her character [ἦθος] must be impeccable [σπουδαῖος]. This, then, shows that the study [πραγματεία] of characters [περὶ τὰ ἤθη] is part [μέρος] of politics and also its origin and principle [ἀρχή], and it seems to me altogether that this study would justly be termed not 'ethical' but 'political'" (1181b1–28).

Among other things, this means that there is no ethical discourse transcending the political order or based on otherwise transcendent premises. To say that a science is "architectonic" means to attribute to it the knowledge of causes, of the *why* (*Metaphysics* 981a30–982a1), that is to say, of the origin. Ethics or politics, in its architectonic character, knows that the causes, the inception, are to be found there where we are, in the midst of our involvements. The principles and values structuring comportment emerge at the intersection of individual inclinations and communal agreements, and the ethical account will always have had to begin there, out of the dynamic play of interdependence between each one and the whole. It is hardly necessary to point out the thoroughly Platonic subtext of these opening considerations. The indissoluble intertwinement of ethics, politics, psychology, and pedagogy will remain a crucial feature of Aristotle's approach to the question concerning human thriving, and beyond.

1.3. On Ethics

1.3.1. Imprecision of Ethics

Aristotle could hardly be more punctilious in his attempt at determining the most proper register of the ethical investigation and repeatedly calls attention to the necessarily approximate character of discourse vis-à-vis the overflowing and ever-changing phenomenon of life. The issue was briefly anticipated in the Prelude and must now be considered more closely. *Logos* can at best grasp some aspects of the exuberant complexity of our experience, but such a discourse is bound to remain incomplete, unable to circumscribe and exhaustively capture its subject matter. It is as though, in its analytical unfolding, *logos* were too coarse, or too schematic, too abstract, to do justice to the taking place of life in its literally infinite nuances, where even repetitions and patterns of regularity indicate neither the permanence of the self-identical nor the reducibility of the manifold to the simple. As transpires from Aristotle's observations, here one finds compounded the difficulties pertaining to becoming (in the sense of phenomena by nature), those pertaining to human action, and, finally, those pertaining to a discourse that, in line with its exquisitely "productive" (poietic, architectonic) character, is actively involved in the very development of occurrences it undertakes to analyze. Indeed, politics is simultaneously concerned with elucidating and bringing forth the good, with illuminating the good and bringing it into appearance, letting it shine in its concreteness, in its "beauty and justice." As a matter of fact, Aristotle even goes beyond the intimation of discourse as essentially poietic, and seems to suggest that discourses themselves are artifacts, that the *logoi* themselves are the outcome of artful production, *poiēsis*, and therefore not all alike in vividness. At the origin of *logoi* as such and sustaining them, thus, would be *poiēsis* or, at any rate, a certain conduct vis-à-vis the asperity of the subject matter. This much seems to be implied by the parallel between "hand made articles" and the investigative discourses (*logoi*):

> Our inquiry [μέθοδος], then, has as its aim these ends, and it is a certain political inquiry; and it would be adequately discussed if it is presented as clearly as is proper to its subject matter [ὑποκειμένην ὕλην]; for, as in hand made articles [δημιουργουμένοις], precision [τὸ γὰρ ἀκριβὲς] should not be sought for alike in all discussions [λόγοις]. Beautiful and just things, with which politics is concerned, have so many differences and fluctuations [διαφορὰν καὶ πλάνην] that they appear [δοκεῖν] to be only by custom [νόμῳ] and not by nature [φύσει]. Good things, too, have such fluctuations because harm has come from them to many individuals; for some human beings even perished because of wealth, others because of

> bravery. So in discussing such matters and in using [premises] concerning them, we should be content to indicate the truth roughly and in outline [παχυλῶς καὶ τύπῳ], and when we deal with things which occur for the most part and use similar [premises] for them, [we should be content to draw] conclusions of a similar nature. The listener, too, should accept each of these statements in the same manner; for it is the mark of an educated human being to seek as much precision in things of a given genus as their nature allows, for to accept persuasive arguments from a mathematician appears to be [as inappropriate as] to demand demonstrations from a rhetorician. (1094b12–28)

A few further remarks concerning this first statement are in order. First, we note the caution marking the affirmation that ethico-political matters may be a matter of convention, of *nomos*, and not by nature, *phusei*. Aristotle does not say that they *are* according to *nomos*, but that they *appear, are thought to be* so. This initial claim concerning the conventional dimension of ethical considerations will, in a sense, find confirmation throughout the treatise. In another sense, however, Aristotle will complicate it by frequently intimating the irreducibility of ethical structures to the order of mere arbitrariness. Indeed, in the course of the treatise, as we shall see, Aristotle will progressively emphasize the "natural" stratum of human comportment, the insufficiency of custom and convention to account for it. However, the reference to nature, *phusis*, in this case cannot amount to a "naturalization" or transcendent grounding of ethics. As will emerge especially in the course of Book Epsilon, on justice, Aristotle problematizes the commonplace according to which fluctuation pertains to custom alone, while that which is by nature would enjoy a certain stability. In a remarkable move, he will surmise that, in fact, that which is by nature may least of all be immobile, secured to an unchanging order. According to this singular orientation, the invocation of nature in ethical matters, then, will not at all establish and warrant the validity of principles (manifest in their intelligible fixity) outside the realm of human determination. We shall consider these matters in due time, but for the moment let us notice the dialectical qualifications of the statement above: ethical matters, in their differences and wanderings, in their nomadic character, "seem" or are "commonly believed" to be a matter of *nomos*. Whether this is so or not remains to be seen.

It is also crucial to underline that the acceptance of what is here proposed, namely that only a qualified accuracy is to be expected of the discourse at hand, rests on the assumption that the interlocutors or listeners have already received the proper education, *paideia*. This is the condition for the acceptance of the premises as such, the condition *before* the premises, *prior to* and *outside* the entire discourse.[3] It is only those who already have a certain degree of maturity who will be able to stop at the principle without asking for further reasons – which would be inappropriate. Education, then, means knowing when to stop in the inquiry concerning the causes, when to recognize something as a principle, that is, without any further causes, and accordingly acknowledge it as a premise regardless of its demonstrability. In this sense, education signifies not so much or not simply formal learning, but character formation, formation of the human being as such. Thus understood, education is necessary in order for the discourse to make a start at all.

Shortly afterward, Aristotle returns to these points, granting them ample articulation. Speaking of the strategy of his *logos*, he says:

> perhaps we should first make a sketch and later fill in the details. When an outline has been beautifully made, it would seem that anyone could go forward and articulate the parts, for time is a good discoverer and cooperator [συνεργὸς] in such matters. It is in this way that the arts advanced, for anyone can add what is lacking. We should also recall what has been stated previously: precision should not be sought alike in all cases, but in each case only as much as the subject matter [ὑποκειμένην ὕλην] allows and as much as is proper to the inquiry. Thus a carpenter [τέκτων] and a geometer [γεωμέτρης] make inquiries concerning the right angle in different ways; for the first does it as much as it is useful to his work, while the second inquires what it is or what kind of thing it is, since his aim is to contemplate the truth. We should proceed likewise in other situations and not allow side lines [πάρεργα] to dominate the main task [ἔργων]. Again, we should not demand the cause in all things alike, but in some cases it is sufficient to indicate the fact [τὸ ὅτι] beautifully, as is also the case with principles; and the fact is first and is a principle. Now some principles are contemplated [θεωροῦνται] by induction, others by sensation, others by some kind of habituation [ἐθισμῷ], and others in some other way. So we should try to present each according to its own nature and should make a serious effort to describe [διορισθῶσι] them beautifully, for they have a great influence on what follows; for a principle is thought to be more than half of the whole, and through it many of the things sought become apparent also. (1098a22–b8)

The proposition here put forth entails, then, producing a schematic outline to begin with, which may provide orientation for subsequent operations of refinement.[4] Again, a comparison with artistic procedures corroborates this position (the arts "advanced" in this way, says Aristotle). Of

[3] On the features distinguishing someone "educated," see *On the Parts of Animals* (639a1–15), *Metaphysics* (1005b3–5, 1006a5–9), and *Politics* (1282a1–12).

[4] See also *Topics* 101a19–24.

course, such a course of action does not always yield the desired outcome, as will become progressively clear in the elaboration of the schematic partitioning of the soul. Apparently unproblematic at first, as the psychonoetic analysis is deepened such a scheme will be revealed as increasingly inconsistent. But we shall address this problem later. We should, for the moment, take notice of Aristotle's insistence on the correlation between precision, on the one hand, and the demands of the matter at stake on the pertinent inquiry, on the other. It is the "subject matter," the "thing itself," the "fact" (*to hoti*) that regulates the discourse and manifests itself through it. Aristotle seems, in sum, to be gesturing toward what could be called an "*ēthos* of inquiry" – a certain sensitivity, on part of the one who speaks and inquires, to the particular, to the singular circumstance, to the peculiar requirements of the theme under scrutiny. This will also be disclosed as the mark of all deliberation that informs action. There is no absolute and all-encompassing set of criteria regulating the inquiring posture and discourse: these find in their own "underlying matter" decisive guidance.

It is because of this that Aristotle almost redundantly emphasizes the importance of "describing" the fact well, "beautifully." Not only concerning practical affairs, but more broadly with respect to first principles, it is inane, indeed inappropriate, to ask for the cause beyond a certain point: in the case of principles overall, because they are the uncaused causes; in the case of a fact, because the *that* of a given situation is "first and a principle," and as such involves no further "why." It should be apprehended in the experience of evidence, in being drawn to assent. Consequently, *logos* cannot fully fathom principles, least of all those principles that are practical matters. It can, at most, describe them, assume them through definition. As we shall surmise later, in the course of the analysis of *nous*, first principles and ultimate particulars constitute the extreme terms delimiting the field of thinking and encompassing the properly scientific procedures. They are the noematic excess to and condition of the scientific discourses strictly understood. This, of course, holds even for the so-called theoretical sciences, for example, geometry: first principles, just as particular states of affairs, cannot be circumscribed, demonstratively owned, but only descriptively indicated. But the prominence of the descriptive practice bespeaks the primacy of dialectical practices in grounding these sciences as well, and hence the primordiality of the ethical dimension vis-à-vis the exercise of the sciences. On the ground of premises thus accepted they may, then, proceed to prove and demonstrate.

As for ethics itself, Aristotle's affirmation that "the fact is first and is a principle" signals, again, that the ethical discourse recognizes and seeks to thematize, to clarify, the dynamic ground on which it rests. Such a ground would be dynamic, in fact shifting and mobile, because intuitively constituted and demanding continuous readjustment. Ethics is, then, about establishing principles, that is, by describing facts. It is in order to account for principles "beautifully," in a way that is less unjust with respect to their multiplicity, unevenness, and locality, that ethics is not "precise." The priority of ethics is determined by the postulation that through principles many things are revealed, become luminous, *sumphanēs*, and according to such a disclosure a host of consequences becomes possible, certain investigations or lines of reflections are seminally prescribed. Indeed, a principle "is thought" or "appears" to be (notice, once more, the dialectical qualification of this statement) "more than half of the whole." Even before proceeding from principles, ethics takes up the task of assessing and formulating principles, according to the distinction of Platonic ancestry, which Aristotle himself recalls, between *logoi* "from principles" and "leading to principles" (1095a31–b2). Ethics, then, is quite genuinely a "science of principles," with all the peculiarity implicit in such a phrase, for a science of principles, let alone first philosophy, cannot be strictly demonstrative. More specifically, in ethics what is at stake is finding principles *in* the familiar, starting from the familiar in order to dig out what is folded there. This issue will be taken up again shortly, in the course of a few remarks on dialectic.

Aristotle insists on the question of precision even later on, in Book Beta, which arguably signals a profound concern with these "methodological issues." We wonder whether such preoccupations are at all to be considered *parerga*, collateral considerations, or whether, in fact, they may lie at the very heart of the task, the *ergon*, taken up when one broaches the discourse of ethics. As though beginning anew, Aristotle recommends:

> But first, let us agree on that matter, namely, that all statements concerning matters of action should be made sketchily [τύπῳ] and not with precision, for, as we said at the beginning, our demands of statements should be in accordance with the subject matter [κατὰ τὴν ὕλην] of those statements; in matters concerning action and expediency, and in those of health, there is no uniformity. And if such is the statement according to the whole [καθόλου λόγου], a statement concerning particulars [περὶ τῶν καθ' ἕκαστα] will be even less precise; for these do not fall under any art [τέκνην] or precept [παραγγελίαν], but those who are to act must always examine what pertains to the occasion [τὰ πρὸς τὸν καιρὸν], as in medical art and navigation [κυβερνητικῆς]. Yet even though our present statement is of such a nature, we should try to be of some help. (1104a1–11)

Aristotle underlines once more the lack of uniformity distinguishing the matter, the *hulē* of ethics, that is, life itself in its becoming. Even more importantly, here he suggests a distinction between (1) the *logoi* of ethics, that is, statements that, still remaining somehow general (*katholou*), frame the field and questions of ethics, on the one hand, and (2) the *logoi* regarding each particular situation, that is, statements bound to be least of all precise, let alone predictable, because pertaining to circumstances that are elusive in their singularity, on the other hand. The first inference that we must draw is that there is no statement that would be as such simply adequate to the mutable subject matter of timeliness and appropriateness, that is, a statement able to adhere without any qualification to the situation in motion and to account adequately for the situatedness or dwelling in the *kairos*. Second, we must conclude that there is no artful technique, *tekhnē*, which would provide a prescriptive ethical system in the strict sense. For the directions for action are to be found, crucially if not exclusively, in specific circumstances and in the intuitive-practical ability to evaluate them. The ethical dissertation, thus, would provide the intellectual analyses and clarifications propaedeutic to a more skilled encounter with what is the case, but could in no way replace practical upbringing (the formation of character), let alone the intuitive assessment of each singular circumstance – of *this* body to be cured, of the course to be taken in the midst of *these* currents, under *this* sky. A priori and for thoroughly essential reasons, ethics cannot be prescriptive, precisely because it cannot embrace all possible circumstances and have in sight the infinite fecundity of time.

The ethical treatises may at best offer "navigational instruments," give instruction, contribute to establish the needed posture to steer "beautifully" through the often raging waters of life (one is reminded here of the simile of the city and the ship in Plato's *Republic*). For what is at stake in living is, as Aristotle notes following Calypso's recommendation, to "keep the ship away from the surf and spray" (1109a2; *Odyssey* XII.219). The virtues, *aretai* – these acquired "postures," these dispositions that one "has" or "possesses" (*ekhein*) as one's own habitus and habitat (*hexis*), which are proper to one in the sense of one's very shape and structure – are formed through repeated practice and there is no discursive shortcut to them. It is this altogether practical substratum that furnishes determinant orientation in action and remains indispensable.

Let us bring these remarks to a conclusion by surmising that imprecision may not be seen as an imperfection. As will become increasingly perspicuous in the course of the unfolding of the treatise, it is *logos*, when alienated from the binds of concrete particulars, which represents a problem. Ethics is imprecise "concerning particulars" just as any other science is. But, unlike the other sciences, ethics recognizes and thematizes this. It understands that it is imprecise *of necessity*, because what is at stake, as in navigation, is to act while considering the *kairos*, the distinctive demand (propriety) of *this* moment and place. It is imprecise because it broadens the spectrum of attention to include all that may concern anyone in any circumstance, but no discourse could adequately circumscribe such a range. Paradoxically, it is precisely because of its imprecision, because it is grounded in world and experience as a whole, with no exclusions and abstractions, that ethics can be first philosophy, in the sense of architectonic, fundamental, and most comprehensive. Again, imprecision is not a limit: if anything, abstraction (dis-anchored *logos*) is. But we shall return to this.

1.3.2. The Always Already of Life

Above we hinted at the importance of prior education in determining the communicational effectiveness of the ethical discourse. The listener who already received the proper education is in a position to be convinced of the principles without much difficulty and, from here, to proceed to infer the rest. But those who are not so disposed will hardly be permeable to what the *logos* says, hardly be touched by it. This is the problem starkly outlined at the very beginning of the *Republic*, where Plato diagnoses the impotence of *logos* vis-à-vis those who cannot or refuse to listen (327c). *Logos* is always and inevitably vulnerable to this possibility. Thus, a certain availability to the experience of listening and, most decisively, a conducive character structure, will determine whether or not the seed of *logos* will find favorable terrain and the soul bear its fruits. But *logos* alone will not force any kind of understanding if the principles, which are a matter of conviction and not demonstration, are not in place – or if one is not prepared to make them one's own.[5] The *Nicomachean Ethics* ends with a series of reflections on this cluster of issues (Kappa 10). After pointing out the insufficiency of *logos* in the task of "making us good," Aristotle proceeds to a sustained articulation of what could be called a certain "passivity of the

5 After noting that "language can say nothing of the indivisibles" or the "simple" and that "no one has been as aware as Aristotle of the limits of philosophical discourse," Pierre Hadot adds: "The limits of discourse are due also to its inability autonomously to transmit to the listener the knowing and, even more so, conviction. On its own, discourse cannot act on the auditor if there is no collaboration on the latter's part" (*Che cos'è la filosofia antica?* [Turin: Einaudi, 1998], 86–7). Here and below, the translation is my own.

ethical," showing how our dispositions and predisposition for the most part elude our self-mastery and capacity for self-determination:

Some think that human beings become good by nature, others think that they do so by habituation [ἔθει], still others by teaching [διδαχῇ]. Now it is clear that nature's part is not in our own power to do anything about but is present in those who are truly fortunate through some divine cause. Perhaps discourse [λόγος] and teaching, too, cannot reach all human beings, but the soul of the listener, like the earth which is to nourish the seed, should first be cultivated by habit to enjoy or hate things beautifully; for he who lives according to passion would neither listen to a discourse which dissuades him nor understand it, and if he is disposed in this manner, how can he be persuaded to change? In general, passion seems to yield not to argument but to force [βίᾳ]. So one's character [τὸ ἦθος] must be somehow predisposed toward virtue, liking what is beautiful and disliking what is disgraceful. (1179b21–32)

As though in a proto-Spinozistic outlook, Aristotle's concern with the passions is rooted in the recognition of their primordial power to prejudge and predetermine. As we shall note again, however, this preoccupation does not result in an articulate analysis of the phenomena of human undergoing.

If Nicomachus ends on such a note, it should also be said that it begins in a similar fashion and is throughout accompanied by this line of reflection. Aristotle repeatedly reminds us that we cannot overstate the importance of experience, *empeiria*, and of having received the pertinent upbringing, *paideia*, prior to being exposed to the ethical discussion. Those who lack the required experience remain indefinite, as it were. They lack limits, a sharp definition, their understanding is unfocused. A listener such as this may at best retain a thoroughly formal knowledge of the discourses and lectures heard, but will be unable to assimilate such a knowledge in its practical significance and teleological thrust toward action:

Now a human being judges beautifully the things he knows, and it is of these that he is a good judge; so a good judge in a subject is one who is educated in that subject, and a good judge without qualification is one who is educated in every subject. In view of this, a young human being is not a proper student of politics; for he is inexperienced [ἄπειρος] in actions concerned with human life, and discussions [λόγοι] proceed from [premises concerning those actions] and deal with [those actions]. Moreover, being disposed to follow his passions [πάθεσιν], he will listen in vain and without benefit, since the end of such discussions is not knowledge [γνῶσις] but action. And it makes no difference whether he is young in age or youthful in character [ἦθος], for his deficiency arises not from lack of time but because he lives and pursues things according to passion. For knowledge about such matters in such a human being, as in those who are incontinent [ἀκρατέσιν], becomes unprofitable; but in those who form their desires [τὰς ὀρέξεις ποιουμένοις] and act according to reason [κατὰ λόγον], it becomes very beneficial. (1094b29–1095a11)

Thus, having listened to *logos* already, that is, having undergone the *logos* informing one's own nature, all the way to one's instincts and desires, makes it possible to listen to the *logos* of ethics in its embodied and experiential resonance. Youth means not having learned to align passion and reason, *pathos* and *logos*. Without such an alignment or harmonization, *logos* is empty, abstract. It neither touches nor otherwise affects action. As Aristotle anticipates, this is the structure of the problem of incontinence, which will be examined later. In a certain sense, then, the end to be brought about, that is, the human being in its harmonious actualization, must be presupposed in deed. The human being that the ethical inquiry attempts to put into sharp focus must be present as the listener of the inquiry to begin with. At a later stage, Aristotle will say that nothing less than the ultimate end, the good, is brought into view by virtue, that is, in a way, determined by character, prior to all analysis. Accordingly, only those who are already virtuous would see it.

Aristotle again emphasizes the function of prior experience as he suggests that we should always start from where we are, from where we have always already started, and establish principles from there where we find ourselves, from what is familiar. Having received an adequate kind of upbringing, in this sense, would amount to a beginning all the more auspicious:

Probably we should begin from things which are known [γνωρίμων] to us. Accordingly, he who is to listen effectively to lectures concerning beautiful and just things and, in general, to subjects dealt with by politics, should be brought up beautifully in ethical habits; for the beginning is the fact [ἀρχὴ γὰρ τὸ ὅτι], and if this fact should appear to be adequate, there will be no further need of the why of it. Such a human being either has or can easily get principles. As for the one who lacks both, let him listen to the words of Hesiod:

> that man is best of all who himself apprehends [νοήσῃ] all;
> . . . he is also good who trusts a good advisor;
> but he who neither can himself apprehend [νοέῃ] nor, listening to another,
> takes what he hears into his heart, this man is useless. (1095b4–13)

The apt formulation or description of the fact, of the *that*, provides a principle, stops the concatenation of causes that would otherwise go on ad infinitum. Once again, we find here an intimation of the sufficiency of reason inherent in action, in *praxis* – of the reason that is at work in a certain mode of being alive, the reason according to which ethical habits, that is, character, are formed. The one who has enjoyed a harmonious beginning, who knows first hand the fact of a "beautiful" education, will know how to recognize a fact as an adequate beginning, without asking for the "why" of it beyond a certain point. In his chagrin at those who neither have principles nor display the ability to acquire them through a correct receptivity, Aristotle quotes Hesiod from *Works and Days* (293ff.). If they lack even the capacity for listening to the wisdom at hand, let them listen to the poet announcing their irrelevance qua human beings. A few centuries later, Sextus (*adversus Mathematicos* 7.132) will have reported a saying by Heraclitus analogously lamenting the inability to listen on part of the many or, more precisely, their lack of comprehension *even after having heard*: "Of this *logos* here, which always is," Heraclitus would have said, "human beings lack understanding [ἀξύνετοι], both before hearing [ἀκοῦσαι] and when they first have heard [ἀκούσαντες] it." They listened to lectures, were variously exposed to *logos*, yet remained untouched and unchanged. They are unable to experience the *logos*, whether in words or in deeds: "for while all comes to be according to this *logos* [κατὰ τὸν λογον τόνδε], they resemble those who lack experience when they experience such words [ἐπέων] and deeds [ἔργων] as I lay out [διηγεῦμαι], dividing [διαιρέων] each according to nature [κατὰ φύσιν] and saying [φράζων] how it holds itself." However, in this experiential impoverishment, one's knowledge remains empty and formulaic, having no vibrant relation to what and how one lives: "But what they do when awake escapes [λανθάνει] them," Heraclitus is said to have concluded, "just as they forget [ἐπιλανθάνονται] what they do when asleep" (22B1).

On Aristotle's part, the warnings against the disconnection between knowledge and action are innumerable. Here is a related moment in *Magna moralia* focusing on the fact that knowledge, in and of itself, does not change one's condition. Of course, this line of thinking constitutes the prelude of the critique of *logos* developed in a more sustained way in the course of the analysis of incontinence, but also pervasive in the treatises of the *Metaphysics*. The author of *Magna moralia* points out:

> One may ask a question of this kind: Supposing that I know all this, shall I be happy? For they fancy they will. But this is not so. None of these other manners of knowledge imparts to the one who learns the use [χρῆσιν] and activity [enactment, activation, actualization] [ἐνέργειαν]; but the habit [ἕξιν] alone [does]. No more in this case does knowing these matters impart the use (for,

as we say, happiness is activity), but the habit; and happiness does not consist in knowing its implications, but comes from using them. However, it does not pertain to the present study to impart the use and enactment of these things; for indeed no other knowledge imparts the use but the habit. (1208a31–b2)

Three times, in this brief passage, it is stated that it is the habit, the possession of a certain psychological and practical formation (*hexis*), which confers the *khrēsis* and *energeia*, the usage and activation, the power to take up that which presents itself and put it to its proper use, letting it follow its course of actualization.[6] This enactment or, in fact, self-enactment, alone can make one happy. On their own, neither the properly ethical discourse *nor any other science* can give the power to actualize oneself, that is to say, to enjoy the fulfillment and fullness we call happiness. Indeed, as we shall see even better in a moment, it is for quite systemic reasons that prior ethical formation is necessary in order to be able to listen correctly to the ethical discourse, to make that discourse substantial and concrete: the ethical discourse, like *any* discourse, *cannot* capture the particulars; no discourse can give the perception, sensible and intuitive, of particulars, facts, and concomitant principles. Hence, when Aristotle says that the aim of this discourse is "not knowledge but action," and hence declares that experiential supplementation is needed in order to *touch* the stratum of lived experience, he is stating a necessity characterizing discourse as such, not something secondary and dispensable. Indeed, we might call prior experience or education, the fact that life has always already taken place, always already shaped, molded one, *the ineffable supplement of logos.* The *logos* that desires to embrace "facts" as they are, to open up to that which it cannot reduce to itself, and, hence, not to remain formal, needs the integration of life in its in(de)finite excess and priority. Or, to put it otherwise, *logos* must be *practically owned.*

Among other things, as was already observed, this is also why Aristotle's *Nicomachean Ethics* and ethical expositions in general are essentially and necessarily non-prescriptive. Circumstances, in their infinite spatiotemporal mutability, cannot simply be discursively contained. Again, the author of *Magna moralia,* by reference to the discussion of the "perfect" syllogism and the constitution of the major (or unqualified) and minor (or particular) premise in *Prior Analytics* A 1–4, addresses the problem of

[6] On happiness as use and actualization, *khrēsis* and *energeia,* of excellent habit, see *Magna moralia* 1184b31–5.

the translation of knowledge into particularity, and the ultimate excess of particularity vis-à-vis discourse:

In turn, this can be made manifest by reference to our analytical treatises. There we said that the syllogism comes to be from two premises, the first being universal [καθόλου], and the second subordinate to it and particular [ἐπὶ μέρους]. For example: "I know how to cure [how to create health in] all the human beings suffering from fever"; "This one here suffers from fever"; "Therefore, I know how to cure this one." Now there are cases in which I know the universal knowledge but not the particular. Here comes to be the possibility of error for the one who has knowledge. [He says:] "I know how to cure all the sufferers from fever; but whether this man suffers from fever, I don't know." Likewise, the same error may occur in the case of the incontinent, who possesses knowledge. It may be that the incontinent has the universal knowledge that such and such things are evil and hurtful, and yet not know which things in particular are evil. Thus, he will make mistakes although he has knowledge; for he has the universal one, but not the particular. (1201b24–40)

The author of *Magna moralia* highlights the ultimate inexplicability of the particular. Learning the principle is impossible if one cannot stop the chain of questioning, if one cannot discern the fact, the "that," in the things themselves. The same inexhaustibility in *logos* can be attributed to the passions, *pathē* – to that undergoing that, under auspicious conditions, that is, in the case of the excellent human being, does not interfere with *nous* carrying out its own work (*ergon energein*, 1208a20), but in fact constitutes the very condition thereof:

"Yes," someone may say, "but what is the bearing of the passions when they do not hinder [*nous*]? And when do they hold themselves in such a way? For that I do not know." It is not easy to reply to a question such as this. Nor is it easy for the physician, when, for instance, he prescribes a decoction of barley "in case," he says, "the patient is feverish." "But how do I perceive [αἰσθάνομαι] that he is feverish?" "When," he says, "you see that he is pale." "How will I discern [εἰδήσω] this pallor?" Thereupon the physician has to understand. "If you do not yourself have the perception [αἴσθησιν] of this," he will say, "there is no [teaching]." The reason [λόγος] is common and equally underlies other cases. The same holds for the knowledge [γνωρίζειν] of the passions. One must oneself contribute toward the perception. (1208a22–30)

Thus, whether considering upbringing and education, experience, or the emotions underlying action as well as intellectual activity, the Aristotelian discourse underlines how the prior psycho-practical formation determines the way in which one will be able to receive knowledge, to listen and understand – and whether such a learning will be effortlessly acquired or, on the contrary, irremediably compromised. Again, in this last passage we almost hear a nascent invitation to a kind of psychoanalysis, or to a phenomenology of lived experience: to an analysis of the passions and emotions, evidently based on intuitive and descriptive beginnings.

1.3.3. Dialectical Ground

The Aristotelian discourse, ethical and otherwise, is so thoroughly dialectical in tenor as to warrant here only the most circumscribed remarks. In the course of our reading we will find many occasions to underline the ubiquity of dialectical qualifications. Dialectic presents itself as a kind of excavation, as a digging into the familiar, into the current opinions and communal stipulations – or as the unfolding, the explication, of what is enfolded, implicated, within the familiar. The movement from priority according to us to priority according to being lies in this operation of deepening, in not going anywhere else, remaining where one already is, only discarding outer layers in order to come closer to the heart of the matter. Starting from the prevalent views, from what "we" say, thus, dialectic yields the principle by clarifying the fact, making manifest in an articulate fashion the common perception of it.

In a statement again making a start from desire as the motivation and moving force of inquiry, Aristotle acknowledges happiness as the highest good to which human beings aspire and, therefore, as the end underlying the investigation of ethics. It is on the "almost" unanimous agreement among humans that this acknowledgment rests. The name concerning which most people agree, however, is filled with quite heterogeneous, even incompatible meanings, determined by one's degree of wisdom and by the mutability of opinions, whether due to the intrinsic fickleness of the human psyche or to contingent factors such as suffering or poverty, in whose power one lives:

> To resume, since all knowledge and every intention desire some good, let us discuss what is that which is aimed at by politics and what is the highest of all goods achievable by action. Most people are almost agreed as to its name; for both ordinary and cultivated people call it "happiness," and both regard living well and acting well as being the same as being happy. But there is disagreement as to what happiness is, and the account of it given by ordinary people is not similar to that given by the wise. For some regard it as something obvious or apparent, such as pleasure or wealth or honor, while others regard it something else; and often the same man changes his mind about it, for when suffering from diseases he regards it as being health, when poor as being wealth, and when he becomes conscious of his ignorance he marvels at those who discuss something great and beyond his comprehension. Again, some held that beside these particular goods there exists something by itself, and that it is this which causes these particulars

to be good. To examine all these doctrines would perhaps be rather fruitless, but it is sufficient to examine only those which are most prevalent or are thought to be based on some reason. (1095a15–31)

Most of the times, then, people are caught within a kind of compensatory logic, such that one may define happiness reactively, only as the counterpart of a reversal of fortune. And yet, at times, when one is no longer preoccupied with such matters, it may happen that one envisages happiness in becoming more acquainted with things marvelous, inducing wonder. This is the case of those who pursue study and discussion – such as the Platonists, for instance, considered shortly afterward, unlike others holding worthless opinions. But the philosophers' opinions are not the only ones that must be taken into consideration. Aristotle could not be more emphatic in recognizing the foundation established through the practice of inclusive dialogue: the very fact of being widespread, or of being "considered" somehow reasonable, in and of itself confers to certain opinions their worth.

As the sustained exercise of communal stipulation, evidently, dialectical involvement reflects the ways of life of those involved. Illuminated, again, is the role of what is always already presupposed in order for discourse and discussion to begin, what is the case always, already, and in a determining way. It is on the ground of life that decisions concerning life, how to live, are made; it is on the ground of what appears, of what is experienced that opinions are formed.

Let us continue from the point at which we digressed. It is not unreasonable that what human beings regard the good or happiness to be seems to come from their ways of living. Thus ordinary people or those who are most vulgar regard it as being pleasure, and in view of this they like a life of sensual pleasure.... Men of culture and action seek a life of honor; for the end of political life is almost this. But this good appears rather superficial to be what is sought; for it is thought [δοκεῖ] to depend on those who bestow rather than on those who receive honor, whereas we presage [μαντευόμεθα] that the good is something which belongs to the man who possesses it and cannot be taken away from him easily. (1095b15–28)

Elusive as this discursive ground may be, Aristotle is very careful not to treat the result of dialectical negotiations as a mere arbitrary matter that, in other circumstances and by reference to other socio-cultural coordinates, could have been resolved in altogether different ways. Here he juxtaposes the twofold source of the belief in principles. On the one hand, one is convinced of a principle, and thereby acquires it, thanks to what "seems" to be the case, what "is opined" (*dokei*). On the other hand, an element exceeding shared opinion, something like a pre- or non-discursive certainty, seems without fail to guide one from within, compelling assent out of its intuitive evidence. Remarkably enough, for this element Aristotle utilizes the language of divination, *manteuomai.*

In the *Topics* dialectic is at first defined as that mode of *logos* or discussion, *sullogismos,* moving from opined premises, *ex endoxōn* (100b18). And yet, dialogical exchange does not simply concern issues that remain subject to contestation or negotiation. Rather, dialectic also gives articulation to those immediate intuitions through which one divines principles that are not doubted; it brings into a spoken outline the unspoken certainty that commands belief. Such a certainty, too, is subject to discussion and receives its definition in virtue of it. Indeed, this would be the proper work of culture. Thus, the difference between principles or premises that are "first and true" and those that are merely opinable hypotheses is rather evanescent. It lies in the fact that the former "carry belief [πίστιν] through themselves and not through others" (100b19–20), that is, need discursive assessment not so much in order to obtain credibility but, instead, in order to be drawn out, described.

It could be said, then, that dialectic is the *speaking of thinking,* or even *the exercise of thinking together.* That by dialectic we should understand that cluster of practices thanks to which intuition, what we divine in virtue of our lived and shared experience, is *formulated,* brought into *logos.* And that what emerges here is a certain irreducibility of thinking to knowing or demonstrating, of thinking to logic, finally the irreducibility of *logos* to itself. For *logos,* overflowing apodictic exercise as well as the self-articulation of reason, in dialectic presents itself primordially as *dialogos,* as that gathering in (de)finitely prior with respect to any human endeavor as such – as the being together heeding which any endeavor may find its beginning. Shortly after the considerations in the opening of the *Topics,* Aristotle explains that the study, the *pragmateia* there proposed, can be useful, among other things,

> in relation to the first principles of each science; for it is impossible to say anything about them from the principles proper to the science at issue, since the principles are first in relation to everything, and it is necessary to deal with them through the opined premises [διὰ δὲ τῶν περὶ ἕκαστα ἐνδόξων] on each point. This pertains peculiarly, or most appropriately, to dialectic; for, being fit for investigation [ἐξεταστικὴ], it has the path [ὁδὸν] to the principles of all inquiries [μεθόδων]. (101a37–b4)

The first principles, those common to all the sciences and making the sciences possible, are in this way revealed in their dialectical character.

Such would be the essential role and continuing task of dialogue, of the weaving that weaves human beings together. Again, it is not the case that ethics alone, in its imprecision and practical focus, can only be dialectically grounded. Rather, the sciences themselves, each and all of them, are ultimately based on dialectically defined principles – where, of course, dialectically defined means articulated through the practices of communication and commonality, and hence essentially belonging in the phenomenality and phenomenology of human *ēthos*.

These findings converge with what was pointed out in the Prelude, concerning the sensible and inductive conditions for the possibility of the sciences (81a38–b9). It is Aristotle himself who, at the very end of the *Posterior Analytics*, in one sweeping gesture intimates the unity of "*nous* as principle of science" (a "principle of principle," because through it principles are acquired) and fact, *pragma*. The sciences would be related to both *nous* and *pragma* in like manner (*homoiōs*) (100b15–17).

1.3.4. Ethics as a Making

Ethics, then, does not admit of abstract generalizations, universal formulations, or reductions to calculation. It rests on previous ethical formation. It is essentially dialectical. Its imprecision "concerning particulars" is due to its adherence to the moment in its absolute singularity, for "those who are to act must always consider what pertains to the *kairos* as in medical art or navigation" (1104a9–10). Resting on such prior practical conditions is by no means distinctive of ethics, but ethics consciously highlights and dwells on this circularity. Ethics is that discourse, that *logos*, which recognizes itself in and as deed.

To speak of the dialectical, in fact altogether ethical terrain of ethics, entails, no doubt, the intimation that one will never have started from knowledge in the strict sense, for there is no knowledge that would encompass the entire spectrum of experience, of the possible, of the singular. Because of this, it was suggested above that ethics cannot be purely prescriptive, for it cannot abstract and generalize matters pertaining to unrepeatable circumstances, which are by definition irreducible. Or it may be that ethics does prescribe, yet not in the sense that it comprehends and anticipates every possible occasion or spatio-temporal configuration, but rather in the sense that it offers points of reference, "navigational tools," orienting suggestions. In this way, prescribing comes to coincide with bringing forth guidelines (laws and regulations) that provide perimeter and parameters for the human venture.

However, the beginning of ethics in the midst of the ethical would also seem to entail that ethics cannot be seen, strictly speaking, as an exercise of *poiēsis*, as a *tekhnē*, an art or artful production – at least, not if we understand *tekhnē* according to the model laid out by Plato in the *Timaeus*, that is to say, as producing by imitating an eidetic object. This is precisely how the celestial demiurge is envisioned at work, bringing forth the *cosmos* thanks to the contemplation and mimetic reproduction of an idea, which would subsist in its integrity prior to and separate from the becoming of the productive effort. It would appear, then, that ethics is not poietic in this sense, for it has no prior idea of that which it sets out to bring about, namely, the happy or good human being.

And yet, Aristotle quite consistently turns to the language of making, of creativity, to characterize the ethico-political discourse and action. "For," he says, "we posited the end of politics to be the highest good, and politics takes the greatest care in making [ποιεῖται] the citizens of a certain quality, that is, making [ποιῆσαι] them good and disposed to beautiful actions" (1099b30–32). In turn, the politician or lawgiver is presented as an *arkhitekton*, a master *tekhnitēs*: "The true statesman, too, is thought to have made the greatest effort in studying excellence, for his wish is [βούλεται] to make [ποιεῖν] the citizens good and obedient to the laws" (1102a7–10). Whether skillfully or poorly done, the aim of the lawgiver is such an intervention in the human surroundings, this way of taking things up, reshaping and reorienting them: "For it is by letting citizens acquire certain habits that legislators make [ποιοῦσιν] them good, and this is what every legislator wishes. But legislators who do not do [ποιοῦσιν] this well are making a mistake; and good government differs from bad government in this respect" (1103b4–6). Of course, let this be said in passing, what is aimed at by the lawmaker is anything but an acquiescent citizen, easily controlled and passively subjected to the rules. This would be, at best, a distorted interpretation of the political operation. In other words, the "architectonic" and creative quality of the lawmaker does not automatically translate into the manipulative sway of the ruler over the ruled, let alone of the control of knowledge over action. For, as Aristotle, echoing Plato, notes in the *Politics* (1282a20–4), ultimately the one who can authoritatively assess something produced is not the maker, but the user. If the fecundity of the lawmaker is understood as the ability to produce laws and other instruments for "navigation," it is the "user," in this case the one who navigates, that is, lives, who "knows" what allows him or her to do so well.

At any rate, what must be underlined here is that Aristotle's repeated affirmations of the productive function of the ethico-political investigation necessitate a re-thinking of *poiēsis*, of *tekhnē* itself, aside from and beyond the model of production following eidetic contemplation. Ethics, therefore, may be acknowledged as indeed productive, but in such a way as to cast a quite different light on production. Far from resting on the clarity of the eidetic, artful production is revealed as starting from a twofold difficulty. In its doubly difficult beginning, the productive undertaking (1) sets out to bring forth what is not yet fully defined and, thus, (2) has to clarify to itself, while already on the way, what is to be brought forth, that is, the paradigm itself of the bringing forth. In this sense, production (ethics itself qua productive) presents itself less as *methodos* than as *hodos* – as that manner of intervention that, venturing to bring forth that which, by definition, is not yet the case, but only a vision thus far indefinite and underdetermined, draws its path for the first time. To put it in strictly Aristotelian language, we might say that the bringing forth that ethics names is architecture without geometry.[7]

Again, this difficulty is, properly speaking, not a limit. It marks the overflowing resources of a science that does not contemplate its object(s) from a distance or from a position of separation, but rather contemplates its own belonging in and with its other(s). Ethics is grafted upon, channeled into the becoming out of which it finds its own beginning. And it is at this most basic, most elementary level that ethics is productive, reveals, brings forth: for all intervention in becoming, all channeling into or grafting upon becoming (and *what* would be excluded from so doing?) is in one sense or another poietic, because it alters becoming, impresses a certain course upon being that becomes. It inscribes itself into being changing it, *making* it what it is. To the extent that a purely

7 Far from reducing politics or action to *tekhnē*, through politics Aristotle shows *tekhnē* as a *poiein* that is no mere presupposition and copying of an eidetic original; the making here at stake is a making without and prior to a paradigm – at the limit, the making of the paradigm itself. Understood in terms of detachment from the practical, as contemplation of the eidetic in order to shape the practical, *tekhnē* seems to be at odds with the thrust of Aristotle's thinking. But *tekhnē* thus understood may already be a myth in Plato himself. In *Resp.* II we witness the building of the city in the absence of any accessible paradigm; the making is undertaken precisely because of the essential impossibility of contemplation and is, therefore, a groping in the dark. The interlocutors produce an *eidōlon* in order to make up for the *eidos* they cannot contemplate. The entire dialogue revolves around such an unsettled making and, even in its concluding Book, reiterates the complexity involved in bringing forth, revealing the measure of making to be not so much an eidetic pattern but the community of "users" (601c). After all, even the "contemplative" maker at work in the *Timaeus* is evoked through a "likely," "imaginal" *logos* or *muthos*. In this light, the Arendtian diagnosis of the Platonic subordination of politics or action to *tekhnē* (to a *tekhnē* understood, with Heidegger, in its knowing, contemplative, and potentially manipulative detachment) appears profoundly problematic. See Hannah Arendt, *The Human Condition* (Chicago: University of Chicago Press, 1958). Consider also John Sallis, "The Politics of the *chora*," in *Platonic Legacies* (Albany: SUNY Press, 2004), 27–45.

theoretical stance is impossible, ethics (indeed, thought or discourse *tout court*) is poietic, unfolds being, is implicated in being's unfolding, does not simply observe. As a primordial, almost imperceptible framing, ethics makes certain shapes of comportment, of community, even of thinking, possible, encouraged, others invisible, unlikely. Ethics or politics, then, emerges as a poietic-performative discourse: it is involved in bringing about and bringing forth the world it tries to encounter and understand. It is implicated in the movement it strives to investigate. It is moved by an understanding of the good, desiring and striving toward the good, even as it tries to inquire about the good.

2. ON HAPPINESS

If the dialectical character of premises is evident throughout the ethics, it becomes most notable in the introduction of the main theme, happiness. Here, proceeding from what is more known to us to what is less known, Aristotle progressively casts light on happiness as the highest good, and, hence, as the highest moment of human finality and projection. Proceeding from what is closer and more known to us means starting by acknowledging the ground of shared conversation, the habit of exchange in virtue of which opinions on the subject are layered. As we saw already (1095a15–31), it is thanks to the virtually unanimous agreement that happiness is established as the highest good to begin with. From here, Aristotle initiates a deepening process whereby the dialectical ground is assessed, the most prominent views examined. The discussion unravels from within the practice of dialectic, that is, as thoroughly immersed in the order of becoming, of the phenomenal, of the experiential. It is here that the shifting of opinions, the instability of agreements, the overall plasticity of the "ground" are heeded.

After a few considerations on sensation, induction, and habituation as ways of perceiving principles, and on principles as "facts" on whose description any inquiry hinges, Aristotle turns to the discussions surrounding happiness. The worth of this most basic dialectical layer is assessed as follows:

We should consider this [principle] not only from the conclusion and from [premises] leading to its definition [λόγος], but also from what human beings say [ἐκ τῶν λεγομένων] about it; for all things that belong to it are in harmony with a true [definition of it], but truth is soon bound to be in disharmony with respect to a false [definition of it]. Now goods have been divided into three [kinds]: those which have been called "external," those regarding [περὶ] the soul, and those

> regarding the body; and we say that those regarding the soul are the most important [κυριώτατα] and are goods in the highest degree. We posit actions [πράξεις] and [psychological] activities [ἐνεργείας] regarding the soul. So our account must have been stated beautifully, at least according to this doctrine [δόξαν], which is an old one and agreed upon by all philosophers. It is also correctly said that the end is certain actions or activities; for it is in such a manner that the goods regarding the soul come to be [γίνεται], and not from the external goods. The statement that the happy human being lives well [εὖ ζῆν] and acts well [εὖ πράττειν], too, is in harmony with the definition of happiness; for we have almost said that happiness is living well [εὐζωΐα] or acting well [εὐπραξία]. (1098b9–22)

To be noticed in this passage is the convergence, almost the coincidence of action, *praxis*, and activity (or actuality, activation), *energeia*. This is further reinforced by the concluding description of happiness, later said to be the excellent "activation or activity of the soul" in its fullness (1102a5–6), as "acting well," *eu prattein* or *eupraxia*. But the co-significance of *praxis* and *energeia* was already clearly announced when the "task" of the human being was said to be an "activity or action of the soul with reason" (1098a14). The implication seems to be that the work of actualization, however psychological, is as such a practical matter, a matter of action. Certainly, the "activity of the soul" according to excellence and not without *logos*, or, in other words, the pursuit of the goods "regarding the soul," will not have been a disembodied matter, detached from worldly involvement. Among other things, this should alert us to the difficulties presented by the term *psukhē*, which we translate as "soul" but should by no means automatically understand as opposed to, let alone separate from, body.

In addition and according to these remarks, let us simply underline again the practical-active ground for the emergence of the highest good. In order rhetorically to provide a confirmation for the position outlined, concerning the highest dignity of the goods pertaining to the soul, Aristotle resorts to the "ancient doctrine," the *doxa palaia* maintained not by the wise, but by all those who pursue wisdom, the philosophers. As for the view that happiness is "living well," its confirmation is based, without further examination, on its dialectical plausibility. What "we almost said" earlier, simply based on what "both ordinary and educated people" say (1095a18–21), is now definitely validated by noting that it "harmonizes" with the definition of happiness, which, in turn, rests on premises crucially dialectical. The strange and inevitable circularity of discourse could hardly be exhibited more lucidly.

2.1. Happiness: The Beyond-Human Perfection of Human Beings

Let us, first of all, attempt to hear the Greek word *eudaimonia*, which we are all too readily inclined to translate as "happiness," in its energy and resonance. The word *eudaimonia* evokes the benevolent and beneficial sway of the *daimōn*, and, hence, the sense of harmonious connection with or attunement to the daimonic. Indicated here is the cluster of conditions supporting a being in its becoming, protecting and promoting it along the trajectory of its unfolding.

As a prefix, *eu-* carries an adverbial value, expressing that something is taking place well, harmoniously. In its nominalized form, *eu* signifies that which is excellent, eminently good. Aristotle, for instance, uses it in this way at 1097b27, where *to eu* is associated with goodness, *tagathon.*[8] He also speaks of *to eu* as final cause, "that for the sake of which," in *On Sensation and Sensibles* (437a1), just as Plato does in the *Timaeus*, when describing how the celestial maker devised the good, *to eu*, in "all that was becoming." *To eu* is here designated as "divine" cause, in contrast to the "necessary" ones (68e).

On the other hand, *daimōn* constitutes a figure of the divine. However, aside from a particular god or goddess, it may more broadly convey the range of phenomena making the deity manifest, the signs of divinity at work, or even the strange, extraordinary quality of altogether ordinary human circumstances. In the *Symposium*, as is well known, the *daimōn* is described as a mediating figure: neither human nor properly divine, it holds together the spheres of the human and the divine by securing the exchanges between them. This is the bridging image of the messenger, of the one who dwells in between and weaves together that which only appears to be mutually extraneous. *Daimōn*, thus, names the subtle work of communication, the manifold propagation of energy, signs, and impulses across heterogeneous domains. In this sense, the *daimonic* both transcends and uniquely concerns human matters. It is irreducible but not at all extraneous to them. In fact, it concerns human affairs precisely to the extent that these are not self-enclosed but distinctively marked by an openness to that which exceeds them, or even surrounds and contains them. It could be said, consequently, that the *daimōn*, whether a divine figure, incomplete deity, or manifestation of divine work,

[8] In Aristotle this nominalization is frequent. See, for instance, *Metaphysics* 984b11, 988a14, 1021b15, and 1092b26.

illuminates the human as that to which an openness to the radically other is proper.

In the *Republic*, the theme of transmission, translation, and interpretation linked to the *daimonic* receives yet another variation. In the concluding vision of the souls' journey from life to death and back again to life, we are shown how the souls are led to choose a life, *bios*, to which they will be bound "by necessity." Making such a fateful choice means at once selecting a *daimōn* (617d–e). In this sense, *daimōn* names the tutelary figure accompanying the soul across the threshold between death and life as well as through the various thresholds and stages of life. It conveys the soul onto the shore of life and, from here onward, it has both the function of guiding and safekeeping. It is both guardian and fate, protective and binding. *Daimōn* is the life itself that one has chosen and will thereby, from birth on, whether consciously or not, begin to unfold. In this connection, we are reminded of Heraclitus' saying *ēthos anthropōi daimōn*, establishing the identity, for a human being, of character and *daimōn* (22B119). For it is indeed *ēthos*, character, which determines the manner of a human being's dwelling and thereby secures one to a certain course of life. Because of this, in the *Topics* Aristotle can say that being happy, *eudaimōn*, is the condition of one "whose δαίμων is effective or excellent [σπουδαῖος]" (112a37). *Eudaimonia*, in this intimation, means being well guided, accompanied through life in an excellent way. In other words, it names the excellent carrying-out of the task of being, that is, of living. According to the connotation of *spoudaios*, suggesting a certain intensity and saturation, *eudaimonia* denotes prosperity, abundance. In relation to the task of living, therefore, it designates flourishing, brimming with health and well-being, thriving.

But there is yet another trait of the *daimonic* that needs to be drawn out, because it carries the utmost relevance in the Aristotelian discussion of *eudaimonia*. In the etymological play that is Plato's *Cratylus*, by reference to Hesiod, Socrates recalls the first human beings to be born, those of the "golden race." They were covered over by fate, *moira*, and now, *daimones* under the earth, they are "guardians of human beings" (*Works* 122ff.). Socrates suggests that those primeval human beings were not said to be golden because made of gold, but because "good and beautiful," that is, also, "prudent," φρόνιμοι. Hence, he concludes, Hesiod called them *daimones* because they were *daēmones*, knowing and experienced, and so "I assert that every man who is good, whether living or dead, is *daimonic* [δαιμόνιον εἶναι], and is correctly called a *daimōn*" (397e–398c). Aside from the plausibility of the etymology, what is crucial in this text is the indication of a perfection that is altogether human, however designated as "golden." To be sure, such a perfection may exceed the condition of most humans as we know them in the current era, that "of iron." Socrates' comparison between the divine human beings of the origins and those of our time, in fact, reminds us of another Heraclitean statement: "a man is called an infant before a δαίμων, like a child before a human being" (22B79).

And yet, Socrates also underlines that a human being, even among those living at present, may actualize the traits of a *daimōn*, that is to say, exercise his or her capacity for excellence, manifesting prudence and goodness in living beautifully. The implication in the Platonic passage is that humans harmoniously supported and supplemented by the *daimonic* would, in a way, be returned to their originary plenitude and perfection, that of the golden kind. In this sense, the mythical time "of gold" is least of all a matter of chronological past, but a possibility that may always be enacted, however "covered over." We could say, consequently, that divinity, the divinity consisting of the goodness and beauty of the first human race, is properly human. More precisely, we can say that, thus understood, divinity is properly human potential. As is variously announced in *Nicomachean Ethics* Alpha and tersely declared in *Magna moralia*, *eudaimonia* is "an end that is complete or perfect [τέλος τέλειον]; and the complete or perfect end is the good and the end of all that is good [τἀγαθόν ἐστι καὶ τέλος τῶν ἀγαθῶν]" (1184a14).

Again, it is toward the utmost perfection and completion (1184b8), toward the sense of full actualization that the human being strives. The thrust beyond itself is proper to the human. Of course, in light of the open structure of the thrust beyond, which is the structure of desire itself, "proper" can in no way simply be a matter of propriety, let alone ownership or property.

2.2. Belonging of Human Life to Happiness

As we saw above, then, happiness means living well, or "doing [acting] well and living well [τὸ εὖ πράττειν καὶ εὖ ζῆν]" (*Magna moralia* 1184b10). Whatever the mode of being at stake may be, happiness entails that the being is or lives in such a way as to give itself over fully to what or who it is, or is to be. Such a way of living is the working of an attunement to what exceeds one, in order more genuinely to be oneself; the relinquishing of one's self-enclosure in order, paradoxically, to find one's completeness and completion. In this sense, living involves setting the necessary (though not sufficient) conditions for something divine, that is, essentially human, to occur, to light up in one's life. It could be said, thus, that such a way of living does not amount to a merely human-made achievement. Or it may be understood in altogether human terms, provided that "human" here designates something more, or less, something other than self-determination. The divine would essentially name the human precisely qua wondrous, not subject to either mastery or control, whether individual or communal.

Aristotle raises the question concerning the character, origin, and attainability of human happiness on a number of occasions. In considering the overall condition of openness to what comes and is not in one's control, he discerns factors that can be designated as "natural" or "divine" and others pertaining to teaching, upbringing, and the manifold of surrounding influences. In *Eudemian Ethics* he states:

> First we must consider in what the good life consists and how it is achieved – whether all those who are designated "happy" [εὐδαίμονες] become so by nature [φύσει], as with tallness and shortness and differing in complexion, or through learning [μαθήσεως], such that there would be a certain science of happiness, or through some training [ἀσκήσεως] (for there are many features belonging to human beings, which are neither according to nature nor to study, but to habituation [ἐθισθεῖσιν] – bad ones for those badly habituated and useful ones for those usefully habituated [χρηστὰ δὲ τοῖς χρηστῶς]). Or does it come in none of these ways, but either through an inspiration breathed upon the possessed enthusiast by a certain *daimonion* [ἐπιπνοίᾳ δαιμονίου τινὸς ὥσπερ ἐνθουσιάζοντες], as in the case of human beings caught by a nymph [νυμφόληπτοι] or a god [θεόληπτοι], or else through fortune [τύχην] (for many say that happiness is good fortune [εὐτυχίαν])? (1214a15–26)

Aristotle surmises that a felicitous configuration of soul, and hence order of living, may be attained by nature, by the rapture inspired by the *daimonic* or divine, by systematic (scientific) study, or by training and habituation. All these manners of self-realization point to factors exceeding one's own autarchic self-positing. Even scientific inquiry, which aims at a rational mastery of the question of happiness and whose intrinsic logic exhibits a certain autonomy vis-à-vis imponderable, extrinsic fluctuations, is ultimately not "self-made," resting as it does on cultural initiation and experientially obtained principles. It is *eudaimonia* that, qua final and most complete end, is "autarchic," self-sufficient, not the human being (1097b8). On the contrary, the human being is inscribed within, belongs to, the all-comprehensive finality that *eudaimonia* names. The human being is constitutively traversed, as it were, by that which remains inassimilable, irreducibly alien. This is quite literally the case, as can be appreciated already in the basic statement, in *Nicomachean Ethics*, that the human being cannot be conceived aside from relational considerations: "By 'self-sufficient' we do not speak of an individual who leads just a solitary life, but of [one's] parents and children and a wife and, in general, of friends and fellow-citizens as well, since a human being is by nature political [φύσει πολιτικὸν]" (1097b9–12). As we shall see later, the condition of interdependence does not simply define the single human being with respect to the rest of the human community, but also humankind as such with respect to the community that may be called "beyond-human" (natural, divine), or "human" in the unique sense just suggested.

However, while consistently underlining the condition of receptivity in ethical formation and hence the passivity inscribed in the realization of happiness, Aristotle just as frequently emphasizes what is in one's power, the moment of responsibility distinguishing the conscious contribution to the fulfillment of the task of living. In the *Eudemian Ethics* he continues the line of thinking just inaugurated by noting:

> For if living beautifully depends on that which is by fortune or by nature, it would be beyond hope for many [human beings], for then its attainment is not through care [ἐπιμελείας] and does not rest upon human beings themselves and is not a matter of their demeanor [πραγματείας]; but if it consists in oneself and one's own actions [πράξεις] being of a certain sort, the good would be more common [κοινότερον] and more divine [θειότερον], more common because it would be possible for more [human beings] to partake [μετασχεῖν] in it, and more divine because happiness would then be in store for those who make themselves and their actions of a certain sort. (1215a12–19)

To be noticed here is the convergence of the common, *koinon*, and the divine, *theion*. The good achieved not by chance or instinctively, but rather through mindful effort, is potentially most widely shared, hence common: it is a possibility available to human beings, defining the human as such. It is also eminently divine, for it marks the coming of happiness to those who have aptly prepared themselves, laying the ground and clearing the space for such an arrival. *Eudaimonia* names precisely the advent or availability, the taking place of a perfection at once divine and properly human, thanks to the predisposition to a certain hospitality, to an openness to what may come. The divine, then, designates neither a predictable, causally determinable outcome nor the purely random occurrence of felicitous episodes, displaying no discernible relation to causes, let alone conditions. The divine presents itself, if and when it does, in contexts that have been appropriately disposed, which make *eudaimonia* likely, although not granted.

It is because of this that happiness, however much designating an exquisitely human potential, remains fleeting and elusive, a wondrous condition that we perceive in its strangeness and extraordinary quality. Aristotle, again in *Eudemian Ethics*, says:

> Owing to this, a different [human being] names "happy" a different [human being] . . . and Anaxagoras of Clazomenae when asked "who is the happiest one?" said: "None of those you are accustomed to consider, but he would appear to you a strange [ἄτοπος] one." But Anaxagoras answered in that way because he saw that the one who asked assumed it is impossible to receive such a name without being great and beautiful and rich, while he himself perhaps held that the one who humanly speaking is blessed is one who lives without pain and in purity following the just, or shares in a certain divine contemplation [θεωρίας κοινωνοῦντα θείας]. (1215b6–13)

In the anecdote reported, Anaxagoras calls into question the conventional view of happiness as resting on external goods, on gifts, natural or otherwise, that are culturally invested with intrinsic value. We should notice here Aristotle's emphasis on "naming," on the attribution of the proper appellation: again, the whole problematic of happiness is broached in terms of dialectic and the dialogical, poly-logical practices pertaining to it. And yet, while in a sense determined by customary and dominant discourses, the phenomenon of happiness also presents a disruptive quality with respect to custom. On the one hand, it is virtually impossible to determine the meaning of "living well," "fully," or "excellently" aside from cultural practices and systems of valuation. On the other hand, however, one who is happy, in the sense of being most completely who or what one is and dwelling in the fullness of living, cannot but be perceived as singularly strange, placeless (*atopos*). Such a human being would hardly find a place within the order and measure of human community as we know it.

Traversed by the divine, partaking in the consciousness or vision (*theōria*) of gods (*theia*), such a human being cannot not interrupt the axiological configuration prevalent within the communal framework, the privilege therein accorded to the extrinsic goods. Both an exemplary point of reference and a transgressive, destabilizing presence with respect to communal agreements, such a man (at these junctures Aristotle's language tends to switch from *anthrōpos* to *anēr*) would be situated at the margins, at the limit of this community, as its outer confine, pointing to divinity. As will often be remarked in the *Politics*, this highly accomplished human being, god-like and heroic, would and would not belong in the *polis*: he would be its lawgiver and king, and under his rule the *polis* would grow in excellence (1284b26ff., 1286a23ff., 1332b17ff.). Otherwise, he would be intolerable for his outstanding traits, ostracized at best (1284a20ff.). Aristotle's thought fruitfully dwells on this tension and derives much of its vitality from it. In the passage just quoted, this is clear from the fact that the almost divine human being, however absorbed in contemplation, indeed, precisely in order to be thus absorbed, must be healthy, enjoy freedom from psychophysical pains. Even a being such as this needs the satisfaction of certain basic material conditions in order to join the deities.

However, the "placelessness," the eccentric character of this simultaneous belonging and transcending, of this presence that at once brings the *polis* into its best outline and ruptures it, can hardly be overemphasized. A statement from the *Politics* must be quoted for its peremptoriness in this regard:

> if there is someone (or few, yet unable to make up a complete *polis*) so exceedingly distinguished in virtue that the virtue and political capacity of all the others cannot be compared to his (or their) virtue and political capacity, then this one (or those few) should not be regarded as a part [μέρος] of the *polis*; for being unequal to the others in virtue and political capacity yet regarded as equal (or equals), he (or they) would be treated unjustly. Such a human being [ἀνθρώποις] would be like a god among them. From this it is also clear that laws must be posited only for those who are equal in birth and capacity, for no law exists for such a human being – *he is himself the law*. It would, indeed, be ridiculous for anyone to try to posit laws for such a man; for he would perhaps say what, in the fable of Antisthenes, the lions said to the hares ["Where are your claws and teeth?"] when the hares were making speeches and claiming equal status for all. (1284a3–18; emphasis added)

2.3. Ways of Living

Almost everyone, then, agrees on designating "happiness" as living well and acting well. As to what these mean, however, there prevail a great many variations of opinion and disagreements. Such differences seem to come "from their ways of living [ἐκ τῶν βίων]" (1095b16). The word *bios* designates precisely the manner and shape of one's living, a definite mode of *zēn*, of metabolic or physiological life. The configuration of one's life is revealing of an axiology in a twofold sense, for it is both determined by and determinative of it, in a play of mutual implication and equiprimordiality. On the basis of these considerations, Aristotle proceeds to discern three ways of living that make manifest three outstanding human possibilities.

The discussion of happiness is progressively deepened, becomes more unfamiliar as the dialectical ground undergoes critical assessment. Such is the thrust of the whole analysis, as is clear from a passage in part examined above and here quoted more fully:

> Thus ordinary people or those who are most vulgar regard it as being pleasure, and in view of this they like a life of sensual pleasure [τὸν ἀπολαυστικόν]. Now there are three kinds of life which stand out most; the one just mentioned, the political [ὁ πολιτικὸς], and thirdly the contemplative [ὁ θεωρητικός]. Ordinary people appear to be quite slavish in choosing deliberately [προαιρούμενοι] a life of beastly pleasures, but their view has support because many men of means share the passions of Sardanapalus. Men of culture and action seek a life of honor; for the end of political life is almost this. But this good appears rather superficial to be what is sought. (1095b16–24)

It should be noticed that, at this juncture, Aristotle does not elaborate on what the third mode of life would be and entail. This will be approached at the end of the treatise, in Book Kappa. For the moment, we are left with a little more than a hint. Indeed, we find a passing anticipatory remark in a passage already considered above, where Aristotle observes that some regard the supreme good as something "obvious or apparent," while others as "something other" (1095a23–4). Then, as though in order to elaborate on the latter, he speaks of those human beings who, upon taking note of their "ignorance," are drawn to "those who discuss something great and beyond themselves [ὑπὲρ αὑτοὺς]" (1095a26–7). It is in such a wondrous striving toward a comprehension leading them over and above themselves, making them more comprehensive, that we recognize the *bios* of seeing, contemplation, even theory. Once again, the nexus of human and divine modes can be divined precisely in this eccentric movement of the human in excess of itself, projected beyond itself. We shall have numerous occasions to return to this, because such a "thrust beyond" will emerge as central in the understanding of the intellectual "excellences" *nous* and *sophia* as well as friendship in its manifold senses. Of course, it will also be crucial in the development of the contemplative life at the end of the *Nicomachean Ethics.*[9]

The hedonistic life keeps one bound to one's drives and compulsions, well beyond the mere and necessary satisfaction of physiological

[9] Regarding the "the paradoxical and enigmatic idea that Aristotle forms of the intellect and of spirit," Hadot notes: "the intellect is that which is most essential in man, and, at the same time, it is *something divine that comes to man,* so that it is that which transcends man that constitutes his authentic personality, as if the essence of man would consist of his being above himself" (*Che cos'è la filosofia ontica?* 78; emphasis added).

necessities. Sensual appetites become the focus of one's pursuits to the point of overindulgence, as in the paradigmatic case of the Assyrian king. The problematic character of this choice is not so much, or not so simply, its attention to sensuous needs, but rather the disproportion and one-sidedness of this emphasis. It is precisely the lack of measure in the satisfaction of these desires that ends up making this life, far from a magnification of embodiment, a corruption of bodily well being, a destructive and unhealthy conduct. On the other hand, the "political" life, the life more consciously devoted to the care of one's essentially political nature, is associated with honor, with the love of magnificence, recognition, and reputation. It remains, therefore, crucially bound to the order of appearances and, most notably, to the vain cultivation of one's own glory. Its limit seems to lie here, and not so much in its "practicality" as such. It is the narcissistic turn of its involvement in action (*praxis*) that makes this life somewhat partial. Concerning the "theoretical" life, besides the anticipation just mentioned, for the moment let us simply signal another passing remark around the beginning of the *Eudemian Ethics*:

> the [things] related to the happy deportment [ἀγωγὴν] being three, the things mentioned first as the greatest goods for human beings – virtue and prudence and pleasure – we see that there are also three ways of life [τρεῖς ὁρῶμεν καὶ βίους] in which all those who happen to be in power choose to live [προαιροῦνται ζῆν], the political, the philosophical, and that of sensual pleasure. Of these the philosophical life wishes [βούλεται] to be about prudence [φρόνησιν] and contemplation [θεωρίαν] of truth, the political life about beautiful actions [πράξεις τὰς καλάς] (and these are the actions from virtue), and the life of sensual pleasure about the bodily pleasures. (1215a32–b5)

The third shape of life, then, is distinguished by a concern with the truth, that is, by the pursuit of wisdom. It is in the context of such a philosophical (desiring and striving) character that the contemplative aspect of this life should be understood. Such a life is moved by the wish to see beyond the phantasmagoria of political standing, and yet entails by no means an abstraction from political involvement. (Let it be said merely parenthetically, for now: Book Kappa, concluding the *Nicomachean Ethics*, constitutes *at once* the *locus* of the discussion of the "theoretical" life and the moment at which the treatment of ethics shifts to its more properly political mode.) The life thus led wishes to bring mindfulness to itself: to enact the virtues (i.e., to live and act excellently) in a more conscious way, developing a prudent awareness of itself. Not simply practicing the virtues, but also illuminating the practice of excellence in this way, the philosophical life opens itself up to the possibility of contemplating beyond itself.

Thus, it should be noticed already that, to whatever degree *theēria* may be attainable, it will not have been without qualification: *theōria* will always have taken place in the midst of the unraveling of life, of *one* life. This is, indeed, the meaning of *bios*: that life, unique and finite, that provides an unrepeatable taking-place of *zēn*, indefinite and all-encompassing life. Qua *bios*, the *bios theōrētikos* is a matter of action, of *praxis*. In other words, *theōrein* is a manner of life, neither outside nor above life, hence always involved in life even as it tries to examine it. *Theōrein* will, in this sense, never have meant separation from life, privation of the implication and enfoldment within it.[10]

2.4. A More Complete Definition of Happiness

Once again, happiness is acknowledged almost unanimously as living and acting well. On this basis, progressive clarifications are proposed. (1) Happiness as living and acting well, to be more precise, indicates a manner of life and of action distinguished by excellence (*aretē*): *eudaimonia* and *eudaimonein*, says the author of *Magna moralia*, lie "in living well [ἐν τῷ εὖ ζῆν] ... and living well in living according to the virtues [ἐν τῷ κατὰ τὰς ἀρετὰς ζῆν]" (1184b28–30). (2) In the *Nicomachean Ethics* we find a further polished description specifying that happiness, that is, the venture of living, is an activity (*energeia*) and that its excellence must be "complete" or "perfect," "perfectly achieved" (τελείαν): "happiness is an activity of the soul in accordance with complete virtue" (1102a5–6). (3) Another remark in *Magna moralia* specifies that activity, *energeia*, occurs in terms of a having, of a possession, *hexis*, set to use, *khrēsis*. In other words, activity occurs in terms of structures acquired through repeated practice, or habits. Whatever is accomplished by habits is accomplished well by those particular habits that are the virtues: "Happiness would be in the use and activity of something [possessed]. For where something is a possession [having, habit] and used, its use and activity are its end. Virtue

[10] It is relevant to point out that Aristotle never uses the direct opposite of the adjective *praktikos*, namely, *theōrikos*. He only utilizes the term *theōrētikos*, which designates at once the modality of knowing for its own sake (and not for extrinsic goals) and the way of life, the *bios*, devoted to the pursuit of such a knowing. Because of this, Hadot notices, "'theoretical' is not opposed to 'practical'; in other words, 'theoretical' may be applied to a philosophy that is practiced, lived, active, bearing happiness.... In this perspective, 'theoretical' philosophy is at the same time ethics," such that, on strictly Aristotelian ground, we may venture the phrase "theoretical *praxis*" (*Che cos'è la filosofia antica?* 79–80).

is a possession of the soul" (1184b32–4). A whole range of terminological and speculative resources is deployed around the theme of happiness, casting light on its various implications. The crucial terms drawn together in these formulations of happiness will demand close inspection: activity, *energeia*; soul, *psukhē*; excellence or virtue, *aretē*; habit, having, or possession, *hexis*; completeness or perfection, *teleiōsis*.

Living is the enactment or activity, the *energeia* of the soul. Living indicates the soul at work, carrying out its task, its *ergon*. Something realizing or actualizing itself means something carrying out its exquisitely unique assignment. For the soul, this is living, and it is in virtue of the soul that anything alive lives (*Magna moralia* 1184b27).

Now, living well, that is, according to excellence, means to live fully, to actualize one's potential completely: to be fully who or what someone or something is. Accordingly, living well indicates that the soul carries out its work excellently. This, in turn, reveals that the soul has been structured and shaped through habituation in such a way that, when it enacts itself, when it has to act, to live, and to measure itself against the various circumstances in which it may find itself, the soul does so well. It does so well thanks to the configuration it has acquired, thanks to those paths and channels that habit has carved within it, as it were – in virtue of those tracks that, though in a sense invisible, make themselves unmistakably manifest in and as the course and design of one's actions. Habits are fully what they are when enacted, activated, and not simply dormant possessions in the psyche. Invisible when merely a latent psychological feature, it is as *habitus*, as outward appearance and manifestation of character in action, that habit is most completely what it is.

One's task is actualizing, realizing oneself. It is the movement from potentiality to actuality, from one's potential to one's self-realization. The fulfillment of the movement to self-realization constitutes one's *telos*, one's end, completion, and perfection. Such is happiness, the highest good. Again, we read in *Magna moralia*: "Since the best good is happiness, and this in activity is an end and a complete end, by living in accordance with the virtues we shall be happy and have the best good" (1184b37–40). What is crucial here is the continuity between belonging in the highest, most embracing finality and actualizing one's own unique, finite potential. Genuinely becoming who or what one potentially already is means at once contributing to and partaking in the good without qualification. In this sense, fulfilling one's potential, setting one's power to work in the fullness of its possibility, points less to a discrete plenitude than to the movement of overflowing into an enveloping, comprehensive attainment that exceeds the singular being. The perfection or completion of happiness, its sufficing to itself and depending on no further factors (*autarkeia*), must be understood in this light. An extended set of considerations in *Nicomachean Ethics* gathers the multifaceted phenomenon of happiness:

> Since the ends appear [φαίνεται] to be many, and since we choose some of them (e.g., wealth, flutes, and instruments in general) because of others, it is clear that not all ends are complete; but the highest good appears [φαίνεται] to be something that is complete. So if there is only one end which is complete, this will be the good we are seeking, but if there are many, the most complete of these will be that good. Now what we maintain [λέγομεν] is this: that which is pursued according to itself is more complete than that which is pursued because of something else, and that which is chosen but never chosen because of something else is more complete than other things which, though chosen according to themselves, are also chosen because of this; and that which is complete without any qualification is that which is chosen always according to itself and never because of something else. Now happiness is thought to be [δοκεῖ] such an end most of all, for it is this that we choose always and never because of something else; and as for honor and pleasure and intellect [νοῦν] and every virtue, we choose them because of themselves (for we would choose each of them when nothing else resulted from them), but we also choose them on account of happiness, believing that through these we shall be happy. But no one chooses happiness on account of these nor, in general, because of some other thing.
>
> The result appears [φαίνεται] to be still the same if we proceed from self-sufficiency, for the perfect good is thought to be [δοκεῖ] self-sufficient. By "self-sufficient" we do not mean [λέγομεν] oneself alone, living a solitary life. . . . Now we posit [τίθεμεν] the self-sufficient to be that which taken by itself alone makes one's life worthy of choice and lacking in nothing; and such we consider [οἰόμεθα] happiness to be. Moreover, we posit happiness to be of all things the most worthy of choice and not capable of being increased by the addition of some other good [συναριθμουμένην], since if it were capable of being increased by the addition even of the least of the goods, the result would clearly be more worthy of choice; for the result would exceed [the initial good, happiness] and the greater of two goods is always more worthy of choice. It appears [φαίνεται], then, that happiness is something perfect and self-sufficient, and it is the end of our actions. (1097a26–b21)

Aside from the frequent qualifications signaling the belonging of this discourse in the order of phenomena and dialectical stipulations, we should note the way in which the intellectual pursuit is illuminated by the logic of progressively encompassing finality. Even manners of intellectual excellence such as *nous* are desired, pursued, because of the happiness they bring. Their self-sufficiency and worth seem to be qualified, in that they are not loved simply for their own sake. Happiness surpasses them in the order of finality, for it is not for the sake of them. Its plenitude alone is found to be unqualified.

The accomplishment of one's task constitutes one's end, that is, ultimately, happiness. But how to determine one's task? The determination of the task, of what or who one is to become, is guided by an insight into one's being, into who or what one is, and hence is to be. Being a certain kind of being already entails a certain trajectory projected toward the fulfillment of such a being. The peculiar potential of the soul, and hence the task it must carry out, is living. But what about the potential distinctive of the human being? For the human being shares the overall task of living with everything else animated, whether plants or other animals. And yet, it is clear that "living well," fulfilling one's potential, will have meant something different according to who or what one may be. Aristotle denounces the vagueness of the elaboration of happiness carried out so far and proposes the consideration of distinctively human purposiveness: "Perhaps to say that happiness is the highest good is something which appears to be agreed upon [ὁμολογούμενον]; what we miss, however, is a more explicit statement as to what it is. Perhaps this might be given if the task [ἔργον] of the human being is taken into consideration" (1097b22–4). Indeed, it must be assumed that the human being as such does have an assignment or function, because the carpenter or the shoemaker do have one, and, "just as an eye and a hand and a foot and any part of the body in general appear to have a certain function, so a human being has some function other than these" (1097b31–4). The assignment at stake, therefore, will have concerned the human being not according to his or her specific occupational profile, let alone according to any particularity pertaining to a finite life, but rather according to his or her humanity.[11] Clarifying the function or task of the human being would deepen our understanding of human happiness, for the measure of one's accomplishment rests in and with one's undertaking: "just as in a flute-player or a statue-maker or any artist, or, in general, in anyone who

[11] The "hierarchy of ends" in the opening page of the *Nicomachean Ethics* (1094a) should be understood in this light. The subordination of bridle-making to horsemanship, and of the latter to military strategy, indicates the inclusion of partial finalities within increasingly more comprehensive ones, and the coming of the various sciences under the science eminently architectonic. As the most architectonic science or faculty, ethics or politics undertakes precisely to illuminate an order of priority inherent in each human being: *before* being anything specific, functionally and professionally delimited, identified with a particular role (e.g., an artist, a scientist), a human being is a human being, and that is his or her highest task and assignment. This work or task is shared in common by all human beings qua human.

has a function or an action to perform, the good and excellence [τὸ εὖ] are thought to be [δοκεῖ] in that function [ἐν τῷ ἔργῳ], so it would appear to be the case [δόξειεν] in a human being" (1097b26–8).

Aristotle proceeds, then, to complete the definition of happiness by reference to the pivotal distinction among the lives of plants, of animals, and of the human animal, a distinction reflecting the threefold division of the soul and the three main shapes of life considered above. Again, the passage is worth quoting extensively:

Now living [ζῆν] appears to be common to plants [as well as to human beings]; but what we seek is proper [ἴδιον] [to human beings alone]. So let us leave aside the life [ζωήν] of nutrition [θρεπτικὴν] and growth [αὐξητικὴν]. Next there would be a certain life of sensation [αἰσθητική]; but this, too, appears to be common also to a horse and an ox and all animals. There remains, then, the life of action [πρακτική] of a being having *logos* [λόγον ἔχοντος]. Of that which has *logos,* (a) one [part] has it in the sense that it may obey it, (b) the other [part] has it in the sense that it has [ἔχον] it or in the sense that it is thinking [διανοούμενον]. Since we speak of part (b), too, in two senses, let us confine ourselves to the life with *logos* in activity [κατ' ἐνέργειαν], for it is this sense which apparently is said to be more important [κυριώτερον]. Accordingly, if the function of a human being is an activity of the soul according to *logos* or not without *logos,* and if we say that the function of a human being is generically the same as that of a good [σπουδαίου] human being, like that of a lyre-player and a good lyre-player, and of all the others without qualification, when excellence [ὑπεροχῆς] with respect to virtue is added to that function (for the function of a lyre-player is to play the lyre while that of a good lyre-player is to play it well [εὖ], and if so, then we posit the function of a human being to be a certain life [ζωήν], namely, activity and actions of the soul with *logos,* and of a good man [σπουδαίου δ' ἀνδρὸς] we posit these to be well [εὖ] and beautifully [καλῶς] done; so since each thing is performed well according to its proper [οἰκείαν] virtue), then the good [ἀγαθὸν] for a human being turns out to be an activity of the soul according to virtue, and if the virtues are many, then according to the best and most complete virtue. And we should add "in a complete life [βίῳ]," for one swallow does not make a spring, nor does one day; and so too one day or a short time does not make a human being blessed or happy. (1097b38–1098a20)

The decisive operation here is carving *bios,* the unity of a finite and individuated life, out of *zōē,* the undifferentiated continuum of physical/physiological life. This means carving human life, each human life in its singularity, out of (1) life as metabolic function, that is, the elemental/elementary stratum of life common to all, even blades of grass, and (2) the life of sensual exposure and sensory stimulation shared by all the animals. It is in this way that the distinctively human work, and hence the traits of human happiness, are incisively captured. Human beings do indeed partake of common metabolic processes as well as sensory life. The latter seems to entail emancipation with respect to the mere maintenance and well functioning of organic life, and it is such an overflowing of sensuous solicitation beyond necessity that makes possible the life (*bios*) of bodily overindulgence discussed above. However, these features do not ultimately seize human specificity. The latter has to be caught in action, *praxis*, and reason, *logos*, in fact, in action according to reason, for the two aspects are introduced in their intertwinement. The being that "has" *logos* is a being that acts, practices, a being whose activity has a distinctively practical character. "Practicing" seems here to designate the uniquely human feature, namely, a comportment exhibiting a deliberate character, consciously accompanied or sustained. For the moment, Aristotle does not dwell on the distinction between the "having" reason that indicates simply the ability to listen, follow, and obey reason and that "having" that is the enactment of thinking, *dianoia*, properly speaking. Instead, he limits himself to underlining that such a "having" *logos* may be latent, that is, inactive or de-activated, as if dormant, or, on the contrary, activated, actualized, at work (*energeia* names precisely this), in brief, practiced.

If, then, the psychological (i.e., in this context, psychophysical) configuration distinguishing the human being entails such a threefold functionality (metabolism, sensibility, action with *logos* or *logos* in action), Aristotle concludes that its proper end and assignment is "activity and action" (*energeia, praxis*) according to *logos* and excellently performed. Here is indicated the human being setting itself to work according to its fullest potential, in a way that encompasses and realizes its being in its manifoldness. Again, it should be underlined that, much as *energeia* and *praxis*, it is said, must be guided by *logos*, take place "according to *logos*" or "not without *logos*" (*kata logon* or *mē aneu logou*), *logos* itself is a matter of *energeia*, is more fully itself when "according to *energeia*" (*kat'energeian*), when operative. And it operates in action.

2.5. Happiness as "Being-at-Work" and "Action"

Let us review what has been found so far. (1) The lyre player's task is playing the lyre; (2) the player's virtue is accomplishing this well, that is, playing well; (3) the player's end is being a good player, a good musician, a musician in the fullest sense. *Analogously*, (1) the human being's task is an activity or action of the soul as a whole according to *logos*; (2) the human being's virtue is accomplishing this well, that is, living well, fully;

(3) the human being's end is being oneself fully, that is, being happy, being good.

(1) *Ergon* may be translated as "function," "work," "task," "assignment," or even "product." The *ergon* of the human being is a certain *energeia*, literally, "being-at-work," also translated as "activity," "enactment," "actualization." Indeed, the *ergon* is articulated in terms of *energeia* and *praxis*. (2) *Aretē*, virtue, broadly speaking designates a sense of excellence. It neither primarily nor exclusively pertains to matters of ethics. It does not even strictly pertain to human matters alone. *aretē* is a having (*ekhein*), that which is possessed and belongs (a structure, an ability), whether activated or not, actual or dormant; it is a *hexis*, a disposition or habit acquired through exercise, repetition, practice. *Energeia* or *praxis* is its awakening and enactment. In other words, virtue designates the "how," the manner or quality of activity, the excellence displayed in carrying out a task. In the excellent carrying out of a task, that is, in an activity marked by excellence, virtue becomes actual. (3) The end names the carrying out of the human task in an excellent way. It is *energeia* or *praxis* in the mode of *aretē*. For the human being as such, this is happiness or the good.

But the identification of the human *ergon* as an *energeia* and the association, or even the interchangeability, of *energeia* and *praxis* carry a crucial implication. Happiness, and this means the good, is a being-at-work, a matter of *praxis*. Far from a detached inertness, it is a being-at-work characterized by excellence and making manifest *logos* in action. Indeed, that in the soul which thinks (*dianooumenon*) shines through such a being-at-work. We will have to remain mindful of this, for here lies the possibility, in fact the necessity, of calling into question the apparently obvious but all too problematic disjunctions of action and contemplation, of the practical and the speculative, of ethics and theoretical discourse, finally, of physics and metaphysics. Indeed, while "reason" or "thinking" may not simply be the same as "action," still they may not be separable from action either – or they may be separable from the practical only in *logos*, in discourse, only provisionally and for the sake of analysis. Accordingly, far from appearing in its partiality and opposition to the theoretical, the practical would have to be seen as that which underlies the moment of contemplative insight or the exercise of reason, that in which reason is nestled and belongs. A remark in the *Politics* is utterly relevant in this connection:

If the above things are beautifully stated and if happiness should be posited as being actions well performed [εὐπραγίαν], then the best life [βίος] for every

> *polis* as well as for every individual [καθ' ἕκαστον] would be the practical life. But the practical is not necessarily in relation to others, as some suppose; and practical thoughts [διανοίας], too, are not only those occurring on account of what comes to be from acting, but much more those which are complete in themselves [αὐτοτελεῖς] and are speculations [θεωρίας] and thoughts [διανοήσεις] for their own sake; for a good deed [εὐπραξία] is an end, and so it is a certain action [πρᾶξίς τις]. Outward actions [ἐξωτερικῶν πράξεων] in the highest sense, too, we say to be mainly those which master artists [ἀρχιτέκτονας] perform [πράττειν] by thoughts [διανοίαις]. (1325b14–23)

Dianoia, thinking as such, is, then, disclosed in its highest dignity as *praxis.* Indeed, Aristotle proceeds to explain more incisively that thinking is *inherently* practical and relational, even when a human being is not relating to others. The suggestion here is that an "individual" is a community – that, just like a *polis*, an individual is composite, one is many, and the structure of thinking is analogous to the exchanges that may take place within a *polis*, however isolated from others. The practical character of thinking has to do with the fact that unity is complex, that the one is not simple:

> Moreover, communities [πόλεις] which are founded in isolation from others and intend to live so, too, are not necessarily devoid of action [ἀπρακτεῖν]; for actions may occur among the parts of the *polis* since there are many associations of those parts with each other. This is similarly true also with any one individual human being, for, if not, god and the whole universe, whose actions are not outward [ἐξωτερικαὶ] but appropriate [οἰκείας] to themselves, would not fare beautifully. (1325b24–30)

Again, the consequences of these reflections are boundless. We shall return to them time and again, especially when considering the relationship between the intellectual virtues of prudence and wisdom and, later on, the "theoretical life."

2.6. Addenda to the Question of Happiness

2.6.1. *Inseparability of Ends and Means*

When Aristotle says that happiness is an activity of the soul according to virtue and that this marks the accomplishment of the human task or function, what he is saying is that happiness is an activity *in and as which* the human task is carried out. The task, *ergon*, is an *energeia*; the work is being-at-work, and being-at-work well is the end – indeed, the highest end: happiness, the good.

In its highest manifestation, then, the end is not an outcome separate from the activity leading to it (we should especially avoid a naïve temporal understanding of finality here), but, rather, the activity itself. The end is manifest in and as the action, from the start. It already informs the unfolding of the activity, of a certain way of living. According to Aristotle, "it is rightly said that the end is certain actions [πράξεις] or activities [ἐνέργειαι]; for it is in such a manner that the goods regarding the soul come to be, and not from external goods" (1098b18–20). The highest end presents itself as inseparable from means, that is, as an activity for its own sake. In this sense, happiness is nothing to be grasped: it is a way of living that constitutes its own end – an end in play at every stage and orienting a certain growth, maturation. As Aristotle also suggests, happiness may be grasped in the unity, in fact, the identity of end, cause, and principle or beginning: "happiness is a principle, for it is on account of this that all actions are done by everyone; and we posit that the principle and the cause [αἴτιον] of good things is something worthy of honor and is divine" (1102a3–4).

After all, it is in and of itself significant that the proportion thanks to which Aristotle casts light on the human being revolves around the figure of the instrument player. Unlike the maker of an external artifact, the lyre player does not pursue an end separate from his or her activity, as the outcome of a productive activity. As "playing well," the end is accomplished in every moment of the musical performance, of the player's enactment as such. Far from entailing a clear-cut distinction between means and ends, that is, a purely instrumental view of activity, Aristotle posits that, in the case of the good or happiness, a certain activity is its own end, task, and product. It is on finality thus understood that happiness casts light.[12]

But even when addressing instances of ends as discrete artifacts, as is the case in the productive activities, such activities are hardly seen as extraneous to their results. Aristotle does not display the terminological resources allowing for a nominalization, for a substantiation and substantive conception of the means. He lacks a noun designating the altogether modern notion of the means as an instrument or expedient leading to an end that may be altogether discontinuous and unrelated. Rather, in these discussions we find the language of that which promotes, sustains, encourages an end, that which is projected "toward" or "relative to" (*pros*) an end.

[12] Granted, Aristotle says that, if and when "ends are apart from [παρὰ] actions, the products [ἔργα] are by nature better than the corresponding activities [ἐνεργειῶν]" (1094a6–7). Yet it is not qua products that they are better (1094a17–18), but qua further, broader ends – because they are the fruit and final cause of those activities, because they are that for the sake of which those activities are undertaken.

It is from the end, from the binding orientation of the end, that the thrust toward the end is disclosed. This necessary alignment between means and ends as well as the understanding of ultimate finality in light of happiness, to be sure, problematize the logic of ends and means understood *more moderno*, not to mention the possibility of objectification that this logic inaugurates. In the "hierarchy of ends," the highest end is not that which presents itself as emancipated from its material conditions (conditions set aside, objectified, and merely used), but rather the end which is most all-embracing, beyond which no further reference to other goals is thinkable, and, most importantly, which remains thoroughly implicated in its conditions.

2.6.2. *The Place and Time of the Individual*

As we saw above, happiness involves the assumption of a "complete life," a sense of continuity and sustained achievement, "for one swallow does not make a spring" (1098a19–20). Aristotle returns to this question shortly thereafter:

> For happiness requires, as we have stated, both complete virtue and complete life, since many changes and all sorts of chance occurrences come to be in a lifetime; and it is possible for the most prosperous human being to suffer great calamities in his old age, as is told of Priam in the Trojan [or heroic] stories, and one who has met such fortunes and has come to a wretched end would not be considered happy by anyone. (1100a5–9)

Happiness is here assumed as concerning "complete" or adult human beings alone. However, the difficulty lies in finding the confines properly delimiting a life as "complete," as a unity enjoying identity and self-sufficiency. Do the beginning and ceasing of physical life define such a unity? How are we to delimit the phenomenon of individuality in its spatiotemporal unfolding? Is individuality a matter of monadic discreteness, or is the individual as such constitutively traversed by concomitant occurrences and lives, a locus of relations and intersecting forces? In the final analysis, the issue broached here is that of a certain immortality, of the qualified endurance obtained through procreation and belonging in familial or communal structures. These inherently human ways of extending oneself, reaching out beyond oneself through one's roots and branches, as it were, entail living on beyond one's allotted biological duration, while being caught in a relational web not in one's control. At stake is nothing less than the possibility of being happy when around us, whether spatially or temporally, reversals of fortune and great sufferings take place. This line of investigation encounters problems at every turn, as Aristotle repeatedly acknowledges:

> Should we consider no human being happy, then, while he is living, but wait, as Solon said, "to see the end" [of his life]? And if we posit also such a requirement, will it not be the case, too, that a human being is happy when dead? But is this not entirely absurd [ἄτοπον], especially since we have maintained that happiness is a certain activity? Now if we do not mean to say that a dead human being is happy and if Solon did not wish to say this, but instead that one might safely consider a human being blessed only when he is already beyond the reach of evils and misfortunes, this too would be subject to dispute; for it seems that something good as well as something bad may come to someone dead, if indeed it does also to someone living when he is not conscious [μὴ αἰσθανομένῳ], e.g., honors and dishonors, and also good actions and misfortunes of children and descendants in general. But this too presents a problem [ἀπορίαν]; for if a human being has lived according to *logos* a blessed life till old age and died as befitted him, many changes may occur in his descendants, for some of them might turn out to be good and to attain the life they are worthy of, while with others the contrary might be the case. It is clear, too, that the distance in the relationship between these descendants and the human being might vary in all sorts of ways. It would thus be absurd [ἄτοπον] if also the dead one were to change along with his descendants and become at one time happy and at another wretched; but it would also be absurd [ἄτοπον] if that which pertains to descendants contributed nothing at all, nor for some time, to the happiness or unhappiness of their ancestors. (1100a10–31)

Aristotle proceeds to point out that, at any rate, even within the limited scope of one life understood as the span of physical survival, we can notice fluctuations in the conditions of happiness: the "same" human being, whatever this may mean, can at one time enjoy good fortune, at another undergo misfortune. However, analogously to the vicissitudes that may befall others (whether friends, ancestors, or descendants), fortune and its demise are extrinsic factors. Fortuitous events as well as the ventures of those who are related to us in space and time affect our lives in a way that we cannot control or can control only very partially. These are factors more removed from our power, which we undergo with a measure of passivity and impotence. Because of this, Aristotle resists the notion that happiness may be decisively based on them: "For goodness [τὸ εὖ] or badness in someone does not depend on these, although, as we have stated, human life needs them, too; but it is the activities in accordance with virtue which play the dominant role in happiness" (1100b8–11). This set of considerations, then, is mainly preoccupied with the coherence and constancy of happiness: "For in none of human actions is there so much certainty as in activities in accordance with virtue, which appear to be more enduring *than even scientific knowledge*" (1100b13–15; emphasis added).

And yet, the uncontrollable fluctuations of fortune and the accidents of fate remain indispensable ingredients in the quest for the attainment and preservation of *eudaimonia.* For, even though an excellent human being may be capable of remaining steady in the midst of difficulty and of bearing "many and great misfortunes with calm and ease, not through insensibility to pain, but through nobility [γεννάδας] and highmindedness [μεγαλόψυχος]" (1100b31–33), the imponderable dynamics in one's environment will not have left one untouched. Aristotle, thus, concludes:

As for the fortunes that may befall a human being's descendants and all his friends, to regard them as not contributing anything at all appears very unwelcome and contrary to the opinions [of human beings].... Now just as some of a human being's mishaps have some weight or influence on his life, while others seem rather light, so the things that happen to all of a human being's friends are similarly related. (1101a23–31)

Although to a limited degree, this is held even for the dead: "Good actions of friends, then, and bad actions similarly, appear to contribute something to the dead, but they do so to such a degree and extent as not to change happy into unhappy human beings or to make some other such change" (1101b6–9). It is through the network of relations that one entertains with family, kin, friends, and others that the individual human being is disclosed. This entails the emergence of a dilated, choral sense of oneself out of the experience of interdependence. Far from self-enclosed, the singular human being articulates him- or herself through the conscious inscription in a community both synchronically and diachronically understood – a community of place and time.

2.6.3. *Critique of the Good of the Platonists*

Aristotle's evaluation of the Platonic conception of the good will be considered here only very succinctly. These brief remarks aim at casting light on the peculiar "critical" strategy vis-à-vis the Platonists and on the comprehension of the good thus delineated.

Aristotle develops his critical assessment without naming names. He refers to "friends," in the plural, who speak of the "ideas" (probably Platonists such as Speusippus and Xenocrates), but never mentions Plato himself. The issue is introduced as follows:

As for the good according to the whole, perhaps it is better to examine it and go over the difficulties [διαπορῆσαι] arising from the way it is stated, although such an inquiry is made with reluctance because those who introduced the forms [εἴδη] are friends. Yet it would perhaps be thought better, and also our duty, to forsake even what is close to us in order to preserve the truth, especially as we are philosophers; for while both are dear, it is sacred to honor the truth above friendship. (1096a11–18)

It should be underlined that here Aristotle is echoing what is written in one of Plato's own "exoteric" writings. Indeed, in Book X of the *Republic*, Socrates is made to declare that, even in light of his friendship with and admiration for Homer, he will pursue the truth above all (595b–c). This does not escape Thomas, who, in his commentary to the *Nicomachean Ethics*, observes with regard to the apparent tension between friendship and truth: "Along the same lines is also the judgment of Plato who, in rejecting the opinion of his teacher Socrates, says that it is necessary to care more for truth than for anything else. Somewhere else he affirms that Socrates is certainly a friend, but truth is even more so (*amicus quidem Socrates, sed magis amica veritas*). In yet another place he says that one should certainly care little for Socrates but a lot for truth" (I.6.5). The *ēthos* of the philosopher seems to entail precisely this: a love of the truth that does not remain caught in dogmatically confirmed alliances or forms fidelity demanding the suspension of questioning. But, as we shall see later, not only the friendship with wisdom, but also friendship *as such* demands this kind of posture: in the philosophical love as well as in the love of another, what is at stake is the sharing of what exceeds the bond between two human beings. In this sense, there is no conflict between philosophy and friendship, because both are animated by the love of the truth. It is indeed the desire for truth, for that which cannot be reduced to the two friends, which the friends share. They find in one another the reminder of that which is irreducible to oneself as well as the other, they love one another precisely because each sees in the other the same overflowing love, the same openness that does not confine them to the exiguous and exclusive bond between two.

Without examining the argumentation in detail, let us simply notice that the central problem diagnosed in the doctrine of the Platonists is the assumption of eidetic separation, *khōrismos*. For, says Aristotle, "even if there is some one good which is commonly predicated or which is separate by itself, clearly it cannot be practicable [a matter of action] or attained by a human being; but it is such a good that we are seeking now" (1096b32–6). In fact, Aristotle goes so far as to deny that the knowledge of a separate and "universal" good would at all be relevant to an investigation into the human good and human action:

Perhaps one might think that the knowledge [γνωρίζειν] of such a separate good would be better for those goods that can be attained and practicable, for having it like a paradigm we shall also know more [εἰσόμεθα] the things which are good for us, and if we know [εἰδῶμεν] them, we shall succeed in obtaining them. This argument [λόγος] carries indeed a certain persuasion, but it seems to be dissonant with respect to the sciences [ἐπιστήμαις]. For *all of them* aim at some good and seek what is lacking, yet they leave out the knowledge [γνῶσιν] of it; and it is unreasonable that all the artists [τεχνίτας] should be ignorant of so great an aid and make no attempt at all to seek it out. (1096b36–1097a8; emphasis added)

Action and, in general, the conduct of human life need not be and are not based on knowledge, on eidetic foundations. *Even in the course of scientific or creative pursuits,* one has always already acted on the ground of an otherwise than scientific knowledge, that is, on the ground, shifting yet no less reliable, of an intuitive and often implicit or imprecise awareness. As in the discourse of Diotima in Plato's *Symposium,* it seems that the desire and thrust toward the good (that which is lacking) need not rest on knowledge. A sense of what is pursued, however indefinite, will suffice.

It should be noticed that, despite the critique of a transcendent good, Aristotle's pursuit is still oriented to the good in a comprehensive (some may be tempted to say "metaphysical") sense. The divergence from Platonism does not signal a less ambitious pursuit, the exploration of some "local" or partial good, but what could be called a difference in method. The polemic here is against the inclination, especially pronounced among certain followers of Plato, to bring any discussion back to the study of number, thus attempting to account for the particular in terms of the abstract ("they demonstrate from numbers that justice and health are good . . . on the assumption that the good belongs in numbers and monads because the good itself is the one" [*Eudemian Ethics* 1218a18–21]). On the contrary, Aristotle insists that it is appropriate to proceed from matters widely agreed on (*ek tōn homologoumenōn*) to more encompassing or "abstract" conclusions: to start, for instance, from things usually experienced as beautiful or good, such as "health, strength, and temperance, and to demonstrate that the beautiful is even more in the unmoving" (*Eudemian Ethics* 1218a21–3).

Thus, the human good sought after in the ethico-political discussion presents itself as neither partial nor secondary. It may be the case that we are seeking neither the "idea of the good" nor the good as "common" (for the former is both "unmoving and impracticable" and the latter is "moving yet impracticable"). Yet the good we are discussing is "the best as end, as that for the sake of which, and the cause of those [goods] subordinate to it and first of all; so the good itself [αὐτὸ τὸ ἀγαθόν] is the end of those [goods] practicable for the human being. This is the good that comes under that [discipline] authoritative [κυρίαν] among all, which is politics and economics and prudence" (*Eudemian Ethics* 1218b7–14).[13] The good that directs the various human goods, thus orienting the human desirous teleology, is, therefore, the proper subject matter of ethics or politics. For this is the discipline that not only aims at the contemplation of the good exceeding human affairs but also, conversely and quite self-consciously, exhibits the awareness of the altogether human, ethical conditions for such a contemplation. We shall return to this, especially when considering more closely the intellectual virtue of wisdom. For the time being, let us simply recall that, as the *Eudemian Ethics* reports, Anaxagoras may have said the noblest human pursuit is "contemplating the sky and the order of the whole cosmos," and yet, such a transcendence of human affairs entails by no means the abstraction from them. On the contrary, it requires "coming into being" and "living" (1216a11–16). The good here at stake is neither separate not abstract, yet no less "universal," according to the whole.

In broaching the theme of the highest good, Aristotle does not avoid the question "what it is" (*Eudemian Ethics* 1217b1), though he also warns us that "what excellence [τὸ εὖ] or the good in living is escapes [διαφεύγει] our investigation" (1216a9–10). These considerations prompt the discussion of the fact that the good, just like being, can be said in "many ways" and that, subsequently, it cannot unproblematically fall under one science (*Nicomachean Ethics* 1096a24–34, *Eudemian Ethics* 1217b27–1218a1). As for the alleged contrast with Plato, however, it is hardly necessary to point out that Plato himself posits something like the "idea of the good" only in a highly qualified fashion. Even though we find such a phrase in the *Republic*, we cannot fail to acknowledge that in that dialogue the good is also said to be "beyond being," that is, also beyond that articulation of being that the eidetic constitutes. Book VI is crucial in this regard: just as the sun is the source of light revealing the visible things, so the good is the source of intellection casting light on intelligible things and thereby disclosing them. Accordingly, the good, far from being an idea among ideas, is the condition for the possibility of the intellectual perception of ideas as well as the lighting up of the ideas – the very source of the intelligible domain, and so of the eidetic. As such a source, the good exceeds the order of knowledge, even the highest segment of the

[13] See also *Magna moralia* 1184a8–14.

so-called divided line. To continue on these terms, we might say that the good constitutes the very possibility of the line, that is, of the ascent to increasing levels of luminosity and apprehension.

2.6.4. Further Questions (On Convention and Nature)

In the wake of what has been said thus far, we are in the position of formulating a series of questions regarding, broadly speaking, the relation between nature and convention, or that which most properly belongs in the sphere of human affairs. It commonly appears that ethical or political matters are "by custom [νόμῳ] alone and not by nature [φύσει]" (1094b16–17). This is due to the "differences and fluctuations" characteristic of them and associated less with natural becoming than with human determinations. While the fact *that* human beings are political and distinguished by certain intellectual powers is given by nature, nature does not seem to prescribe *how* such "logo-political" potentials are to be developed and actualized, that is, *what* they (and, thus, the human being) are to be. In this sense, the various and variable human constructions, the many ways in which human beings interpret their task and potentiality, appear to *supplement* nature, to make up for the void of natural determinations, to extend order and structure there where nature remains silent or inscrutable. As Aristotle puts it, "every art and [kind of] education wishes to fill up [ἀναπληροῦν] nature's deficiencies" (*Politics* 1337a2–3).

But how, then, is such a supplementation related to that which it sets out to supplement? In what way, and with what entitlement, would the human being or, more precisely, a human community, undertake to extend natural order, as though making up for what nature has not ordained and, thus, "completing" the work of nature? For any constitution and institution of political order as such lays such a claim, because its self-presentation in terms of mere contingency and arbitrariness would by definition preclude its authority and establishment. Moreover, the human being, considering its psycho-physiological endowment, finds itself necessarily bound to acknowledge its belonging in nature, even if exceeding to some degree the scope of nature's mechanical causality. Hence, it finds itself bound to wonder about the continuities or discontinuities in the trajectory from natural determination to what we call human freedom. In this connection, Aristotle seems to suggest, however obliquely, that the human supplementation of nature may aptly be grasped in terms of imitation, of an imitative interpolation into nature. Much as he emphasizes the role of culture and custom in the discussion of ethical matters, Aristotle displays little or no propensity toward a relativism that would superficially reduce human institutions to purely random shapes. Despite their multiplicity and transient character, the determinations of human convention aim at prolonging the operations of nature, claim to parallel nature, to mirror it, and to belong in the same logic. Because of this, the character acquired through education and upbringing is designated as a "second nature." For the same reason, Aristotle speaks of "natural virtue," *aretē phusikē*, which is latent or unconscious, and which human practices undertake to make explicit, turning it into "virtue in the main sense" (1144b1–1145a11).

In this perspective, the articulation of human construction would bespeak an attempt at reading what is not immediately readable, at making nature accessible there where it seems to withdraw into an enigmatic silence. In effect, at times Aristotle seems to resort to the figure of the wise human being precisely in order to recompose the apparent rift between nature and human matters. Thus, for instance, he observes that "things which give pleasure to most human beings are in conflict with each other because they are not by nature such. But things which give pleasure to those who love beautiful things [φιλοκάλοις] are by nature pleasant; and such are the actions according to virtue, and these are both pleasant to such human beings and pleasant according to themselves" (1099a12–15). The suggestion that the excellent human beings (or "lovers of the beautiful") may enjoy a privileged access to nature and thereby provide a standard in the quest for truth, is echoed later on: "a serious [σπουδαῖος] human being judges things correctly, and in each case what appears to him is the true; for there are beautiful and pleasant things which are proper to each disposition [ἕξιν], and perhaps a virtuous human being differs from others most by seeing the truth in each case, being like a standard [κανὼν] and measure [μέτρον] of them" (1113a30–35).[14] Thus, while human custom at large, despite its claims and self-assertion, can hardly be referred to nature in any linear way, that which virtuous human beings perceive and practice seems to carry intrinsic value. However misrecognized, these human beings constitute a normatively authoritative point of reference, for their opinions tend to converge in such a way as to distinguish themselves from convention. Indeed, they approximate nature.

If convention, the shape of human coexistence, aims at supplementing nature, filling a void or underdetermined margin left by it, however, we must in addition pose the question concerning individual self-determination. To be sure, above we have shown that individuality

[14] See also, e.g., *Eudemian Ethics* 1215a3.

emerges from certain Aristotelian texts in a problematic fashion, as the intersection of communal as well as genealogical influences, and thereby demands the utmost caution around notions such as unqualified self-mastery or monadic autonomy. And yet, even in light of such an expanded view of the individual, we still wonder about the possibility for a human being (in the utter singularity, if not absolute autarchy, of his or her configuration and circumstance) to break through necessitating forces, whether natural or cultural. What is at stake is the capacity of a human being to puncture, or even to disrupt, the automatism following either natural necessities or cultural formation broadly speaking. In other words, this is a question concerning the possibility of change in spite of established conditions that would seem to impose a certain course. This will lead us to consider the phenomena of volition, intention, deliberation, and, more generally, the relation between drive, motivation, moving forces, on the one hand, and reason, *logos*, on the other.

We should highlight ulterior facets of the question of the relation between *phusis* and *nomos*. The human being is crucially, if not exclusively, determined by surrounding conditions. The focus of the ethical discussion is the treatment of the exquisitely communal or political conditions. And yet, what about natural or "biological" factors? We should not ignore the role of this order of necessity in ethical matters, merely on account of its being hardly intelligible and of the disquieting consequences of biological determinism in various guises. Concomitantly, how are we to think through the distinction, whether in kind or degree, between humans and other animals? This, in turn, leads us to ask: How is reason, *logos*, related to embodiment, broadly speaking to animality? Does rationality require, belong to a physiological support? How does reason give itself in and through the living? How is life inflected through such a "having"?

We will elaborate on these issues as we proceed in our analysis of the Aristotelian discussion. For the moment, however, in a merely suggestive fashion, I would like to recall a passage near the beginning of the *Politics* in which Aristotle tightly weaves together matters pertaining to the essentially logo-political character of human beings and considerations pertaining to human embodiment and that which a particular physical conformation makes possible. The reflection starts with an acknowledgment of the teleological reliability of nature (an acknowledgment literally ubiquitous in *De anima*):

> It is clear, then, why the human being is more of a political animal than a bee or any other gregarious animal; for nature, as we say, does [ποιεῖ] nothing in

vain [μάτην], and the human being alone, of all animals, has [ἔχει] *logos.* Voice, of course, serves as a sign [σημεῖον] of the painful and the pleasurable, and for this reason it belongs to the other animals also; for the nature of these advances only up to the point of *having the sensation* of the painful and the pleasurable and of signaling [σημαίνειν] these to one another. But *logos* is to make clear what is beneficial or harmful and so what is just or unjust; for what is proper [ἴδιον] to the human being compared with other animals is this: the human being alone *has the sensation* of what is good or evil, just or unjust, and the like, and it is a community [κοινωνία] of such beings which makes [ποιεῖ] a household and a *polis.* (1253a7–19; emphasis added)

Neither randomly nor by folly, then, did nature endow the human being with *logos.* It is such an endowment that constitutes the distinctive human trait and makes human beings unique vis-à-vis other animals. Aristotle attempts to provide a sharp demarcation between the human and other animals, locating it in the shift from voice, *phōnē,* and sign, *sēmeion,* to *logos.* Such a shift entails the transition, mysterious in its discontinuity, from the immediacy of the vocal signal, from a vocal sound conveying a present experience, to an altogether other order of communication entailing the mnemonic stabilization of contents, noetic elaboration, and the possibility of an infinitely more refined articulation. For the communication that *logos* designates, a communication granting the communal character of humans, entails the retention and projection of pleasure and pain in terms of that which brings about benefits and harms, and hence of the just and unjust.

And yet, despite his eagerness to underline the propriety and exclusiveness of *logos* as human endowment, Aristotle preserves the language of sensation and sensibility, *aisthēsis,* to connote both the mere power of vocalization common to many animals and *logos* proper. *Aisthēsis* emerges here as if continuously underlying the allegedly discontinuous shift from *phōnē* to *logos,* so much so that both the perception of pleasure and pain and the perception of good and evil are said to be a manner of sensation. In this way, the difference between *phōnē* and *logos* may be understood less in terms of kind than in terms of degree (indeed, the very difference between difference in kind and difference in degree becomes an issue). After all, even the mere fact that the term *logos* semantically ranges from reason, informing order, to discourse, speech, articulation of sound conveying meaning, sums up the problematic relation between *phusis* and *nomos,* between *sōma* and *psukhē,* and so forth. To be most concise here, let us simply note that the in *De anima* this problem is further amplified. At the end of Beta 8, the intertwinement of voice (as "sound of an animal" and "sound that signals," *sēmantikos*) and *logos* is viewed in its indissolubility and decisively cast in terms of its physiological conditions (apparatus of the pharynx, oral cavity, and tongue, which allows for the emission of a certain acoustic variety, and breath, whose work is communication or articulation, *dialektos*, that is, the vocal explication of thought, *hermēneia*). What is noteworthy, in this discussion, is that it is nature itself that is said to "use" (*katakhrētai*) the process of inhalation for the sake of the outcome of *logos*, which situates the phenomenon of *logos* within natural teleology. As an ulterior sign of the "physical" character of signification, we are told that *logos* is voice, the sound produced by an animate being, "accompanied by imagination," *phōnē meta phantasias* (420b6–421a7).[15]

3. ON THE SOUL

Through the introductory remarks and the discussion of happiness, an analytic of the soul imposes itself as necessary and begins to find a delineation. As seen above, happiness, the highest good, is principle, cause, and end. It is *energeia* of the *psukhē* according to *aretē*. *Aretē*, excellence, belongs to the soul, indicates the way in which the soul properly enacts itself: in this light we may understand excellence as a possession, property, or propriety of the soul, as a *hexis* – that which the soul "has" and, when in action, *shows*. To gain an insight into the virtues, therefore, we must project, at least in broad terms, a comprehension of the soul. Aristotle states the necessity of a psychological investigation in connection with the political task of shaping human beings:

> it is clear that the human being involved in politics [τὸν πολιτικὸν] should understand [εἰδέναι] in some way that which pertains to the soul, like a doctor who cures the eyes or the whole body, and to the degree that politics is more honorable and better than medicine. Now the cultivated among the doctors endeavor [πραγματεύονται] to acquire knowledge [γνῶσιν] of the body. So the political human being, too, should contemplate [θεωρητέον] that which pertains to the soul, contemplating it both on its own account and as much as is adequate to what is sought, for greater precision is perhaps rather burdensome in view of what he is aiming at. (1102a19–28)

Politics is more architectonic than medicine, for it comprehends the human being as a whole, not merely as a bodily organism, however much ensouled or animated. In the wake of this reflection Aristotle undertakes

[15] On these issues, see also the connected discussions in *Categories* 4b34–5a1 and *On Interpretation* 16a20–17a8.

to present the structure of the soul construed most broadly as that which informs the phenomenon of living as a whole. Even without considering here in detail the difficulties of Aristotelian psychology, let alone the controversies marking the history of its transmission, for the sake of counterbalancing an almost irresistible tendency we should emphasize that, in this context, nothing is to be assumed *less* straightforwardly than a notion of *psukhē* as a personal spiritual principle.

3.1. Living

Psukhē names the vitality of the living being, including the automatic metabolic processes, whereby life is maintained, and unconscious emotional contents, feelings, thoughts, and so on. In his analytic of the *psukhē*, Aristotle proposes that two "parts" may be distinguished within it, at least in *logos*, that is, in the order of discourse or inquiry. This proviso is a crucial reminder of the caution necessary when speaking of "components" of the soul: "It makes no difference for the present whether these parts are distinct [διώρισται], like the parts [μόρια] of a body or of any other divisible whole [μεριστόν], or whether they are two for *logos* [τῷ λόγῳ] but inseparable [ἀχώριστα] by nature, like the convex and the concave in the circumference of a circle" (1102a30–34). The issue of separability is not developed further here. For practical-political purposes, it may not be essential to know whether that which can be separated or discerned in *logos* is substantially separable or separate. However, this comment signals a problem that we, even if and precisely because under the spell of *logos* and its operation of "taking apart," would better not forget. This taking apart in and by *logos* properly defines the mathematical strategy as such, as we read in the *Metaphysics*: "Something can best be contemplated if that which is not separate [κεχωρισμένον] [from the thing] is laid down [θείν] as separate [χωρίσας], and this is what the arithmetician and the geometrician do" (1078a21–23). However, in that context Aristotle also warns that, while "prior in *logos*," the "mathematical [objects]," that into which something is analyzed, are neither "substances to a higher degree," nor "prior in being," nor yet "capable of being separately [κεχωρισμένα]" (1077b1–17).

Following the "mathematization" of the *psukhē* provisionally attempted in *logos*, we find a first distinction between an irrational part, *alogon*, and one that is rational, that has *logos*, *logon ekhon* (1102a29–30). The former would designate the physiological stratum shared by all that is alive. *Logos* would appear to be grafted upon a layer of life discontinuous with *logos* because lacking it (receiving it at most, but without possessing it, as we shall see). In this investigation concerning the soul, then, *logos* attempts to embrace itself as well as its other, that dimension of the soul that remains foreign to it, in which it does not dwell.

Thus, the human soul, that manner of animation distinctive of human beings, may be understood in terms of its rational and irrational components. In the course of these considerations (1102a5–1103a4), however, the twofold structure of the soul receives further elaboration. In one sense, indeed, it could be said that the life of nutrition and growth as well as sensation is irrational, while the part that has *logos*, the part where *logos* dwells, is the properly rational part. And yet, in another sense, it could be said that the strictly irrational part of the soul is the nutritive one, that pertaining to organic sustenance, while the life of sensation and appetite may be with or without *logos* or, better, with or against it. To the extent that the life of sensing and instinctual drives exceeds the bounds of the necessary (of metabolism), it may both be against and follow, resist and listen to *logos*. The seat of desire (*orexis*, *epithumia*) may be subjected to *logos*, neither indifferent nor impervious to *logos*, and may therefore adjust to it. In this limited sense, it could be said that the "part" of the appetites and desires "has" *logos*: it does not itself possess *logos* but may be informed and determined by it. It has the ability to entertain an exchange with *logos*, to hear it. What remains to be seen is whether such a dialogue, such an exchange between *logos* and that which is irreducible and partially foreign to *logos*, is merely a matter of "obeying" *logos*, as a child does his or her father, or whether *logos* and desire may communicate with one another, listen to one another, inflect one another, indeed, entertain a relation of *mutual affection*. This would be the case if, for instance, *logos* were itself an "object" of desire and not extraneous to the order of pleasure.

The soul, then, is articulated into a threefold structure, involving the life of the organism, the properly desiring aspect, and *logos*. Of course, this analysis corresponds to the distinctions among plants, animals, and the human animal mentioned above. As for the ways of life available to human beings, the hedonistic life rests on the activation of the first two parts, the metabolic and the desiring, while the life of honors and the life pursuing contemplation both require the activation of the third factor, *logos*, albeit to different degrees and in different ways. This illuminates yet another problem concerning the life of pleasures: devoting one's life only to the satisfaction of bodily desires entails living *beneath* a human being's potential, not enacting oneself as a whole, as a human being, but remaining at the level shared in by other animals. As Aristotle says in the

Politics, "all other animals live by nature most of all, but few of them live also by habit [ἔθεσιν], and to a slight extent. The human being lives by *logos* as well, for it alone has *logos*" (1332b4–6).

What is at stake, then, is self-realization without residue. It is important to notice that such a complete self-enactment, if it ever were attainable, would *at once* pertain to the human being as that particular individual and to the human being as such. It would involve no contrast between singularity and humankind, for belonging in humankind, being human in the fullest sense, signifies to respond and act excellently in any given circumstances, at any given time. It signifies a fidelity, an adherence to place-time and its fluctuations, at all times. This we shall see better in the course of the analysis of virtue as middle.

We should also notice that, through this set of considerations, *logos* itself emerges as a matter of "having," as an *ekhein* – to put it more starkly, as a *hexis*, habit. Once again, we wonder about *logos*, thus continuing on the line of questioning broached above. What does it mean to "have" (*ekhein*) *logos*? What does it mean to activate or actualize oneself according to *logos*, if *logos* itself must be acquired or stabilized into a habitual shape? How does *logos* belong to a living body, that is, how can an animal, a growing, sentient, and desiring organism "have" *logos*? What is the relation between *logos* and embodiment, animality – *life* itself? What does it mean to enact that mode of animality that "has" *logos*? How is this peculiar animal that the human being is related to other living beings? These questions lie at the heart of the present investigation, and we shall return to them at various junctures. The discussion of Book Zeta, devoted to the intellectual virtues, through which the "part" that thinks and "has" *logos* is articulated, will be crucial in the elucidation of some of these issues. But we can already see a few anticipations of these themes in Books Beta, introducing the virtues, and Gamma, on voluntary action and deliberation.

3.2. Excellences

3.2.1. Acquisition

The distinction between ethical and intellectual virtues rests on the "mathematization" of the soul just laid out (1103a4–10). Book Beta opens with an explication of this difference:

Since virtues are of two kinds, intellectual [διανοητικῆς] and ethical [ἠθικῆς], an intellectual virtue comes to be [ἔχει καὶ τὴν γένεσιν] and grows [αὔξησιν] *mostly* from teaching and, in view of this, it requires experience and time, whereas an ethical virtue is acquired by habituation [ἔθους], as is indicated by the name "ethical," which varies slightly from the name *ethos*. From this fact it is also clear that none of the ethical virtues comes to be in us by nature, for no thing that is by nature can be changed into something else by habituation; e.g., no stone, which moves downward by nature, can be habituated to move upward, even if one were to keep on throwing it up countless times, nor can fire be similarly habituated to move downward, nor can anything else that is by nature be altered by habituation. Hence virtues come to be in us neither by nature nor aside from nature [παρὰ φύσιν]; but by our nature we can *receive* [δέξασθαι] them and perfect them by habituation. (1103a14–26; emphases added)

We will consider in a moment the decisive traits of the virtues of thinking succinctly signaled already in this inception. For now let us simply note, without downplaying the distinction between teaching and habituation, that they both are modalities of repeated practice, of practical exercise. So much so that Aristotle makes it explicit that teaching is an experiential and temporal matter, not to mention the materiality involved in all education. It could indeed be said that the phenomenon of teaching and learning should be understood as a species of habitual training and that it would differ from, say, habituation in matters such as eating, only in terms of varying degrees of awareness involved. Thus, *to the extent that* the virtues of the intellect come to be from teaching, just like those of character they come to be through practical formation (*ēthos*). In time, they become stabilized as "possessions," acquired structures or dispositions of the soul (1105b20–1106a13). This is what *hexis* and *diathesis* signify.

Neither by nature nor against it, neither within the compass of nature nor beside it, the virtues come to be thanks to our receptivity, to our being by nature exposed to and informed by our environs, whichever they may be. Thus, while the susceptibility to conditions is by nature, the unique conditions affecting one's life from birth onward are not. This means that the acquisitions of certain habits rather than others does not occur as a transition from potentiality to actuality, as is the case for natural endowments:

Again, of things which come to us by nature, we first bring along the powers and later exhibit the [corresponding] activities. This indeed is clear in the case of sensations; for it is not by seeing often or hearing often that we acquired the [corresponding powers of] sensation, but conversely: having [the power] we used it, and not: using it, we came to have it. In the case of the virtues, on the other hand, we acquire them as a result of prior activities; and this is like the case of the other arts, for that which we are to perform [ποιεῖν] [by art] after learning, we first learn [by performing], e.g., we become builders by building and lyre players by playing the lyre. Similarly, we become [γινόμεθα] just by doing [πράττοντες] what is just, temperate by doing what is temperate, and brave by doing brave deeds. (1103a27–b3)

What is by nature requires no exercise in order to be enacted: to begin with, one has the power of seeing and sees. To be sure, one's ability to see can subsequently be refined and trained further, but the enactment of such a power is immediate and unintentional. In matters of habituation, instead, one proceeds from the acquisition of an activity to its further reenactment, from actuality to actuality. Or, to put it even more sharply, instead of the transition from potentiality to actualization, in matters of virtue it is the acquisition of actualities that gives rise to our power. Not only, then, do we receive an actuality and enact it ourselves, but our very receptivity with regard to what surrounds us, our exposure to the worldly and communal circumstances, frees our potentiality as human beings. It is in this way that we genuinely become who and what we are and are to be, that human potential may as such be released.

Aristotle could hardly insist more emphatically on this apparent circularity, according to which one must "have" already what one is in the process of acquiring, becoming, or learning, so that a certain "having" appears to be both beginning and end of one's endeavor, both necessary condition and final cause:

Again, it is from the same [actions] and because of the same [actions] that every virtue comes into being or is destroyed, and similarly with every art; for it is by playing the lyre well or badly that human beings become good or bad lyre players, respectively. In the case of architects and all the rest, too, the situation is analogous; for human beings become good architects by building houses well, and bad architects by building houses badly. For if such were not the case, there would not have been the need for a teacher, but all would have become good or bad [artists]. Such indeed is the case with the virtues also; for it is by our actions with other human beings in transactions that we are in the process of becoming just or unjust, and it is by our actions in dangerous situations [ἐν τοῖς δεινοῖς] in which we are in the process of acquiring the habit of being courageous or afraid that we become brave or cowardly, respectively. It is likewise with desires and with anger [ὀργάς]; for, by behaving in a way or in the contrary way in [corresponding] situations, some human beings become temperate or intemperate, good tempered or irascible. In a word, it is by similar activities that habits come to be [in human beings]; and in view of this, the activities in which human beings are engaged should be of quality, for the kinds of habits which develop follow from the [corresponding] differences in those activities. So in acquiring a habit it makes no small difference whether we are acting in one way or in the contrary way right from our early youth; it makes a great difference, or rather all the difference. (1103b7–25)

This extensive quotation occasions various remarks. First, we should highlight the parallelism, repeatedly proposed, between the productive endeavors (the arts) and the acquisition of virtues and vices, of the habits in general. Living is thereby disclosed as a making – to be sure, not simply a matter of making oneself, let alone creating or inventing oneself, if indeed the notion of individual autarchy was effectively shown above as implausible in this context. And yet, however heteronomous and disseminated its moving forces, the work of living shapes, brings one forth throughout life. So much so that we may say that awareness regarding one's living, the conscious steering and coming together according to both one's thrust and enveloping conditions, constitutes a kind of architecture. However, this statement requires some qualification – and thus we come to our second point. An architect becomes an architect by doing what architects do. This is so, says Aristotle, for the arts in general, and most notably for that architectonic endeavor that is human living or becoming. But this, very much in line with what we already surmised above, involves a quite significant shift in the understanding of making or production – the shift that earlier led us to speak of ethics as architecture without geometry. Far from resting on the separation between intelligent agency and material execution, or eidetic determination and its reproduction, the *poiein*, the performing or producing here at issue emerges as a practice that is always already under way, prior to the fixation of an intelligible end or guiding principle. In other words, *poiein*, doing and making, does not unfold according to the directives of a contemplated *eidos* subsisting aside from action. Rather, *poiein* is disclosed as a bringing forth simultaneous with the investigation/clarification of that which is to be brought forth, a bringing forth that demands to be thought in terms of the interpenetration of purposive projection *and* receptivity to available solicitations and/or deflections – that is, in terms of the ability to divine surrounding possibilities *and* respond to necessities. In this sense, *poiein* appears as the methodic pursuit and, at once, the finding (or discovery) of an *ergon*.

This is clearest in ethical and political matters: here bringing forth, whether the constitution of communities or the formation of individuals, means working through present conditions in order to realize a vision of that which is not yet, a vision that itself arises from said conditions. One is making, bringing forth, prior to any firm knowledge of one's making and that which is to be made. Needless to say, this does not at all amount to some random initiative. Lack of ultimate and guiding knowledge should not be equated with mere groping in the dark. But this should be evident. While we need to be just in order to be together in the most conducive ways, we must come together in order to become just. We will always already have been together as we pursue the ongoing task of justice to come. The making of ourselves and of our togetherness will as such always already have taken place by reference to the not yet (justice) and, by the same token, have provided the parameters for the pursuit thereof.

A third issue to be underlined is the centrality of teaching and learning in the human experience. The human being is illuminated as essentially teachable, as a being eminently capable of learning. This also makes the human being especially vulnerable to kinds of teaching and upbringing that spoil or even pervert one's potential by conveying unskilled habits. As Aristotle notices, receiving this kind of direction from early age may be utterly compromising. It is the crucial figure of the teacher who, aside from natural "gifts" in the one who receives teaching, will determine the quality of his or her acquisition and capacity for re-enactment. It is teaching broadly understood, one's environment and vicissitudes as a whole, that in every respect will transmit habits of one kind or another, virtues or vices. Likewise, it is by teaching, whether in the form of verbal instruction, practical exercise, or otherwise, that desires and even emotions can be reached, touched, led. This domain of the soul, not altogether unconscious and yet, for the most part, rarely and dimly illuminated by awareness, can as well be available to transformation. Teaching (training) provides habits as "second" nature, the soul's acquired nature and structure. When the structured soul en-acts itself, what would otherwise be a mere possession, property, or latent state constitutes the guideline of such an enactment, the course that such an enactment follows.

The habits, then, whether excellent or otherwise, are acquired in this way. In order to have a virtue, one must have it already, enact it to begin with. Virtue appears to be necessary before virtue: it is always already actual in the environment, in the teacher from which or whom one acquires or learns it.

3.2.2. Virtue before Virtue

Aristotle devotes considerable attention to the problem of the necessity of virtue in order to obtain virtue. These considerations will lead to a deepening of the phenomenon of learning and "acquiring." They announce as well a perplexing case of infinite regress, which Aristotle, contrary to his usual alertness to this issue, allows to remain latent. The difficulty is diagnosed yet again:

> not only does each virtue come to be, or grow [αὐξήσεις], or undergo destruction from the same and by the same [kind of actions], but also the activities [according to each virtue] will depend on that same [virtue], for such is the case with other things which are more apparent, as with strength; for not only does strength come into being by taking much nourishment and undergoing many exertions, but it is also the strong human being who is most able to do such things. Such too is the case with the virtues; for from abstaining from [excessive] pleasures we become temperate, and, in turn, when we have become temperate we are most able to abstain from such pleasures. And similarly with bravery; for by becoming habituated to show contempt for and endure what is fearful we become brave, and when we have become brave we are most able to endure what is fearful. (1104a27–b3)

But the restatement of this problem does not signal an indulgent reveling in paradox. Rather, Aristotle is preparing to bring the examination of the process of learning and acquisition to a further depth. True, the process unfolds from a "having" to a "having," through the enactment of a "having": "One might raise a difficulty [ἀπορήσειε]: how can we say that human beings should do what is just in order to become just, and act temperately in order to become temperate? For if they do what is just or temperate, they are already just or temperate, just as if they do what is grammatical or musical, they are already grammarians or musicians, respectively" (1105a17–21). Yet, on closer inspection it becomes clear that what is at stake is a certain transmission, or even translation, of a given "having."

A certain activity is transferred from the outside to the inside, as it were. Someone learning takes something in and makes it one's own. Whether a way of acting is acquired from a teacher or from prevalent custom, the principle of action (that which directs and subtends it) is brought inside from the outside, substantially assimilated. Both in the case of the arts and in the case of habituation or education, acting in a certain way is not enough: a certain inner modality or awareness accompanying the outward action is needed. Indeed, even in the case of the arts, whose work is either a separate object or a performance "having their excellence [τὸ εὖ] in themselves," we say that someone is genuinely a maker (a musician, a grammarian) when we perceive that he does what he does with lucidity and skillfulness. This is all the more the case if an action does not lead to an end separate from itself, to a product. For a product may in itself appear quite well executed, and yet be achieved by chance, even without actual virtue, while in matters of action

> things [done] according to virtue... are done justly or temperately not [only] if (1) they themselves are of a certain quality, but also if (2) the one who acts holds together in a certain way when acting, namely, (a) when he knows [εἰδώς] what he does, (b) when he intends [προαιρούμενος] to do what he does and intends to do it because of itself, and (c) when he acts with certainty and firmness. Now with the exception of (a) knowledge [εἰδέναι], these [b, c] are not taken into account as requirements in the possession of the various arts; but in the possession of the virtues knowledge has little or no weight, while the others [b, c] count for not a little but for everything, for it is indeed from repeated practice of what is just and temperate that [virtue] results [περιγίνεται]. (1105a29–b5)

Thanks to time and consistent exercise a kind of autonomy may be acquired. One becomes one's own source and point of reference, comes to have the actuality of habitual structures inside. One does not begin in this way, but only appears to, while in fact imitating without fully possessing and understanding what one is doing. At this juncture, Aristotle emphasizes the full integration of practice and awareness, which only time can yield. Without genuine training, a practice is unskilled, a knowledge formal and empty. That is to say, in the initial stages of learning or taking up a particular practice, one presents the appearance of dexterity, while depending on the examples furnished by an outside guide. The trajectory, thus, leads one to increasing degrees of independence, as it were – although, again, we would do well to remain mindful of the constitutive heteronomy of the individual, of the fact that one will significantly have been constituted by interactions and common practices.

Thus, one learns to continue on one's own. The capacity for deliberate and skillful action is activated in one, and one is transformed. At some point, in some way, a shift occurs, an authentic quantum leap: one is no longer following and imitating, but fully carrying out a given action. What is learned by practice and consistently lived out is unforgettable, cannot be reabsorbed into latency, *lēthē* (1100b17). One is being cultivated, cultivating oneself. Once again, Aristotle seizes the opportunity to underscore the irreplaceable role of *praxis* in such a development and the danger of "philosophizing" as a withdrawal from action:

> while things are said [to be] just or temperate if they are such as a just or temperate human being would do, a just or temperate human being is not one who [just] does these, but one who also does them as a just or temperate human being would. So it is well said that it is from doing what is just or temperate that a human being becomes just or temperate, respectively; and no one who is to become good will

become good unless he does good things. Yet most human beings do not do these; instead, they resort to talking [λόγον] about them and think that they are philosophizing and that by doing so they will become serious [σπουδαῖοι], thus behaving somewhat like patients who listen to their doctors attentively but do none of the things they are ordered to do. And just as these patients will not cure their body by behaving in this way, so those who philosophize in such a manner will not better their soul. (1105b5–18)

We already had more than one occasion to call attention to Aristotle's warning against the alienation of *logos* from worldly engagements. We shall encounter this preoccupation time and again, most articulately exposed in the course of the discussion of incontinence, *akrasia*. For the moment, let us, instead, conclude by casting light on a latent problem regarding this whole genetic analysis of habits. We understand very well how the foregoing reflections illuminate the transition from childhood and adolescence to adulthood, and more broadly, in any given domain of endeavor, the movement from the stage of initiation to that of mature and stabilized practice. The beginner, whether in a specific work or in the work of living, receives an initiation from the outside and learns to own it. One always finds oneself in the midst of established cultural contexts and lines of transmission, always late with regard to one's "background," as we call it. Whatever the guise, the source of formation is there prior to one's arrival on the scene. There will always already have been a set of activities to be acquired, re-enacted, and even transformed. One will not have started from nothing. And yet, if this is the case, we should notice the following. Referring an activity back to a prior activity ends up effecting a transposition of the whole issue from the order of singular human beings to the order of humankind as such. Moreover, such a trajectory back to the previous cause is no mere logical pursuit, but entails an ineliminable chronological dimension. For, if what is passed on from generation to generation is a practical patrimony, which can be received through time and exercise alone, the issue of beginning cannot be easily disengaged from its temporal and historical dimensions. The question concerning the beginning remains irreducibly genealogical in character. However, what is relevant in this connection is that, in tracing an actuality back to its antecedent, and so forth, we follow a backward trajectory without coming to stop. We end up wondering about the coming to be of humankind's originary activities – of those first habits that would have inaugurated humankind as such, constituted the beginning of humankind's education out of its capacity, by nature, for learning and teaching. However, we find no answer in which to rest.

In this shift from the individual child or apprentice to humankind as a whole, the developmental logic that underlies the phenomenology of the virtues poses the problem of infinite regress. Indeed, the infinite regress of the source of instruction is implicit here, for the analogy between humankind and a singular human being is interrupted by the severe difficulty involved in envisioning the former's infancy and childhood, let alone its parents or teachers. Indeed, whence would humankind as such have first learned and developed the various forms of habituation and manners of *logos*? Who or what actuality would have led and guided humankind into its growth? No definite beginning is posited here or even sought after – unless we think of the good as final end, and, hence, as beginning, but this can as such hardly be that which bestows cultural formations. Thus, the regress is possibly disclosed as even more vertiginous, for, finding no inaugural mark decisively setting humankind aside from other manners of animality, it may, in its pursuit of the habit before a given habit, continue well into the domain of those animals proximate to the human animal, which, even though to a lesser degree, live "by habit" (*Politics* 1332b4–6).

Thus, referring back to earlier and earlier moments along the line(s) of transmission, we broach the question of the *arkhē*, the question of a first actualization of the natural potentiality for growth, education, transformation – of a first attempt to articulate an aspect of being not prescribed by nature, to respond to a void or lack of determination on part of nature. Not only do we not find a relevant reply to such a question, but the formulation of the question is itself arduous, awkward. We are left with a reference to the next cause, in an asymptotic approximation to the beginning.

What can be said with a degree of confidence is that, in Aristotle, there is no coming to be of any kind of actuality or activity, let alone knowledge, ex nihilo. Rather, these appear as acquired, whether wholly or mostly, from previous actualities, in a process of transmission that is not equivalent to the simple, linear conveying and receiving of what is there. Aristotle at crucial junctures evidences that the actuality of comportments, including the exercises of knowledge, in fact, the reception and cultivation of *logos tout court*, must be seen as a genuinely historico-genealogical phenomenon. The following statement from *Metaphysics* Alpha Elatton deserves to be recalled for its paradigmatic character:

> It is just to be grateful not only to those with whose opinions we might agree, but also to those who have expressed rather superficial opinions; for the latter, too, have contributed something, namely, they have handed down for us the

habit [ἕξιν] [of thinking]. If there had been no Timotheus, we would not have much lyric poetry; and if there had been no Phrynis, there would have been no Timotheus. The same may be said of those who spoke about the truth; for some of them handed down to us certain opinions [δόξας], but there were others before who caused [αἴτιοι] them to be what they were. (993b11–19)[16]

As is clear in the development of the *ēthos* of knowledge and inquiry, but also in the formation of customs and beliefs broadly speaking, the acquisition of actualities amounts to taking up the past, to inheriting, in a gesture that is essentially a matter of interpretation and critical consciousness. Indeed, hermeneutical sophistication appears to be a crucial requisite in communication at large and, most particularly, in the communication across time thanks to which we commune with our "forefathers" and receive their "opinion" (*Metaphysics* 1074b1–14). In such an interpretive reception, knowledge is both transmitted and changed, inaugurated and found – made, not from nothing, but from previous teachings. Now, previous knowledge is the problem with which the *Posterior Analytics* begins (71a1–11). It is precisely the question concerning whence, ultimately, knowledge proceeds, which opens the treatise. Yet, as we saw, endless regress is ruled out there because of the compelling character of the things themselves. The fundamental intuitive apprehension of what is grounds discursive or syllogistic knowledge and, more broadly, the practices of teaching and learning. However, in the present course

16 Al-Farabi will have proven especially receptive to this strand of Aristotle's thinking. In "The Attainment of Happiness" he formulates a similar awareness of the intertwined themes of transmission, communal sharing, the genealogy of practical as well as rational formations, of communities as well as communities of inquiry. In a powerfully synthetic gesture, he situates such issues in the context of the innately political character of human beings, of the primordiality and necessity of political bonds, and, in the final analysis, of friendship: "each man achieves only a portion of that perfection [he should achieve], and what he achieves of this portion varies in its extent, for an isolated individual cannot achieve all the perfections by himself and without the aid of many other individuals. It is the innate disposition of every man to join another human being or other men in the labor he ought to perform: this is the condition of every single man. Therefore, to achieve what he can of that perfection, every man needs to stay in the neighborhood of others and associate with them. It is also the innate nature of this animal to seek shelter and to dwell in the neighborhood of those who belong to the same species, which is why he is called the *social* and *political* animal." In considering this remarkable statement, it is worth recalling that al-Farabi had no access to Aristotle's *Politics*. We should also consider the note immediately following the passage quoted, in which al-Farabi hints at the priority of political science, at political science as the achievement crowning human inquiry: "There emerges now another science and another inquiry that investigates these intellectual principles and the acts and states of character with which man labors toward this perfection. From this, in turn, emerge the science of man and political science" (*Alfarabi's Philosophy of Plato and Aristotle*, 23).

of investigation we are inquiring not about the foundation of discursive and scientific procedures, but rather about these procedures themselves, along with the other habits. In other words, we are inquiring about the very fact of inquiring, teaching, and learning, about the originary habits of teaching and learning necessary to turn the potentiality for teaching and learning into an actual *praxis.* Most comprehensively, the inquiry concerns the habit or practice of transmitting habits, that is, ways of doing things, of living, of learning, teaching, transmitting. Infinite regress seems inevitable in this regard.

3.2.3. *Seeing the End*

The end moving human beings, that for the sake of which they do what they do and live the way they live, is a hypothesis – a hypothesis formulated thanks to the actuality of virtue, whose origin, in turn, remains elusive because of the phenomenon of infinite regress considered above. Indeed, it is the virtues that determine the end, which bring it into view and fix themselves on it. Virtue, which is a condition or quality of soul both enabling action and brought about through action, makes the end perspicuous, recognizes the end as principle and orientation. Or, if any habit assumes an end, it could be said that virtue, qua excellent habit, is that thanks to which the end in view either coincides with the good or is "right," *orthon,* aligned with the good.

During the discussion of deliberation, *bouleusis,* in the *Eudemian Ethics,* Aristotle observes that, "since one who deliberates always deliberates for the sake of something, and someone deliberating always has some aim in view [σκοπός] in relation to which he contemplates [σκοπεῖ] what is conducive, nobody deliberates about the end, but this is a beginning [ἀρχὴ] and hypothesis [ὑπόθεσις], like the hypotheses in the theoretical sciences" (1227a6–10). The end, then, cannot be determined through reasoning and logistical considerations. Rather, it must be assumed hypothetically, posited as a postulate, and thereby accepted as a beginning. Reasoning takes place for the sake of it and thanks to it. The assumption of the end is made according to the psychological structures in place, to the excellences:

> Does virtue bring forth [ποιεῖ] the aim in view or that which promotes the aim in view? Our position is that it brings forth the aim in view, because this is not a matter of syllogism or *logos,* but in fact this must be laid under as a beginning. For a doctor does not contemplate whether his patient ought to be healthy or not, but whether he ought to take walks or not, and the gymnastic trainer does not consider whether his pupil ought to be in good condition or not, but whether

he ought to wrestle or not. Similarly no other [discipline] [deliberates] about its end. For, as in the theoretical [sciences] the hypotheses are beginnings, so in the productive [sciences] the end is beginning and hypothesis; since so and so ought to be healthy, if that is to be so it is necessary for such and such [a thing] to be provided, just as [in mathematics], if the angles of a triangle are [equal to] two right angles, such and such [a consequence] is of necessity. Therefore the end is the beginning of thought [νοήσεως ἀρχή], the completion [τελευτή] of thought is the beginning of action. (1227b23–34)

The end, whether the proximate end of a particular action or the most complete end, which is happiness or the good, is not the object of scientific examination. The vision of the end occurs thanks to the "acquired structures" of the soul. Thus brought forth, the end underlies the processes of reasoning whereby one determines what might lead to that end, what might sustain and encourage it. Analogously to the procedure of the sciences in the strict sense, the articulation of *logos* rests on that which exceeds it, which is otherwise than demonstratively accepted as principle. So much so that, despite Aristotle's concluding remark on the end as *arkhē* of thought and on the fulfillment of thought as the *arkhē* of action, it could be said that thought, *noēsis*, and action, *praxis*, emerge from this line of thinking in their interdependence. In other words, thought and action appear not to be related according to the former's priority and the latter's derivative character, but rather to be mutually determining. For, while deliberation determines the course of action appropriate to the end, action is implicated in the formation of the virtues that, in turn, identify the end and make it visible. And it is the end that provides the non-deliberated ground of deliberation. That is also why, as Aristotle variously points out in Book Alpha of *Nicomachean Ethics*, one should be virtuous to begin with, in order most profitably to engage in the study of ethics. For the excellent conformation of the soul would allow one to frame issues in a most conducive way – to understand and at once to embody a certain orientation to the good. On such a terrain the *logos* of ethics would thrive.

Again, the interdependence of *praxis* and *noēsis* points to the peculiar character of ethics or politics as a productive discourse. For ethics undertakes to bring forth that which it is in the course of investigating. In this perspective must be understood its peculiar teleology.

3.2.4. More Remarks on the Virtues

Two more words on the virtues are in order. In the first place, it seems worth noticing that in these discussions a great deal of emphasis is placed on teaching and training as radically formative, indeed, transformative practices. In this respect, Aristotle is luminously representing a long tradition tending to attribute to the human being a nearly unlimited plasticity, thus following the saying ascribed to Periander, according to which "through practice all can be obtained." One discerns here what one would be tempted to call a felicitous naïveté of Greek ancestry, minimizing the physiognomic or unconscious datum to the advantage of pedagogy, of practice in its forming and molding power – to the advantage of education in its nearly infinite creative power, which supposes the body as indifferently versatile. Only a culture so ready to acknowledge the adaptability of the human being, to understand the soul as almost nothing aside from its cultivation, could develop such a refined, articulate body of reflection on upbringing, *paideia.* Only the disquieting experience of vulnerability, of pliability vis-à-vis the surrounding conditions, could have demanded such a concerned attention to the construction and stabilization of conducive psycho-physiological traits.

And yet, this posture reveals a sort of blind spot, for it leads to the assumption of the unconscious not only as shared, common, but, perhaps too quickly, as neutrally malleable. So much so that in this tradition, at least at this stage of its development, we find that the enormous emphasis on education or training is hardly counterbalanced by a comparable analysis of psycho-physical conditions. To be sure, the Aristotelian analysis, in *Problēmata,* of the psycho-physiology of melancholy in superior human beings constitutes an exemplary attempt in this direction. However, we remain under the impression that a full-fledged study of the physiological or even physiognomic basis of cultivation is lacking, and the same can be said for psychological contents, such as emotions, desires, or, broadly speaking, the passions. Again, this appears to be all the more remarkable precisely because Aristotle himself underlines the role and power of the desirous element in all matters human, and especially in the phenomenon of incontinence, as we shall see. In this connection, the overpowering force of the desires is acknowledged and examined in its structural function, yet is not phenomenologically analyzed. Aristotle diagnoses desire's capacity to make one blind and reason inactive – as though reason would retreat into latency, become disconnected from the body of desires, and therefore from the origin of action, from life itself. As we shall have the occasion to see when considering this later discussion, because of the vehemence of the passions, the human being is in a condition analogous to sleep or drunkenness. These states constitute a sort of black out, mark the intermittence of reason, that is to say, a lack, a negativity. But this is not quite enough. It would be necessary to go beyond, to delineate an in-depth study of the positive phenomenon, of the *fact* of overwhelming desires in their constitution, peculiarities, and unfolding. We shall return to this.

One final word must be devoted to the ethical virtues as the middle between extremes. Excellence aims at the mean in the sense of a perfect equilibrium in carrying out one's work:

> If, then, this is the manner in which every science accomplishes its task well, namely, by keeping an eye [βλέπουσα] on the mean [τὸ μέσον] and working toward it (whence arises the usual remark concerning excellent works, that nothing can be subtracted from or added to them, since both excess and deficiency destroy the excellence in them, while the mean preserves it), and if, as we say, it is with an eye on this that good artists do their work, and if virtue, like nature, is more precise and better than any art, then virtue would be aiming [στοχαστική] at the mean. I am speaking here of ethical virtue, for it is this which is concerned with feelings [πάθη] and actions, in which there is excess, and deficiency, and the mean. (1106b8–17)

Human beings aim at making themselves into excellent works. This means that, in their work of living, they aim at encountering each circumstance and unfolding themselves into each context in a way that is excellent each time, perfect in the sense of balanced, measured, both practically and emotionally. It should be underlined that the middle is neither some neutral point in between, nor some calculable intermediate in a geometrical space, nor a mathematical average, let alone a going only halfway. For, "when related to us, it neither exceeds nor falls short, and this is neither one nor the same for everyone" (1106a32). Again, the mean one pursues is "not the mean with respect to the thing itself [πράγματος] but the one related to us" (1106b7). The middle is what is right, or just, at a given time and place, in that particular circumstance and in that respect:

> For example, we may have the feelings of fear, courage, desire, anger, pity, and any pleasure or pain in general either more or less than we should, and in both cases this is not well; but to have these feelings at the right times and for the right things and toward the right [human beings] and for the right purpose and in the right manner, this is the mean and the best, and it is precisely this which belongs to virtue. In actions, too, there is excess, deficiency, and the mean in a similar manner. Now a virtue is concerned with feelings and actions, in which excess and deficiency are errors and are blamed, while the mean is a success [succeeds in being right] [κατορθοῦται] and is praised; and both success and praise belong to virtue. (1106b18–26)

The middle, thus, indicates what is harmonious, attuned, open – a quality of wakefulness, of insight into the situation. It is a qualitative shift, an altogether different way of being and relating: at any given moment, it is the one and only way: being there fully, ready to embrace that condition without reservations; ready to *be* that condition, to affirm it, as if for all time, for it completely is what it is, lacks nothing, is perfect. This is so even though circumstances are ever changing and the equilibrium ephemeral, even though perfection is never attained once for all and one's experience reflects such an ongoing dynamism. Thus, the middle bespeaks neither grabbing hold of whatever may be the case nor letting it slip away, but, rather, holding the present circumstance in care and attention. In the wake of these reflections, Aristotle begins to formulate a definition of the ethical virtues:

> Virtue, then, is a kind of mean [μεσότης], at least having the mean [μέσου] as its aim [στοχαστική]. Also someone may make an error in many ways (for evil, as the Pythagoreans conjectured, belongs to the infinite, while goodness belongs to the finite), but he may succeed in one way only; and in view of this, one of them is easy but the other hard. It is easy to miss the mark [σκοποῦ] but hard to hit it. So it is because of these, too, that excess and deficiency belong to vice, but then mean [μεσότης] to virtue. For human beings are good [ἐσθλοὶ] in one way, bad in many. (1106b27–35)

Of course, the one way of succeeding, that is, of being right, "hitting the mark," must be understood in light of infinity, as the unity and uniqueness of the perfection pertaining to each of the infinitely many arrangements of place and time. Because this concerns comportment as well as the quality of emotional contents, virtue names being disposed to both effective action and equanimity. A comprehensive understanding of virtue may now be gathered:

> Virtue, then, is a habit of deliberate choice [προαιρετική], being at the mean relative to us, and defined by *logos* and as a prudent human being would define it. It is a mean between two vices, one by excess and the other by deficiency; and while some of the vices exceed while the others are deficient in what is right in feelings and actions, virtue finds and chooses [αἱρεῖσθαι] the mean. Thus, according to its substance or the *logos* stating its essence [τὸ τί ἦν εἶναι], virtue is a mean, but with respect to the best [τὸ ἄριστον] and to excellence [τὸ εὖ], it is an extreme. (1106b36–1107a8)

We shall consider shortly the issues of deliberate choice and of *logos* that are mentioned here as decisive in the coming to be of ethical virtue. Here let us simply add that, as Aristotle will point out much later on in Book Iota, the life of a human being who is thus determined by excellence is "good" and "delightful," and such a human being "wishes himself to live and be saved." Echoing the Platonic statement regarding the soul that is harmonized in all its components, characteristic of one who has become "one's own friend" (*Republic* 443c–e), Aristotle adds that such an individual "wishes to live together with himself, for he does so with pleasure" (1166a18–26). Such is the condition of the human being who finds the measure in the environing circumstance – who senses the measure surfacing in him- or herself.

3.3. Excellences of *Logos*

3.3.1. The "Power" of Logos

The excellences pertaining to the "thinking part" of the soul will be considered in Book Zeta. Only a few preparatory remarks are in order at this point, connecting issues raised above to the later discussion. As we have seen, the virtues of character, *ēthos*, pertain to the part of the soul that has reason in the sense that it does or may listen to it. The virtues of the intellect or of thinking, *dianoia*, pertain to the part of the soul that has reason in the sense that it itself properly thinks and is the "seat" of *logos*. Regarding the intellectual virtues, we also saw that they "mostly" "come to be" and "grow" "from teaching" and, hence, require "experience and time" (1103a15–17). We shall come back to this qualification, "mostly" or "for the most part," *to pleion*. Here let us simply recall that, to the extent that the intellectual virtues originate from teaching, they are a matter of *praxis* no less than the ethical virtues. Actualizing oneself, whether according to *logos*, that is, under its guidance, or in terms of the development of *logos* itself, takes time and consistent exercise, that is, habitual practice. Again, let us think of the inheritance of the "habit of thinking" from our predecessors, in the genealogical considerations put forth at the beginning of *Metaphysics* Alpha Elatton (993b11–14). The trait of humanness emerges as essentially grown, cultivated, cultural: as the process of maturation leading to the fulfillment that could be called adulthood, as the adulthood not simply reached in virtue of time alone but rather requiring practical supplementation.

Logos, then, in its various aspects or excellences, comes to be in certain living beings, mostly through their altogether temporal and embodied practices. In a certain sense, *logos* is a possession of a body, a having, *ekhein*, of an animal – a having that, as it were, comes to be had. To the extent that it comes to be in virtue of teaching, and is not immediately activated in its fullness, what was previously observed concerning the virtues of character can be restated concerning *logos* and the virtues articulating it: *logos* is not, or not simply, by nature and constitutes a potential or power in a very peculiar sense. In the case of the powers of sensation, for instance, nature disposes their activation without preparatory training. In the case of *logos,* the fact *that* it can be acquired and developed, that is, the fact *that* it is potential, is given by nature; however, *what* or *how* it may be is not determined by nature. Nature hosts it, as it were, without regulating or legislating about it. *Logos* is a strange gift, harbored within nature, in accord with nature, yet not thereby ruled – not, at least, in any humanly discernible way. It is given in its indeterminacy, given as an assignment, given to human beings in order to receive determination. Nature provides no further points of reference for human beings to develop it one way or another. In this regard, it seems to love to hide.

For *ta phusei onta,* the beings by nature and of nature, to realize themselves means to realize their nature, the potential inscribed within them, to become themselves. In each case, a being by nature develops toward its own *to ti ēn einai,* "what it was to be," thus fulfilling it. Yet for human beings this is not simply the case. Inexorably becoming what each was to be, human beings simultaneously enjoy what can be called a certain freedom. The possibility of *logos* bespeaks at once the multiplicity of possible actualizations or enactments of *logos,* its coming to be "in many ways." For *logos* is a strange endowment, a "having" that entails a lack of clarity concerning who, what, and how a human being is to be and, subsequently, a lack of automatism concerning what and how a human being is to do. In a way, we could say, we have a nature. Yet it does not simply, not fully determine us and decide for us – at least, not in a way that is intelligible to us. It is our nature not to be in an unqualified way resolved by nature. It is our nature to enjoy (or undergo) a margin of indeterminacy, as if a condition of solitude before the task of determination and self-determination, of unraveling and unveiling the possible. In our condition, the fulfillment of one's "what it was to be" is not unmediated. Nature does not guide the human being to his or her completion or fullest actualization in the way in which it leads other beings. Accordingly, all the appeals to nature in ethical matters are bound to be rather problematic.

Whatever the difficulties pertaining to the full actualization of the animal "having" *logos,* however, it may minimally be said that such an actualization is attained only in a community, *polis.* The mutual implication of *logos* and *polis* is acknowledged at the very outset of the *Politics,* where it is stated that clearly "the human being is more of a political animal than a bee or any other gregarious animal; for nature, as we say, does nothing in vain, and the human being alone of all animals has *logos*" (1253a8–10). In view of this, reflection on the *polis* becomes indispensable to the investigation of the human being and the cultivation of its peculiar potentiality. Thus, while in the "genetic" (*phusei*) account Aristotle starts from the couple and family, in the order of final causality he recognizes the priority of the *polis.* In line with the Platonic view (*Republic* 369b), the human being is seen as essentially not self-sufficient, and hence first of all and "by nature political" (*Politics* 1253a3): "It is clear, then, that a *polis* is by nature and is prior to each [of its parts]; for if each human being is not self-sufficient when separate [from a *polis*], he will be like other parts in relation to the whole; and one who cannot commune [with others] or does not need [an association with others] because of self-sufficiency is no part of a *polis* but is either a brute or a god" (1253a25–9).

In this perspective, it could even be said that, aside from and beyond the comprehensive designation of the human being as "political," it is the *politēs,* the citizen, who interprets most fully the potential of the "animal having *logos.*" Indeed, being *politikos* and being a *politēs* do not amount to the same. The former defines the human condition as such, a condition common to all, slaves, women, and children included. But being a citizen bespeaks being free, having the chance (or burden) of exploring what is left underdetermined by nature, necessity, or mechanism. Being a slave or a woman, then, means precisely being deprived, either in part or in full, of the ability to explore human potential – whether this phenomenon be explained in terms of natural privation or political deprivation (and both explanations, of course, are essentially political, determined by the operative interpretation of the meaning of *polis*). Freedom, precisely in being defined by contrast to the condition of slaves and women, emerges primordially in the *polis,* reveals itself politically as the highest human possibility. Troubling as it may be, this distinctive human trait emerges precisely through communal arrangements that structurally deny its being shared in common and, in fact, establish it as a relatively infrequent merit. Through the divisive dynamics establishing hierarchy and privilege in the community (establishing *community as* the structure of hierarchy and privilege), freedom becomes manifest as an issue. After all, only within the framework of the *polis* does leisurely time become possible, in virtue of which the exercise, unfolding, and investigation of human potential become available to some. In a typically compressed statement near the beginning of the *Metaphysics,* Aristotle weaves together the motif of freedom (understood as a mark of both certain human beings and certain human endeavors, namely, those pursued for their own sake) and that of leisure:

> it was when almost all the necessities [of life] were supplied, both for comfort and activity [διαγωγήν], that such thinking [φρόνησις] began to be sought. Clearly, then, we do not seek this science for any other need; but just as a human being is said to be free if he is for his own sake and not for the sake of somebody else, so this alone of all the sciences is free, for only this science is for its own sake. (982b22–7)

Freedom, then, bespeaks the order of the highest finality, that which is for its own sake, with reference to nothing further and no one else. Of course, the physical, material, and political conditions for such an "emancipation" from conditions, for such an allegedly unconditional independence, are quite perspicuous. As Aristotle states again in the *Politics*, it is in virtue of the "use of slaves" (1255b32) that a few human beings can "attend to political matters or philosophy" (1255b37).

This is what seems to be at stake, then, in the quest for privilege or elevation within the communal organism: a certain liberation from hardship, from the binding aspects of toil, from the slavish (i.e., passive) posture in the face of necessity. Externalizing the burdensome maintenance of life, attributing this function to a specific group within the group (slaves and manual workers), in a gesture of denial of that which remains nevertheless inevitable for each, the free catch a glimpse of a human possibility, of a condition not unlike that of gods. The pursuit of investigation for its own sake, because of the pleasure that the pursuit itself grants, is the mark of such a condition:

> the possession of this science might justly be regarded as not befitting the human being; for human nature is servile [δούλη] in many ways and so, as Simonides says, "god alone should have this prerogative," and it would be unworthy of a man not to seek the science proper to his nature. If, then, there is something in what the poets say and the deity is by nature jealous, he would most probably be so in this case, and all eminent human beings would be unfortunate. But neither is it possible for the deity to be jealous... nor need we suppose that there is a science more honorable than this one. For the most divine science is the most honorable. (982b28–983a5)

The free citizens affirm freedom as a distinctive human possibility over against the condition of slavishness. Yet the discovery of human freedom occurs at the price of a division internal to the human community, a rift between the free and the slaves – at the price, that is, of the denial of human nature as shared by all human beings. This, of course, exposes the boundaries between the human and other animals to potentially permanent contestation and negotiation.[17]

3.3.2. Logos and Polis

In line with these considerations, then, we should at the very least underline the inherently political character of the "having" of *logos.* It is only in a community that human beings can actualize their potential (humans are "by nature political"). *Logos, polis,* and *anthrōpos* emerge in their indissoluble intertwinement. Within this framework is situated Aristotle's elaboration of human nature, an elaboration whose aporetic structure is illuminated by the contrast between the being of the citizen and that of the human being as such.

More often than not, Aristotle seems to imply an understanding of the human being in its singularity, as a "this," a unique being whom it is often arduous to refer back to a comprehensive conception of the human. On the one hand, in fact, the human being essentially and by nature belongs in the *polis.* On the other hand, the political constitution of the human being does not obviously dictate an understanding of the individual as an indifferent and interchangeable unit. In other words, the individual is seen both as a "this," whose singular identifying features by definition remain to be assessed, and as political in the sense of neither self-constituted nor yet autonomous. This appears to be the converse of what will have been the modern conception of the subject – construed, on the one hand, as free and absolved from heteronomous conditions and, on the other hand, as utterly homogeneous with respect to any other subject.[18] The subject at once distinctively and indifferently rational, that is, characterized by the power of reason while least singular, least differentiated by reference to this power, this subject bespeaking the possibility of undifferentiated intersubjectivity, remains unthinkable for Aristotle. On Aristotelian terms, being human per se entails minimal automatic assumptions and, hence, minimal automatic entitlement to

[17] In this regard, see D. J. Depew, "Humans and Other Political Animals in Aristotle's *History of Animals,*" *Phronesis* 40 (1995).

[18] Aristotle's incipient elaboration of the difference between "natural slave" and other human beings in terms of the difference between "beasts" and human beings, or between "body" and "soul" (*Politics* 1254b17–20), and even the remark to the effect that the bodies of the most excellent men are "useless" in carrying out necessary labors (1254b30), foreshadow the modern conception of the subject as disembodied and essentially rational. However, as will be shown, because of the problematic status of such remarks in the context of the discourse as a whole, the Aristotelian vision remains crucially irreducible to the developments it may have made possible.

sharing rights and privileges in common. Privileges and goods, as well as responsibilities, are assigned to individuals not in virtue of their being individuals, but on the ground of a kind of axiological calculus, as we shall see in the analysis of justice. So much so that, for Aristotle, not every human being is a citizen, and we pervasively notice an attentive resistance against the conflation of the two.

And yet, while such an emphasis on the "this" dictates an understanding of community in which no numerical equality can be simply presupposed, the assumption that the differences among human beings are by nature and that the political hierarchies merely reproduce natural differentiations does not follow at all. As a matter of fact, such an assumption is even at odds with the demand of close scrutiny of each individual, for the reliance on a straightforward natural classification would make the alertness regarding the individual unnecessary. Indeed, the relevance of such an alertness as well as the essentially political status of *logos* suggest that, far from determined by nature (i.e., evident from birth), who one is and will become (the degree of perfection or accomplishment) will crucially be determined by *opportunity* and evident to us only retrospectively. Regarding issues of communal stratification, Aristotle, attempting to square the implications of his own line of thinking with conventional wisdom as he finds it, provides a discussion torn by unresolved conflicts.

The claims, in the *Politics*, that barbarians and, most remarkably, slaves are "by nature" (1252b1–9, 1254a14–17, 1254a18–1255a3) are exemplary of a certain passive acceptance of contemporary practices and conventions. Again, the "having" of *logos* must be nothing too widely shared if, as we are told, some human beings differ from others "as much as beasts do from human beings," and these "are by nature slaves, and it is better for them to be ruled despotically," for "a slave by nature is a human being who can belong to another . . . and who can participate in *logos* [κοινωνῶν λόγου] to the extent of apprehending [αἰσθάνεσθαι] it but not possessing [μὴ ἔχειν] it" (1254b15–23). Implied here, to limit ourselves to the exemplary line of thinking on the subject of slavery, is the complete lack of *logos* in some human beings: "the slave does not have [οὐκ ἔχει] the deliberative [part of the soul] [βουλευτικόν] at all [ὅλως]" (1260a12).

And yet the reference to nature can hardly settle this problem. The "having" of *logos* must be nothing too self-evident, if indeed sustained interaction, *dialogos*, is needed in order to discover such a "having" in action. Aristotle intimates this much when, calling into question his own hypothesis that it is possible to discern "immediately after birth" the slave from the ruler by nature (1254a23), he affirms that "it is not so easy to perceive the beauty of the soul as it is to perceive the beauty of the body" (1254b39–1255a1). Indeed, nature does not always work in linear, legible ways:

> Nature, too, tends to make the bodies of the freemen and of slaves different, making those of slaves strong for the necessities [of life] but those of freemen upright and useless for such services but useful for political life, whether for war or peace. But often the contrary, too, happens, for some [slaves] have the bodies of freemen but some freemen have the souls [of slaves]. (1254b27–34)

Of course, the only partial legibility of nature, the fact that nature may do "nothing in vain" (1256b21) yet remain inscrutable in its purpose, entails that human institutions cannot claim to be aligned with natural determinations, let alone grounded on them. Human beings, in sum, may present radical differences in terms of their psychological organization and endowment. But how such differences come to manifest themselves, and hence be read, ordered, juridically regulated, remains precisely a problem requiring sustained reflection.

Accordingly, Aristotle concedes that it is for good reasons that some argue that slavery rests on a conventional ordering and is "by law" (κατὰ νόμον) (1255a3–b16). At stake is not simply claiming the natural or conventional status of political hierarchies and classifications, but, above all, recognizing that both claims are equally political and a matter of political contention, in the sense that both rest on presuppositions regarding the political, its nature, purpose, and excellence. Both rest on the *logos*, on the capacity for articulate discernment that comes to be (comes to be "had") in the *polis*. To such an extent does Aristotle counter his main claim about the "natural" status of the slave, that he even calls for the liberation of slaves as a "reward" for their merit (1330a34) – which presupposes that slaves are not simply deprived of *logos* or deliberation, but rather, *if given a chance*, may develop these powers and deserve emancipation (see also *Oikonomikōn* 1344b15–16). This is evidently in line with the notion that *logos* is essentially, if not exclusively, "cultivated" and that it is only in light of the outcome of training that the extent and character of the having of *logos* can be evaluated.

However, these argumentations signal Aristotle's reluctance to grant essential presuppositions, to rely on an absolute determination of the human being as such without further qualification and inspection. He displays a heightened caution vis-à-vis any abstraction regarding what it would mean to be human and what would properly pertain to such a manner of being. Nothing seems to be pre-judged, as though the discovery of a being such as the human, "having *logos*" in some way, whether by nature or by law/convention or both, were still recent and astonishing.

In light of the assumption that no essential psychological characteristics should automatically be attached to a body with a given conformation, even the institution of democracy comes to be disclosed problematically. Democracy entails the transitivity of one body, one subject, one vote, and this seems to be at odds with the suggestion that no intrinsic features are obviously common to those who appear in human guise. Moreover, the question of the distinction between human beings and other animals, already broached in the previous considerations on *logos* and voice, is confirmed in its difficulty. Statements to the effect that "the use made of slaves, too, departs but little from that of other animals; for both slaves and tame animals contribute to the necessities of life with the aid of their bodies" (1254b25–7) only bring us back to the elusiveness of an effective differentiation of the human from proximate modes of animality. The attribution of *logos* to human beings, far from securing a definition of human nature, leaves open the question whether humankind may in fact be discerned in terms of kind at all. In fact, if anything, difference in kind appears to be internal to humankind: "for a ruler and a subject differ in kind [εἴδει διαφέρει], and this difference is not one of degree at all" (1259b37). The reflection on slavery paradigmatically exposes the crisis of the definition of the *anthrōpos* as *logon ekhon.*

Thus, the human is examined in every single case, every single "this." Some human beings may not have *logos* in any prominent or significant sense. In the end, in our undertaking to capture the human in its distinctness, we are left with no formulation of essence, but only with the *fact* of an operative human community, of a community at work, recognized as human despite (or because of) the mutable shapes it gives itself and the fluctuating outcomes of the communal quest for self-understanding and other negotiations. To "have" *logos* is never simply to speak, to utter articulate sounds, but to do so having learned from others, and exhibiting a capacity to mean and understand, hence to listen and interact. *Logos* is essentially *dialogos,* and this is the meaning of being "by nature" *politikos.*

Of course, the question remains pressing, concerning the way and direction according to which *logos* would best develop. For it can grow in disparate directions, pernicious as well as beneficial. It bespeaks at once a healing power and danger:

> for just as the human being when perfected is the best of all animals, so he is the worst of all when separated from law and justice. For the most cruel [χαλεπωτάτη] injustice is the one which has weapons to carry it out; and the human being, born

[φύεται] with weapons to be used with prudence and virtue, can misuse these for contrary [ends] most of all. Because of this, a human being without virtue may be the most unholy, the most savage, and the worst for lust and gluttony. (1253a32–8)

Logos is such a dangerous "weapon," indifferently amplifying magnificence and bestiality alike. The good, said to orient *logos*, is by definition excessive with respect to it. Overflowing as it does any attempts at discursive grasp, the good thereby remains the object of debate.

3.4. Volition

3.4.1. Willing the Virtues

But let us consider more closely an issue thus far noted only marginally. We observed, in that which is by nature, the priority of potentiality over actuality. In ethical matters, however, we saw how actuality proceeds from actuality (virtue from virtue). No habits are simply by nature. *That* we are capable of developing and acquiring habits is a kind of gift from nature. But the gift does not prescribe *what* those habits should be. In other words, human beings are not bound to necessity absolutely or in an unqualified way. They enjoy a margin of "freedom" that is at once a source of perplexity, a lack of direction. In this perspective, in the previous analyses we repeatedly underlined the role, in ethical formation, of convention and dialectical agreement. Yet the acquisition of the virtues pertaining to thinking is not merely a matter of practical training. As Aristotle cautiously puts it, these virtues are "mostly," but not only, the fruit of teaching. Their belonging in the practical and temporal order of transmission is, thus, qualified. So much so that, as already pointed out, Aristotle seems to divine in the excellent exercise of thinking a trace of objectivity, if not universality, and to refuse to reduce the wise assessment of things to a merely arbitrary phenomenon, which could just as well be otherwise. In their evaluation of experiences and vicissitudes, the wise tend to agree, to speak at one, in marked contrast with the many whose opinions on such matters widely differ (1099a12–15, 1113a30–5). Accordingly, it might perhaps be said that human beings are free, but less in the sense that they are not subject to necessity than in the sense that they are free to discover their necessity. Such a discovery seems to bespeak freedom as a more intimate understanding of nature.

The *Eudemian Ethics* is even more extreme in granting to *logos* and the virtues pertaining to it a certain emancipation from conventional conditioning, indeed, a certain naturalness. In the following statement, *logos* is associated with desire and recognized as naturally inhering in us:

> by nature we have both [parts]; since λόγος belongs by nature, for it will be in us if our development [γενέσεως] is allowed and not inhibited, and also desire [ἐπιθυμία] [is by nature], for it accompanies and is in us from birth; and these are, broadly speaking, the two features by which we define that which is by nature; it is what accompanies everybody straight [εὐθὺς] from birth, or what comes to us if development is allowed to go on straightforwardly [εὐθυπορεῖν], for example gray hair, old age, and other such things. (1224b29–35)

The development of *logos* is said not positively to depend on teaching, but to come to be of its own accord, naturally, if only upbringing and other conditions do not prevent it. The emphasis here switches from teaching as a positive informing practice to negative conditions, that is, conditions not hindering the natural development of *logos*. In this perspective, *logos*, similarly to any other natural unfolding such as aging, would only take time.

The fact that the intellectual virtues are "mostly" but not exclusively generated by teaching makes even more tense and questionable the relation between arbitrary convention and natural necessity – for, while irreducible to each other, they are far from simply opposite. Indeed, they are intertwined in ways worth examining closely. Moreover, in the tension between human institutions and nature can be located the question of individual self-determination, of the singular human being's ability to steer his or her own course, even beyond the education received and conditions undergone. What is intimated here is the human power to interrupt, albeit in a qualified way, the determining work of circumstances shaping the human being as if this were a completely inert patient. Aristotle goes so far as to affirm that, to an extent, we are individually responsible for our acts, even the cause of our own habits. If, indeed, once a habit is established it carries the necessitating force of nature (of a second nature), the formation of such a habit is in the final analysis up to one. The issue of volition is thus introduced:

> in the case of an unjust and an intemperate human being, it was up to them at first not to become such, and so they are voluntarily [ἑκόντες] such; but having become such, it is no longer up to them not to be such [now]. Not only are the vices of the soul voluntary, but for some human beings, whom we censure, those of the body also; for no one censures those who are ugly because of [their] nature, but we do censure those who are ugly because of lack of exercise or because of negligence. (1114a19–25)

Action and habituation, thus, result from (1) convention (dialectically determined rules and customs), (2) natural factors, and (3) individual responsibility. In other words, human beings are not simply, passively determined by their upbringing and surroundings. There is something like responsibility for one's own virtues and, in general, habits, and hence for one's subsequent behavior. In a sense, and to a degree, one is one's own moving cause: "If, then, as it is said, the virtues are voluntary [ἑκούσιοι] (for we ourselves are partly responsible [συναίτιοι] for our habits, and it is by being human beings of a certain kind that we posit the end as being of a certain sort), the vices, too, will be voluntary for a similar reason" (1114b23–5). This is so in spite of and beyond nature, second nature, and the crystallization of habits. Or, more precisely, this is so because of the irreducibility of nature to second nature – an irreducibility that keeps second nature and its crystallizations mobile, subject to re-evaluation and re-negotiation already at the individual level, that is, at the level of "one's nature." It is the commitment to unfolding one's own nature, to let it become manifest, take shape, unravel in its legibility, it is such a commitment to confront nature's unintelligibility that allows for a certain emancipation from the factors demanding conformity, from conformism in general.

To summarize, while stating that ethics is (1) by *nomos* and not by nature, Aristotle also recognizes in it (2) an element of "objectivity" or "naturalness," a non-conventional dimension. He discerns, furthermore, (3) an element of responsibility, a factor at work which is neither conventional nor genetic, but rather like an ability, or a determination, to break through. The latter could be understood as a daimonic element pervading, even disrupting, the *polis,* traversing the *polis* and potentially suspending its normativity. Again, this force *in the polis* would be irreducible to political determination – it would be, rather, an *eudaimonic* operation aligned, if anything, with nature. In the framework of the *polis,* such a force would indicate the human possibility of not being completely absorbed within the customary, the margin allowing human beings to step back and assess that through which they nevertheless become who they are. It would indicate the possibility of metamorphosis, of recognizing communally formulated finalities as hypotheses – for, as seen above, the end is and remains a hypothesis, caught within the circularity of actions and habits both determined by the end and revealing the end, making it perspicuous, bringing it forth. As a working hypothesis, the end presents itself as an infinite task, requiring ongoing inquiry. Ethics is not only a matter of habitual formation, but also contemplates transformation, the renewal always possible through insightful breakthrough.

3.4.2. Ignorance and Evil

The phenomenon of volition requires closer inspection. Aristotle distinguishes voluntary actions from those performed "by force" (τὰ βίᾳ) or "through ignorance" (δἰ ἄγνοιαν) (1110a1). The latter are said to be not voluntary (*oukh hekousion*), whether involuntary (*akousion*) or nonvoluntary (*oukh hekon*). The distinction internal to what is not voluntary is based on the emotional response to what one unwillingly did and caused:

Everything done through ignorance [δἰ ἄγνοιαν] is not voluntary [οὐχ ἑκούσιον], but if it causes pain and regret, it is involuntary [ἀκούσιον]; for the one who through ignorance did something, whatever this may be, but is not displeased at all by that action, though he did not act voluntarily [ἑκὼν], as he did not know [what he was doing], neither did he act involuntarily [ἄκων] if he is not pained. So of a thing done through ignorance, if the agent regrets it, he is thought to have acted involuntarily [ἄκων], but if he does not regret it, since he is different, let him be called "nonvoluntary" [οὐκ ἑκών]; for since he differs, it is better for him to have a special name. (1110b18–24)

Ultimately, what determines the quality of an action not voluntarily performed is the psychological posture revealed by the psychological response to the consequences of one's action. It is only the regret at the realization of one's own ignorance and its consequences that can make a given action properly involuntary. The case of the one who does not display any pain or concern after the fact is different; and so is the case of the one who acted "in ignorance" and not merely "through ignorance":

Again, acting through ignorance seems to be different from acting in ignorance [τοῦ ἀγνοοῦντα]; for he who is drunk or angry is not thought to be acting through ignorance but through one of the causes stated, not knowing [εἰδὼς] his act but in ignorance [ἀγνοῶν] of it. Thus every evil human being [μοχθηρὸς] is in ignorance [ἀγνοεῖ] of what he should do and what he should abstain from doing, and it is through such error that human beings become unjust and in general bad. Now the term "involuntary" tends to be used not whenever a human being is ignorant [ἀγνοεῖ] of what is expedient, for ignorance [ἄγνοια] in intention [προαιρέσει] [of what should be done] is a cause not of what is involuntary but of evil [μοχθηρίας]; and [involuntariness] is not universal ignorance (for through universal ignorance human beings are blamed), but ignorance with respect to particulars [καθ' ἕκαστα] in which action is and with which action is concerned. For it is on these particulars that both pity and pardon [συγγνώμη] depend, since one who is ignorant [ἀγνοῶν] of some of these particulars acts involuntarily [ἀκουσίως]. (1110b25–1111a2)

An essential connection is here asserted between the problem of evil and ignorance. What is at stake, however, is not the ignorance of the peculiar details making each circumstance unique. Indeed, exhaustive knowledge of (and, hence, control over) a situation in all its variables cannot be and is not assumed. There may always be an idiosyncratic, strictly unpredictable factor setting off an undesirable chain of events, despite one's careful assessment of the situation. This is the case with involuntary actions, performed through ignorance. Instead, the ignorance associated with evil is the complete black-out regarding one's circumstances, which can be compared to states of altered or dimmed consciousness. In this sense, evil appears as a more fundamental problem than vice, which entails rational effectiveness oriented to questionable goals. A comprehensive lack of awareness of one's situation and potential impact over it, a lack that is not inevitable but due to systematic negligence, constitutes the genuine mark of evil. In other words, it is disregard that is evil, the lack of interest in and commitment to one's context, and the presumption that one may act in that condition nevertheless. Evil emerges here as a manner of being in the world characterized by willful ignorance or, at least, carelessness of the things of the world. And while evil thus understood can conceivably be the result of unfavorable upbringing and other compromised circumstances, it is in no way to be justified as the permanent condition of a human adult.

In this connection, once again, we are reminded of the image of the city-ship in Plato's *Republic* (488a–489a), of the way in which "navigation" requires knowledge of sea, earth, and sky, that is, the ability to read the context within which one finds oneself living, moving, and acting. It is from this watching or "reading" that one derives guidance, instead of acting in ignorance. It is from this attention and solicitude that one draws the awareness of interconnectedness, of the ripples caused by one's actions, of the systemic repercussions of one's comportment. Evil, *mokhthēria*, thus, amounts to irresponsibility and lack of conscious commitment.

3.4.3. *Qualified Willing*

Needless to say, in this context the language of willing and volition indicates neither what will have been called "free will" nor, again, the power of unlimited self-determination. As was just observed, one never has complete control over a given situation and, thus, one's comportment, intention, and evaluation of conditions always encounter a certain resistance or opacity in the surroundings. However, even more radically, it appears that, as "moving causes," volition and intention or deliberate choice operate in their indeterminate intertwinement with no less moving, indeed, compelling factors such as desires, passions, and, more broadly, irrational or unconscious motifs. Volition, therefore, cannot be understood as a solely rational function. In fact, Aristotle remains rather ambivalent concerning the ability of humans simply to govern themselves. His perplexity is due above all to the difficulty in discerning, at the root of human comportment, self-causation and natural causation, each in relation to the other as well as in its distinctness:

One might say that all human beings aim at the apparent good [φαινομένου ἀγαθοῦ] but cannot control [κύριοι] what appears [φαντασίας] [to them to be good], and that the end appears [φαίνεται] to each human being to be such as to correspond to the sort of human being one is. Now, if each human being is in some way the [moving] cause [αἴτιος] of his own habit, he is also in some way the cause of what appears [φαντασίας] [to him]. But if not, then no one is the cause of his doing what is bad but each does these through ignorance [δι᾽ ἄγνοιαν] of the end, thinking that by doing them he will attain the best for himself, and the aiming at an end is not self-chosen [αὐθαίρετος], but one must be born [φῦναι δεῖ] having [a power, such as] vision, by which he will judge beautifully and will choose [αἱρήσεται] the good according to truth [κατ᾽ ἀλήθειαν]; and so a human being is well born [εὐφυής] if he is from birth beautifully endowed [καλῶς πέφυκεν] [with this power], for that which is greatest is also most beautiful, and that which can neither be received nor learned from another but is disposed to function in the manner which corresponds to its quality from birth, if it be well and beautifully endowed, will be by nature a perfect and true [ἀληθινὴ] disposition [εὐφυΐα]. (1114a30–b12)

Aristotle ends up avoiding to take a clear position in this regard. He concludes that the human being is at least in part responsible (*sunaitios*) for his or her own habits, and hence self-causing. In this sense, one is in a way the cause of the end one pursues, that is, one envisions and posits a certain end in virtue of the kind of human being one is (1114b23–5). However, responsibility without qualification remains out of the question. It is also worth noticing that, in this argumentation privileging natural gift over against rational self-determination (an argumentation that Aristotle never simply rejects in full), (1) discerning and choosing (*hairesis*) function analogously to the powers of sensation, such as sight, and, consequently, (2) truth is not a function of knowing understood as a merely human construction.

That acting voluntarily may not be a purely rational matter is also made explicit by certain decisive references to beings other than human adults, such as children and other animals. Aristotle observes:

Since that which is involuntary is done by force or through ignorance, the voluntary would seem to be that whose [moving] principle is in oneself [ἐν αὐτῷ], [in the one] who knows [εἰδότι] the particulars in which the action [takes place]. For surely it is not beautiful to say, as some do, that whatever is done through temper [θυμὸν] or desire [ἐπιθυμίαν] is involuntary. For, first, none of the other animals would do anything voluntarily, not even children. (1111a22–7)

A voluntary action reveals that the moving principle is (in) the one who acts, although it may not be rational, that is, not in the order of self-mastery. So much so that the ability to "will" a certain course of action is attributed to animals other than the human and to children ("incomplete" human beings). Desires and emotional contents, in other words, are integral to the voluntary initiative and altogether consistent with appropriate as well as desirable action. For "we should be angry with certain people and we should desire certain things, such as health and learning" (1111a31–2). Acting voluntarily, then, rather than being solely a matter of reasoned determination, appears in some sense to include acting on impulse, acting under the compulsion of passions that, however endogenous, cannot be brought within the compass of calculation. Aristotle insists: "it seems that passions, which are non-rational [ἄλογα], are not less human, just as those actions which are from temper and desire also belong to the human being. It would be absurd, then, to posit them as being involuntary" (1111b1–3). Volition seems to designate, more precisely, a volitional drive.

However, things seem to stand differently with intention, or deliberate choice, *proairesis*. Thus is indicated that which precedes (*pro*), promotes, and is relative to (*pros*) action, the precursor of action that most properly manifests virtue and reveals character even more than action itself. For intention designates that which animates and motivates action, and not the merely external performance (1111b6–7). This is carefully distinguished from volition: "Now intention appears to be volition but is not the same as volition, since the latter is wider; for children and other animals share [κοινωνεῖ] in volition, but not in intention, and things done on the spur of the moment [τὰ ἐξαίφνης] are said to be voluntary but not according to intention" (1111b7–11). It is because of its exquisitely deliberative character that intention must be set aside from volition. It is also to be distinguished from wish, *boulēsis,* both in terms of its aim and in terms of its modality. Wish is of what imposes itself on one as eminently desirable, of what moves one to a given pursuit, whereas intention determines the manner of the motion, of the pursuit toward (*pros*) that which is wished:

a wish is rather of the end, while intention is of that which pertains to the end [τῶν πρὸς τὸ τέλος]; e.g., we wish to be healthy but we choose after deliberation [προαιρούμεθα] that through which we may become healthy, and we wish to be happy and speak of this, but it does not befit us to say that we choose after deliberation [προαιρούμεθα] [to be happy] and, in general, intention seems to be concerned with that which can be brought about by us. (1111b27–31)

Intention, then, is considered aside from wishing and the desirous as well as compulsive quality characteristic of it. It is elucidated as the process in virtue of which one identifies and chooses the path to a certain outcome, the way of action most conducive to a certain desired end. Indeed, "intention [is formed] with *logos* or thought [μετὰ λόγου καὶ διανοίας], and the name [προαιρετόν] itself seems to suggest that it is something chosen [αἱρετόν] before [πρὸ] other things" (1112a16–17). And yet, even the deliberative operation of intention intersects significantly with desire. So much so that we could say that it derives its operative effectiveness from the element of desire it incorporates:

Since that which is intended is that which is deliberately desired [προαιρετοῦ βουλευτοῦ ὀρεκτοῦ] and which is in our power to attain, intention too would be a deliberate desire [βουλευτικὴ ὄρεξις] of that which is in our power to attain; for having discerned [an alternative] after deliberation, we desire [ὀρεγόμεθα] [that alternative] in accordance with that deliberation. (1113a9–13)

It could be said that, without the moving impulse provided by desire, here understood both as (1) wish for the end and as (2) deliberate desire of the specific traits of the action to be carried out, intention or deliberate choice would remain formal and without consequence. For, while such a choice is a principle of action, it is so less in the sense of a moving cause than in the sense of a principle determining the way, the *how* of motion.

If, then, *praxis*, action, is *kinēsis*, motion (*Eudemian Ethics* 1220b28), these are the factors causing and determining its course. The virtues, themselves formed through actions in their orientation, make the end perspicuous, but do not set one in motion. It is the desires, instead, whether volitional drives or other manners of impulsion, which move. Motion being thus compelled, its way, its *how* is delineated, necessitated by the structures of habituation and excellence – more precisely, by the intentional/deliberative capacity. As the most genuine expression of habitual structures, intention decides on the outlines of action, but, again, it derives its governing authority from desire in its "deliberative" mode – from the drive toward that which is envisioned as the desirable path. It is not deliberation or intention alone that bring about motion, let alone acting. Our thinking does not move us, we cannot simply (i.e., in a purely rational fashion) will ourselves one way or another.

4. ON JUSTICE

We have variously insisted on the fact that ethics is politics. For (1) the human being is by nature political, and (2) education (habituation as well as teaching) is a task of the community, not a private matter.[19] We come, thus, to the discussion of justice,[20] *dikaiosunē*, this unique virtue said to be "complete" and distinctively concerning the relation to an other, that is, coexistence, commonality, community. Justice names the open, communal field of the working and practice of virtue. It names the psychological state *at work* relationally, *enacted* in the *polis*. Accordingly, in the *Politics* it is said that "the political good is that which is just, this being that which is of common benefit to all (*koinēi sumpheron*)" (1282b17–18).

Let us recall again the immediately political dimensions of ethics, by turning to a few remarks in the *Politics*. The treatise opens with a pertinent reflection:

> We observe that every *polis* is a sort of association [κοινωνίαν], and that every association is formed for the sake of some good (for all human beings always act in order to attain what they think to be good). So it is clear that, while all associations aim at some good, the association which aims in the highest degree and at the most authoritative [κυριωτάτου] of all [goods] is the one which is the most authoritative [κυριωτάτη] and contains [περιέχουσα] all the others. Now this is called *polis* and it is a political association. (1252a1–7)

As the all-embracing and, therefore, most authoritative manner of communion, the *polis* harbors the human pursuit of the highest good. It constitutes the place of such a pursuit, indeed, its very condition. It is

19 I deliberately emphasize the language of the "common," *koinon*, over against the posterior terminology of the "public," in order to underline the comprehensive anthropological connotation of the former. The *locus* of justice is irreducible to "public space" understood in its opposition to the "private." See *Politics* 1337a22–7.

20 Among the texts variously providing the background for the considerations here put forth regarding justice, I especially recall the following: Otfried Höffe, *Politische Gerechtigkeit. Grundlegung einer kritischen Philosophie von Recht und Staat* (Frankfurt am Mein: Suhrkamp, 1987); Eric A. Havelock, *The Greek Concept of Justice from Its Shadow in Homer to Its Substance in Plato* (Cambridge, Mass.: Harvard UP, 1978); and Franco Volpi, "Che cosa significa neoaristotelismo? La riabilitazione della filosofia pratica e il suo senso nella crisi della modernità," in Enrico Berti, ed., *Tradizione e attualità della filosofia pratica* (Genova: Marietti, 1988), 111–35.

in such a context that something like the orientation to the good, and hence "living well," become at all an issue:

A complete association composed of many villages is a *polis*, an association which (a) has reached the limit of every self-sufficiency, so to speak, (b) comes to be for the sake of living, but (c) is for the sake of living well. Because of this, every *polis* is by nature, if indeed the first associations too [were by nature]; for the latter associations have the *polis* as their end, and nature is the end. For that which each [thing] is at the end of a generation is said to be the nature of that [thing], as in the case of a human being, or a horse, or a house. (1252b28–1253a1)

The *polis*, then, is the end, that is, the nature, of any and every association: it is the being of an association, what this is and, therefore, is to be. We should notice right away the problematic status of self-sufficiency and completeness attributed to the *polis*, for it is far from clear when and by what criteria an association of villages would be judged "complete," and hence called a *polis* proper, or how the condition of "self-sufficiency" in every respect would be satisfied. This issue is far from marginal, because, later in the treatise, the morphological and quantitative profile of the *polis* will be shown to be intimately connected with the question of justice. Let us briefly follow this line of thinking in its basic implications.

By reference to the image of the ship, Aristotle will insist on the importance of observing a "moderate or measured magnitude" (μεγέθους μέτρον) for the *polis*, lest it be deformed, deprived of its "power" and of its "nature" (1326a37–40): for a ship, too, "will no longer be a ship if it is a foot long or a quarter of a mile long, and it will do badly as a ship if it deviates from its proper size by a certain magnitude either in the direction of smallness or in that of excess" (1326a41–b2).[21] What is at stake is the unity of the *polis*, the possibility of the *polis* as such. And the *polis* limited according to the proper measure is "most beautiful," because "the beautiful" can be found "in number [πλήθει] and magnitude [μεγέθει]" (1326a35–6). Thus, only the *polis* aptly growing to the appropriate size can function at its best, and this has to do with the peculiarly human character of such an organism:

[21] In *Nicomachean Ethics*, in the course of the discussion of friendship, Aristotle wonders: "should there be as many friends as possible [πλείστους κατ᾽ ἀριθμόν], or is there, as in the case of a city, a certain measure [μέτρον] to them? For neither would ten human beings make a city, nor will it remain a city if increased to one hundred thousand. Perhaps the quantity is not one particular [number], but all those between certain limits [μεταξὺ τινῶν ὡρισμένων]" (1170b30–5).

of cities which are thought to be beautifully governed, none is observed to be indiscriminate in the size of its population. Conviction through speeches [λόγων], too, makes this clear. For law is a certain order [τάξις], so good law must be a good order; but a very excessive number [ἀριθμὸς] [of human beings] cannot partake of order, for to do so would be a task for the divine, which also holds together all [συνέχει τὸ πᾶν] ... whereas the beautiful [for human beings] usually comes to be in number and magnitude. (1326a28–36)

The *polis*, despite its "most authoritative" encompassing character (*periekhein*), remains altogether other than the all-embracing gesture (*sunekhein*) of the divine. Thus, Aristotle will suggest that the size of the territory and population must be contained according to the ability of the *polis* to carry out its task optimally (1326a12–14) and that, in general, the *polis* should be large enough to be self-sufficient, but small enough to be visible "at a glance" (*eusunoptos*) (1326b24–5) and to allow military leaders or heralds to communicate effectively (1326b6–7). The *polis*, then, will be understood as a "community of sensibility," held together by the parameters of sensible sharing – a community that can be held in view by each of its members and within which communication can circulate (be heard) without hindrance. In turn, the possibility of mutual acquaintance among citizens will be found to be a condition for the possibility of justice:

In judging what is just and distributing offices according to merit, the citizens must know each other's characters; for, wherever this does not happen to occur, both that which pertains to offices and the judgments [of what is just], being done without adequate preparation and so unjustly, are necessarily bad; and evidently such happens to be the case whenever populations are very large. (1326b14–21)

The possibility of justice, then, will appear to be rooted in the concrete, embodied prerequisites for genuine and meaningful exchange within the community. It is these material conditions that lay the ground for the cohesiveness and harmonious articulation of the community. Though regulating communal living beyond particular inclinations, predilections, and bonds of affection, and as such contrasted to friendship, justice appears not to be merely a matter of indifferent normative imposition. Rather, it presupposes and results from a certain tenor of human relations, a certain socio-relational climate, as it were. Justice as legality, which is said to order the *polis*, to hold it together and grant its continuing unity, requires for its operation that certain numerical-structural features be in place, that the *polis* be one. Justice as the exercise of normativity presupposes justice more primordially understood, that is, justice as constitutive of the togetherness and integrity of the political organism.

Of course, in line with these considerations on self-sufficiency and, hence, on the "perfection" of the communal organism, we are led to wonder how each relatively accomplished *polis*, each of these poles (*polos*) around which revolves (*pelein*) the life of human beings gathered together, would commune with others. That is, we wonder how things stand concerning the communication among communities, whether justice names the practice of the virtues with respect to an other even when alterity presents itself under the guise of an other political center and not of an other individual. Of course, implied in this questioning is the examination of the possibility of dialogue, of balanced exchange among diverse interpretations and instantiations of the political. Preoccupations of this kind acquire a particular sharpness in light of remarks such as the one added, almost as a mere afterthought, to the passage just quoted. After connecting the exercise of justice to the size of the political body, Aristotle notes that, whenever the number of inhabitants is inappropriately large, "foreigners and resident aliens would easily be able to share in the government; for it is not difficult to do so without being detected [τὸ λανθάνειν] because of an excess of population" (1326b21–3). There is, thus, an essential problem in measureless or, at any rate, disproportionate gatherings: beyond a certain number, transparency becomes impossible and the surveyed circulation of information hindered. Acquaintance is increasingly superficial, and this makes even relevant issues disappear, fading from view. We shall return to this.

Taking note of these concerns, for the moment let us simply say that justice is the virtue of the *polis*, its perfection and realization. Indeed, justice, *dikaiosunē*, is "political, for *dikē*, that is, the discernment of what is just, is the order of the political association" (1253a38–40). As virtue of the *polis*, justice indicates its organization. As the exercise of "complete virtue," that is, the practice of all the virtues, justice indicates customs, rules, and laws in their genuinely formative, pedagogical role. In this sense, laws would not merely be a matter of restraining viciousness and correcting its consequences, thus re-establishing a prior order, but, rather, they would have a positively informing function, they would demand excellence, prescribe or, at least, encourage it in each case. They would outline a vision of excellence, trace an envisioning of order. Let us also signal the terminological bifurcation into *dikaiosunē* and *dikē*, for it may pertain to the non-coincidence, which we shall have to examine later, of any juridical syntax and justice itself.

4.1. The Manifold Meaning of Justice

4.1.1. Justice as Legality

Justice, we are told, "has many meanings," presents a certain equivocity (1129a27–9). Primarily, the just (*dikaion*) is "that which is lawful [νόμιμον]" and "that which is fair [ἴσον]" (1129a34–b1). In the latter sense, it points to the posture of one who is neither grasping nor driven by the passion for indiscriminate acquisition. At stake in both cases is the search for balance and measure in the relation to another or among others. As com-position of many (literally, the self-positioning and taking place of many together), community requires a management of difference in the mode of peaceful articulation. This is what distinguishes an organic manifold from a random collection of fragments, and the conduciveness of relative stability from the threat of ongoing disintegration.

In this discussion, once again, we should note Aristotle's way of proceeding from the more to the less familiar. The gradual, relentlessly vertical character of the Aristotelian inquiry, to be sure, means proceeding from common, even superficial opinions to increasingly more layered and problematic formulations, according to the insight that what is first in the order of being comes later or is last in the order of knowledge, that is, in the process of coming to know. However, in the case of justice, starting from the more familiar also means starting from injustice, in order progressively to gain an understanding of justice. Hence, the first point of reference is the "unjust human being," who is "thought to be," broadly speaking, a "lawbreaker" and, more narrowly, someone "grasping or unfair" (1129a33). It is from these two main commonly held views of injustice that follow two corresponding ways of understanding justice, namely, as lawfulness and as fairness.

Aristotle first elaborates on justice understood as legality, which he takes to be justice in the broader sense. The system of laws and regulations is here seen as the structural support of the community. It is that through and as which the vision sustaining communal articulation is itself articulated. As usual, the inception of the inquiry is dialectical in register:

> it is clear that all lawful things are in some sense just; for the things specified by the legislative [art] [νομοθετικῆς] are lawful, and we say that each of them is just. Now the laws deal with all matters which aim at what is commonly expedient, either to all or to the best or to those who have authority, whether with respect to virtue or with respect to some other such thing; so in one way we call just those things which produce [ποιητικὰ] or preserve [φυλακτικὰ] happiness or its

> parts in a political community. Thus the law orders us to perform the actions of someone brave . . . and similarly with respect to the other virtues and evil habits, commanding us to do certain things and forbidding us to do others; and it does so rightly [ὀρθῶς] if it is rightly framed [κείμενος ὀρθῶς], but less well if hastily framed. (1129b12–25)

The just is equated with the order of legality, for the body of laws grants the well-being of community and discrete human beings alike: it promotes that which is advantageous to the political aggregation and is formative of the individual. Already from these introductory remarks, however, we notice a symptomatic caution. The legal system may sustain the development of the *polis* in many ways, in certain cases favoring all those involved without restrictions, in other cases only those distinguishing themselves for their qualities, in yet other cases those detaining power, whether thanks to their individual excellence or to less than essential considerations. We are already warned that "common expediency" may be and is, in fact, interpreted in different ways; that what is said to be for the sake of the community may take place under radically heterogeneous guises; and that, above all, the best and those in power may not coincide. The power to order the *polis* may be in the hands of undeserving individuals whose inadequacy or, worse, self-interest will be reflected in the measures they establish (indeed, as the saying of Bias advises, "the way one rules will show him up" [1130a2]). The concern with the good of the community may be distorted and laws conceived to further the disproportionate privilege of a few.

This cluster of problems is suggested here only in minimal terms, but the implications are already clear: no sooner is the coincidence of justice and legality stated than doubt is cast upon it. We see Aristotle begin from the commonly held view of the coincidence of justice and legal system and, immediately, pose certain qualifications, provisos, or cautionary remarks around it. The law does indeed appear to be an expression of virtue in its entirety, and hence of justice, that is, complete virtue. For it is the laws that determine which virtues are to be cultivated and that grant the pertinent education or habituation. Yet laws can be framed not well, hastily, not rightly. Hence, they may not (in fact, do not) coincide with justice, capture and express justice fully. And this is not simply because of contingent errors or dispensable accidents. The very possibility of perceiving a law as unjust or to be corrected proves the gap between justice and legality as such. But that the laws may satisfy their political and pedagogical function well or less well, for they may be laid down well or less well, does not simply indicate the non-identity of law as such, without any further qualification, and justice. It also indicates that law, to the extent that it may fall short of justice, hence be somewhat unjust (i.e., not coextensive with justice as a whole), is not even necessarily a part of justice (i.e., something that is just). Aristotle will return to this set of issues shortly.

Justice as legality is clarified further. We are told that "this kind of justice is complete virtue" (albeit "not in an unqualified way [ἁπλῶς]") and designates the exercise of the virtues "in relation to another [human being]" (1129b26–7): "And it is a virtue in the most complete sense, since the use of it is that of complete virtue; and it is complete, since the one who possesses it can use it also toward another and not only for oneself" (1129b31–3). The attainment of one's highest potential, and this means the most complete expression of virtue, is a relational matter. It is by acting with respect to others, that is, through interaction, through one's manifest attitude toward others' experiences and demands, that one carries out one's task and becomes who one is in the fullest sense. In general, actions with particular repercussions at the communal level reveal in a magnified way the character traits of the one who performs them – whether virtuous or vicious. They may prove to be most beneficial or most damaging, according to the psychological order of the one performing them:

> And for the same reason justice alone of the virtues, by relating to another, is thought to be another's good; for [the just human being] acts for what is expedient for someone else, whether for a ruler or a member of the community. The worst one, then, is the one whose evil habit relates both to himself and to his friends, while the best one is one whose virtue is directed not to himself but to others, for this is a difficult task. Accordingly, this kind of justice is not a part of virtue but the whole virtue, and injustice, which is its contrary, is not a part of vice but the whole vice. (1130a4–11)

Justice names the manner of the thrust toward (*pros*) another. As legality, it constitutes the phenomenal, worldly manifestation of the character of the legislator(s); it makes visible, transposed into communal interactions, the habitual as well as deliberative structures of the *psukhē* that has envisioned a certain community and brought it forth, given it shape; it is a political vision manifest and at work.

On the one hand, indeed, the legal system prescribes a course of action, encouraging the exercise of the virtues defined according to the values shared in a given community and constituting its identity: "perhaps most lawful things are those done from the whole of virtue, since the law orders us to live in accordance to each of the virtues and prohibits us from living according to each of the evil habits" (1130b23–5). On the other hand, far from simply reflecting an implicit axiological arrangement, the legal system is also somewhat productive of it, in the sense that it contributes to its coming into being and fixation. We are, indeed, told that "other lawful things are those which have been enacted and produce [ποιητικὰ] the whole of virtue, and they are concerned with education for the common [good]" (1130b25–7). Rooted in custom and communal practices, legality brings their working normativity into focus, clarifies its margins and assumptions, in a work of interpretation involving no mere transcription, but decisive and reorienting construction. It is with respect to the pedagogical function of legal measures that, once again, Aristotle warns against collapsing justice itself and any juridical norms, thus continuing with the double strategy of identification *and* differentiation of justice and legality. Being a "good citizen," that is, embodying the legal projection of a virtuous active member of the *polis*, he observes, may not mean the same as being a "good human being." Again, this would depend on the manner in which a body of norms is laid down or "framed": "As for each individual's education, in virtue of which a human being is good without qualification, we must determine later whether it belongs to politics or to another inquiry; for perhaps to be a good human being is not the same as to be a good citizen in every case" (1130b27–9).

The issue will appear properly to belong to the political investigation – for, much as the non-coincidence of good citizen and good human being remains an issue, we find that we cannot access any determination of the human being as such aside from altogether essential and constitutive political considerations. *Politics* Theta is in its entirety devoted to the issue of education "of the young" (1337a11) and makes it clear that the cultivation of *logos* (both [1] the capacity for receiving *logos* and forming character accordingly and [2] the enactment of *logos* itself) is an essentially political matter. Whether in its determinate informing function or in its actuality, *logos* is a fruit of politics. At the same time, however, in the same treatise Aristotle displays considerable argumentative effort in order to show human virtue in its non-identity with respect to the virtue of the citizen. As he says,

> the virtue of a citizen must be referred to the government [πολιτείαν]. Accordingly, since there are many forms [εἴδη] of government, it is clear that the perfect virtue of [various] good citizens cannot be one. But we say that a man is good according to his one perfect virtue. It is evident, then, that a virtuous citizen does not necessarily possess the virtue of a virtuous man. (1276b30–6)

Just as governments vary widely in their structures and informing values, so do their respective projections of the perfect citizen. And, although being a good human being may not be incompatible with excellence in carrying out a particular function (and, hence, with being a good citizen), but rather exceeds and includes the partial functions, the two may not indicate the same. This means that, in their constitution and self-presentation, the various manners of government only approximate the conditions for the full attainment of human excellence, and their legal orders only strive toward justice. At a later stage, Aristotle will say that only in the most excellent *polis*, whether governed by the best citizens (*aristoi*) or by one king, would the good human being coincide with the best citizen, for there the law would finally coincide with justice, and to be virtuous with respect to one order would entail to be virtuous with respect to the other (1288a32–b2). Thus, while under all other forms of government the excellence of human being and citizen do "not necessarily" coincide, that is, may do so only accidentally, in the best form of government they would coincide "of necessity" (1288a38). But the argumentation lacks perspicuity in this regard. For Aristotle does not make fully clear whether the "aristocratic" *polis* would be a hypothesis or a manner of government humanly possible, let alone historically exemplified. Nor does he explain whether various instantiations of "the best" could admit of variations and peculiarities or, on the contrary, whether "the best" would by definition designate an invariable legislative order and communal organization – thus, as it were, being "the same everywhere."

Moreover, even if we were to leave aside these problems, Aristotle himself comes to a quite opposite conclusion in this same context. Rather than stating that, in the best constituted *polis*, "good citizen" and "good human being" "necessarily" signify the same, he turns to the best constituted *polis* precisely in order to demonstrate the non-identity of the two. The argumentation here is twofold, if less than limpid. In the first place, it is taken as self-evident that even the best government "cannot [ἀδύνατον] be composed only of virtuous human beings" (1276b38). In its lack of any further elaboration, this is a striking assumption.[22] Second, it is pointed out that, even aside from the diversity among various manners of government, within the best *politeia* citizens would still be unlike one another in their proper function: "and since it is impossible for all citizens to be alike, the virtue of a citizen and of a good man is not one" (1276b41–1277a1).

22 In light of the conclusion at 1277a4–6, the proposed emendation of *adunaton* into *dunaton* seems altogether unconvincing.

While this statement would already, in and of itself, confirm the view of the irreducibility of "political" and "human" excellence, Aristotle proceeds to a conclusion, drawing together the two argumentative strands: "for the virtue of a virtuous citizen should belong to each of the citizens (since it is in this way that the state is necessarily the best), but the virtue of a good man cannot [ἀδύνατον] belong to all citizens since necessarily not all of them are good men in a virtuous state" (1277a2–6). The argument concerning the relation between good citizen and good human being seems to shift from the result that the two are *not necessarily identical* to the result that they are *necessarily not identical*. The excellence of the human being seems as such both elusive (even unimaginable) and irreducible with regard to the excellence pertaining to a political function. Once again, this signals the elusiveness and irreducibility of justice with regard to any and every juridical system. However, before considering at further length the relation between justice and law, we must – most succinctly – attend to the second main sense of the word "justice."

4.1.2. Justice as Fairness

Justice may be understood in a more "specific" sense. Justice narrowly construed "has the same name, for its definition falls within the same genus" (1130a34–b1). While, qua "taken as a whole" (1130a34), justice gathers the work of all the virtues, qua specific virtue it concerns acquisitions, regulates grasping. In this sense, it indicates what is fair in exchanges. Distinguishing the two corresponding kinds of injustice, Aristotle says: "the narrow one is concerned with honor or property or safety or something (if we had a single name) which includes all these and has as its aim the pleasure which comes from gain, while the other [the wide one] is concerned with all the things with which someone virtuous is concerned" (1130b2–5). Again, the just as the fair is related to the just as the lawful as a part to the whole (1130b12–13).

Justice as that which is fair indicates balance in relating to one another, in giving and taking: giving or taking neither too much nor too little. It expresses a kind of mean, of harmony or measure in exchanges. More precisely still, as we shall see, it entails reciprocity proportional to individual worth. These are the features involved in Aristotle's discussion of the distributive and corrective functions of justice thus understood:

> One kind of justice in the narrow sense [κατὰ μέρος], and of what is just according to this justice, concerns itself with the distributions [διανομαῖς] of honors or property or the other things that are to be shared by the members of the *polis*

(for it is these who may be so related that some of them possess a fair share and others an unfair share). Another kind is that whose aim is to correct [the wrongs] [διορθωτικόν] done in exchanges [συναλλάγμασι], and it has two parts; for of exchanges some are voluntary but others involuntary. (1130b30–1131a3)

As distribution, *dianomē*, justice regulates (*nomos*) the space of interaction, the space in between (*dia*); it structures transmission and reception in the exchanges among community members, thus constituting, in a manner of speaking, the nervous system of the communal organism. As correction, justice attempts to make right, *orthos*, various manners of wrong-doing; it seeks to repair what was broken through unbalanced or violating interactions, to heal what was wounded, by punishing the perpetrators and compensating those who were damaged. If it is impossible to restore the situation prior to the injustice, if signs and scars are bound to remain, corrective justice nevertheless seeks to re-establish some kind of order, so that the organism may plausibly live on. In this twofold modality, justice is disclosed as that which holds the *polis* together, which keeps the organism of the *polis* alive, unified, and functioning effectively. While distribution entails sharing in advantages and responsibilities (whether material or otherwise) in the right proportion and, hence, establishes *normal* interaction, correction means making unjust interactions just, bringing them back to sustainability.[23] It is worth following Aristotle's catalogue of the exchanges, voluntary as well as involuntary, that do or may require correction:

Voluntary exchanges are such things as sale, purchase, loan, security, use of property loaned, deposit, and hiring; and they are said to be voluntary, since they are initiated voluntarily. Of involuntary exchanges, (a) some are clandestine, such as theft, adultery, poisoning, procuring, enticing slaves away from their masters, assassination, and false witness, but (b) others are violent, such as assault, imprisonment, murder, seizure, injury, defamation, and besmirching. (1131a3–9)

Assumed in this context is the measurability of the various matters to be distributed or corrected, along with the calculability of the relative worth of those involved in the distribution or correction. Enjoying gains or undergoing losses, even in cases such as the infliction of emotional pain or taking someone's life, is taken to be a reckonable matter, and so is the assessment of one's character in terms of merit, standing, and entitlement. In other words, Aristotle is presuming, and thereby positing, the convertibility of quality into quantity, for the sake of equalization, that

[23] See G. Koumakis, "Die 'korrigierende' Gerechtigkeit bei Aristoteles," *Dodone* 14, no.3 (1985): 21–31.

is, of establishing equality not based on number (each human being as one) but on worth:

> the just is necessarily a mean [μέσον], and fair [ἴσον], and in relation to something, and for certain persons.... The just, then, necessarily depends on at least four things; for the persons to whom it happens are two, and the things are distributed into two [parts]. And it is the same equality that is with respect to the persons and with respect to the things, for as the latter are related, so are the former, for if the former are not equal, they will not have equal parts. Again, this is clear from what happens with respect to merit. (1131a16–25)

We notice here, once more, Aristotle's reluctance to consider human beings in terms of numerical equality, that is, of presuming homogeneous rights simply in virtue of being a human being, of counting as one. On the contrary, he suggests, in each case human beings must be subjected to an axiological assessment. Only thus may interactions be regulated in a fair way. The rule cannot be the mechanical reciprocation of whatever one receives or undergoes: "To take an example, if a magistrate [ἀρχὴν ἔχων] strikes another, he should not be struck in return, but if someone strikes a magistrate [ἄρχοντα], he should not only be struck in return, but also be punished" (1132b28–30). This is so even in light of the difficulties involved in such a quantification – difficulties whose ramifications we will consider only most tangentially, as they clearly exceed the scope of this study. Let us simply notice Aristotle's own observation that "all agree that what is just in distribution should be according to merit [ἀξίαν] of some sort, but not everyone means the same merit" (1131a25–7). The agreement *that* merit should figure in the evaluation of a given situation does not at all imply the self-evidence of *what* this would mean. The issue of merit, thus, is bound to be variously contended in the political arena: "democrats assert that this is freedom, oligarchs that it is wealth, others that it is high lineage, and aristocrats that it is virtue" (1131a27–9).[24] Yet regardless of the problems involved in practicing this kind of calculus, it is maintained that "what is just, then, is something

[24] See L. Guidi, "Sulla giustizia distributiva," *Studium* (1940): 349–99; William Mathie, "Political and Distributive Justice in the Political Science of Aristotle," *Review of Politics* 49 (1987): 59–84; William Mathie, "Justice and the Question of Regimes in Ancient and Modern Political Philosophy," *Canadian Journal of Political Science* 9 (1976): 449–63; and D. Keyt, "Distributive Justice in Aristotle's *Ethics* and *Politics*," *Topoi* 4 (1985): 23–45. The latter article appears in a conspicuously revised version under the title "Aristotle's Theory of Distributive Justice," in D. Keyt and Fred D. Miller, Jr., eds., *A Companion to Aristotle's* Politics (Oxford: Blackwell, 1991), 238–78. See also D. McKerlie, "Aristotle's Theory of Justice," *Southern Journal of Philosophy* 39 (2001).

in a proportion of some sort [ἀνάλογόν τι], for a proportion [ἀναλογία] is a property not merely of numbers with units as elements [μοναδικοῦ ἀριθμοῦ], but of numbers as a whole; for it is an equality of ratios [ἰσότης ἐστὶ λόγων], and it is in at least four terms" (1131a29–32). According to that which is just, one should give and receive in proportion to one's value.

Thus, even if complicated by the assumption that not all human beings may carry equal weight and worth, the practice of justice (whether of granting or reestablishing justice) is presented as a matter of reckoning. Although no numerical reciprocity is assumed between two people interacting, it is nevertheless the case that a common ground is posited underlying the interaction, a shared continuum involving the commensurability of the experiences on both sides of an exchange. Even the abysmal discontinuity between the victim and the perpetrator of a crime seems to leave open the possibility of being overcome, of adequate reparation. In turn, the hypothesis of calculability and commensurability across the most profound differences presupposes the logic of the marketplace, the possibility of evaluating anything in terms of quantity. Both the attribution of value and that of price operate according to this logic. Everything can be brought back to a basic unit of exchange, so that exchange may be controlled and kept fluid, current. This is precisely what currency does. In this way, thanks to justice as fairness and the legal administration thereof, the human gathering comes to acquire a stabilizing homogeneity: it becomes a *polis*. *Polis* bespeaks the communal fabric into which differences and disaggregating drives, however radical, are woven together. Thanks to justice thus understood, fissures within the community may be mended. Justice is revealed as a principle of cohesion.

Aristotle makes the connection between the administration of justice and mercantile operations explicit:

> In view of this, all things should have a price on them; for in this way an exchange [ἀλλαγή] is always [possible], and if so, also an association [of human beings]. A coin [νόμισμα], then, like a measure [μέτρον], by making [things] commensurate [σύμμετρα], equalizes [ἰσάζει] [them]; for neither would an association of human beings be without exchange, nor exchange without equalization, nor equalization without commensurability. (1133b15–19)

The coin, *nomisma*, is the rule, *nomos*, common to all, that into which everything can be converted, by reference to which everything can be counted, measured, and regulated. The coin or exchange unit, then, grants the appropriate circulation (and, accordingly, transformation) of energy and resources within the body politic.[25] Accordingly, exchange in all its guises and community emerge as coextensive. Once again, Aristotle insists on justice as the computation and observation of proportion in transactions, and on its concomitant role in animating the *polis*, making it cohere, unified and alive:

> in associations for exchange, that which is reciprocally just and holds [human beings] together [συνέχει] is not the one according to equality but the one according to proportion [κατ᾽ ἀναλογίαν]; for it is by an action that is reciprocally proportional [ἀντιποιεῖν γὰρ ἀνάλογον] that a *polis* continues to hold together [συμμένει]. For what [human beings] seek is either to return something bad – otherwise they consider their position as one of slavery – or that which is good [τὸ εὖ], failing which there can be no give-and-take [μετάδοσις]; and it is by give-and-take that [human beings] hold together [συμμένουσιν]. (1132b32–1133a3)

However, this line of reflection concludes with a certain overcoming of the mercantile logic that contemplates the reducibility of all matters exchanged to a price, of all people involved to a quantifiable relevance, and of all exchanges to proportionally equalized giving and taking. Immediately after stating that it is by give-and-take, by returning what is owed and receiving back what was given, that human relations are instituted and stabilized, Aristotle adds: "And it is in view of this that [human beings] set up the temple of the Graces [Χαρίτων] in prominent places [ἐμποδὼν], so that [human beings] may give back [ἀνταπόδοσις], for a proper mark of grace is this: to return a service to one who has shown grace, and later to take the initiative in showing grace" (1133a3–6). In the most comprehensive sense, then, justice does not simply name returning what was received. Beyond the mere re-balancing of a debt by paying it back, justice, and hence the strength and constancy of a communal bond, bespeaks the availability to giving more, to giving spontaneously, graciously, without owing or being forced to do so. Above and beyond making even uneven exchanges and honoring what is due in transactions, justice names the gratuitous initiative of solidarity, the acknowledgment of a togetherness that far exceeds all calculation. The occurrences of grace thus understood hinder the mechanical reproduction of calculable exchange; indeed, they constitute irruptions into it and interruptions of it.

[25] See Gianfranco Lotito, "Aristotele su moneta scambio bisogni," *Materiali e discussioni per l'analisi dei testi classici* 4, 5, and 6 (1980–1): 125–80, 27–85, and 9–69, respectively.

4.2. "What Is Just without Qualification"

4.2.1. Political Justice between Law and Nature

Before returning to the central discussion of unqualified justice and its irreducibility to law, we must attend to a remarkable terminological proliferation introduced in *Nicomachean Ethics* Epsilon 6–7 (1134a17–1135a15).[26] This segment proves to be exceptionally dense and worth examining closely.

After considering the phenomenon of justice in its distributive and corrective functions, Aristotle recalls the main task at hand:

> We have stated previously how reciprocity is related to what is just; but it must not escape us that what is sought is the just without qualification and the politically just [καὶ τὸ ἁπλῶς δίκαιον καὶ τὸ πολιτικὸν δίκαιον]. This is among those who share a life in common oriented toward self-sufficiency and who are free and equal, whether according to proportion [κατ' ἀναλογίαν] or according to number. So what applies to those who do not possess these prerogatives is not what is politically just but only what is just in a qualified way or in virtue of some likeness [καθ' ὁμοιότητα]; for what is just [without qualification] belongs to those who come under the law also, and the law applies to situations where there may be injustice, for a verdict is a judgment [δίκη κρίσις] of what is just or unjust. (1134a25–32)

The categories of what is just "without qualification" and what is just "politically" are announced, yet left undeveloped in the thrust of the discussion. It is, subsequently, unclear whether they are simply juxtaposed or, on the contrary, indicated in their synonymity. What can and should be emphasized is that the pair of unqualified (simple, absolute) and political justice does not lend itself to being superimposed to the previously considered pair of complete (comprehensive) and partial (particular) justice. Political justice regards the citizens of a *polis*, those who are equal, free, and pursuing a self-sufficient life – those who "by nature live according to law" (1134b15). Political justice, thus, articulates itself in virtue of and *as* a body of laws and norms. Therefore, if presents the same problems diagnosed earlier about legality. Legality or, broadly speaking, normativity is clearly irreducible to a narrow understanding of justice as fairness, whether distributive or corrective. This is especially perspicuous in passages such as 1129b12–25, 1130b2–5, and 1130b23–5, stating that the laws prescribe

[26] It has been argued that 1134a24–1135a8 may be the insertion, into the lecture notes constituting the *Nicomachean Ethics*, of a page from an earlier exoteric text by Aristotle, possibly the dialogue *Perì dikaiosúnēs*. See, e.g., Gianfrancesco Zanetti, *La nozione di giustizia in Aristotele* (Bologna: Il Mulino, 1993), 32–5.

the practice of the virtues, a certain way of living, and do not merely regulate exchanges. At the same time, as pointed out above, legality may not simply coincide with justice in the comprehensive sense as such. Thus, political justice, in its legal or normative expression, *both* exceeds the narrower sense of justice *and* falls short of justice in its complete sense. Rather than corresponding to partial and complete justice, the juxtaposition of political and absolute justice brings to the fore, yet again, the simultaneous association *and* irreducibility of legality and justice as such. Rather than in terms of part to whole, political justice (legality) appears to be related to justice as such in terms of asymptotic approximation, of a striving toward perfection, completion, and accomplishment that would bespeak the identity of law and justice.

If, on the one hand, the relation between political and absolute justice may not be a matter of pure disjunction, the hypothesis of their simple conjunction or synonymity appears to be problematic as well. This is so for reasons that exceed the mentioned irreducibility of justice to law. The hypothesis of the co-extensiveness of what is just simply (*haplōs*) and the politically just (the just pertaining to those whose relations are structured by the law) presents problems because political justice, indeed, the category of the political thus construed, is not all-inclusive. As pointed out above, political justice embraces the lives and interactions of citizens. Consequently, it does not include those who fail to reach the status of free male adulthood, particularly women, children, and slaves – and, hence, the domains of the familial and the economic. Indeed, vertical relations and, in general, matters pertaining to the family seem not to be a part of political justice. And yet, in the very context in which Aristotle observes such an exclusion, thus intimating the limited domain of political justice, the identity of political and "simple" justice seems to be affirmed:

> What is just for a master [δεσποτικὸν] or a father [πατρικὸν], on the other hand, is not the same [as what is just for citizens] but is similar [ὅμοιον] to it; for there can be no unqualified injustice [ἀδικία πρὸς τὰ αὑτοῦ ἁπλῶς] toward what belongs to oneself since a man's possession or child (till it reaches the age when it becomes separate) is like a part of himself.... Hence what is just or unjust [for a master or a father] is not political; for the politically just or unjust was stated to be according to law [κατὰ νόμον] and to be among those who by nature live according to law [ἐν οἷς ἐπεφύκει εἶναι νόμος], and these were stated to be equal in ruling and being ruled. Hence, what is just is toward one's wife more than toward one's children or possessions, for this is what is just in a household [τὸ οἰκονομικὸν δίκαιον]; but this, too, is distinct from what is politically just. (1134b9–18)

Here, what is just in hierarchical relations (the "economic just") is shown to lie outside the politically just as well as the simply (unqualifiedly) just, as though in order to intimate their identity. In addition to this difficulty, we should note that even these domains said to be excluded from unqualified justice and/or political justice, that is, from the field of legality, are regulated by laws. For even the relations among those who are unequal (those cases in which the condition of inequality is normatively inscribed, i.e., not brought about by an unjust deed, accidentally) are regulated by law. To be sure, here the function of the law is not so much the preservation of reciprocity or the re-establishment of numerical equality, but, rather, guarding the inequalities prescribed and instituted. Indeed, even within the household, the *oikos*, Aristotle recognizes *nomos* at work, whether understood as customary structures or laws. The justice pertaining to this domain he calls *oikonomikē*. Following these remarks, we may conclude that, as a whole, legality is irreducible to political justice construed as the regulation of the interactions among citizens.

In the final analysis, what remains most perplexing in these passages is precisely the suggestion of the coinciding of legality and political (let alone unqualified) justice. In the first place, as was just emphasized, legality seems to exceed the domain of norms regulating citizenry. Second, and on altogether Aristotelian grounds, the political itself would seem to exceed the legal. For the *polis* (not this or that *politeia*, not a *polis* in its unique *genesis* or constitution, but the *polis* as such) is by nature, and this means that it is irreducible to convention, to the dimension of the *nomikos*, of customary as well as formal or juridical norms. Convention is always *this* – singular and historically determined. This is so even if convention simultaneously tends to understand and impose itself as general, abstract, even "natural" – if it must at all command authoritatively. Its authoritative command seems structurally to rest on the surreptitious denial, indeed, the betrayal of singularity, above all its own. The somehow arbitrary, finite character of the legal or conventional is often covered over or forgotten: it is in this way that convention preserves and enforces itself.

In line with these concerns regarding the irreducibility of *polis* to *nomos*, Aristotle introduces yet another specification, effectively interrupting or qualifying the identity of political and legal justice. The category of the natural is brought into the discussion:

> That which is politically just may be natural [φυσικόν] or legal. It is natural if it has the same power [δύναμιν] everywhere and is not subject to what one thinks of it [τῷ δοκεῖν] or not; it is legal if originally it makes no difference whether it takes

one form or another but, after a form is posited, it does make a difference, e.g., the specification that a prisoner's ransom shall be one mina, or that a goat shall be sacrificed and not two sheep, and in addition, all laws passed for individual cases, like that concerning a sacrifice in honor of Brasydas or any particular decree. (1134b18–24)

The "naturally" just is that which is common to all, despite differences in language, formation, and articulation. The virtually arbitrary comes to supplement nature there where nature provides no clear direction. In this sense, then, political justice is the work of integration of natural and conventional motifs. Just as (1) *logos* comes to be for the most part through teaching but is irreducible to it, so (2) the politically just involves both a natural and a legal or conventional dimension. The former is "mostly" acquired through participation in the community of *dialogos*, in the exercise and practice of *logos*. The latter is "mostly" acquired through participation in the community of practices and subtending legislative-normative structures. Both exhibit a certain excess vis-à-vis any specific discourse or context (this particular dialogue, this particular set of practices). But, of course, *logos* and justice do not merely enjoy structurally parallel developments: for the explication of justice, in fact, the institution of justice as such is crucially a matter of *logos*, of the spoken practices and psychological powers signified by this single word.

Because structure is essential to communal practices, customary formations, once established, require the relative stability approximating that of nature. Aristotle is eager to underline, however, that the acknowledgment of the twofold character of political justice, indeed, of the political as such, entails by no means the contrast between natural immobility and conventional instability. On the contrary, the politically just is said to involve both natural and customary dimensions *despite* its evident overall variability, fluctuation in formulation, and so on. Indeed, with regard to things pertaining to justice and, broadly speaking, to *ēthos*, nature appears to be no less subject to change than human customs:

There are some who think that all kinds of justice are such as these [i.e., legal], in view of the fact that what is by nature is unchangeable and has the same power everywhere, like fire, which burns here as well as in Persia, but that things which are just are observed to be subject to change. Such is not the case, however, although there is a sense in which this is true. Perhaps among the gods, at least, this is not the case at all, but among us there is something that is just by nature, *even though all of what is just is subject to change.* Nevertheless, some of what is just is by nature, some not by nature. Now of things which can be otherwise, what kind are by nature and what kind are not by nature but by law or convention, if indeed they are alike in being both subject to change, is clear from the examples that follow; and the same distinction applies to the other cases. The right hand is by nature stronger, although it is possible for everyone to become ambidextrous. As for the things that are just by convention or expediency, they are like standard measures; for measures of wine or of corn are not everywhere equal but larger on wholesale and smaller in retail markets. Similarly, what is just according to human beings and not by nature is not the same everywhere, since forms of government, too, are not all the same; nevertheless, there is only one form of government which is by nature the best everywhere. (1134b25–1135a5; emphasis added)

Nature presents a distinctive plasticity: it can be modified through repeated practice, replaced by another, a "second" nature. Even more remarkably, though the naturally just has "the same power everywhere," it manifests itself in different ways, at different times and places, if it is true that "all of what is just is subject to change." The "same power" takes place and form (becomes actual, enacted) in irreducible ways. This means that, while something named the "naturally just" is liminally intuited as "the same everywhere," it actually qua identical has no place anywhere – just as the "one form of government which is the best everywhere," the excellence in political constitution that is said to be unique and self-identical, is nowhere to be found.

The just by nature, then, is not unchangeable – or, minimally, it is not recognized as such. Again, the point here is manifestly not whether or not "natural laws" (as distinct from natural phenomena) would be immutable. Indeed, the very distinction between phenomenon and underlying "law" or cause can hardly be posited, given the elusiveness and unintelligibility of the "same everywhere." Rather, at stake is showing that even that which is, in the realm of ethics, by nature, is not changeless, not uniformly manifest, not manifest in one form. Indeed, there may be nothing changeless in ethical matters – neither that which is by nature nor, a fortiori, that which is legal or conventional.

Thus, the reference to nature here should not be read as a turn to a sanctioning ground, as a "naturalizing" move that would found the system of legal justice and cast laws in their immobility, fixity, and absoluteness. This move amounts, at most, to inserting laws into the context of nature, which involves motion and transformation – introducing laws into the motility or dynamism of nature. Aristotle refuses to choose between the two dichotomous conceptions of nature, as either (1) the random, indifferent, and unfair, against which human laws would provide the necessary protection, or (2) the static horizon grounding all self-enforcement and any authority claiming to carry the sanction and necessitating force of the natural. In this connection, we observe Aristotle's desire to transcend both superficial relativism and jus naturae in its dogmatic essentialism. At the very least, we recognize his desire to reach beyond facile arbitrariness *as well as* his inability simply to identify immutable, natural foundations for ethical-legal matters.[27] In its unfolding, this meditation discloses, articulates, and keeps open a space between these extremes. The meditation on justice results in an attempt at doing justice to human experience, to the mobility yet composure of life.

4.2.2. The Aporia *of Justice*

We finally return to the perplexing equation of justice, as a whole and as such, with law. Left unqualified, such an equation would attribute unlimited power to the lawgivers and judges. This scenario reminds us of Plato's *Republic* 1, in which Thrasymachus argues that justice is what the rulers (those in power, determining, if not making, the laws) decide it to be. The sophist maintains, in other words, the purely arbitrary status of justice: it is the laws furthering the advantage of those who make them, of the stronger, the rulers themselves.

We saw that the politically just can be analyzed into a natural and a legal aspect. The natural may be understood as that within which any singular legal construct is nestled, and by which it is necessitated. It indicates the necessity of the *polis* and the order it names, and hence the necessarily political character of human beings, due to the lack of self-sufficiency distinguishing them from gods and beasts. Such a "natural ground" of the just, however, allows for indefinitely many legal interpretations, that is, contemplates the legal precisely in its formal multiplicity. Just as *logos*, justice is indeed said (spoken, articulated, enacted) in many ways: it both comes to be in many ways and is irreducible to any of them. Thus, the transcendence of justice with regard to the texts and contexts of legality will at once signify the transcendence of *logos* with regard to any human instantiation thereof, that is, the transcendence of *logos* with regard to itself.

[27] Already Max Salomon diagnosed the problems involved in reading a theory of *jus naturale* into the Aristotelian text. By this author, see *Der Begriff der Gerechtigkeit bei Aristoteles* (Leiden: Sijthoff, 1937; rpt., New York: Arno, 1979), 55; "Le droit naturel chez Aristote," *Archives de philosophie du droit et de sociologie juridique* 7, nos. 3–4 (1937): 120–7; and "Der Begriff des Naturrechts in der 'Grossen Ethik,'" *Archiv für Rechts- und Sozialphilosophie* 41 (1954–5): 422–35. See also Bernard Yack, "Natural Right and Aristotle's Understanding of Justice," *Political Theory* 18, no 2 (May 1990): 216–37, and P. Destrée, "Aristote et la question du droit naturel (*Eth. Nic.*, V, 10, 1134b18–1135a5)," *Phronesis* 45, no.3 (August 2000).

It was intimated above that it is not simply because of the variety of governments or constitutions and the elusiveness of the "best" form thereof, that the authority of laws can consistently be diagnosed as discrepant with respect to justice itself. Actually, even the falling short of governments vis-à-vis the rule of the best may hardly be anything "simple," an unfortunate contingency. Rather, in their inevitability such shortcomings may reveal an essential trait of the political as such (of the coming into being of human togetherness) and, at the same time, the fleeting character of that which would abide, "the same everywhere." But aside from these considerations, we must now show that it is the law as such, as a written text, which appears intrinsically, essentially, and necessarily unfit to coincide with justice. For even in the "perfect" or "best" *polis*, Aristotle suggests, the laws would have a problematic status. It is the genetic and operative horizon of legality (how laws are given and subsequently enforced, i.e., read and interpreted) that presents difficulties. As we shall see, the coming into being and functioning of the law has to do with the work of legislator and judge alike, that is, with the figures of the one who institutes the law and the one who, in virtue of his or her living presence, re-enacts the law, enlivens it and brings it to life, to the specific circumstances of life. Such operations prove to be eminently questionable.

The examination of the discrepancy between law and justice is forced by a perceived inability of the law to do justice to action, to discern its infinite richness and singularity. Aristotle notes that "if one gave a judgment in ignorance," that is, being unable to contemplate the details of an action, "neither does he act unjustly according to what is legally just nor is his judgment unjust (though his judgment is unjust in a certain sense, for what is legally just is distinct from what is just in the first sense)" (1136b32–5). In other words, if one would evaluate a circumstance without grasping its particular features, one would in so doing adhere to the legally just. It does, indeed, pertain to legality to predispose judgment in ignorance of the particulars. Such an approach to the assessment of circumstances, however, cannot but be unsatisfactory, whether in strictly judiciary contexts or in the process of evaluation and judgment involved in all deliberation. For, while not unjust according to the legal text, judgment "in ignorance" of the particulars is hardly just vis-à-vis the circumstance considered. It amounts to a somewhat mechanical application of the established rule. This is why the law as "universal" statement needs to be supplemented and perfected, indeed, corrected there where it cannot *by definition* be adequate.

The discussion of the equitable and equity, *epieikeia*, belongs in this set of concerns.[28] It does indeed appear that, in its function as a corrective of law, equity more closely approximates justice, although it is not unqualifiedly the same as justice (1137a34–5). The thrust of the reflection indicates that just action or evaluation stems from a source irreducible to law: even there where legislation does not reach, when facing unlegislated details or circumstances not legally contemplated, one is not without guidance. As such a guidance, equity surpasses legal directions, transcends them – indeed, it works in their absence, supplementing their limitations:

> the equitable is just although it is better than one sort of what is just, and it is better than what is just not by coming under another genus. So the just and the equitable are the same, and though both of them are good [σπουδαίοιν], the equitable is superior [κρεῖττον]. What causes the problem [ἀπορίαν] is the fact that the equitable is just not according to law but as something which is a correction [ἐπανόρθωμα] of what is legally just. (1137b8–13)

The privileged relationship of law to justice is, thus, called into question due to some intrinsic limitation inherent in law as such. Aristotle seems to show law *at once in its necessity and impossibility* or, at least, in its necessary insufficiency vis-à-vis singularity. It could also be said that it is the concrete situation that is inherently flawed because of its overflowing, irreducible particularity, but this would hardly make a difference. For the problem or flaw at stake here is the inability of the law to contain, contemplate, and include the practical manifold:

> The cause [of the equitable being better than, or a correction of, the legally just] is the fact that all laws are according to the whole [in statement] but about some things there is no speaking correctly according to the whole. So in cases in which it is *necessary* to speak according to the whole but *not possible* to do so correctly, the law grasps what is mostly or in the majority of cases correct, without ignoring that there is error in so doing [τὸ ἁμαρτανόμενον]. And in doing this, it is nonetheless correct, for the error lies neither in the statement of the law nor in the lawgiver, but in the nature of the matter at stake; for right away the matter [ὕλη] of actions [which are performed] is of such a nature. (1137b13–20; emphasis added)

The problem or flaw at stake is, then, the discrepancy between the universality of the law and the subject matter to be legally regulated. *The impossibility in principle to close the gap between universality of statement and materiality of action is the flaw.* This should be underlined: the law's limit does not or does not simply lie in its falling short of the universal, that

[28] See Giulio Maria Chiodi, *Equità. La categoria regolativa del diritto* (Naples: Guida, 1989).

is, in its partiality or particularity. Rather, precisely because of its claimed universality, the law falls short of the overabundance of the practical and the material. The universal statement proves to be limited, one-sided, as it were, vis-à-vis life in its open, in(de)finite character. Consequently, justice comes to be illuminated not as the universal that all concrete legal formulations would fail to capture, but, rather, as that which eludes the universal, or at least universal formulation. Just like singularity in its teeming multiplicity, justice transcends the universal. In turn, the written law that is the fruit of political/dialectical negotiation owes its authority and enforceability qua universal precisely to the oblivion surrounding its own historicity and all too contextual character. The law is the instrument for the assessment of particular circumstances, which operates in virtue of the denial of its own circumstances. So much so, indeed, that the law even claims not to ignore its own ignorance and error, and re-inscribes them within the predictable. Legality or convention is always singular, contextual. Yet to the extent that it must be general, abstract, in order to have any normative power at all, legality constitutes the betrayal of singularity.

Aristotle draws the consequences of these considerations and suggests that, precisely because perceived as not fully just, or even possibly unjust, by definition the law is subjected to ongoing revision. There belongs to law an infinite process of rewriting, a process that is never over. For the law (this writing, this *logos*) entails perfectibility, and therefore contestation, transgression, and re-determination. These define the law *as such.* Justice seems to exceed such a dialectical arena and ongoing debate. It names that for the love of which the infinite debate takes place:

> So when the law makes a universal statement [about something] but a case arises which does not come under that universal statement, then it is right to correct the omission made by the legislator when he left some error in his unqualified statement; for the legislator himself would have made that correction had he been present, or he would have legislated accordingly if he had known. Thus the equitable is just; and it is better than a certain kind of what is just, not the unqualified just but that which has error because it is stated in an unqualified manner. And this is the nature of the equitable, namely, a correction of the law insofar as the law errs because it is [or must be] stated universally. And the reason why not all things come under the law is this, that it is impossible to lay down a law for some things, and so a decree is needed. For of that which is indefinite, the rule too is indefinite, like the leaden rule [κανών] used in Lesbian construction; for the rule here is not rigid but adapts itself to the shape of the stone, and so does the decree when applied to its subject matter [πράγματα]. (1137b20–33)

Stating its pronouncements in an unqualified manner, the law is always exposed to the possibility of missing the unqualified. Suggested here is a certain ineffability of the unqualified, of justice in the unqualified sense: indeed, it is in its unqualified mode that a statement errs. Again, the impotence or inability of the law before actions not exactly corresponding to universal typologies is not a contingent, unfortunate incident. It defines the law essentially and as such. In the *Politics,* Aristotle reformulates this point in light of the discussion of rule of law:

> no other thing than the laws, when rightly laid down, should be the authority [κυρίους], and the ruler [ἄρχοντα], whether he be one or whether there be many, should have authority over matters about which laws cannot be stated with precision, because it is not easy for laws, which are stated according to the whole, to clarify every particular. What is not yet clear, however, is what such laws which are rightly laid down should be.... (1282b2–8)

When error is detected in the enforcement of the universal legal statement, the appropriate adjustments must be made. Law enforcement is anything but the automatic application of a universal on the particular. Rather, it is a matter of bringing the law to bear on the singular circumstance in such a way that the law is made alive again, recovered in its animating intent, as though the founding insight of the legislator would shine through again. Bringing law to bear on life means bringing law to life again. In this sense, the intervention of the judge, of the one in power, or of anyone called to evaluate a situation, constitutes the repetition of the law-giving act. In every enlivening conjunction of legal text and practical circumstances, in every legal consideration infusing the law with the intelligence that gave it origin, the founding act is re-enacted.

Thus, on the one hand, "we do not allow a human being to rule, but the law," because a human being tends to be greedy and self-interested or "to become a tyrant," while the ruler who refers to the law "is a guardian of what is just" and "a preserver of what is fair" (1134a35–b3). And yet, on the other hand, the law will always have involved more than preservation: it will have demanded mindful assistance so that the vision it harbors may be awakened and released. In thus being stirred up, its vision encounters previously unforeseen particulars and is thereby perfected, prolonged beyond itself. Without such a contribution on part of the human being, the legal text, very much in accord with certain Platonic pronouncements (*Phaedrus* 278b–d), is dead letter, a universal formulation disconnected from this life. It is in this operation, whereby a law is conceived together with a particular situation to be assessed, that we catch a glimpse of justice. It is not the law that is justice, but the work of judgment, the incessant assessment of practical configurations that rests on the intimate understanding of them. In other words: the assessment of life taking place in life. This is why Aristotle says that "to go to a judge is to go to what is just, for a judge tends to be something which is just and ensouled [δίκαιον ἔμψυχον]" (1132a21–2). Again, in the *Politics* we are told that, while the rule of law may be preferred because "passion does not belong in law, whereas it necessarily resides in every human soul," still "it might be said, conversely, that deliberation concerning particulars is more beautiful" (1286a19–22). Ultimately, it is that which undergoes passions, the human soul, that can deliberate otherwise than universally, that can intelligently discern and evaluate each singular event: "It is clear, then, that this [the best human being] must be a lawgiver and that laws must be laid down, but that these laws should have no authority insofar as they deviate [from equity], although in the rest of cases they should be authoritative" (1286a23–4). Preserving the law means keeping it in line with life, lest it go astray.

Speaking of the irreducibility of justice to law, then, means pointing to a certain injustice (failure, error) of law and to justice as constant revision and rewriting of the law, as the questioning of what presents itself as above questioning if it has to have any authority at all. Justice emerges, then, as the work of a certain deconstruction, as Derrida has also suggested. Among other things, the *aporia* of justice makes it possible to catch a further glimpse of the difference between legal and natural justice. As we saw, the legal and the natural cannot be contrasted in terms of mutability and constancy, respectively. For both move and change. Their difference may perhaps be sought in the contrast between universality (abstractness) and singularity. Nature may indeed name the whole, yet not in the mode of *universalitas.* Once again, the *logos* speaking from out of an intimacy with justice (with life, *phusis*, the *phusis* of *praxis*) is, unlike the legal text, that articulation open to its own disarticulation and overcoming.

4.3. The Place of Justice

From the foregoing discussion emerged a certain elusiveness or, literally, ineffability of justice as such. In its positivity, *logos* seems essentially inadequate to capture it, which means that justice does not properly belong in the order of eidetic or conceptual simplicity that *logos* aims at fixating. Aristotle returns to this point in the context of a remark on the difference between (1) being just or unjust and (2) sporadically performing a just or unjust act:

Human beings think that it is in their power to act unjustly, and hence that it is easy to be just also. But such is not the case; for to lie with one's neighbor's wife or strike someone in the vicinity or deliver money into someone's hand is easy and in our power, but to do these by being disposed in a certain way [ὡδὶ ἔχοντας] is neither easy nor in our power. Likewise, human beings think that one does not need to be wise [σοφὸν] to know [γνῶναι] what is just and what is unjust, since it is not hard to understand [ξυνιέναι] what the laws state [λέγουσιν]. It is not these [the laws or what they state], however, that are just, except accidentally [κατὰ συμβεβηκός], but the manner in which just things are done or distributed, and to do just things in a certain manner is a greater task [ἔργον] than to know [εἰδέναι] what produces health – although even here it is easy to know that honey and wine and hellebore and cautery and surgery heal, but to know how to use these, and for whom, and when, etc., in bringing about health, is as much a task as being a doctor. (1137a5–17)

Aristotle opens this reflection by gesturing toward the difficulty of his earlier statement, in Book Gamma, regarding the voluntary character of the virtues and, hence, the relative responsibility of adult human beings vis-à vis how they act and who they have become (1114a19ff.). Once a certain order of the soul is established through habituation and one holds and comports (*ekhei*) oneself in a certain manner, it is no small task, if indeed at all feasible, to reconfigure oneself. This is why, while performing an occasional just act may be possible for someone unjust, truly to act justly, that is, to *become* just, to reorient one's whole being from injustice to justice (or, for that matter, vice versa), represents an altogether different challenge. However, what is here decisive to the present discussion is the statement that the laws, or their pronouncements, are just only in a secondary sense, according to an attribute. Primarily, justice is not to be found in the laws or in their content (the prescribed actions). These are not the *locus* of justice, where justice strictly speaking can be found. Rather, justice is to be found in the *how* of certain actions – not in the prescription thereof, not even in the bare performance of them, but in the psychological structure in which certain actions are rooted and out of which, as though effortlessly and of their of accord, they flow.

What is at stake in justice, then, is not a merely formal knowledge of what might be just, but the capacity for carrying out a certain action in alignment with a certain preparation and predisposition to justice. This, quite crucially, entails the ability not simply to apply an abstract knowledge of justice, but to assess, to judge, in every single case, what the best, that is, just, course of action may be. This much is revealed by the comparison with the art of healing, which is altogether irreducible to the abstract knowledge of that which heals. It appears, consequently, that it is in action, in life itself, that justice properly understood resides. Infinitely receding before the advancing of the law, ultimately inaccessible to legal statements, justice is a matter of aliveness, lives in action – in a certain manner or quality of action or life.

Equally to be underlined is the suggestion that wisdom, *sophia*, may not be merely a matter of understanding laws, of formal comprehension. Just as it is not the same to be just and to perform a just act, so it is not the same to know (*gignōskein*) what is just and to understand (*xunienai*) the statements of the laws. Wisdom is associated with the former, with the ability to discern the just from the unjust, and is a matter of knowledge, *gnōsis*, in the broadest sense. Being wise, even more than genuinely being a doctor, means possessing a firm knowledge, on the basis of habitual practice and experience, of *how* to respond to the unique demands of any single circumstance. A formulaic cognition of what the laws command will never constitute an adequate basis for such a skilled and opportune response. Indeed, if abstract knowledge were sufficient to propel one toward a certain behavior, one would be in the position of determining oneself to act in such and such way at will. However, habitual formation is a much more stable ground of practical determination. Aristotle reiterates this point, as though to insist on its relevance:

> For that very reason, too, human beings think that it is in the power of someone just to act unjustly... since the just one is not less but even more able to do each of these unjust things; for he is able to lie with a woman or to strike someone, and a brave man can throw away his shield and turn to flight in this or that direction. Yet, to act in a cowardly way or unjustly is not simply to do these things, except accidentally [κατὰ συμβεβηκός], but to do so by being disposed in a certain manner [ὡδὶ ἔχοντα], just as to practice medicine or to heal is not just to use or not use a knife, not just to give or not to give medicine, but to do so in such-and-such a manner [ἀλλὰ τὸ ὡδὶ]. (1137a17–25)

Situating justice, the exercise of virtue as a whole, in action means emphasizing that the pursuit of the good as such is a matter of practice, irreducible to mere intellectual contemplation. Identifying justice with a certain *how* of action, rooted in practical formation, means understanding that the orientation to the good will never simply have been a matter of rational grasp – that, rather, the turn to the good rests on one's ethical constitution and the rational clarification (and concomitant systematic development) of such a turn will necessarily have been successive to it. As we shall see, it is the appropriate (i.e., excellent) kind of habituation that makes the end in view right beforehand, which originarily discloses the good to be pursued. In lack of such a desirable formation, speculation will be deprived of meaning, that is, superficial, disconnected from life. After all, Aristotle had already anticipated in Book Alpha that "in none of human deeds [ἔργων] is there so much stability [βεβαιότης] as in the activities [ἐνεργείας] according to virtue, which appear to be more enduring [μονιμώτεραι] than the sciences themselves" (1100b12–15). The next chapter, focusing on Aristotle's discussion of the intellectual virtues, will provide ample opportunity to deepen these outcomes.

5. THE VIRTUES OF THE INTELLECT

The previous investigation regarding justice has cast light on the limits of language as well as purely rational determination, *logos*, and on the exuberance of life in its sensible and practical dimensions.[29] This does *not* simplistically mean that, because things pertaining to human comportment are mutable and fluctuating, there can be neither purely contemplative grasp nor geometrically precise exposition of them, while, regarding other fields of inquiry, such a grasp and exposition would remain viable and retain their primacy. Rather, it means that the speculative endeavor cannot not be inscribed within essentially and basically practical conditions. Nor does this entail that that which pertains to life and experience enjoys a priority merely in the order of becoming or of knowing, that is, a genetic priority that would only reconfirm the priority of the "metaphysical," as it were, in the order of being. Quite on the contrary, while the phenomenon of life and ethical formation is to be acknowledged in its priority vis-à-vis subsequent speculative articulations, the *awareness* of such an ethical ground seems to come last in the order of knowing. Indeed, the ethical condition is as such made explicit only in the properly ethical reflection, which fully elaborates motifs incipiently raised in the inquiries on "logic" and "first philosophy." In other words, ethics clarifies and further develops the insight regarding ground and conditions already announced in the "metaphysical" discussions but left underdeveloped in those contexts. It is in this sense that the reflection on ethics may be seen as first in the order of being and, hence, as first philosophy.

[29] A seminal version of this section appeared under the title "The Nature of Reason and the Sublimity of First Philosophy: Toward a Reconfiguration of Aristotelian Interpretation," *Epoché* 7, no 2 (Spring 2003): 223–49.

The analysis of Book Zeta will set a number of issues already noted thus far into sharper relief. In this sense, it constitutes a culminating moment in the present discussion. Reading this segment of the *Ethics* will provide an opportunity to observe more closely the relation between the "part" of the soul said to pertain to character and its formation and that other "part" said to be the seat of *logos*. Thus, it will allow us to articulate a more refined understanding of the relation between comportment and reason, that is, to deepen the question of the difference between agreeing with *logos* (self-actualization or self-activation according to *logos*) and "having" (*ekhein, hexis*) *logos*. If it were to turn out that the two are not ultimately distinct and self-contained, that their relation has the form of a certain interpenetration, *then* we would have to call into question the very possibility of rational autonomy, pure agency, unqualified freedom, and emancipation from body, animality, nature. Again, at stake is the relation of *logos* to body and animality, to the life that bears, carries it – that "has" it.

We saw how the ethical virtues belong to the desiring "part," while the intellectual ones belong to the thinking "part." Yet we also saw that *both* are a matter of practice and time. To actualize oneself *according to logos* entails habituation. But *having logos*, too, is "mostly" (Aristotle says) a matter of habituation, more specifically of learning (*Nicomachean Ethics* 1103a15). Both, then, entail experience, which belongs in the world and time, that is, is embodied and lived. "Having" *logos* seems to be less a matter of mere possession or property than a matter, again, of habit (*hexis*), of coming to have – as Aristotle intimates in the *Metaphysics*, in his remark on thinking as a habit handed down to us (993b14). Now, in Book Zeta Aristotle is focusing especially on the virtues of the intellect, on the "part" of the soul that *in itself has logos*, that is the seat, domain, or proper dwelling of *logos*. *Logos* is that thanks to which we grasp the mean, the middle point characterizing virtuous action, which leads to and *itself is* happiness. But is *logos* an autonomous principle, unaffected and affecting the rest of the soul? Or is thinking always *of* this world, *of* the body, in such a way as never to be free from this binding exchange? May thinking and its disourse entail a dimension of passivity and affection, too?

In connection to this line of questioning, which problematizes the viability of a clear-cut separation and hierarchical relation between the "parts" of the soul, this investigation will encourage us to wonder about the relation among the excellences internal, as it were, to reason, that is, to wonder about the structure of the allegedly rational "part." In particular, we will be compelled to articulate an understanding of *phronēsis* and *sophia* (and, concomitantly, of *praxis* and *theōria*) in their belonging together. At stake in doing so is the possibility of overcoming the traditional opposition of these terms, an opposition preserved even by those thinkers who have emphasized the practical over against the theoretical simply by inverting the order of the hierarchy.[30]

That Aristotle may undeniably accord a certain primacy to *sophia* may not amount to a privileging of the "theoretical" understood in terms of abstraction, that is, in terms of disembodied perception transcending conditions human and otherwise. For if, as will be suggested below, *sophia* at once embraces and is informed by *phronēsis*, their differing is not a matter of opposition, let alone of separation. And if the theoretical is always informed by a set of practices, by the modality of one's comportment to phenomena, then encountering phenomena, the world, nature in its measureless, even transcendent, disclosure is always a matter of *ēthos*. To give to the analysis of Book Zeta the centrality and prominence it deserves, it will be opportune to recapitulate, in their main delineations, a few issues already encountered in our reading of earlier moments in the ethical discussion. They will provide the broad framework wherein the examination of the intellectual virtues unfolds. Such an examination vertically delves into the heretofore unanalyzed "having" of *logos* – into the belonging of *logos* in and to life. Let us, then, begin again.

5.1. The "Most Authoritative and Architectonic" of the "Sciences or Faculties"

The *Nicomachean Ethics* opens with the statement, "Every art [τέχνη] and every inquiry [μέθοδος], and similarly every action [πρᾶξίς] and every intention [προαίρεσις] seems [δοκεῖ] to aim at some good [ἀγαθοῦ τινὸς]; hence it was well said that the good is that at which all things aim" (1094a1–3). The whole range of human activity, of modes of human self-manifestation, appears to "aim at a certain good." Nothing is left out that would not relate to, stretch out toward, or strive for the good. At the same time, again, we should notice the dialectical tenor of this initial statement setting the tone for the rest of the inquiry. This opening is

[30] For a recent contribution along these lines, see Christopher P. Long, "The Ontological Reappropriation of *Phronēsis*," *Continental Philosophy Review* 35 (2002): 35–60. By the same author, see also "The Ethical Culmination of Aristotle's *Metaphysics*," *Epoché* 8, no. 1 (Fall 2003): 53–72, and *The Ethics of Ontology: Rethinking the Aristotelian Legacy* (Albany: SUNY Press, 2004).

based on consensus (*sensus communis, koinē aisthēsis*), on common (i.e., shared, agreed on) views. Though not assumed a-critically and, in fact, necessitating thorough questioning and elucidation, nevertheless such a doxic ground discloses the encompassing domain of the inquiry and prescribes its course.[31] The investigation ensuing can be seen as an attempt at thoughtfully engaging the shared perception (often unthematic, even unconscious) of the centrality of the good in human undertakings – in other words, at deepening the reflection concerning the pursuit of *eudaimonia*, the pursuit that *eudaimonia* (understood as thriving, attunement, or harmonious relation to the daimonic, to what exceeds one) itself is.[32]

Ethics, Aristotle observes in these preliminary remarks, is the study of the good as ultimate finality, as that which sustains and structures all doing. Ethics pursues a knowledge, a *gnōsis* of the good, the *agathon* that culminates in *to ariston*: the best, as it were, highest good. As such a study, ethics (that is to say, already, politics) presents itself in its "most authoritative and architectonic" character. Ethics-politics is indeed such a most comprehensive "science or faculty," *epistēmē* or *dunamis* (1094a19ff.).[33] First in the order of being, ethics is, indeed, last in the order of knowledge, most encompassing – for it entails humans' self-reflexivity about their own endeavors, their coming back full circle to reflect on their own undertakings, most remarkably on their own reflective exercises (e.g., scientific investigations of *phusis* and "beyond," logical or rhetorical analyses, or the study of the soul).

It is at this point that Aristotle introduces, albeit in an abbreviated fashion, the psychological account that will remain a point of reference throughout the *Ethics*. For the activity of the human *psukhē*, its unfolding into action, its giving itself (according to its being) in and as *ēthos* is precisely what is at stake in the ethical inquiry. Indeed, it seems that,

31 Aristotle could hardly emphasize more how the dialectical "ground" of ethics demands an appropriate methodological approach, admitting neither of generalities nor of abstractions (1094a19–b27; 1098a22–b9; 1098b10–22; 1104a1–10).

32 In terms of a fundamental orientation toward the question of the good, the concurrence of the *Ethics* and Plato's *Republic* should be noticed. In both cases, the good (source of being and becoming in the *Republic*, that which informs and occurs as eudaimonic growth in the *Ethics*) exceeds scientific-theoretical perception. It is neither, in Platonic terms, an "object" of eidetic contemplation (indeed, it is not, strictly speaking, an *eidos*) nor, in Aristotelian parlance, the highest attainment of the "theoretical" life. It grants knowledge, while remaining irreducible to it, unknown.

33 Notice the indefinite terminology designating the ethical discourse. Such discourse is a kind of knowing, something humans are capable of, something for which they have the power.

in the anthropological context, *eudaimonia* should be understood as the most excellent (skilled and, in this sense, virtuous) carrying out of the human task, *ergon*. But the exquisitely human *ergon*, far from being limited to the purely vegetative life or the life of sensation, would consist in a certain activation (self-enactment, *energeia*) of the *psukhē* according to reason (*logos*), or not without it. It is *such an enactment* that would distinguish the human from other living beings (once more, we will have to return to this). The human would be characterized, literally, by a certain soulfulness, by the fullness and spaciousness of soul not confined to bodily or sensory functions, embracing while exceeding the functioning of the organism (which still belongs *in* soul, is en-souled). The activation of soul in the plenitude of its properly human power constitutes the properly human assignment.

The psychological exploration, then, incisively configures the question of human endeavor and concomitant excellence. For, says Aristotle, in the right proportion psychology is an integral part of ethics-politics (1102a5–26). What thus surfaces is an understanding of the *psukhē* in its basically three-fold structure. This initial psychological tripartition into metabolic life, life of the senses (sensibility), and enactment according to reason gives rise to a division more precisely reflecting the relation of the "parts" to *logos*. At a basic level, Aristotle says, the *psukhē* can be seen partly as having *logos*, partly as *a-logon*. But, in turn, each of these two "parts" presents a further division, that is, can be taken in two senses. Let this well-known (indeed, "exoteric," 1102a28ff.) analysis be recalled in outline.[34]

The nutritive part of the soul, common to all living, is said to be purely non-rational. The part ("nature," 1102b14) of the soul where appetites and, in general, desire (*epithumiai, orexis*) reside in a way can be said to be irrational and driven by sensibility, but in another way seems to participate (*metekhein*) in reason, for it is able to subject itself to reason even though it does not possess it as its own. It has the capacity for the recognition of reason as such, and this acknowledgment seems to exert a certain compelling power over it. According to the well-known image of

[34] *Morion* (meaning "piece," "portion," "constituent," "member," "part" in the broadest sense) is the term Aristotle mostly employs (although not without exception, e.g., 1102b14) to refer to the partitions of the soul. Aristotle also stipulates that, "at present," it is a matter of indifference whether the rational and non-rational components of the soul be understood as separable (analogously to parts of a divisible whole) or as aspects or modes of the same, i.e., "by nature inseparable" and appearing to be two only "to *logos*" (1102a30–4).

filial piety, this part is said to be capable of following reason "like a child listening to a father" (1103a3; also 1102b30ff.). The desirous part, then, is in one sense irrational and in another rational. Consequently, the part of the soul that has reason can also be viewed in two ways: as that which has reason in a qualified way, which is somewhat available to the claim of reason (such would be the desirous, driven element) and as that which has reason in itself (in which, properly and strictly, reason abides). This composite articulation of the difference between the rational and the irrational indicates their dialectical (non-contradictory) relation and, by the same token, the dialectical relation between what is by nature and what is not by nature.

It is according to such view of the domains of the soul that the *aretai*, the dispositions denoting excellence in various modes of comportment (i.e., excellent habits, stable structures of the soul acquired through repeated practice), are classified. Aristotle will devote part of Book Gamma and Book Delta in its entirety to the so-called ethical virtues, virtues pertaining to character (*ēthos*), that is, the appetitive (desiring) "region" of the soul. After the discussion of justice, in Book Zeta Aristotle will turn to the intellectual virtues (*aretai dianoētikai*), virtues of (or through) the intellect (*nous*), that is, of the part of the soul where *logos* dwells.[35] It is on the latter discussion that we must now focus.

5.2. The Abode of *Logos*

The inceptive phases of the *Ethics* have been schematically recalled because, in the first place, it seemed opportune to situate the analysis of the intellectual virtues (of reason *tout court*) within the broader scope of the discussion. Second, however, having this framework starkly in view is crucial because what was initially announced as an unproblematic structural account of the *psukhē* will, on closer inspection, occasion considerable perplexity. Zooming into the domain of reason, with its formations and excellences, will considerably complicate what at first seemed a relatively clear-cut schema. It will reveal the soul in its mobility, aliveness, and irreducibility to the static, in fact, mathematical partitioning earlier delineated. Indeed, in the course of this discussion we will find difficulties analogous to those noticed in the analysis of intention and volition – difficulties having to do with an ever fleeting and elusive distinction between

35 It should be underscored that *nous* already announces itself as the "environment" of *logos*, reason. The two terms are far from coextensive.

rationality and desire as well as with the alleged hegemony (hierarchical superiority) of *logos.*

The Book opens by referring back to previous discussions, the latest of which at 1137a5ff., regarding the manner of excellent action or, more precisely, excellence as a matter of balance between extremes. The turn to *logos* is, thus, introduced specifically by reference to *orthos logos*, right reason. *Orthos logos* names the ability to reckon with the mean, that is, to envision the most effective, appropriate way of action in order to achieve the end in view: "Since we have stated earlier that one should choose the mean and not excess or deficiency, and since the mean is such as right reason [λόγος ὁ ὀρθὸς] declares [λέγει] it to be, let us go over this next" (1138b18–21). Indeed, Aristotle adds, "the mean . . . is in accordance with right reason [κατὰ τὸν ὀρθὸν λόγον]" (1138b23–5). It is *logos* that grasps and reveals the mean, that is the way of actualizing the end (the good, happiness), thus realizing oneself. Consequently, the task at hand will entail a close consideration of the "having" or possession of such an endowment and the manners in which it enacts itself excellently.

Before viewing in detail the taxonomy of the virtues pertaining to *logos,* two noteworthy issues concerning the part of the soul "having" *logos* should be considered at least in passing. Such issues undermine the apparently straightforward logic of paternal authoritative speaking and filial obedient listening, by revealing the highly controversial status of the distinction between the domain of desirous sensibility and that of reason; so much so that we may begin to wonder whether these "parts" are indeed clearly separate and relating according to the parental model or whether, instead, they may entertain a dialogue with one another, a play of *mutual affection* making them, if not the same or indiscernible, at the very least inseparable, involved in a bond of mutual implication. "Mutual affection" here would indicate the mutual undergoing that binds and unifies the soul. In virtue of such a mutually affective bond, the soul could be or could become one, not in the sense of simple, but in the sense of cohesive and in accord with itself – united in friendship, as it were. As the consideration of the soul of the continent and incontinent will make especially clear, nothing less than such an attuned cohesiveness would be required of the excellent soul.

5.2.1. Desiring Principle

First of all, in broaching this discussion (1139a18 ff.), Aristotle points out that it is the chiasmic interpenetration of intellect (at this juncture variously designated as *nous, dianoia, bouleusis, logos*) and desire that originates deliberate choice (hence, action, the formation of habits, and ultimately the virtues) and provides the final cause (end, informing motivation). This is declared along with the exclusion of sensation, *aisthēsis,* as a possible principle of action: "sensation is not a principle of any action, and this is clear from the fact that brutes have sense but do not participate in action" (1139a19–20). Action, *praxis,* is as distinctively human as the "having" of *logos.* Quite obviously, then, the ethical reflection should be the privileged *locus* for the analysis (or, in fact, self-analysis) of *logos.* Now Aristotle elaborates on the intertwinement of rational and appetitive motifs:

> Now what affirmation and denial are to thought [διανοίᾳ], pursuit and avoidance are to desire [ὀρέξει]; so since ethical virtue is a habit through deliberate choice [ἕξις προαιρετική], while deliberate choice is desire through deliberation [ὄρεξις βουλευτική], reason [λόγον] should, because of these, be true [ἀληθῆ] and desire should be right [ὄρεξιν ὀρθήν], if indeed deliberate choice is to be good [σπουδαία], and what reason asserts [φάναι] desire should follow [διώκειν]. (1139a21–7)

If the choice directing action, and hence habituation, is to be good, both desire and intellect must concur at their best: the latter by conveying the truth and the former in its rightness or correctness, that is, in its alignment. The contribution of desire, however, is no mere obedience or adjustment to the orders of the intellect. Indeed, on these conditions desire would hardly constitute a principle. If, on the one hand, Aristotle speaks of desire as having to follow reason's assertions, on the other hand he speaks of the task of the part of the soul both "practical [πρακτικοῦ] and thinking [διανοητικοῦ]" as "truth in agreement with right desire" [ἡ ἀλήθεια ὁμολόγως ἔχουσα τῇ ὀρέξει τῇ ὀρθῇ] (1139a30–32). In a elucidatory attempt, Aristotle restates and amplifies:

> Now the principle of action is deliberate choice (but as [a source of] motion and not as that for the sake of which), whereas that of deliberate choice is desire and reason for the sake of something; hence deliberate choice cannot be without intuition [νοῦ] and thought [διανοίας], nor without ethical habit [ἠθικῆς ἐστὶν ἕξεως], for acting well [εὐπραξία] or its opposite cannot be without thought [διανοίας] and character [ἤθους]. It is not thought [διάνοια] as such that can move [anything], but thought which is for the sake of something and is practical, for it is this that rules productive thought also. (1139a32–b2)

The appetites, as well as the structures of character in which they inhere, are crucial as *moving* principles. Alone, thought could not be a principle of action in the sense of inducing action. It is the envisioning of and striving toward the end that initiate the motion, and these pertain to the desiring domain of character. Thought is here seen as essentially regulative of such a stretching out, of such a purpose that incites to action – as if reason were an auxiliary resource allowing for a *more focused* apprehension of the end and a *more expedient* pursuit of it. In its sharpening function reason would listen as much as it would speak (*legein*), would be affected as much as it would affect. Something blind is here adumbrated, an unexplainable drive moving to action and involving even reason, such that reason would apply itself to that which it is not, to that which is *already* there (as another principle, beginning), to that which it cannot reduce to itself.

Again, thought appears to be less implicated in the origination of action than in the *how* of the action, in its balance and appropriateness. The truth it contributes regards the way to achieve a certain end lucidly and effectively. The end, however, is brought into focus through character, that is, through that domain of the soul in which the habits (virtuous or otherwise) come to be established on the basis of the desires. We shall return to this. For the moment, we should simply underscore two important consequences of these observations: In the first place, just as necessitation and modality of an action can hardly be considered as separate, so desire and thought, though discernible from one another, appear to be at one. Second, while, on the one hand, it can be said that desire abides by the directions of reason, on the other hand reason makes itself "similar" to desire, that is, accords itself to desire in order to calculate how to reach the desired end. In the latter sense, the work of reason appears to be grafted on the determining ground of desire, that ground that has determined in advance what is worthy of being pursued as an end. In the course of the following analysis we will have to verify whether this dialogical (dialectical) relationship holds only between desire and specifically practical thinking, leaving speculative thinking free from such an implication, or whether, on the contrary, no thinking can possibly be emancipated from such a bond with action, habituation, and driving impulses.

Far from playing a secondary, ancillary role, then, the desires seem to be inextricably intertwined with rational (at least practical-deliberative) processes and as constitutively determinant as these. Aristotle concludes: "But an object of action [is an end without qualification], for a good action is [such] an end, and this is what we desire. Hence deliberate choice is either a desiring intellect [ὀρεκτικὸς νοῦς] or a thinking desire [ὄρεξις διανοητική], and such a principle [ἀρχή] is a human being" (1139b4–7).

As a coda to these observations, let us simply signal that the author of *Magna moralia* will take a considerably more extreme position and will attribute to the desires an even more fundamental function. In this treatise it is stated that "virtue . . . is found when reason [λόγος], well conditioned, is in symmetry with the passions [πάθεσιν] possessing their own proper excellence, and the passions, in turn, with reason" (1206b10–12). Far from being a matter of paternal speaking and filial listening, the relation of reason and desire or passion is said to be a matter of *sumphōnein* (1206b13), of speaking in harmony and together. But, more decisively and in deliberate polemic with what "others" say, the author makes the "unqualified" statement that "reason is not the principle [ἀρχὴ] and leader [ἡγεμών] of virtue, but rather the passions. For, first, an irrational impulse [ὁρμὴν ἄλογον] toward the beautiful [πρὸς τὸ καλὸν] must (and does) come to be, then, subsequently, reason must cast its vote and judgment" (1206b18–22). It is in virtue of the "impulses of the passions" (ὁρμαὶ τῶν παθῶν) that one is moved "toward a beautiful [end]" (πρὸς τὸ καλὸν) (1206b24). On the contrary, "when from reason the principle reaches toward the beautiful [πρὸς τὰ καλά], the passions do not [necessarily] follow with their assent, but many times they oppose it. Hence, when well disposed, passion, more than *logos*, seems to be the origin promoting virtue [πρὸς τὴν ἀρετὴν]" (1206b26–9).

5.2.2. *Divisions*

The second issue to be noticed is the fact that Aristotle offers two accounts of the structure and subdivision of the part of the soul that "in" itself "has" *logos* (1139a5ff.). According to the first, the rational part is divided into a "scientific" (*epistēmonikon*) and a "deliberative-estimative" (*logistikon*) component. Shortly thereafter, a varied account follows, according to which the rational part of the soul consists of three sub-fields, the "theoretical" (*theōrētikon*), the "practical" (*praktikon*), and the "productive" (*poiētikon*). We wonder, to begin with, (1) whether the two-fold and the three-fold divisions may at all fit together. Indeed, one tends to understand the designations "scientific" and "theoretical" as synonyms in this context, and the terms "productive" and "practical" as bifurcating the comprehensive heading of the "estimative" (which concerns what admits of being otherwise). However, Aristotle does not explicitly establish such a simple equation. The terminological proliferation at this stage seems to be symptomatic of a less-than-clear delineation of the topography of reason, in fact, of its formidable difficulty. Even aside from this, we should wonder (2) why the practical-productive (estimative) functions would be situated here, in this domain said to be of reason as distinct from the desires. For would the operations pertaining to what can be otherwise not belong in the domain of sensibility and passion? After all, is this not the reason why belief and opinion are not accorded a legitimate place in the abode of *logos* (1139b18)? A concomitant question arises (3) concerning virtues such as art and prudence, which seem to pertain to the sensible and variable, yet are classed among the virtues of the intellect. Indeed, at 1140b26–27 and 1144b14–15 the part of the soul to which *phronēsis* (along with "shrewdness," δεινότης) pertains is called *doxastikon*, "that which forms opinions." Given the earlier exclusion of matters related to *doxa* from the domain of *logos*, the schematism here emerges as less than limpid.

Eventually, we must wonder (4) whether or (in fact) not the theoretical or scientific part (*if* the two terms do indicate the same) may be free from the involvement in desire marking the practical or deliberative part. In other words, even conceding the entanglement of "practical reason" in sensibility, would there still remain, in the domain of *logos*, at its core, the precinct of science or theoretical exercise, as it were, a citadel unvanquished, totally intact, not compromised by worldly engagements? Last but not least, we have to ask (5) how, if at all, each "intellectual" virtue (and "intellectual" has here come to denote a quite broad, heterogeneous range of dispositions) would fit into this scheme. Indeed, what virtue would belong in what subfield of the either three-fold or two-fold subdivision of the rational domain? Or might it be the case that the attempt at properly placing each virtue in the configuration(s) provided would reveal such schematism of the rational as unlikely and untenable?

5.3. The Aporetic Order of the "Intellectual Virtues"

In marking a fresh start for the inquiry (*arxamenoi oun anōthen . . . palin*), Aristotle lists five "intellectual" virtues thanks to which the soul "attains the truth" (ἀληθεύει) "when it affirms or denies." These are *tekhnē* (craft, art, artful production), *epistēmē* (science), *phronēsis* (prudence), *sophia* (wisdom), and *nous* (intuition or intellect) (1139b14–17). Following Aristotle's elucidation of them, we shall elaborate further on the questions broached above and encounter new ones. We should also notice that, in enumerating the virtues of the intellect, Aristotle decisively declares that, from this point onward, we will leave aside *hupolēpsis* and *doxa* – or so it seems (1139b18).

5.3.1. Tekhnē

Aristotle's discussion of "art" in this context is strangely truncated and, like any discourse marked by elision, invites close inspection as well as supplemental reference to other texts. Art is defined as "a habit bringing forth with true reason" (ἕξις μετὰ λόγου ἀληθοῦς ποιητική) (1140a11).[36] Art is, therefore, a kind of *poiēsis*, production, or bringing forth. As such, just like that which pertains to action, that which pertains to bringing forth is concerned with "those that admit of being otherwise" (1140a1). The only other specifications that Aristotle offers here are (1) the distinction between the practical and productive spheres, (2) the differentiation between natural bringing forth and artful (i.e., human) production, and (3) the connection between art and luck. Regarding (1), Aristotle is curiously emphatic. In a few lines, he states that "bringing forth [ποίησις] is different from action [πρᾶξις] ... and so practical habit [ἕξις πρακτική] with reason is different from habit bringing forth [ποιητικῆς ἕξεως] with reason" (1140a2–6); that, "therefore, the two exclude each other, for no action is a bringing forth and no bringing forth is an action" (1140a6–7); and that, "since bringing forth and action are different, art must be concerned with bringing forth and not with action" (1140a17–19). This distinction appears somewhat overstated, especially in light of the above quoted statement that it is "thought" (*dianoia*) understood as "practical" and "for the sake of something" that "rules productive [thought] also" (1139a36–b2). Aristotle is here underscoring the difference between end in itself and end as an external, separate outcome. Yet action, however much its own end and performed for its own sake, may still indicate a finality beyond itself, may still be for the sake of a more comprehensive outcome, just as a work of art or product may point to and be for the sake of a further end, for example, living well.

Aristotle's insistence on the mutual exclusivity of *praxis* and *poiēsis* is all the more suspect in light of the pervasiveness of the language of *tekhnē* in the ethical discourse, as noticed above. In a decisive sense, ethics is a

[36] In the *Metaphysics*, art is defined by reference to power or faculty, *dunamis*. More specifically, it is said to be a power accompanied by reason: "all the arts or productive sciences [ποιητικαὶ ἐπιστῆμαι] are powers [δυνάμεις]; for they are principles which can cause a change in another thing or [in the artist himself or herself] qua other. And every power with reason [μετὰ λόγου] [may bring about] both contraries, but every non-rational power only one; for example, heat [can cause] only heating, but the medical art sickness as well as health" (1046b2–7). Reason, *logos* as well as *epistēmē* (1046b7–8), discloses something and its contrary indifferently, in one and the same gesture. The discourse of ethics aims precisely at aligning the power of *logos* with the broader orientation to the good.

kind of making. What in Book Zeta is given a cursory and almost dismissive elaboration appears to be in fact crucially at work in the discussion of ethics, indeed, of the "architectonic" discipline. We previously pointed out the incidence of the language of *tekhnē* in the exposition of apparently remote themes, such as political constitution, law-making, and statesmanship in general (e.g., 1099b30–3, 1102a8–10, 1129b18–19, 1141b23). In this connection, we also suggested that a much more complex understanding of *tekhnē* emerges, according to which bringing forth would not be merely a matter of eidetic contemplation *applied* to matter. Aristotle himself intimates that bringing forth may not so much be a matter of forging matter according to the directives of an eidetic model autonomously known. First, rather than being simply founded on knowledge, bringing forth at once brings forth knowledge and is, in this further sense, formative. This is why the arts can transform and evolve. Second, if knowledge does indeed somehow guide bringing forth, at stake seems to be less a self-subsisting and prior knowledge than the knowledge yielded by experience and practice, indeed, by use.[37] Aristotle cautiously suggests these issues in the *Politics*, where he says that there are "certain cases" in which "the artist would be neither the only nor the best judge [ἄν κρίνειεν] . . . for example, knowledge [γνῶναι] of a house is not limited to the one who makes it, for the user [χρώμενος] is even a better judge [κρινεῖ] of it (for it is the household manager who uses [χρῆται] it), and, similarly, the pilot is a better judge of the rudder than the carpenter [τέκτονος], and the guest is a better judge of the dinner than the cook" (1282a18–23). But an even more incisive statement to this effect is offered in the *Physics*:

> there are two arts [τέχναι] which rule over matter and have the knowledge [γνωρίζουσαι] of it – the art which is concerned with use [χρωμένη] of it and the master-art of bringing forth [τῆς ποιητικῆς ἡ ἀρχιτεκτονική]. Thus the art concerned with use is also in a sense a master-art, but as a master-art it differs from the other insofar as it knows the form [τοῦ εἴδους γνωριστική], while the art that brings forth knows the matter; for the steersman knows what kind of form the rudder should have and orders [its production], but the other knows from what [kind of] wood [it should be produced] and how it should move." (194b1–7)

In this context, then, the knowledge of form must be understood not so much in autonomous and separate terms but, rather, as nested within the practical, most notably within use. Again, besides decisively broadening

[37] The suggestion is, of course, Platonic (*Republic* X).

the semantics of *tekhnē*, passages of this tenor draw out the complexities of the knowledge involved in bringing forth and, thus, complicate the analysis of the exercise of art.

Aristotle also acknowledges the essential function of the arts for both the life of the *polis* and the being of the *anthrōpos*. In the *Politics* he observes that without the arts, *tekhnai*, it would be "impossible to inhabit the city" (1291a2–3). Indeed, among the *tekhnai*, "some must necessarily belong [in the *polis*], others contribute to luxury or to living beautifully [καλῶς ζῆν]" (1291a3–4).

But let us return to the succinct discussion of *tekhnē* in the *Ethics*, specifically to the remark on (2) the differentiation between natural and human bringing forth:

> Every art is about coming into being [γένεσιν], and to pursue an art [τεχνάζειν] is to contemplate [θεωρεῖν] how to generate [γένηται] that which admits of being and not being, and whose principle is in the one who brings forth and not in that which is brought forth; for art is not concerned with things that are or come to be by necessity, nor with things according to nature, for these have the principle in themselves. (1140a12–17)

The bringing forth occurring through and as *tekhnē*, then, is only one modality of bringing forth. *Poiēsis* per se exceeds the domain of human artful production.[38] Indeed, in the broadest sense *poiēsis* comes to coincide with the comprehensive realm of coming into being and passing away, of becoming, *genesis*. In other words, *poiēsis* demands to be thought in its irreducibility to *tekhnē*, most notably to the technical or theoretical mastery involved in the skilled generation of the various crafts. Thus, the issue is understanding the "practice" of *tekhnē* in its relation and contrast to the bringing forth of *phusis*. While *tekhnē* names the bringing forth of beings that may or may not be and come to be according to the principle in the artist, *phusis* names the generation of beings according to the principle in themselves, that is, according to (their) necessity. The limits of *tekhnē* as human bringing forth are thereby marked: *tekhnē* is the generation of beings that are not alive, not animated or ensouled – that do not live and grow, do not live in the sense of grow. For to live and grow means having the principle of becoming within itself. In the spectrum of human experience, we should notice the difference between *tekhnē* and, for example, the *poiēsis* that brings forth children – a making in which humans are involved, but not in the mode of laying down a

[38] In the *Metaphysics*, Aristotle specifies that "[a]ll productions [ποιήσεις] are from art [τέχνης], or from a power [δυνάμεως], or from thought [διανοίας]" (1032a27–8).

project, not as authors, masters of a skill, carrying out a calculated plan based on the contemplation of the end.

In the *Physics*, the nature of the relation between art and nature is addressed by reference to imitation: "art imitates nature," Aristotle surmises at 194a22. The issue, however, is more complex than it seems, and certainly does not lend itself to any straightforward, formulaic understanding. While it may not be opportune to deepen this set of considerations here, let us simply signal a twofold complication of the imitative model. In the first place, art is consciously acknowledged as providing an access into nature, determining the way in which nature is analyzed and, hence, disclosed. For instance, just as the artist must possess the knowledge of both the eidetic and material dimensions involved in his or her art, so, Aristotle says, "physics must know [γνωρίζειν] both natures [i.e., *eidos* and *hulē*]" (194a22–7). It is, therefore, the human involvement in bringing forth that opens up certain paths of inquiry and molds the investigative posture. To the extent that what is apprehended of *phusis* is the fruit of investigations structurally informed by the "technical" exercise, far from viewing art as imitating nature, we might rather say that "nature imitates art." Second, besides being a matter of imitation, art emerges also, as it were, as a supplement to nature. Aristotle notes:

> In general, in some cases art completes [ἐπιτελεῖ] what nature cannot carry out to an end, in others it imitates nature. Thus, if things done according to art are for the sake of something, clearly also those according to nature [are done for the sake of something]; for the later stages are similarly related to the earlier stages in those according to art and those according to nature. (199a15–21)

Thus, the exercise of *tekhnē* not only shapes the manner in which human beings perceive the workings of *phusis*, but, moreover, completes these workings. As is evident in the exemplary case of the work of healing, art effects what nature cannot fully bring about. While clearly irreducible to one another, the *poiēsis* of *tekhnē* and that of *phusis* cannot simply be understood as starkly separate. Rather, *tekhnē* should be understood as ultimately belonging in *phusis*, completing *phusis* there where *phusis* seems to allow for an unregulated margin of indeterminacy, or there where its directives are not legible. After all, it is according to *phusis* that human beings display the "creative" aptitude.

The above signaled "technical" shaping of the human investigative posture (e.g., in physics) resonates with motifs introduced in our Prelude. Already in that context we insisted on the non-autonomy of the sciences strictly understood, on their resting on essentially non-scientific grounds. As we pointed out, the opening lines of the *Posterior Analytics* clearly indicate this: "All teaching and learning through discourse or thinking proceed from previous knowledge. This is evident if we examine all [the kinds of such teaching and learning]. For such is the way through which the mathematical sciences are acquired and each of the other arts. And it is likewise with reasonings [λόγους], whether these be through a syllogism or induction" (71a1–6). Science and art alike rest on a ground not simply their own. The same point is emphasized at the end of the treatise, when the principles from experience are said to underlie the sciences as well as art: "Again, from experience or from every universal which is now stabilized in the soul [produced in us by induction or sensation, 100b6–7] ... [there arises] a principle of art or of science, of art if it is a principle about generation, but of science if it is a principle about being" (100a6–9). We already noted how the language and scrutiny of art is prominent at the beginning of *Metaphysics*, even though the aim of this exposition is establishing scientific or theoretical knowledge in its hierarchical primacy (980b27–982a3). Indeed, in this genetic account of the emergence and differentiation of human faculties, the founding and formative role of art receives conspicuous amplification. Thus, not only does the thinking of *poiēsis* inform the reflection on ethics and politics, but it constellates the discourses of science, first philosophy, and even, as we shall see, the analysis of the noetic excellences.

In conjunction with the foregoing observations, we should once again emphasize that, despite the genuinely "scientific" knowing involved in *tekhnē* (e.g., *Physics* 194a23), theoretical mastery is limited or highly qualified in the exercise of art. To put it in other words, the *theōrein* of art may not be simply a matter of scientific or theoretical contemplation. Indeed, *tekhnē* makes the distinctions implicit in the language of *theōrein* and *epistēmē* quite blurred, because both science and contemplation must here be understood in relation to becoming, bringing forth, and that which admits of being otherwise. Above all, they must be understood in relation to luck, *tukhē* – and we thus come to (3) the connection between art and chance announced above. Aristotle broaches this issue in the conclusion of his brief review of *tekhnē*, when pointing out that chance or luck is not accidentally associated with artful bringing forth: "in a certain sense, both luck and art are concerned with the same things; as Agathon says, 'art is fond of luck, and luck of art'" (1140a19–20). This is what crucially distinguishes art from the bringing forth carried out by *phusis* itself, which brings itself forth from out of itself and according to necessity (according to itself as necessity).[39] The thoughtful bringing forth carried out by humans is pervaded, indeed, even promoted by the intervention of uncontrollable factors and chance discoveries. The interplay with what is unknown (for this is what *tukhē* names) is essential to the "inventive" comportment. It is also because of this that Aristotle mentions "erring willingly [ἑκὼν]" as an integral dimension of *tekhnē* exercised excellently (1140b23). Of course, considerations of this tenor make it arduous to see how *tekhnē* would, strictly and without any further qualification, belong in the domain of the soul that "has" reason.

In light of what we observed so far, we might discern, within the range of human *poiein*, a manner of bringing forth that can be assimilated neither to instrumental, technical production nor to physiological reproduction: a kind of "spiritual" fertility distinctive of what we could call the "visionary animal," the animal that plays with possibility and wrests fragments of the possible out of latency.[40] At stake in this creativity is the ability to envision, to entertain a certain inner vision and give phenomenal birth to it: the ability to give body, to draw out into the light. In this way, the human being intervenes in the fabric of worldly things (in the structures and conditions of human living) and affects or transforms it. To be sure, in the context of the Greek experience production is understood more in terms of transmission, of learned skill, than in terms of individual

39 This problematizes the reflection on *tekhnē* in *Metaphysics* Zeta, 1032a25ff. As if according to a kind of semantic inversion, in the latter context chance and luck (*automaton, tukhē*) are associated not with art but with the "generations from nature [ἀπὸ φύσεως]" (1032a28–30). In keeping with this inversion, generation by art is more schematically treated as entailing the dichotomy of eidetic knowledge and material production. Indeed, Aristotle states that "things generated by art are those whose form [εἶδος] is in the soul (by 'form' I mean the what-it-was-to-be [τὸ τί ἦν εἶναι] of each thing and the first substance [πρώτην οὐσίαν])" (1032a32–b2). He then elaborates on the terminology: "in a sense health is generated from health and a house from a house, that is, the house that has matter from the house without matter, for the medical art and the building art are the form [εἶδος], respectively, of health and of the house; by 'substance without matter' I mean the what-it-was-to-be" (1032b11–14). The "form in the soul," thus, would be the knowledge of something in its essence. Aristotle continues by sharpening the contrast between the "theoretical" moment and production: "Of the generations and motions just considered, one of them is called 'thinking' [νόησις] and the other 'bringing forth' [ποίησις]; thinking occurs from the principle or the form, bringing forth from the end of thinking and thereafter" (1032b15–17). Needless to say, if, e.g., in the case of the art of building, the "form in the soul" must be that of the house, we have to wonder how such form could possibly be contemplated aside from and prior to the experience of building, and, even before that, of seeking a shelter, of exposure to disruptive events, etc.

40 I owe the expression "visionary animal" to Ramano Màdera, *L'animale visionario* (Milan: Il Saggiatore, 1998).

imaginativeness and "creativity." It does retain the character of "originality" in the sense that it "originates," conceives, incubates, and brings to light, or uncovers something in an originary way. But here "originality" is the function of a "choral," collective generativity. Creativity emerges as an anthropological datum, rather than as the exclusive prerogative of a few individuals. To be sure, there may be departures from the traditional transmitted patterns, and there is a margin for experimentation. The artist may "err willingly," and this is preferable to erring by ignorance (1140b23); "erring willingly" means deliberately setting out to allow for change, to explore different practices and manners of engagement with materiality (from stone to sound) and its secrets. Here, then, resides one of the distinctive features of the "visionary animal": in the capacity for this open-ended engagement with the world, an engagement that cannot be self-contained because always having its fulfillment outside of itself, in what is brought forth, and because always disclosing heretofore unfathomed possibilities, like gaping openings calling for further exploration. Perhaps it is out of profound insightfulness that common parlance, as Aristotle notes, attributes wisdom, *sophia*, to those who excel in the exercise of their art, as in the case of "Phidias the sculptor" and "Polyclitus the statue-maker" (1141a9–12).

5.3.2. Epistēmē

The exploration of *epistēmē* begins with a peremptory prescription. To clarify "what knowledge is," Aristotle calls for precision in speech and avoidance of "similitudes." Curiously enough, however, he goes on to expound a belief, a shared opinion: "We believe [ὑπολαμβάνομεν] that the thing which we know cannot be other than it is" (1139b19–20). The distinction between science and what it is not mirrors the distinction between the scientific and the estimative (deliberative, doxastic) components: unlike what is opined, what can be known does not admit of being otherwise. Yet one should not disregard the dialectical, belief-based character of what is said about science – in spite of the fact that Aristotle explicitly purported to leave belief and opinion outside this discussion. Indeed, it seems that they may be left out as themes, but not as modes of discourse and inquiry, as the *ēthos* of this inquiry.

Epistēmē is said to be "a habit pertaining to demonstration" (ἕξις ἀποδεικτική) (1139b32). In this context, Aristotle also insists on the indemonstrable character of scientific principles. Science is demonstrative, but proceeds from indemonstrables. Syllogism (demonstration), whose conclusion is demonstrated, unassailable knowledge, rests on induction (*epagōgē*, which leads from particulars to universals), that is, begins from the universal inductively given. In other words, the ground for universal-apodictic procedures is the particular, which requires sensation and experience (1139b26ff.).[41] Such is the *arkhē* of *epistēmē*. Aristotle underscores the primary importance of the conviction and trust (*pisteuein*) thanks to which universals may be induced. Indeed, "it is when one is both convinced [πιστεύῃ] and is familiar [γνώριμοι] with the principles in a certain manner that he has knowledge, since he will have knowledge only by accident if he is not convinced [of the principles] more than of the conclusion" (1139b34–5). This claim is repeatedly echoed in the *Posterior Analytics*. Near the beginning of the treatise, Aristotle meditates on the beginnings of demonstrative knowledge:

> since this syllogism proceeds from certain [principles] which are, it is necessary not only to know [προγιγνώσκειν] the first [principles], whether all or some, prior [to the fact or conclusion], but also to know them to a higher degree [than the fact or conclusion]; for that [i.e., the cause] because of which something is always is to a higher degree than that thing, e.g., that because of which we love a thing is loved more than the thing. So if indeed we know [ἴσμεν] and also have conviction [πιστεύομεν] [of a fact or conclusion] through the first [principles], then we know and are convinced of these to a higher degree [than the fact or conclusion], since it is through these that we also [know and are convinced of] what follows. (72a27–33)

First principles are those starting points that, aside from and prior to all demonstration, compel our assent. It is such an experience of trust that makes possible and sustains the subsequent operations of reason yielding knowledge. The "fact" (πρᾶγμα, 72a26) that is subjected to analysis, the fact the scientific knowledge of which constitutes the conclusion of the deductive process, is, to begin with, known as such, affirmed in its most basic constitution in virtue of a certain being disposed (διακείμενος, 72a35), in virtue of the posture of trust. Aristotle must find this inceptive intuition startling, for he immediately restates his point:

41 Let us recall, once again, a crucial statement from the *Posterior Analytics*: "It is also evident that if a faculty of sensation [αἴσθησις] is absent from the start, some corresponding science [ἐπιστήμην] must be lacking, seeing that a science cannot be acquired if indeed we learn either by induction or by demonstration. Now a demonstration proceeds from universals, whereas induction proceeds from particulars. But universals cannot be investigated except through induction . . . and it is impossible to learn by induction without having the power of sensation. For of individuals there can be sensation, and no knowledge of them can be acquired; and neither can we demonstrate conclusions from universals without induction, nor can we acquire universals through induction without sensation" (81a38–b9).

> it is necessary for one to be convinced [πιστεύειν] more of the principles [ἀρχαῖς], whether of all or some of them, than of the conclusion. And if one is to have knowledge [ἐπιστήμην] through demonstration, not only should one know [γνωρίζειν] and be convinced of the principles more than of what is proved, but, relative to the statements opposed to these principles, from which statements there can be a syllogism of a contrary mistake, there should be nothing other than these principles of which one is more convinced and knows to a higher degree, if a knower without qualification [ἐπιστάμενον ἁπλῶς], as such a knower, is to be unchangeable in his conviction [ἀμετάπειστον]. (72a37–b4)

In its unshakable character, conviction transcends itself and its own epistemic insubstantiality, gives itself as a knowing (however ineffable) of principles, as the inceptive knowing (*gnōrizein*) with respect to which demonstrated knowing (*epistēmē*) seems somehow secondary (in fact, derived as well as derivative). Thus understood, conviction constitutes the ground of living and acting in its most primordial liminal manifestation. The beginning emerges as or is constituted through an affirming, a confiding in one's circumstances, before having analyzed and known them. Indeed, all subsequent analysis and knowing will have rested on such confident constitution. Compared with the force of such a fundamental trust, it is the logic of *epistēmē* that is exposed in its fragility or insubstantiality.

The same set of problems is acknowledged in the *Metaphysics* as well, and it is important to emphasize these reiterations. It is as though the same concern would recursively return to haunt investigations apparently remote from each other in character. In the Prelude we variously highlighted the preoccupations, pervasive in this text, surrounding the non-scientific ground of science and the need to re-inscribe the scientific enterprise within the context of sensibility, intuitive-inductive evidence, and, broadly speaking, the experiential and practical domain. At this juncture, let us briefly consider yet another moment in this work, analogously suggesting the excess of first philosophy vis-à-vis science and the difficulties harbored in the apparent separability of demonstrative discourses from the confidence or trust (*pistis*) in their ground, constituting their ground as such. We are at the beginning of Book Eta, in which Aristotle restates the task of first philosophy, namely, seeking "the principles and causes of beings, but clearly qua beings" (1025b3–4). The statement of purpose is variously reformulated in the course of the *Metaphysics*, however, what is at stake in such an endeavor remains gaining an insight into the "end" or "good," that is, into "first causes," finally into "beingness" or "substance" (οὐσίας) (996b12–14). Such a task would seem properly to belong to the sciences, because "every science which proceeds by thinking [διανοητική] or participates in thought [διανοίας] to some extent is concerned with causes and principles" (1025b6–7). However, Aristotle immediately proceeds to offer the following diagnosis of scientific inquiry:

> But all these sciences, marking off some being or some genus, conduct their investigations into this [part of being], although not into unqualified being nor [into their part of being] qua being, and they do not bring forth [ποιοῦνται] any discourse [λόγον] concerning the what-it-is [τοῦ τί ἐστιν]; but starting from the what-it-is [of their subject], which what-it-is in some sciences is made clear by sensation but in others is laid down by hypothesis, they thus proceed to demonstrate more or less rigorously the essential attributes of their genus. (1025b7–13)

The consequences are clear: it rests upon first philosophy to address the primary question (the question regarding the primary) left unaddressed by and within the various sciences. Nevertheless, first philosophy is not science:

> Consequently, it is evident by such induction from these sciences that there is no demonstration of beingness [οὐσίας] or of the what-it-is, but that there is some other way for the clarification [δηλώσεως] [of these]. Similarly, they say nothing as to the being or non-being of the genus they investigate, and this is because it belongs to the same thought [διανοίας] to make clear [δῆλον ποιεῖν] both the what-it-is and the being [of a genus]. (1025b14–18)

The affirmation of being as such, as well as the elaboration of what it is, are less a matter of knowledge, especially of scientific knowledge, than of a certain illumination, of a making perspicuous, manifest (*dēlon*). At stake in the question of principles or beginnings is the issue of primordial evidence.

Yet the "object of knowledge" (i.e., the apodictic conclusion), Aristotle asserts in the discussion of scientific knowledge in the *Ethics*, "exists of necessity" and is "eternal," "ungenerable and indestructible."[42] But this is so as long as and wherever the premises or principles hold. As long as this is the case, the conclusion is indeed necessary, unavoidable in its deduction. In this sense alone is it eternal and immutable. However, principles do not necessarily have these qualities – they may not be unqualifiedly eternal, ungenerable, and so on. This is evident from a moment in the *Posterior Analytics* in which the eternity of scientific conclusions is at once claimed and qualified:

[42] It may be worth specifying that the things that are eternal are not separate, but only are always (e.g., numbers, objects of mathematics). As we shall consider shortly, active and passive intellect is not two, let alone two separate entities.

> It is also evident [φανερὸν] that, if the premises from which syllogism proceeds are universal, also the conclusion of such a demonstration and, we may add, of an unqualified demonstration is of necessity eternal [ἀΐδιον]. Hence there can be no unqualified demonstration and no unqualified knowledge of destructible things, but there may be [a syllogism regarding them] as if in an accidental manner, namely, not universally, but at a certain time and in a certain way. And whenever there is [such a syllogism], the other [minor] premise must be destructible and not universal; it must be destructible in view of the fact that it is by being destructible that also the conclusion will be destructible, and it must not be universal since it will be [true] of whatever is said under certain circumstances but not under others, and so the syllogism is not carried out universally but only regarding something being at this or that moment. (75b22–30)

Scientific conclusions are, indeed, eternal, but only as long as the principles or premises are genuinely universal, that is, incorruptible and not subject to any change. That is why, Aristotle concludes, scientific knowledge has the status of eternity and immutability only regarding matters analogously eternal and immutable. Of all the rest (less than eternal and incorruptible matters), scientific knowledge is as necessary and stable as its principles (i.e., the acceptance thereof) are.

Yet, even with regard to the "universal principles," we should note that their universality means nothing more than their being "according to the whole": they are gathered in accordance to the whole of singular occurrences and, while here we are employing the language of particularity and that of singularity somewhat interchangeably, on the ground of our considerations thus far we should keep in mind that the relation between universal and particular cannot in any way be understood in terms of the concept and its temporal/historical instantiation. In this context, rather, the "universal" arises out of the whole of singularities. In turn, the particulars or singulars impose themselves as other than derivative and indifferently equivalent representations of the same and self-subsisting – as irreducible to posteriority and predictability vis-à-vis the universal. Of course, already such an understanding of particulars in terms of singularity announces the difficulties pertaining to the status of the whole and the possibility of grasping it as such. Indeed, only the assumption of the priority of the universal may grant a viable sense of the whole – of the whole to begin with and of the "as such" itself.

Thus, what should be underlined is, in principle, the relative instability of principles – induced as they are from sensibility, from singularity, and the object of trust or conviction. It is true that, qua principles (i.e., achieved universals, i.e., universals inductively achieved), they differ from particulars and cannot be reduced to them. However, their genealogy or provenance prevents us from thinking that universals and particulars are separable, separate, or even opposed. It also prevents us from considering (superficially, no doubt) the particular as explainable by reference to the universal, and from thinking that there is a logical, and that means essential, priority of the principle or universal over against the particular. In an important sense, the principle is not a beginning, but is, rather, an outcome: that vision "according to the whole" the apprehension of which involves sensibility. As such, it displays a certain paradoxical secondariness.

At any rate, the eternity and immutability of scientific knowledge must be clearly qualified, situated in the broad, comprehensive context of the mobility or changing of principles and in nature. Concerning all beings belonging in this domain, the axiomatic ground is bound to be shifting. Even the knowledge regarding geometrical objects may not be unquestionably stable: even geometry may not in an unqualified way proceed from strictly eternal and immovable principles, since the acceptance of its postulates is indeed subject to negotiation (consider, for instance, the most controversial assumption of Euclidean geometry, namely, that regarding parallelism). Of course, the science of numbers does present itself as a model of universality and immutability; and yet, here we should keep in mind the pervasive reservations that Aristotle advances, concerning its abstractness and formality, its proceeding by ignoring the being(s) in which numbers inhere. In its security, arithmetic entails an alienation from content, that is, from being, which Aristotle does not cease to find perplexing to say the least. In other words, the security or universality of arithmetic is but the counterpart of its partiality or one-sidedness. We are, thus, bound rigorously to conclude, with Aristotle, that only concerning the eternal and divine, that is, the cosmos, the spheres, their circular motion, the first mover(s), can there be science strictly speaking.

Yet again these are, strictly speaking, principles. They are what is studied in and by the "science of wisdom" or first philosophy, which, being the study of principles, is hardly a properly demonstrative discourse. The knowledge that subtends all the sciences, that is, perception of those principles that are common qua eternal and immutable, is not itself science. It is neither a science among sciences nor the science of sciences. Hence, surmising, as Aristotle does in the passage from *Posterior Analytics* just quoted, that demonstrative knowledge *aplōs*, without qualification, is only of indestructible, eternal things (75b24–7), entails an inherent tension or even impossibility. For it is precisely of indestructible, eternal matters that there strictly is no demonstration, because such matters are principles. This is also made magnificently conspicuous in the *Metaphysics*: precisely when the question of the eternal and divine (the unmoved, *nous*) is broached, demonstrative knowledge is shown in its limits, giving way to mythical elocution. It is at this juncture, in Lambda, that Aristotle, with a move as uncharacteristic as it is spectacular, turns to the evidence of myth, or myth as evidence (1074b1–14). "Eternal things" in which, alone, would inhere appropriately enduring and universal principles, seem not to yield to knowledge – neither to give themselves according to the logic of knowledge nor plainly to disclose to knowledge the requisite premises for its beginning. Thus, there seems to be no science, no deductive discourse, adequately presenting the scientific requirements of fixity and necessity. Or else, these concepts must be reframed: science and necessity may be taken to indicate neither formulaic abstraction nor unqualified stability. (Of course, there remains to examine the immutability and immovability of those principles that constitute not the premises of demonstration but the structure and articulation of demonstration, the *how* of the apodictic discourse. This is the crucial issue of the axioms informing derivation, at work in any demonstrating, if you wish, the "logical" rules. On the nature and apprehension of the laws of discourse, ultimately seen as the laws of being, *Metaphysics* Gamma is of course central. We will shortly examine it in detail.)

In light of the foregoing considerations, the question arises concerning where to situate knowledge, *epistēmē*, in the context of the partitions of the rational domain of the soul. It would seem that knowledge rather precisely corresponds to the scientific (theoretical?) part. So far, this "part" appeared to be apart from involvement with desires, embodiment, and sensibility – the only enclave, in the rational region, possibly untouched by the *praxical*. But the preceding remarks on the sensible foundation of *epistēmē* hardly allow for such view of the scientific-theoretical endeavors.[43]

5.3.3. Nous

The inquiry concerning *nous* is introduced as follows: "Since scientific knowledge is *belief* [ὑπόληψις] of universal and necessary things, and since there are principles of whatever is demonstrable and of all scientific knowledge . . . , a principle of what is scientifically known cannot be

[43] On the possibility of considering *epistēmē* as a differentia of trust or conviction (*pistis*), see *Topics* 128a30–8.

scientific knowledge. . . . [W]e are left with intuition [as the disposition] of those principles" (1140b31–1141 a 9; emphasis added). It is significant that, consistent with William of Moerbeke's institution of the Aristotelian Latin terminology, *nous* should be rendered as either "intellect" or "intuition," depending on the context. *Nous* undecidably oscillates in the semantic range disclosed by both terms, while being exhausted by neither. It names the virtue (the "excellent disposition") allowing one to grasp first principles. The intersection of *nous* and aisthetic perception provides the beginning and end (the principle and fulfillment) of induction. That is to say, *nous* presides over the "inductive synthesis" originally connecting particulars and universals, drawing the latter from the former.[44]

If *aisthēsis* provides the ground of induction, *nous* names the intelligent pervasiveness, the movement seeing through the perceived, thanks to which the perceptual object can be traversed, laid bare, and intimately understood. It yields the perceived in its nakedness and transparency, not as an object that has been cognitively mastered, but rather as that which announces itself onto the threshold of awareness in its sudden evidence, disclosing itself in an inarticulateness indeterminately prior to the discursive articulations and mastering mediations. As the sudden, immediate intuition of the universal inherent in the particular, *nous* bespeaks the grasping of axioms and definitions – hence its role in granting principles and, subsequently, in the grounding of science. Across science and sensation, interspersed in both, *nous* lights up the range from sensation to perception of the universal or definition. *Nous* is the element of insight.

Most remarkably, then, *nous* is said to be non-discursive, non-linear, that is, to entail a certain immediacy.[45] As Aristotle repeatedly puts it, it does *not* involve *logos*, "[f]or *nous* is of definitions [ὅρων], for which there is no *logos*" (1142a26–7). This is shortly afterward reiterated in a passage remarkable in particular for its association of *nous* with judgment,

44 On the connection between sensation and perception of universals, see Alexander of Aphrodisia's commentary on *De anima* (83, 2–13), in which it is said: "This comprehension, *perilēpsis*, and the grasping of the universal by means of the similarity among particular objects of sensation, is thinking, *noēsis*; for the synthesis of similar things is already a function of *nous*."

45 The activity of *nous*, simple and indivisible intuition, is often referred to as *thinganein*. Considerations of truth or falsity cannot pertain to such a non-composite touching or reaching out (*Metaphysics* 1051b16–26 and 1072b21).

intelligence, and the practical-deliberative virtue of *phronēsis*, let alone for its rapprochement of the language of nature and that of virtue, habituation, experience. Such considerations represent an outstanding development in the treatment of *nous* and deserve to be quoted extensively:

> Now all matters of *praxis* [τὰ πρακτά] pertain to the order of particulars [τῶν καθ' ἕκαστα] and ultimates [τῶν ἐσχάτων]; for a prudent man should know them, and also intelligence [σύνεσις] and judgment [γνώμη] are concerned with matters of *praxis*, which are ultimates. And *nous*, too, is of ultimates, and in both directions, for of both primary terms [definitions] and ultimates there is *nous* and no *logos*; and *nous* according to demonstrations is of immovable [ἀκινήτων] definitions and of that which is primary, whereas in practical [matters] it is of the ultimate and variable objects and of the other [i.e., minor] premises, since these are principles of final cause; for it is from particulars that we come to universals. Accordingly, *we should have sensation* [αἴσθησιν] *of these particulars, and this is* nous. (1143a33–b6; emphasis added)

Nous pertains to the domain enclosed within the extremes of particularity, on the one hand, and definitions, on the other. Such extremes bound and delimit the space of thinking. In this sense, both extremes are ultimate: they mark that threshold beyond which noetic grasp no longer occurs. In one direction, the ultimate names what is primary or first, that is, the synthetic grasp providing the premises or principles with which demonstration begins and about which demonstration is. In the other direction, the ultimate names what is last or particular, that is, contingent "facts" (*pragmata*), minor premises expressing any variable. *Nous* is of both, and the distinction between *nous* as perceiving definitions and *nous* as perceiving singularities is only perspectival: seen from the operation of demonstration, *nous* provides the principle, the universal; seen from the operation of practical deliberation, *nous* provides the perception of the circumstances to be assessed. Here we come to appreciate the twofold nature of *nous*, as intellectual *stricto sensu* and intuitive or, in fact, sensible. In both cases, *nous* names a certain grounding. Of such an intellectual-sensible grounding there is no discursive knowledge, no *logos*. Indeed, it constitutes the ultimate limit of *logos*, that which remains inassimilable to *logos*.

It is important to underline that Aristole here is not proposing a dichotomy of "practical *nous*" and "theoretical *nous*," as it were, so much so that he emphasizes the fundamental role of particulars in the formulation of universals, and, hence, the implication of sensation in intellectual perception. Indeed, because of this he intimates the conjunction, if not the simple identity, of *nous* and *aisthēsis* – a conjunction that it will be hard to write off as solely applying to some subdivision of *nous* that would concern practical matters alone.[46] After stating the concomitance of *nous* and sensation, Aristotle continues:

> In view of this, it is thought that these [powers] are natural [φυσικὰ] and that, while no one is by nature wise, one [by nature] has judgment and intelligence and *nous*. A sign of this is the fact that these [powers] are thought to follow certain stages of our life, e.g., that such-and-such an age possesses *nous* or judgment, *as if* nature were the cause of it. Hence intuition is both a beginning and an end; for demonstrations come from these and are about these. Consequently, one should pay attention to the undemonstrated assertions and opinions of experienced [ἐμπείρων] and older and prudent human beings no less than to demonstrations; for they observe rightly because they gained an eye from experience [ἐκ τῆς ἐμπειρίας ὄμμα ὁρῶσιν ὀρθῶς]. (1143b6–14; emphasis added)

That *nous* should be "both a beginning and an end" corroborates the unity of *nous* as a matter of both intellectual and sensible perception. Indeed, the beginning-and-end character of *nous* need not even be referred to the practical-theoretical distinction, but can be appreciated by reference to the deductive procedure alone. *Nous* is "both beginning and end": this is so, first of all, because demonstrations "come from" intellectually given premises and "are about" variable issues that, through scientific analysis, come to be clarified in the statement of the conclusion. Qua expressed in the statement concluding demonstration, the variable particulars are "last." Second, however, the reverse is also the case: at a most basic level, variables are in play in the formation of the universals, indeed, the latter are "from particulars." In this second sense, the particulars would be "first" and the universals "last."

We should also highlight that the coincidence, if not the identity, of *aisthēsis* and *nous* is situated within the broader framework of a certain, however qualified, belonging of *nous* in the order of the "natural."[47] According to these suggestions, it would seem hardly possible even to understand *nous* as a virtue in the strict sense of the term. The *aporia* of *nous* begins to be manifest. On the one hand, *nous* comes to be disclosed as

46 Contra Heidegger's claim, in his lectures on Plato's *Sophist* (Martin Heidegger, *Plato's* Sophist, trans. Richard Rojcewicz and André Schuwer [Bloomington: Indiana UP, 1997]).

47 In the *Physics*, an interchangeability of *nous* and *phusis* seems at times to be signaled by certain terminological oscillations: for instance, in the passage 198a6–13 the conjunction of *nous* and *phusis* occurs three times, intimating their equivalence as "first or prior cause" of "the all" (τοῦ παντός).

somewhat discontinuous with the dimension of habituation and repeated practice defining the virtues. It is said to belong in the order of *dunamis*, indeed, to be (*like* sensibility, or even *as* sensibility) a power actualized by nature. In this sense, *nous* designates the unmediated intelligence at work in and as sensation. Yet, on the other hand, the activation of noetic insight, however "natural," appears to be neither automatic nor simply immediate. In fact, the insightful "eye" of *nous* becomes actual *through* time, as though refined and fulfilled by experience. Aristotle insists on this distinction between *nous* and what is simply by nature, "observing" that those with "natural dispositions" but "lacking *nous*" are like a "mighty body" that "mightily stumbles" because "lacking vision" (ἄνευ ὄψεως, μὴ ἔχειν ὄψιν) and that only if one "acquires intellect [λάβῃ νοῦν]" will one's disposition, "though similar to the corresponding natural disposition," be "a virtue in the main sense" (1144b9–14).[48]

Oddly enough, then, *nous* must be understood by reference both to (1) the immediacy of its activation and operation and to (2) a process of "acquisition" in virtue of which *nous* seems to be grasped, to ripen, as it were. The statement that we should "pay attention to the undemonstrated assertions and opinions of the experienced" once again suggests a certain secondariness and non-self-sufficiency of the sciences, recognizing the non-scientific condition of scientific-discursive articulations. Most important, it implies that experience, age, prudence itself are involved in coming to "have" *nous*, in a certain "correctness or conformity of the gaze" – in the "seizing" or "apprehending" (*lambanō*), as it were "at a glance," which noetic perception names. This is in line with another remark just preceding the passage now considered, where Aristotle remarkably associates wisdom with the investigation of nature (physics) and contrasts them to mathematics, which can be practiced even by the inexperienced:

> a young man is not experienced, for much time makes [ποιεῖ] experience. (And if one were to inquire why it is possible for a boy to become a mathematician but not wise or a physicist, the answer is this: the objects of mathematics are by abstraction while the principles of philosophy and physics are from experience; and the young have no conviction [πιστεύουσιν] of their principles but [only] speak [λέγουσιν], while the what-it-is [of the objects] of physics and of wisdom is not unclear.) (1142a16–21)

48 Virtue "in the main sense," here said to be acquired through *nous*, is shortly afterward said to come to be thanks to *phronēsis* (1144b15–17). Aristotle seems somehow to intimate a convergence of the latter and *nous*. As we shall see below in further detail, *phronēsis* seems to exhibit an *insightful, illuminative* function analogous to that of *nous*. See also *Part. an.* 686a28.

Philosophy in its highest accomplishment manifests itself as the practice of reason aware that its own principles exceed reason. It consciously proceeds from experience and recognizes experience as its beginning. This realization constitutes the difference between wisdom and the merely scientific posture (here exemplified by mathematics). In this perspective, philosophy as the exercise of (directed to) wisdom is at one with physics, the study of nature. Indeed, if the principles are a matter of experience, in no way could the pursuit of wisdom be construed as "metaphysics." The latter enterprise would remain an issue, at most, for boys and those who can develop their reasoning only in abstraction from its experiential ground, that is, from content. In this case, *logos* becomes formal, divorced from being, from the trust on which *logos* rests and of which *logos* speaks.[49]

Nous must, then, be understood within the compass of *phusis* or, at any rate, in continuity and coextension with natural-physical motifs. As for the concomitance, if not the identity, of *nous* and *aisthēsis*, let us mention, in the margins of the present discussion, that this hypothesis is further corroborated in the *Physics*. In arguing that the being of nature is a matter of primordial self-evidence, Aristotle says:

> As far as trying to prove that nature is, this would be ridiculous, for it is evident [φανερὸν] that there are many such beings; and to try to prove what is evident [φανερὰ] through what is not evident [ἀφανῶν] is a mark of a man who cannot judge what is known through itself from what is known not through itself. That this can take place is not unclear [ἄδηλον]; for a man born blind may make syllogisms concerning colors, but such a *logos* must be about names without intellectual perception [νοεῖν] [of what the names indicate]. (193a3–9)

The immediacy of the apparent imposes itself, its phenomenal evidence compels assent. Such is the force of what is more known by nature, in virtue of itself, of its being. One, Aristotle urges, must know when it is appropriate to stop asking for demonstrations: demonstrations come to an end at some point, coming to rest in that which cannot be demonstrated, indeed, that which, if attended to, does not require any further discursive effort (to such an extent is discourse, most notably philosophical discourse, pervaded by silence). If/when unable to recognize the ground of evidence and rest in the ensuing trust, one produces uprooted reasonings, alienated from what is. Just like the inexperienced young

[49] See *Republic* 409b–e, in which it said that "the good judge must not be young but old, a late learner of what injustice is."

one considered above or the blind man making syllogisms about what he cannot experience and, hence, cannot conceive (*noein*), in this case one speaks without knowing what one is talking about.

After all, even in the *Metaphysics* we find indications to the effect that noetic apprehension is still thoroughly involved in the sensible and phenomenal. For the moment, let us limit ourselves to mentioning a couple of statements. The first is near the beginning of Alpha Elatton, where Aristotle observes that the attainment of truth may be difficult, for, "as the eyes of bats are to the light of day, so is the intellect of our soul to the objects that in their nature are most evident [φανερώτατα] of all" (993b9–11). The second is in Kappa, where it is said:

> In general, it is absurd to form [ποιεῖσθαι] our judgment of the truth from the fact that the things about us [δεῦρο] appear to change and never to stay the same. For, in hunting [θηρεύειν] the truth, we should start from things that always hold themselves as the same and suffer no change. Such are the heavenly bodies [τὰ κατὰ τὸν κόσμον], for these do not appear to be now of one kind and now of another, but are always the same and share in no change. (1063a10–17)

What can be drawn from both moments is the irreducibly phenomenal character of evidence, and hence of the ground or beginning. Even the intellection of that which is immutable entails a contemplation altogether implicated in sensibility, namely, the contemplation of those (in the plural) that are "most phenomenal," "most apparent" – those that "most shine forth." They, the celestial bodies, are eternal and unchangeable, yet visible. They are unchangeable, and yet they move – whether returning every night in the same configuration (as the fixed stars do), or wandering and changing their positions with respect to one another, all the while exhibiting a certain regularity in their orbiting and always returning back to the same point (as the planets do). Their eternity and immutability are due not to absolute fixity but to a more tenuous manifestation of self-sameness – to the phenomenon of a celestial body coming back to the same, repeating the same course in such a way as to remain by itself, close to itself, endlessly reasserting the same course in proximity of itself and through the same beginning point. The noetic perception, then, seems to be not so much a matter of transcending phenomenality in order to attain a contemplation of the purely intelligible but, rather, a matter of a certain reorientation of the gaze from the things "here," "about us" (*deuro*) to the shining bodies in the sky – a reorientation not leaving the sensible behind, as it were, but thoroughly consistent with it. We shall return to this shortly, when considering the virtue of wisdom.

The concurrence of *nous* and *aisthēsis,* however succinctly addressed here, raises problems analogous to those occasioned by *De anima* 430a11–12 and 24–5, which gave rise to the Peripatetic and neo-Platonic contrast between active (productive) and passive, or actual and potential intellect. So far, despite the tension thus engendered, we have emphasized the coincidence of *nous* and sensibility, while, at the same time, maintaining the unity of *nous* (i.e., suspending the subdivision of *nous* into "practical" and "theoretical"). This means understanding *nous* in its inseparability from embodiment, experience, and practical considerations, in accordance with a number of Aristotelian remarks analyzed. However, precisely by turning to *De anima* and the dominant interpretive tradition, one might object that Aristotle does acknowledge there the distinction between agent and patient intellect as well as the separability (and immortality) of the former. To this paradigmatic objection we must reply by proposing an incipient problematization of the distinction and separation at stake here. Of course, a close consideration of these passages would lead us into the enormous complexities of Aristotelian psychology and theology, which have engendered centuries of interpretive battles and a virtually endless scholarly literature, not to mention trials and executions at the stake.[50] As a study of such matters clearly exceeds the scope of the present work, we shall limit ourselves to delineating our reply in the barest, most minimalistic terms.

The passages in question must be brought to our attention, not so much in order to rely on their clarity, but rather so that their obscurity

50 It has frequently been noticed that the section of *De anima* under consideration (430a10–25) constitutes the pinnacle of Aristotelian psychology and that no other segment from an ancient philosophical text has given rise to such a range of disparate readings. Düring has pointed out that, rather than clarifying Aristotle's doctrine in this text, most commentators have expounded their own thought on the subject. See Willy Theiler, De anima: *Über die Seele* (Berlin: Akademie-Verlag, 1959), and Ingemar Düring, *Aristoteles: Darstellung und Interpretation seines Denkens* (Heidelberg: Winter, 1966). See also Franz Brentano, *Die Psychologie des Aristoteles, insbesondere seine Lehre vom nous poietikos* (Mainz, 1867; rpt., Darmstadt: Wissenschaftliche Buchgesellschaft, 1967). Exemplary of the recent debates, see J. M. Rist, "Notes on *De anima* 3.5," *Classic Philology* 61, no. 1 (1966); S. Broadie, "*Nous* and Nature in Aristotle's *De anima* III," *Proceedings of the Boston Area Colloquium in Ancient Philosophy* 12 (1996); V. Caston, "Aristotle's Two Intellects: A Modest Proposal," *Phronesis* 44 (1999); J. Sisko, "On Separating the Intellect from the Body: Aristotle's *De anima* iii.4, 429a10–b5," *Archiv für Geschichte der Philosophie* 81 (1999); and A. Kosman, "What Does the Maker Mind Make?" in Nussbaum and Rorty, eds., *Essays on Aristotle's* De anima (Oxford: Clarendon, 1992).

may be appreciated.[51] Aristotle introduces the distinction between potentiality and act, and, based on this, between passive and active or productive *nous*:

Since in each genus of things there is something, e.g., matter, as in the whole of nature (and matter is that which is potentially each of these things), and also something else which, by bringing forth [ποιεῖν] all [those things], is the cause and that which brings forth [ποιητικόν], as in the case of art [τέχνη] in relation to matter, these differences must belong in the soul also. On the one hand, the intellect becomes all things [πάντα γίνεσθαι] while, on the other, it makes all things [πάντα ποιεῖν], just like a certain [ἕξις] habit, as with light; for in a certain sense light, too, makes [ποιεῖ] potential [δυνάμει] colors be actual [ἐνεργείᾳ] colors. (430a10–17)

The role of *tekhnē* in the characterization of a certain aspect ("part"?) of *nous* should deserve our attention, especially because, as we noted above, within the framework of Aristotle's reflection on the subject it may be arduous to understand *tekhnē* in purely active terms. Indeed, as we saw above, art may not necessarily, or not at all, proceed unaffected, simply imposing on matter a certain eidetic pattern: creativity and receptivity or responsiveness may demand to be thought together. Along these lines, of course, the recognition of a "productive" mode of *nous* may hardly amount to the isolation of a purely active intellect opposed to a purely passive one. Also, in light of the discussion preceding the passage just quoted, it is unclear whether the intellect would potentially be and become all objects, both in their intelligibility and in their materiality, or only in their intelligibility (429b30ff.). The former would seem problematic, given that even sensation is said to be perception "without matter" (425b24). Finally, the parallel between the bringing forth of *nous* and the work of light reveals "production" in a highly qualified sense. According to this analogy, bringing forth appears to be less a matter of constitution than of laying bare, shedding light on, unveiling in the sense of discovering and uncovering. Such is the sense of the transition from potency to act. In this sense, making is making actual. Aristotle continues:

And the latter intellect is separable [χωριστὸς] and is impassible [ἀπαθὴς] and unmixed [ἀμιγὴς], and in beingness [οὐσίᾳ] it is as an actuality [ἐνεργείᾳ]; for that which brings forth [ποιοῦν] is always more honorable than that which undergoes [πάσχοντος], and the principle [ἀρχὴ] than matter. (430a18–19)

[51] W. D. Ross comments on the relatively negligent writing of chapter III.5 (Aristotle, *De anima*, edited with introduction and commentary by David Ross [Oxford: Clarendon Press, 1961], 296).

It is curious and remarkable that the argument on the separability of the *nous* that brings forth should be based on issues of worth and honorability. Indeed, we could say that this is no argumentation at all – that the separable, unaffected, and homogeneous character of *nous* thus understood is simply posited. Let us continue:

> Actual knowledge [κατ᾽ ἐνέργειαν ἐπιστήμη] is the same as the thing [πράγματι] [known]; potential [κατὰ δύναμιν] [knowledge], however, is prior in time in the one [ἐν τῷ ἑνί] [individual], but, as a whole [ὅλως], it is not [prior] in time. But the [active intellect] is not at one time thinking [νοεῖ] and at another not thinking [οὐ νοεῖ]. When separated [χωρισθεὶς], it is as such only that, and only this is immortal [ἀθάνατον] and eternal [ἀΐδιον] (but we do not remember [οὐ μνημονεύομεν], for, although this is impassible, the passive intellect [παθητικὸς νοῦς] is destructible), and without this nothing thinks. (430a20–5)

Without even broaching the strictly textual difficulties in this section, (e.g., [1] how to understand the temporal priority of potential knowledge, whether or not what is at stake here is the contrast between the experience of a single individual and knowledge experienced collectively, "as a whole"; or [2] the nature of the "it" without which "nothing thinks"), let us simply highlight the clause "but we do not remember." Added as a parenthetical remark, it is hardly marginal. In no uncertain terms, it announces the impossibility, for human beings, of overcoming the strictures of the "passive" or "destructible" intellect – that is to say, the inability simply to transcend the finitude and impurity of human intellect, simply to remember and maintain all intellectual activity in the fullness of its exercise (*ergon*).[52] "But we do not remember" means: whatever we may speculate around an intellect that would never relapse into inactivity, whose insight would never fall back into latency or oblivion, we know nothing of it, at least nothing straightforward. We do not have any such simple experience. We are such that, in virtue of what we essentially are, we forget. And all we may venture to say regarding the simply creative, active intellect, immortal and untouched by mortal conditions, is marked precisely by that – by our forgetfulness, by our inability fully to comprehend and fill with meaning the phrase "active intellect."[53]

52 In this connection, see also the earlier passage at 408b24–9.

53 Following the passages here briefly considered, we encounter even more severe problematizations of the possibility of separation understood in terms of disembodiment. Indeed, while "practical" and "theoretical" *nous* may be discerned according to their different ends (433a14–17), yet Aristotle signals the persistence of the imagination, *phantasia*, even in contemplation, *theōria*. Although the *noēmata* are certainly not *phantasmata*, still, he says, the former cannot be without the latter (432a3–14). It appears, then, that

It is in the crevices of such problems that the battles are fought, most notably between the broad fronts of Thomism, on one side, and Averroism, on the other side (the latter inheriting certain unorthodox Peripatetic motifs, especially through Alexander of Aphrodisia and Themistius). It is here that comprehensive contrapositions come to be crystallized, for instance, that between (1) the view upholding the separability, and hence eternity and immortality, of the whole intellect (passive and active), that is, of the "personal" or individual soul, and (2) the views variously maintaining that what is separable and immortal is transcendent in the special sense of common, shared, received "from outside," as it were, and hence in no way "personal" – whether this is to be understood as (a) the active intellect only (Alexander, Avicenna, possibly the Averroes of the commentary on *Metaphysics* Lambda) or as (b) both the active and passive intellect, where the latter is "in us" but belonging in the intellect transcending us (Averroes). These latter positions, and particularly Averroes' so-called monopsychism, hold noteworthy implications regarding the question of separation and, more broadly, the focus of the present work. Their elaboration of separation does not require dualistic assumptions: the immortal, eternal, and separate is understood not in terms of disembodiment but as non-individual, impersonal. It may be separate in the sense that it is separate from *me*, from *this* particular being that I am. It may be transcendent in the sense that it transcends me, even as it is "in me" ("in the soul"). But then, separation or transcendence comes to indicate commonality, sharing in common – with vital consequences concerning the basic approach to the political.[54]

But let us, to conclude, come back to our reading of *Nicomachean Ethics* Zeta. In addition to the complex cluster of problems laid out above, the further question arises concerning the proper location of *nous* within the

the phenomenon of *phantasia* may not be safely confined to the "practical" intellect (431a14–20). See also 431b13–19, regarding the relation between sensuous/categorial intuition (the "snub-nosed") and perception of geometrical/mathematical beings ("concavity"). Here Aristotle leaves open the question whether or not the non-separate *nous* can intuit that which is separate.

54 Despite many prejudices to the contrary, on Aristotelian terms not even the transcendence of *nous* as the god of *Metaphysics* Lambda should be taken as absolutely unqualified and uncontroversial. On the one hand, Aristotle says that the first immovable mover ("the first what-it-was-to-be) "has no matter, for it is actuality" (1074a35–6). On the other, he also states that this "beingness," however "eternal," "immovable," and "separate from sensible beings," as well as "without parts and indivisible," nevertheless "has infinite potentiality," for it causes motion for "an infinite time" (1073a3–8). In Mu, Aristotle also says that "the good is always in action [ἐν πράξει]" (1078a32).

domain of *logos*. Situating *nous* in the context of reason now appears to be both necessary and impossible: necessary because, as an intellectual virtue, *nous* would pertain to the rational part of the soul, to the part that "has" *logos*; and impossible because, as has become manifest, *nous* is non-discursive and without *logos*. Strictly speaking neither communicative nor communicable, yet the condition of communication, *nous* indicates a non-logical operation in the region of *logos* – a trace, divine indeed, having in itself *nothing to do* with the various doings, with the commerce, negotiations, and procedures of discourse, including demonstrative discourse and practices.[55] Thus, the situation or situatedness of *nous* within the rational "part" is highly problematic, indeed, unrepresentable – for *nous* presents itself as radically discontinuous, even interruptive, with respect to *logos*, even if such a disruptiveness need not entail the separation or separability of *nous*. Thus, we are left with the task of thinking transcendence as otherwise than separation, in fact, as the radical differing of that which belongs together, as the breaking through of that which comes from an outside infinitely unlocatable and placeless, "through the door" (θύραθεν, *Gen. Anim.* 736b28, 744b21).

Above all, what is disclosed in this way is the questionability of the map of the rational domain, both in its internal divisions and in its general designation as "rational." For it turns out that the part that "has" *logos* is not (or not simply) thereby rational or logical. It turns out that the authority of *logos* is not coextensive with the region it inhabits or that such a region exceeds considerations pertaining to extension. *Logos* dwells "there" less as an absolute ruler than as a guest. *Nous*, which is said to be "both beginning and end, for demonstrations come from these and are about these" (1143b10–11), remains somehow impervious to *logos* and lends itself to discourse only in a highly qualified way. Because of this, to whatever extent it may develop in the direction of *phusis*, Aristotle's discourse on *nous* can hardly be seen as a kind of "philosophical naturalism" or, in general, as a "naturalizing," legitimizing move. Indeed, far from discursively appropriating the natural and setting it to work in the service of discursive logic, Aristotle is here exploring the limits of such a logic, those borders at which discourse meets silence and its own end (or origin), the way in which speaking (in its very articulation) is traversed by the unspoken and unspeakable.[56]

55 As pointed out above, *nous* is the condition for *logos*, its abode – that through which, in virtue of which (*dia*), *logos* as well as *dianoia* and all dianoetic exercise become possible.

56 An unspoken or unspeakable so radical, indeed, as to be irreducible to what would "remain to be said," to the projection of a future task.

5.3.4. Phronēsis

"Concerning *phronēsis,*" Aristotle says, "we might arrive at it by looking at [θεωρήσαντες] those whom we call prudent" (1140a24–5). To the fore, in this case as well, is the inductive-dialectical foundation of the discussion. In what we could call an incipient phenomenology of prudence, Aristotle stresses again the reference to the appearances of prudence in a human being:

> A prudent man seems [δοκεῖ] to be one who is able to deliberate well concerning what is good and conducive [συμφέροντα] for himself, not with respect to a part, e.g., not the kinds of things which are good and useful for health or strength, but the kinds of things which are good and conducive to living well on the whole [εὖ ζῆν ὅλως]. (1140 a 25–8)

Phronēsis[57] names a certain power with which the living is endowed, the capacity for a certain sight: the ability of the living to envision itself in its possibilities and most comprehensive finality. It orients the living toward its highest achievement and self-realization (its own good). It has to do with estimation (deliberation), that is, with the root of choice and, hence, of *praxis.* Again, qua bridge between character and rational end, between driving desire and reason, *phronēsis* is not properly, strictly, or purely a part of the rational part of the soul (if there were a clearly demarcated one, that is). Rather, it constitutes a kind of interface between character (action) and *logos.* It is here that we see, in its most multifaceted manifestation, their interaction and intertwinement. As a matter of fact, in the context of the relation of *phronēsis* to the formations of character, *phronēsis* is even addressed in terms of "belief," *hupolēpsis.* It is from the habit named *phronēsis,* says Aristotle,

> that temperance [σωφροσύνην] derives its name, as indicating something which saves or preserves [σῴζουσαν] *phronēsis.* And temperance does preserve [σῴζει] such a belief [ὑπόληψιν]; for it is not any kind of belief that the pleasant and the painful destroy or pervert, like the belief that the triangle has or has not its angles equal to two right angles, but only those concerned with that which pertains to action. (1140b12–16)

As a certain manner of action, that is, of living, temperance preserves *phronēsis,* the belief relative to the good in human life. The relation between *phronēsis* and the virtues of character broadly understood is even reinforced by this remark, for not only is a certain coextension of *phronēsis*

57 I especially refer to the recent and comprehensive study on *phronēsis* by Carlo Natali, *The Wisdom of Aristotle* (Albany: SUNY Press, 2001). See also P. Aubenque, *La prudence chez Aristote* (Paris: PUF, 1963), and P. Ricoeur, "À la gloire de la *phronèsis,*" in J.-Y. Chateau, ed., *La vérité pratique: Aristote,* Ethique à Nicomaque, *Livre VI* (Paris: Vrin, 1997).

and the ethical virtues suggested (*phronēsis* is a belief concerning practical matters), but, moreover, such a coextension is not, as might be expected, a matter of *phronēsis* controlling and informing the other virtues. Nor is it a matter of mere interdependence of *phronēsis* and the virtues. Rather, it is the exercise of the virtues of character, paradigmatically of temperance (excellence in confronting issues of pleasure and pain), which "saves" the belief that *phronēsis* names. The vision yielded by *phronēsis* is rooted in and preserved by excellent comportment.

These considerations lend themselves to further elaboration. *Phronēsis* "gives orders, for its end is what should or should not be done" (1143a9). However, more incisively, phronetic excellence entails a certain effectiveness in pursuing the end. In other words, *phronēsis* "makes us do those things that bring about the end" (1145a6). With *phronēsis*, reason assists in the attainment of the *telos*, and, thus, the accord between deliberation and ends is granted. Again, this minimally entails a kind of interdependence bringing together *phronēsis* and the structures of character. Aristotle asserts that a human being "cannot be good in the main sense without prudence, nor can one be prudent without ethical virtues" (1144b31–3). The same kind of co-implication is restated shortly afterward: "when *phronēsis* is, at the same time [ἅμα] all the others are also" (1145a2–3). But more than this seems to be at stake. Indeed, it appears that *phronēsis* is concerned with the attainment of that which is already brought into view in virtue of the formations of character: "[a human being's] work is completed [ἀποτελεῖται] by prudence as well as by ethical virtue; for while virtue makes the end in view [σκοπὸν] right, prudence makes that which promotes the end right" (1144a7–8). At stake, then, seems to be a certain priority of the ethical virtues (thanks to which the appropriate end would come to light) with respect to the intellectual virtue (whose function would be controlling the conformity and correctness of the means). This necessity of *virtue before virtue*, of virtue before purely *intellectual* virtue, had already been anticipated and will be consistently reiterated.

For instance, in relation to the issue of our responsibility for our own actions, we were reminded that "it is by being persons of a certain kind that we posit the end as being of a certain kind" (1114b24–5; see also 1100b12–15 and 1114a29–b13). And following the mentioned remark on the relation between *phronēsis* and temperance, Aristotle had noted that "the principles of action are that for the sake of which the action is. But to one who is corrupted because of pleasure or pain the principle does not appear [οὐ φαίνεται], nor is it apparent that he should choose and do everything for the sake of this and because of this principle;

for vice is destructive of the principle" (1140b17–20). Vice entails a certain blindness or inability to discern the proper beginning and end of action. In other words, vice (lack of virtue) entails the disappearance of the "principle or origin," which is the moving and motivating force prompting an action. In being "destructive of the beginning" and end, vice makes *phronēsis*, the rational pursuit of the end, irrelevant. In this sense, *phronēsis* cannot be "saved" but only perverted, turned into calculation in the service of vicious goals. Again, Aristotle will say that the end (that is, "the best") as such "does not appear [οὐ φαίνεται] to the one who is not good, for evil habit [μοχθηρία] perverts him and causes [ποιεῖ] him to be mistaken about the principles of action. Hence it is evident [φανερὸν] that one cannot be prudent if one is not good" (1144a33–7). The good is manifested as transcendent in the peculiar sense that it transcends rational grasp. In one and the same gesture, ethical integrity is posited as condition for the possibility of prudence, of correct intellectual assessment. Allowing for the discernment of the end (of the good qua end), the structures of character have always already determined the teleological orientation of the human being as a whole. In fact, "someone prudent is disposed to [right] action (for he is concerned with the ultimates [i.e., particulars]) and [already] possesses the other virtues" (1146a8–10). This insight can be brought to such extreme consequences that, in a rather clamorous gesture, it may even be stated that,

> as there are in the soul two parts which have *logos*, prudence would be a virtue in one of them, that which can form opinions [δοξαστικοῦ]; for both opinion [δόξα] and *phronēsis* are about things that admit of being otherwise [i.e., may or may not be]. And yet, *phronēsis* is not just a habit with *logos*; and a sign of this is the fact that there may be forgetfulness [λήθη] of a habit with reason, but not of *phronēsis*. (1140b25–30)

Needless to say, this connection of *phronēsis*, and hence of the *logistikon* (estimative "part" of the rational "part"), with *doxa*, and hence character, exacerbates the aporetic aspects of the psychological schematization. Indeed, it problematizes the ethical discourse in its systematic delineations. What emerges is the all-too-practical character of *phronēsis*, its inseparability vis-à-vis the domain of the soul addressed as character or desire.

At any rate, the outlook of *phronēsis* has a view to aligning the good of the particular individual in particular circumstances with the finality of the species. It is because of this that *phronēsis* is said to be "a habit with true reason [ἕξιν ἀληθῆ μετὰ λόγου] and ability for actions concerning what is good or bad for human beings" (1140b6–7). Such would be the *theōrēma* of *phronēsis*, that which *phronēsis* keeps in sight. The effectiveness of *phronēsis* would be, in sum, an "effectiveness with a vision," differing in this from mere shrewdness or expediency just as virtue proper differs from natural virtue. The "glance at the *kairos*" here indicated would not be a matter of mere opportunity, but a vision oriented to, guided by, striving for the good. Again, in noticing the difference and connection between *phronēsis* and shrewdness, *deinotēs*, Aristotle observes: "Now prudence is not the power [of shrewdness], but neither can it be without this power. And this habit [prudence] develops by means of this eye of the soul [τῷ ὄμματι τούτῳ γίνεται τῆς ψυχῆς], but not without virtue" (1144a28–30).

It is while elaborating on this point that Aristotle makes explicit the genuinely contemplative, indeed, "theoretical" dimension of *phronēsis*.[58] As he observes, it is because of what was said of *phronēsis* so far "that we consider Pericles and others like him to be prudent, for they are able to contemplate [δύνανται θεωρεῖν] what is good for themselves as well as for others" (1140b8–10). Shortly thereafter, Aristotle mentions again the "power of vision" characteristic of *phronēsis*, when stating that "a prudent being is one which contemplates well [εὖ θεωροῦν] matters which are for its own good and they [who belong in the same species] would entrust those matters to that being" (1141a26–7).

If, however, *phronēsis* is crucially theoretical, where to situate it in the schematism of reason? As readily appears, not only can it hardly be placed in that schematic order, but it even seems to disrupt such order, for it seems to be *both* theoretical *and*, as was demonstrated, all too practical. To complicate the matter further, it should also be noticed that prudence does not appear to be an exclusively human patrimony, as becomes evident in the comparison of prudence to wisdom. After defining wisdom as the knowledge and intuition of the highest objects, Aristotle adds that

> it would be absurd to regard politics or prudence as the best [dispositions], if the human being is not the best of beings in the universe. If indeed what is healthy or what is good is different for humans and for fishes, while what is white or what is straight is always the same, everyone would say that what is wise is always the

[58] Here and in the rest of the discussion, the terms related to *theōrein* are employed according to the primordial meaning of this verb: "to see," "to contemplate," "to witness." Aristotle himself utilizes this language in its everyday connotation. To be sure, in *Nicomachean Ethics* Kappa the language of *theōrein* is most emphatically not associated with *phronēsis* – but neither is it associated with *sophia* per se, and hence with *epistēmē*. Rather, in that context it recurs in conjunction with *nous*.

same while what is prudent may be different.... [59] It is in view of this that people say that some beasts too are prudent, namely, those which appear to have the power of foresight [δύναμιν προνοητικήν] with regard to their own way of life. (1141a21–9)

The capability for a certain *pronoia,* for such a phrono-noetic vision may not be an exquisitely, that is, uniquely human trait. But then, how could it be said, as was indeed said, that deliberate choice (which occurs thanks to prudence and is that over which prudence presides) is an exclusive prerogative, not even of all humans, but of the fully developed human adult (unlike volition, which was said to be common to animals and children) (1111a20ff., 1111b9ff.)? Obliquely and in a fragmentary fashion, in the margins of his main discourse, Aristotle seems to outline a questioning of human specificity with respect to other animals. This means not that human uniqueness is denied but that it is questioned precisely as one tries to delineate it, that the specifically human mode of animality remains *in* and *as* question, that its boundaries are transgressed precisely as they are traced and present themselves in their dynamic shifting.[60]

5.3.5. Sophia

Wisdom, *sophia,* is introduced both as pertaining to the artistic-productive practices and as understood in the strict sense, that is, without qualification. In the latter sense, it is said to be the union of *nous* and *epistēmē,* knowledge coupled with the unclouded perception of its own ground (we variously saw above how the trust in first principles, which is yielded by *nous,* is granted priority over deduced knowledge). Thus, *sophia,* as a reminder of the ancillary role of science, points to knowledge in its perfection, completeness, and regality:

So clearly wisdom would be the most accurate of the sciences. Thus the wise man must not only know [εἰδέναι] what follows from the principles, but also *enact, be the truth* about the principles [ἀλλὰ καὶ περὶ τὰς ἀρχὰς ἀληθεύειν]. Wisdom, then,

59 Though Aristotle does not elaborate further on this, the hypothetical tone would seem to suggest that *sophia* may not be "always the same." At any rate, in and of itself the sameness of that which exceeds reason poses peculiar challenges to thinking.

60 Exploring this topic would involve a consideration of questions concerning the meaning of "having *logos*"; the interpolation of *logos* into animality and, broadly speaking, nature; the difference yet inseparability of reason and nature, hence the manifestations of reason in/as nature. It should also be noticed that the relation of *logos* to animality and nature is analogous to its relation with *nous.* On the question of "having *logos,*" especially in its political implications, see Barbara Cassin, *Aristote et le* logos. *Contes de la phénoménologie ordinaire* (Paris: Presses Universitaires de France, 1997), in particular chap. 2, pp. 25–57.

would be intuition and scientific knowledge of the most honorable objects, as if it were scientific knowledge with its own head [κεφαλὴν]. (1141a16–20; emphasis added)

With *sophia* the convergence of noetic perception and trust (conviction, belief) is accorded the appropriate prominence: in this convergence, *sophia* recognizes its own guide. But, more distinctively still, *sophia* is a kind of knowledge (of *gnōsis*, in the comprehensive sense of the term) extending beyond the realm of exquisitely human concerns. It has to do with the situatedness of humans in what is not human, with the question of the proper place of humans in the *kosmos*. Aristotle's intimation was quoted above, according to which humans may not be "the best of beings in the universe" (1141a22). This suggestion is further elucidated:

And if one were to say that the human being is the best of the animals, this too would make no difference; for there are also other things much more divine in [their] nature than the human being, like the most visible objects [φανερώτατα] of which the cosmos is composed. From what has been said, then, it is clear [δῆλον] that wisdom is scientific knowledge [ἐπιστήμη] and intuition [νοῦς] of the objects which are most honorable by [their] nature. It is in view of this that Anaxagoras and Thales and others like them, who are seen to ignore what is conducive to themselves, are called wise but not prudent; and they are said to have understanding of things which are extraordinary [περιττὰ] and wondrous [θαυμαστὰ] and difficult [χαλεπὰ] to know and daimonic [δαιμόνια] but which are not instrumental for other things, for they do not seek human goods. (1141a35–b8)

On the basis of similar statements, it would not be inappropriate to say that, through the analysis of *sophia*, Aristotle is outlining a kind of critique of anthropocentrism (let alone of androcentrism, to the extent that *anthrōpos* ends up being a certain kind of *anēr* endowed with a certain *logos*). While prudence has to do with the perception, the contemplation of matters concerning one's own good, or at most the good for oneself qua human and, hence, for one's fellow human beings, *sophia* entails the realization that human good is not the good without qualification – that what is good in human terms is not necessarily good vis-à-vis the other-than-human. *Sophia* would, then, have to do with the good (*eudaimonia*) *as such*. It is, of course, of the outmost importance to emphasize that, far from entailing what will have been called a "purely theoretical" posture (demanding transcendence of or withdrawal from worldly engagements), in stretching out beyond matters of human utility *sophia* remains bound to phenomena and orients reflection toward the glowing brilliance of what shines forth. The posture of *sophia* will have been "theoretical" or contemplative in the broad, literal sense of looking at what appears.

Transcendence of the human, the thrust beyond the human, need not amount to a pointing beyond the sensible. Rather, in pointing to the other-than-human, *sophia* is the memory and reminder of the irreducibility of the universe to humans.

In this sense, the contemplation of the good beyond the uniquely human good, that is, of the good *as such*, may not be a matter of "metaphysical" insight, let alone of the contemplation of (and commitment to) some "cosmological" principle – as though, in the final analysis, it were impossible to think together the good at stake in the ethical treatises and that, say, in *Metaphysics* Lambda. Immersed in the contemplation of that which pervades and yet indeterminately exceeds the human, the human being may catch a glimpse of the good as the fulfillment of potential, in each irreducible case, that is, in each even non-human case. That is to say, the human being may glimpse at the good as the realization of possibility according to the uniqueness of each manner of being – at the good as thriving in accordance with the unique range of possibility pertaining to each being, whether each may be gathered by similitude into a class or species or considered in its utter singularity. Contemplation of the good as such would, thus, bespeak a vision of all beings pursuing their own realization, each according to its both specific and individual trajectory.

As was noticed above when discussing *nous* (*Metaphysics* 993b9–11 and 1063a10–17), then, what is at stake in the noetic gaze, which is the gaze guiding and sustaining *sophia*, is not a movement beyond phenomenality, but a movement *beyond us* – where "us" means both each individual as well as the human community as such. What is pointed at, thus, is community beyond human community, belonging beyond human relations and constructions. The gaze of *sophia* is a gaze at what appears – not only near us and among us, here (*deuro*), but all around (*peri*) us, beyond our daily involvements, further away. With *sophia*, the gaze reaches out, pierces through our exiguous settings, glimpses at our broader surroundings, at the cosmos we inhabit, which holds (*ekhei*) us, finally at that which surrounds in the sense that it holds everything together, *periekhei* (*Metaphysics* 1074b3). *Ta phanerōtata*, the shining bodies in the sky, signal precisely that which moves around us at the farthest reaches of the *cosmos*, the fire illuminating and thereby revealing, making manifest the form of our abode. Our wonder at the cause and origin of what we perceive every day, the wonder we harbor, which makes us strive to reach beyond what we perceive and traverse it, as if what we perceive were never enough, never self-contained, as if it would always point beyond itself, as if we ourselves could not be exhausted within the horizontal domain of the everyday – this wonder has less to do with abandoning the phenomenal surroundings than with broadening them, deepening our perceptual field. This wonder prompts us to lift our gaze. It is in such a movement, in taking in the sight of the sky, that we address our questions concerning the fact that all is, and what it is, and why. This "daimonic" awareness lies at the heart of *sophia*: it is the knowledge of things not ordinary and strange, the beyond-human and yet exquisitely human knowledge that knows how to "put us in context." In this perspective, we can envision ourselves, in our pursuits and unique concerns, alongside with that which is utterly other to us, discontinuous and unfamiliar. *Sophia* would name such a "daimonic" knowledge of our distinctiveness as well as our belonging in and with "other."

In connection with the contemplation of the good as exceeding even the human good, we observe a certain overcoming of *phronēsis* – or, if you will, a certain thrust of *phronēsis* itself beyond itself, what could be called a "self-overcoming" of *phronēsis* in view of wisdom. As Aristotle states, prudence "sees to it [ὁρᾷ] that wisdom comes to be," it "gives orders for the sake of wisdom but does not give orders to wisdom" (1145a7–11). In light of such profound accord of the two virtues and, in general, of the analyses carried out so far, it is clear that emphasizing *sophia* can in no way mean abandoning the dimension of the practical in favor of the theoretical.[61] For, on the one hand, prudence was shown as inherently "theoretical" (to be sure, according to the broad semantic range of the Greek term), while, on the other hand, wisdom is shown crucially to rest on sensible-intuitive evidence.[62] Human understanding remains situated even when (in fact, all the more when) at stake is a vision that is not human-centered. Such a vision amounts not to a denial of (or abstraction

[61] The relation between *phronēsis* and *sophia* may be illuminated by that between the medical art and health. In *Eudemian Ethics*, we are told that "medical art is a principle in a way, and health in another way, and the former is for the sake of the latter" (1249b12–13). Their relation points to a certain twofoldness of the principle. The principle ruling action is not reason alone, isolated, as it were, but reason embodied, the reason of (in, as) nature, we might say. Again, the principle is a matter of lived experience. In sum, the point is not whether practical reason (prudence) or "theoretical" reason, wisdom, is prior in Aristotle's discourse, but that theoretical knowledge, wisdom, is inherently practical, and the practical is pervasively theoretical, lit up by intuitive insight and moving for the sake of it.

[62] On the integration of contemplative and practical modes (hence, on the questioning of the theoretical/practical distinction in terms of unaffected contemplation vs. affected involvement in action), see Amélie Oksenberg Rorty's "The Place of Contemplation in Aristotle's *Nicomachean Ethics*," in *Essays on Aristotle's Ethics* (Berkeley: University of California Press, 1980).

from) human positionality but to a broadening of human seeing, to an insight becoming more comprehensive.[63]

With regard to *sophia* as well, the question must be raised concerning its placement in the rational context of the *psukhē*. This most noble manifestation of *logos* (the distinctively human power) points beyond the human. With *sophia, logos* points beyond itself – at least beyond itself qua distinctive of humans. That *sophia* should prove to be exorbitant with respect to *logos* is, in the final analysis, only fitting, if indeed *sophia* is "led by" *nous*, which is not *logos*-related.

Among other things, this understanding of *sophia* contributes to a further elucidation of the meaning of *eudaimonia*. For, indeed, *eudaimonia* signifies an attunement to the daimonic – the movement of humans (qua humans) beyond themselves, in a harmonic merging with that which surrounds them, with that *in which* they belong.[64] At their best, that is, in their fullest realization and manifestation, humans would interrogate themselves about their own position, their own task and destiny, understanding themselves in the midst of and pervaded by that which indeterminately exceeds the human – that which they can neither own nor properly bring back to themselves. This, indeed, would be happiness. In Aristotle's words, wisdom (or the synergy of *phronēsis* and *sophia*, 1144a1–4) "brings forth happiness; for being a part [μέρος] of the whole of virtue, wisdom brings forth [ποιεῖ] happiness by its possession and activation or

63 If, according to what I have proposed heretofore, we consider both (1) the indissoluble bond of *phronēsis* and the structures of character and (2) *sophia* as never entailing a separation from phenomenal-ethical conditions, then the long-standing debate on whether, in Aristotle, we should attribute the primacy to *sophia* alone or to all the virtues together can be seen as less substantial than it appears. Indeed, it seems to be motivated by an all-too-unproblematic reliance on the schematization of the virtues and, in general, on an overly schematic psychology. On the position of "intellectualism" vs. that of "inclusivism," see Stephen White, *Sovereign Virtue: Aristotle on the Relation between Happiness and Prosperity* (Stanford: Stanford UP, 1992). Exemplary of the former position is Richard Kraut, *Aristotle on the Human Good* (Princeton: Princeton UP, 1989). Representative of the latter position are J. L. Ackrill, "Aristotle on *Eudaimonia*," and T. Irwin, "The Metaphysical and Psychological Basis of Aristotle's Ethics," both in Rorty, ed., *Essays on Aristotle's Ethics*; Martha Nussbaum, *The Fragility of Goodness* (Cambridge: Cambridge UP, 1986); and White himself. See also A. MacIntyre, *After Virtue* (Notre Dame: Notre Dame UP, 1988), and John M. Cooper, *Reason and Human Good in Aristotle* (Indianapolis: Hackett, 1986) and *Reason and Emotion: Essays on Ancient Moral Psychology and Ethical Theory* (Princeton: Princeton UP, 1999).

64 Encompassed within such daimonic excess to the human (an excess still most human, yet as such least visible), *logos* and *epistēmē* are disclosed as many-modal, themselves irreducible to a single ground. It may indeed be only with modernity that *logos* is isolated in its logicality, de-naturalized, made both neutral and neuter.

enactment [ἐνεργεῖν]" (1144a5–6). It is in this way, then, that the highest good or happiness, the good as such, is not only envisioned but brought forth and *lived* in virtue of *sophia* (in its essential intertwinement with *phronēsis* and, hence, the structures of character).

Aristotle gives particular prominence to the fact that, thanks to *sophia*, the bond between knowledge and intuition is (re)affirmed. During the discussion of this virtue as well as in later developments, his preoccupation could hardly be more explicit regarding the problem of logico-scientific procedures dissociated from the intuitive directives. This is evident in a passage already quoted in the course of the discussion on *nous*. Here, in drawing a connection between the pursuit of *sophia* and the work of the physicist, Aristotle again emphasizes the involvement of *sophia* in the order of sensibility and experience, in one word, of *phusis*:

> And if one were to inquire why it is possible for a boy to become a mathematician but not wise or a physicist, the answer is this: the objects of mathematics exist by abstraction, while the principles of philosophy and of physics are acquired from experience; and young men have no convictions [οὐ πιστεύουσιν] of their principles but only speak [λέγουσιν], while the nature of the objects of physics and of wisdom is not unclear [οὐκ ἄδηλον] to physicists and wise men. (1142a17–21)

It is, then, possible, within the bounds of mere abstraction, to speak and even derive syllogistic conclusions literally without knowing what one is talking about. It is always possible for *logos* to alienate itself from the matter at stake (from time and experience) and proceed alone (only speaking), while to the "wise or physicist" the matter is "not unclear" – indeed, it may even be perspicuous precisely in its inexplicable inscrutability.

Such considerations will receive further confirmation in Book Eta, which primarily focuses on the issue of continence and incontinence. In the course of that analysis, Aristotle significantly reflects on a certain mode of *logos* dissociated from comportment, that is, a certain *ēthos* of discourse without *ēthos* (without time, practice, and the corresponding psychological resonance), oblivious of itself *as ēthos*.[65] Aristotle acknowledges the danger of such an abstract and ultimately empty *logos*, of its logical claims and self-assertiveness – the danger of a *logos* severed from the context of wisdom (a context irreducible to reason and its discourses). In portraying the incontinent human being, the following remark brings to the fore the problematic character of that potentiality of *logos*, according to which *logos* always inherently *can* turn into formal logic:

[65] Aristotle polemically confronts the sophists as much as Plato does.

> [I]n having but not using [ἔχειν μὲν μὴ χρῆσθαι] that knowledge we observe such a difference in his habit that in one sense he has but in another sense he does not have that knowledge, as in the case of a man who is asleep or mad or drunk. Now such is the disposition of those who are under the influence of the passions; for fits of anger and sexual desires and other such passions clearly disturb even the body, and in some they also cause madness. So it is clear that incontinent human beings must be disposed like these. The fact that such people make scientific statements [τὸ δὲ λέγειν τοὺς λόγους τοὺς ἀπὸ τῆς ἐπιστήμης] when so disposed is no sign that they know what they are saying; for even those under the influence of the passions [i.e., drunkards, madmen] utter [λέγουσιν] demonstrations and verses of Empedocles, and also beginners [in science] string together statements [leading to a conclusion] [τοὺς λόγους], but they do not quite understand what they are saying, for these expressions must sink in [συμφυῆναι], and this requires time. So incontinent people must be regarded as speaking [λέγειν] in the way actors [ὑποκρινομένους] do on the stage. (1147a11–24)

What is here delineated is the arrogance, indeed, the madness of rational self-assertion oblivious of its conditions – what could be designated as a hypertrophy of *logos.* Aristotle could not be more peremptory in calling for extraordinary vigilance around this "logical possibility" – this possibility for *logos* of becoming disembodied and disengaged from worldly commitments (or, more precisely, of construing itself in that way). Let this be noted, in the margins of the present discourse: it is this same *logos* that, in the delusion of its autonomy, can turn to our desirous life and, without any effort to understand and attune itself to it, impose itself on this life. This is precisely what happens in the case of the continent person, and in such a scenario we see the antithesis of the prerequisites of human excellence (and of the perversion thereof, viciousness): we see not the accord of desires and intellectual light, their mutual infusion and intertwinement, but, rather, their dichotomy and conflict, the misery (indeed, the poverty) of dissociation and disintegration, a rift tearing life apart and one apart from one's own life. In the contrast of virtue to both continence and incontinence, then, what is at stake is the distinction between being wise and merely knowing, between being grounded and lacking the contact with the intuitive ground that, alone, sustains and substantiates.

5.4. *Marginalia* on Continence and Psychoanalysis

As a matter of fact, the difference between continence and incontinence merely lies in the management of the conflict lacerating a soul. In the case of incontinence, the conflict is manifest in the open contraposition between desires and rational awareness: reason is "overpowered," as it were, unable to speak or speaking but not heard. In the case of continence, the appearance of an acceptable or even conventionally virtuous comportment is obtained at the price of a violation of the desiring "part" (what Freud will have described as living beyond one's psychological "means," fulfilling societal demands thanks to the repression of instinctual contents). This "part" undergoes the repressive self-assertion of rational determination, which curbs anything in its way and, obsequious to form, devotes no attention to the truth of the psychological condition. In both the case of continence and that of incontinence, communication between the two "parts" and, hence, the possibility of reunion are compromised. Of course, to mend such a situation it would be necessary not only to shake *logos* from its delirium of omnipotence, but also to undertake a thorough analysis of the desiring *psukhē*. Indeed, to bring intelligence and intellectual resources to bear on their own worldly condition (on the *psukhē*, embodied and desirous) would precisely be therapeutic with regard to both *logos* and the *pathē* of the soul. Indeed, if continence as well as incontinence signal a disharmony between reason and desire, such that either reason stays "dormant" or desire is forcefully mastered, these questions need to be asked: Why and how is this the case? What are the desires that can cause this, that can be destructive and lead to an overpowering of reason? For not all desires may operate in such a way. Where does the analogy between destructive desire and sleep or drunkenness break down? For, indeed, configuring incontinence simply in terms of an intermittence of reason, such that reason would momentarily become latent, unavailable, inactive, is not enough. An in-depth investigation of the forces capable of causing such an obscuration is called for. But this means an attempt at a genuine understanding of instincts, drives, and unconscious motifs.[66] Only on the ground of such a comprehension might it be possible to reshape the desirous landscape of the soul, to re-habituate the desires – to cultivate and not fight them.

In the Aristotelian ethical treatises, such an incipient psychoanalysis is not thematized but implicitly acknowledged in its urgency. The emphasis on the difference between virtue and continence makes it abundantly clear that a resolution of conflict between diverging "parts" of the soul is desirable as well as necessary and that the pursuit of the good or

[66] In this regard, see *Magna moralia* 1208a21–30.

happiness will not have rested on any manner of repression of (i.e., ignorance regarding) the passions.[67] More on the analysis of the *pathē* moving us, on this life in and with us, can be found in the *Poetics* and *Rhetoric*, where various manners of elocution, versification, and dramatization are examined also in their affective power. Of course, the necessity of coming to terms with the psycho-physiology of such uncontrollable forces is already announced in Plato. In *Republic* IX, he has Socrates "recognize" that "surely some terrible, savage, and lawless form of desires is in everyone, even in some of us who seem to be ever so measured" (572b).[68]

5.5. Concluding Remarks and Open Questions

Book Eta of the *Nicomachean Ethics* is markedly haunted by Aristotle's concern with the dissociation of *logos* from *praxis*, that is, with a *logos* whose relation to the noetic (i.e., as seen above, experiential) beginning is suspended or latent. At stake is the perplexing interruption of the interplay between *logos* and deportment or character (*ēthos*), an interruption paradigmatically manifesting itself in the psychological configuration of incontinence. In this mode, *logos* can neither acknowledge comportment as its ground nor, subsequently, compellingly guide comportment. *Logos*, that is, presents itself as if it had no ethical provenance and were of no ethical consequence – a *logos* wandering and dangerous. Passages such as

67 In *The Therapy of Desire: Theory and Practice in Hellenistic Ethics*, Martha Nussbaum contrasts the Aristotelian posture vis-à-vis the passions to positions prevalent in later Hellenism. While the latter aim at a transformation of beliefs and passions through rational argument, the former views emotions not as blind, brutal forces, but as "intelligent and discriminating parts of the personality . . . responsive to cognitive modification." Furthermore, Aristotle "calls for cultivation of many emotions as valuable and necessary parts of virtuous agency" (78). See also, despite a one-sided emphasis on the emotions' responsiveness to reason, N. Sherman, "Is the Ghost of Aristotle Haunting Freud's House?" *Proceedings of the Boston Area Colloquium in Ancient Philosophy* 16 (2000).

68 In *The Greeks and the Irrational* (Berkeley: University of California Press, 1964), E. R. Dodds, on the one hand, underscores the apparently reductive Aristotelian assimilation of passion to sleep, drunkenness, or madness. On the other hand, in addition to Aristotle's study of dreams, he reports the interest, shared by Theophrastus and other first-generation students of Aristotle, in the therapeutic value of music. Viewing human life as diverging from the contemplative, solitary simplicity enjoyed by the god, Aristotle recognizes that the question concerning "us" can crucially be broached by examining the non-rational dimensions of our being and comportment. Dodds also points out that, after the impulse provided by Aristotle and his school, these fields of research will undergo extended neglect. See also Jeanne Croissant, *Aristote et les mystères* (Liége: Fac. de Philosophie et Lettres, 1933).

the following elaborate on the simultaneous privilege and responsibility involved in "having" a language (reason):

> animals have no power of deliberating or judging [λογισμόν], but their nature lies outside of these, like that of madmen. Brutality [bestiality] is less bad than vice, but more fearful; for there is no corruption of the best part of a beast, as it is in a human being, since beasts do not have such a part. (1149b35–1150a1)

Accordingly, just as the "mighty body" moving without vision "stumbles mightily," the damage that may be provoked by those having considerable yet corrupted assets is considerable: "[T]he badness of that which has no principle is always less harmful than the badness of that which has a principle, and the principle here is the intellect [νοῦς ἀρχή]" (1150a5–6). Indeed, "a bad human being might do a great many times as much evil as a beast" (1150a9).[69]

While a consideration of Aristotle's immensely ambivalent treatment of animality, however urgent, remains collateral in the present investigation (indeed, an adequate treatment of it would deserve extensive argumentation), the remarks just quoted occasion a few concluding observations. In those reflections, Aristotle appears to suggest a sharp distinction between humans and other animals. Such an essentially hierarchical distinction in kind (indeed, the kind of distinction whose original formulation has typically been taken as unproblematic and unproblematically attributed to Aristotle) would define the animal in terms of privation, that is, the lack of *logos.* And yet, toward the end of the same Book, when considering the possibility of understanding the highest good in conjunction with pleasure, Aristotle once again turns to the question of animality – this time gesturing in a quite different direction. "Again," he says, "the fact that all animals, both beasts and humans, pursue pleasure is a sign that pleasure is in some sense the highest good" (1153b25–6). For, he continues, "all pursue pleasure. And perhaps what they pursue is not the pleasure they think or say they do, but the one which is the same for all, for all [animals] have by nature something divine in them" (1153b32–4). Analogously to the intimations examined above about *phronēsis* as a "having" perhaps not exclusively human, this rapprochement of divinity and animality enormously complicates the relation of humans to the other living beings as well as the connection between the divine and life. Of

69 Maimonides will emphatically recall the possibility of bestiality or brutality in human beings. For, indeed, the desiderative principle may be both generative and destructive.

course, these issues can here only be adumbrated in the faintest, most anticipatory fashion.[70]

What is relevant in the present context is that such a vision, situating the human in the context of the beyond-human (whether the animal or divine or both) and explicating the human by reference to what exceeds it, seems to be allowed by *sophia*. The highest good is perceived by a power indeterminately surpassing *logos*, and that is *logos* guided by *nous*. It is *sophia* that checks the remarkable and also dangerous, potentially destructive privilege of *logos*, orienting it to the good (however the good may be understood, if not known), that is, keeping it rooted in aliveness, in being-alive. For, in and of itself, *logos* would be indifferent to the question concerning the good. And we have thus come full circle to the considerations laid out at the beginning – on ethics as first philosophy; on science as that which structurally *cannot* account for *nous*, for it rests on it; on metaphysics itself, qua investigation into the divine (*nous*), as irreducible to science; on *nous* in its non-rational and non-discursive character, that is, as only liminally speakable, marking the limits of *logos* while remaining *beneath the limen* of *logos*, subliminal with respect to the threshold of knowledge, provoking discourse from out of its literally sublime imperviousness; on *nous* as relating to embodied experience of what is primary and what is ultimate – as ultimately belonging in life, with the living, in action.

70 In this perspective, it would be desirable to read those passages, especially in the second part of Book Theta, where the theme of friendship is developed by reference to communal gathering, as that which structures the political organism in its functional diversity, finally as a figure of the bond of cosmic unity bringing humans together with "the whole of life" in view, within nature or the divine (see, e.g., 1160a8–29, 1162a4–8).

3

Interlude

Metaphysics Gamma

Metaphysics Gamma[1] opens by addressing the first of the *aporiai* laid out in Book Beta, namely, the question: does it belong to one or many sciences to investigate the causes, or principles (995b4–6, discussed at 996a18–b26)? As Aristotle notes, the issue was already anticipated in Book Alpha:

All believe that what is called wisdom is concerned with the first causes and principles. So, as stated before, someone experienced seems [δοκεῖ] to be wiser than one who has any of the sensations, an artist [τεχνίτης] wiser than one who is experienced, a master artist [ἀρχιτέκτων] wiser than a manual worker [χειροτέκνου], and the theoretical [sciences seem to be wisdom] to a higher degree than the productive [sciences] [αἱ δὲ θεωρητικαὶ τῶν ποιητικῶν μᾶλλον]. Clearly then, wisdom is the science of certain causes and principles. (981b28–982a3)

Aristotle proceeds to illuminate this point further when he speaks of "the science taken in the highest degree":

such is the science of that which is knowable [ἐπιστητοῦ] in the highest degree; and that which is knowable in the highest degree is that which is first and the

[1] In elaborating the discussion of this treatise, the following studies have been especially relevant: Emanuele Severino, trans., introduction, and commentary, *Aristotele: il principio di non contraddizione.* Libro quarto della *Metafisica* (Brescia: La Scuola, 1959); T. H. Irwin, *Aristotle's First Principles* (Oxford: Clarendon, 1988); and the remarkable introductory essays by Barbara Cassin and Michel Narcy in their critical edition of the text of *Metaphysics* Gamma (*La décision du sens: le livre Gamma de la* Métaphysique *d'Aristote* [Paris: Vrin, 1989]). I have also fruitfully consulted, among others, the following essays by Enrico Berti: "Il principio di non contraddizione come criterio supremo di significanza nella metafisica aristotelica," in *Studi Aristotelici* (L'Aquila: *Methodos* 7 [1975], 61–88); "Il valore 'teologico' del principio di non contraddizione nella metafisica aristotelica," in ibid., 89–108; and "La critica allo scetticismo nel IV libro della *Metafisica* di Aristotele," in *Nuovi Studi Aristotelici,* vol. 2 (Brescia: Morcelliana, 2005), 195–207.

causes, for it is because of these and from these that the other things are known [γνωρίζεται], and not these because of the underlying subjects. Finally, the most commanding [ἀρχικωτάτη] science, and superior [μᾶλλον ἀρχική] to any subordinate science, is the one which knows [γνωρίζουσα] that for the sake of which each action is done, and this is the good in each case [τἀγαθὸν ἑκάστου], and, comprehensively, the highest good [τὸ ἄριστον] in the whole of nature. (982b1–7)

The convergence of the language of cause and that of the good is of utmost importance. The pursuit of the highest, first, and ultimate principles and that of the good coincide, and are "science in the highest degree," that is, not any kind of demonstrative procedure. Note, indeed, how such a science is said to know in the mode of *gnōrizein*. Aristotle continues to illuminate the character of this science shortly thereafter. Oscillating between the language of *phronēsis* and that of *epistēmē* (982b19–24), he observes that "clearly, then, we do not seek this [science] for any other need; but just as a human being is said to be free if he or she is for his or her own sake and not for the sake of somebody else, so this alone of all the sciences is free, for only this science is for its own sake" (982b24–8). A further elaboration of this follows almost immediately:

the most divine [science] is the most honorable, and it would be most divine in only two ways: if god above all would have it, or if it were a science of divine matters. This science alone happens to be divine in both ways; for god is thought [δοκεῖ] by all to be one of the causes and a certain principle, and god alone or in the highest degree would possess such a science. Accordingly, while all the other sciences are more necessary than this, none is better. (983a5–11)

We should highlight the terminological proliferation characteristic of Aristotle's attempts to articulate such a science. As recalled, the science of wisdom is said to pertain to (first) causes and principles (or origins), to that which is "knowable in the highest degree," to the divine (and that means to the god, the good, and the ultimate end). However, we should anticipate that the science of wisdom is also addressed as the science of being(s), the science of substance(s), the science of demonstration, the science of nature (and that may mean [1] of nature itself, [2] of nature as that which is, [3] of the nature of that which is). In the final analysis, this designates that which we call philosophy in its highest, primordial, and governing sense: first philosophy, itself "most divine."

The varied terminology encountered in this context is noteworthy, in that it seems to indicate not so much the heterogeneity of the treatises gathered under the heading of *Metaphysics* (as has been paradigmatically argued by Werner Jaeger), let alone Aristotle's inconsistency or lack of rigor. Rather, at stake seems to be the essential complexity inherent in the subject matter; for the subject matter seems to admit of (indeed, seems to require) being said in many ways. Thus, we are confronted with a subject matter that yields itself essentially in light of many-ness. We are confronted with the essential many-way-ness, if not the equivocity, of being or of what is first. At stake is, from the start, the relation between what is first and *logos.*

1. *APORIAI* OF THE SCIENCE OF "BEING QUA BEING"

As pointed out, then, Book Gamma begins by addressing the first *aporia.* The elaboration it provides, too, is in line with the discussion in Book Alpha recalled above. It pertains to one science to investigate first principles and causes:

> There is a certain science which contemplates [θεωρεῖ] being qua being [τὸ ὂν ᾗ ὄν] and what belongs to it in virtue of itself [καθ' αὑτό]. This science is not the same as any of the so-called "partial sciences"; for none of those sciences examines [ἐπισκοπεῖ] being qua being [τοῦ ὄντος ᾗ ὄν] according to the whole [καθόλου], but, cutting off some part of it, each of them contemplates [θεωροῦσι] the attributes of that part, as in the case of the mathematical sciences. Now since we are seeking the principles and the highest causes, clearly these must belong to a certain nature [φύσεώς τινος] in virtue of itself [καθ' αὑτήν]. If, then, also those who were seeking the elements of beings [στοιχεῖα τῶν ὄντων] were seeking these principles, these elements too must be elements of being [τοῦ ὄντος], not according to an attribute, but qua being. Accordingly, it is of being qua being that we, too, must find the first causes. (1003a21–32)

The task at hand is lucidly formulated: investigating being qua being means individuating (its) first principles or causes – the first principles or causes of being qua being, or (which is the same) first principles or causes as such. The science of being, then, is to investigate into the first and highest elements of being, and is to do so by investigating beings.

This is of the utmost relevance. The difference between the "partial sciences" (such as mathematics and, we may add, physics narrowly understood) and the science of being is not a shift in focus from beings to being, as though the investigation regarding being were other than and separate from that regarding beings. Rather, the shift at stake in the science of being is from the examination of a part, aspect, or attribute of being to the examination of being as such, as a whole, that is, of what belongs to being not according to an attribute but in virtue of being itself considered in its wholeness. What belongs in such a way is understood as principle or cause. It is this transition from the partial or accidental to the whole, and hence to principles, that marks the science of being. As for the way in which this science is carried out, it still regards beings. It is through the consideration of what belongs to beings (to a being, to "a certain nature") in virtue of themselves that being may come to be contemplated. It is through the consideration of the principles, of the highest "elements of beings," that being is approached and glimpsed. For, qua principles, "the elements of beings . . . must be elements of being . . . qua being" (1003a28–31). The shift from mathematics to the science of wisdom is not thematic (from one "subject matter" to another) but concerns *how* the *same* is contemplated.

We should note, in this discourse, the gathering of the language of being and beings as well as, even more crucially, of being and nature. The latter juxtaposition is amplified in the lines immediately following this initial statement. Here Aristotle defines more decisively the connection between being and nature or, minimally, between being and nature understood in a certain way: "Being is said in many ways, but all of these are related to a certain nature, one and single [πρὸς ἓν καὶ μίαν τινὰ φύσιν], and not equivocally" (1003a33–4). The science of being may be decisively connected with physics, at least with physics comprehensively construed, that is, not as a "partial science."

Shortly thereafter, Aristotle proceeds to address the second *aporia* laid out in Book Beta, addressing the question: would such a science as that just defined pertain only to the first principles of substances, or also to the first principles of demonstration (995b5–10, discussed at 996b26–997a15)? A conspicuous part of Book Gamma addresses this question. I confine myself to quoting the following segment:

> We must state whether it belongs to one or to a different science to inquire into what in mathematics are called "axioms" and into substances. It is evident that the inquiry into these belongs to one science and to the science of the philosopher; for the axioms *belong to all beings and are not proper to some one genus apart from the others.* And everyone uses them, since they *are of being qua being,* and each genus is [a being]. However, they use them only to the extent that they need them, that is, as far as the genus extends, with regard to which they carry out demonstrations. So, since it is clear that the axioms *belong to all beings qua beings* (for this is common to them), the contemplation [θεωρία] of these axioms belongs also to one who is to know [γνωρίζοντος] being qua being. Because of this, no one who examines only a part of being, such as the geometer or the arithmetician, tries to say anything about them, whether they are true or not, except for some physicists who have done so for an appropriate reason [εἰκότως]. (1005a19–32; emphasis added)

Again, Aristotle underscores that it is through the examination of what belongs to "all beings qua beings," that is, through the examination of what is common to beings as a whole, that one may come to know "being qua being." The statement also hints at the proximity between such an inquiry and that of "certain physicists." Irreducible to a "specialized" science, physics may be *par excellence* the study of beings as a whole, that interrogation of beings that is concerned with their principles.

Quite robustly, the statement asserts the unity and inseparability of formality and substantiality, of the structure of logico-mathematical procedures and the investigation into that which is – of logic and ontology. The axioms "belong," inhere in beings as such, as a whole. More precisely, they are what all beings share in common. In this distinctive sense, the inquiry regarding axioms is at one with that regarding being itself, indiscernible with respect to it. Again, far from exhibiting the partiality characteristic of the mathematical disciplines, physics (the investigation concerning *phusis*) appears to address the question of being and that of the axioms precisely in their belonging together, and to do so for altogether not accidental reasons. This suggests a certain convergence of physics and philosophy or, indeed, first philosophy. Aristotle continues:

> Clearly, then, it is the task of the philosopher, that is, of the one who investigates all substances insofar as they by nature come under his or her science, to examine also the principles of the syllogism. Now, it is fitting for one who is to have knowledge in the highest degree [μάλιστα γνωρίζοντα] concerning each genus to be able to state the most certain principles of things in that genus, so that one who is to have such knowledge of being qua being, too, must be able to state the most certain principles of all things. This is the philosopher, and the most certain principle of all is that about which it is impossible to think falsely; for such a principle must be most known [γνωριμωτάτην] (for all may be mistaken about things which they do not know [γνωρίζουσιν]) and also be non-hypothetical. For a principle which one must have if one is to understand anything is not a hypothesis; and that which one must know [γνωρίζειν] if one is to know [γνωρίζοντι] anything must be in one's possession for every occasion. (1005b5–17)

The sequence of considerations examined thus far announces the discussion of the ultimately first, most certain, and most known principle: the principle informing all axiomatic structure as well as the articulation and unfolding of being qua being, that is, qua "all beings." Let us try to follow Aristotle as he begins to uncover such a supremely eminent principle. What will come to light, and this is crucial to the thesis sustained throughout this study, is precisely a certain ethical stratum sustaining the entire discussion and assertion of the absolutely first axiom. Let it be restated that the first and ultimate principle, which is by definition "most known," cannot as such be demonstrated. Knowledge of principle(s), which is knowledge in the highest degree, is not scientific knowledge, *epistēmē*, in the strict (syllogistic, demonstrative) sense. Again, the pervasiveness of the language of *gnōrizein* should not go unnoticed. First philosophy is science (of wisdom, of being) in a highly qualified sense. Yet that which, from a strictly scientific point of view, would be qualified knowledge is the most authoritative, most commanding knowledge – the knowledge that, while not scientific, grounds science.

2. THE PRINCIPLE "BY NATURE"

Aristotle proceeds to lay out the absolutely first principle in the following terms:

> Clearly, then, such a principle is the most certain of all; and what this principle is we proceed to state. It is: The same thing cannot at the same time both belong and not belong to the same object and in the same respect (and all other specifications that might be made, let them be added to meet logical objections). Indeed, this is the most certain of all principles; for it has the specification stated above. For it is impossible for anyone to believe something to be and not to be, as some think Heraclitus says; for one does not necessarily believe what he says. If, then, contraries cannot at the same time belong to the same subject (and let the usual specifications be added also to this premise), and if the contrary of an opinion is the negation of that opinion, it is evident that the same person cannot at the same time believe the same object to be and not to be; for in being mistaken concerning this that person would be having contrary opinions at the same time. It is because of this that all those who carry out demonstrations make reference to this as an ultimate opinion. This is by nature a principle also of all the other axioms. (1005b17–33)

That which will have been called "principle of non-contradiction" finds here its first thematic formulation (though it is anticipated already in Plato's *Republic*). On the ground of what has been laid out so far, a few observations are in order. We should, first of all, investigate further the relation between being and axiom – more pointedly, between being and the principle of non-contradiction. The latter applies to beings, to things in their multiplicity and singularity and, at once, also yields a structural insight into being as such, as a whole. Indeed, we may venture to say that this principle *is* being, in the sense that it is indiscernible from being. Once again, investigating being qua being, according to the whole, means investigating its principle(s). The principle of non-contradiction is indiscernible from being qua being, that is, qua "all beings": it is indiscernible from being in its becoming, that is, in and as spatio-temporality. In other words, this principle may be understood as the mode and condition of being's eventuation – that is to say, the very mode of being's self-articulation into and as beings in their becoming. Indeed, we need to underline these ineliminable indices of perspective and temporality, which we could call aspectival and temporal indices: any thing, indeed, all things, cannot be and not be characterized in a certain way *at the same time* and *in the same respect.*

2.1. Principle as Being

Thus, in one and the same gesture, the principle of being is exhibited as a principle of beings, of substances in their particularity. It is exhibited as belonging to being and to beings, or, rather, as a principle of *being qua beings*, as a principle of *being qua becoming*. It makes manifest the common (shared) structure of the becoming of beings, revealing its most basic truth. Aristotle is suggesting that being (or a being) in its occurring cannot admit of self-denial: not at the same time and in the same respect. To be sure, self-denial (along with the concomitant contradictory beliefs) does mark the spatio-temporal unfolding of being – the flowing of any thing into alterity, any thing ultimately being resolved into another, even its other, its dissipation. Contradiction, then, bespeaks temporality and signals finitude, the ephemeral character, instability, and reversibility of all that is – for the becoming of any thing does indeed entail constant oscillation between contraries and even development as self-negation. However, at any given moment and in any particular respect, contradiction is impossible, in fact, inconceivable.

The principle of non-contradiction does not amount to a denial of irreducible complexity, to a constitutively metaphysical attempt at capturing the flow of becoming, its infinite richness, within the logic of contraries, of binary oppositions, of the contrast of being and non-being. Rather, the irreducible complexity inherent in becoming, in its time and manifoldness, is what the principle at once makes possible, does justice to, and explicates. In stating the impossibility of contradiction at the same time and in the same place (*hama*), the principle grants differentiation and determinacy and, thus, safeguards radical difference, the utter singularity and uniqueness of each moment of becoming, in each facet, however relentlessly passing away. For, far from being a matter of indeterminacy or confusion, complexity and difference take place in and as the ongoing mutability of the determinate. As Aristotle will notice later on, in Book Kappa, "the thing in motion must be in that from which it will be moved and not be in itself, must then be moving into another thing, and must finally become in it; but then two contradictories cannot be true of it in each of these at the same time" (1063a19–21).

2.2. Principle as Thinking

At the same time, the principle of non-contradiction is constitutive of thinking, in the sense that it lays bare the most basic structures of thinking. For such a principle concerns not only beings in their being, but also our experience, indeed our beliefs and opinions thereof. Such a principle concerns not only the being of beings but also, most importantly, the being of this being that we are – the being of this being that perceives beings as such and perceives itself as a being. In other words, the principle informs *what* we undergo, think, and say as well as the structure, the *how*, of our undergoing, thinking, and speaking. The principle of being, or principle as being, at once structures the manner and communication (transmission, propagation) of our perceiving, whether sensible, intuitive, or otherwise. Thus, such a principle signals the unity of thinking and content: of thinking, understood as the constellation of perception in the broad sense, but also as intending, pointing toward, wanting to say (meaning); and of content, as that which is perceived, meant, and said. Just as things cannot be and not be such and such in the same respect and at the same time, so one cannot mean and not mean a certain content in the same respect and at the same time.

What becomes prominent in this context is a certain psycho-phenomenological stratum of signification, in fact, the psycho-phenomenological ground and origin of signification. Propositions cannot be empty, merely formal. The speaker must mean what she says, must discern what she says as meaningful. One speaks only from belief, that is to say, from conviction regarding some thing or other, thereby intending or meaning some thing or other. Differently put: perceiving, opining, and their articulation through and as *logos* are understood in their unity as well as in their coherent following things as they unfold. In their unity, thinking and speaking adhere to the dynamic configuration of things, to their self-disclosure, which admits of no contradictory view at the same time and in the same respect. When such an adherence to things, to beings in their becoming, is suspended, one faces meaninglessness, or even folly, that is, uprootedness vis-à-vis the necessity of what is.

Being, thinking, and meaningfully speaking appear, thus, to share the same condition(s). They are indissolubly intertwined in the discussion in Book Gamma.

To recapitulate, there is one science about both principles of being and principles of demonstration. For, indeed, axioms belong to being qua being in its articulation, in its spatio-temporal unfolding, and hence to all beings qua beings. First philosophy is not only the science interrogating beingness, *ousia*, but also the science interrogating itself as it interrogates beingness, that is, the science thinking itself in its possibility and principle(s). Thus, it harbors a self-reflective character.

2.3. The Ethics of First Principle(s)

2.3.1. Indemonstrability

Aristotle goes on to say that the principle of non-contradiction just laid out cannot as such be demonstrated. At stake, once more, is the defenseless undeniability of first principles. They compel assent *in deed*, aside from and prior to the logic of defense (or logic *as* defense). And yet that which, in the order of *logos* (of science qua syllogism), appears as the defenselessness and fragility of the indemonstrable, is the prerogative of that which is in and of itself "most known," prior in the order of being. That which is "most known" enjoys such a primacy *in the order of being* that, indeed, it is prior *to the order of ontology* strictly understood, that is, understood as the discourse of the knowledge of being. Ontology does not exhaust the question of being.

That which is "most known" cannot be known demonstratively, for it is indeterminately prior to demonstration. However, those who argue against such a principle *can* be refuted. They can be refuted not on their own terms, that is to say, not merely in *logos*, but rather on the ground of their behavior in context. The argumentation by which Aristotle proceeds to delineate the possibility, indeed, the inevitability of such a refutation, is not apodictic. Instead, in its gesturing to that which is irreducible to demonstration, in its appealing to evidences prior to demonstration, such an argumentation remains open: a *logos* open to that which exceeds *logos*, or, which is the same, a *logos* showing in its openness the irreducibility of *logos* itself to demonstration. Indemonstrability entails neither paralysis, whether discursive or practical, nor the indifference of relativism: there where *logos* cannot proceed demonstrably, it can be guided by experience and speak out of such an otherwise than scientific determination.

As we shall see, Aristotle's argumentation at this juncture is twofold. In the first place, he will state that the education that each has received is prior to scientific inquiry and argument. That is to say, education shapes the outlines, delineation, and limits of scientific inquiry and, more broadly, of discourse. On a most basic level, education has always already determined the recognition of what can and what cannot be demonstrated. Second, it will turn out that, to the extent that the opponents of the principle of non-contradiction argue against it, they are not indifferently also arguing in its support. That is, they do not indifferently hold a position and its contrary, for, if they would do so, their speaking would lack meaning and they would be saying nothing at all. Thus, in defending their position and not also, at the same time, its contrary, they in fact destroy their position and show it as untenable. For they confirm the principle they set out to reject, that is, confirm the impossibility of contradiction at the same time and in the same respect. Ultimately, despite what people say when they reject the principle of non-contradiction, they themselves cannot believe what they say. While they may hold this position, they do not act according to their own *logos*. Their actions reveal the abstractness and alienation of their words from *praxis*. They either do not realize what they are saying or speak contentiously.

Here we finally come to illuminate the ethical or practical substratum of the entire discussion. For these people who argue against the principle of non-contradiction, propositions are empty – for their propositions are dissociated from their perceptions, experiences, and actions. Their propositions contradict the way they live as well as the way of things. But let us follow Aristotle's twofold elaboration, starting with the issue of education:

> There are some who, as we said, say that it is possible for the same thing to be and not to be and also to believe that this is so. Even many physicists use this language. We, on the other hand, have just posited that it is impossible to be and not to be at the same time, and through this we have shown that it is the most certain of all principles. Some thinkers demand a demonstration even of this principle, but they do so because they lack education; for it is a lack of education not to know [γιγνώσκειν] of what things one should seek a demonstration and of what one should not. For, as a whole, a demonstration of everything is impossible (for the process would go on to infinity, so that even in this manner there would be no demonstration). If, then, there are some things of which one should not seek a demonstration, these thinkers could not say which of the principles has more claim to be of this kind. (1005b35–1006a11)

Seeking demonstration of everything betrays a lack of education, indeed, of speculative rigor. For demonstrating everything is impossible. It is here that the problem of infinite regress intersects with the discussion of non-contradiction. The principle of non-contradiction brings regress in the demonstrative chain to a halt. In turn, the argument of infinite regress explains the indemonstrability of the principle. Aristotle continues by highlighting the nonsensicality of the opponents' position:

That the position of these thinkers is impossible can also be demonstrated by refutation, if only our opponent says [λέγῃ] something; and if he or she says nothing, it is ridiculous to seek an argument [λόγον] against one who has no argument insofar as he or she has no argument [λόγον], for such a person as such is indeed like a plant. Demonstration by refutation, I may say, differs from demonstration in this, that one who demonstrates might seem to be begging the basic question, but if the other party is the cause of something posited, we would have a refutation but not a demonstration. The principle for all such [arguments] is not to demand that our opponent say that something is or is not (for one might believe this to be a begging of the question), but that what he or she says should at least mean [σημαίνειν] something to him- or herself as well as to another; for this is necessary, if indeed he or she is to say anything. For if what he or she says means nothing, such a person could not argue either by him- or herself or with another. But if one grants this, there will be a demonstration; for there will already be something definite [ὡρισμένον]. But the one who is the cause [of something granted] is not one who demonstrates but one who submits [ὑπομένων]; for while he or she denies argument he or she submits to argument [ἀναιρῶν γὰρ λόγον ὑπομένει λόγον]. Besides, one who has granted this has granted that something is true without a demonstration, so that not everything can be so and not so. (1006a11–28)

Such a refutation of the opponents does not require that they say anything specific – that they affirm (or, correspondingly, deny) this or that. They would not be willing to grant anything of that kind, precisely because they wish to assert that one may indifferently assert and deny something at the same time and in the same respect. However, the refutation does not rest on *what* they say, but simply on the fact *that* they say anything, that is, that they mean something, that what they say has meaning, whether they are speaking to themselves or to another. There can be no meaning, no meaningful speaking, in holding a position and its contrary at the same time and in the same regard. In fact, listening itself, listening with understanding, would become impossible under such circumstances. The conditions would be lacking for communication – for conveying meaning, whether across oneself or across the space shared with others. In other words, denying the principle of non-contradiction means denying the very operation of *logos*, in *any* of its enactments. If the principle of non-contradiction grants the conditions for *logos*, rejecting the principle amounts to rejecting *logos* – being "like a plant." Accordingly, regarding the opponent who says something, anything whatsoever, Aristotle observes: "while one denies *logos* one submits to *logos*" (1006a26).

Once again, we are brought to contemplate how the principle of non-contradiction constitutes the very condition of meaning. Meaning bespeaks orientation, non-indifference, things being "this way and not that," the taking place and taking shape of determinacy, which may be undone but not at the same time and in the same respect – which may be undone according to time and aspect. The bare phenomenon of "taking a stand" (one stand and not also, simultaneously, its contrary) will always already have practically revealed the principle of non-contradiction at work.

2.3.2. *Meaning*

Aristotle emphasizes dialectic – the dialectical and pre-demonstrative dimension of interaction and, in fact, of *logos* itself. Here *logos* itself is elaborated in terms that exceed *logos* qua strict syllogistical or demonstrative procedure, in terms of the ability to engage in speaking, which involves listening, taking in what is said. Meaning emerges prior to the processes that provide proof. It emerges out of experience and its circulation, its being shared. Prior to *logos* as proof, *logos* presents itself in and as *dialogos*.

Logos is meaningful: it "has" meaning, it carries a configuration of meaning, and this means a directionality. That *logos* is neither meaningless nor indifferently admitting every content and its contrary is demonstrated by the very fact that even the alleged opponents of the principle (of non-contradiction) have an argument. They do so precisely *qua opponents*. They hear the *logos* of the principle in its meaningful definiteness and respond with their own *logos*. In articulating an argument, in discussing and exposing their discourse, in listening and replying to the one they oppose, they performatively demonstrate that they take meaning (determinacy, definiteness) as the condition of the engagement. But the possibility of meaning is precisely what the principle of non-contradiction sets out to explicate, ground, and preserve. Hence, the opponents are refuted by their *ēthos* itself, by their practical and factual involvement in dynamics of meaning, that is, in its dialogical articulation. In taking a stand against the principle and arguing for the indifferent possibility of meaninglessness, they speak in a way that is dissociated from their comportment. What their posture shows is contradicted or negated by their words.

It is difficult, in this connection, not to recall the discussion of incontinence in the *Nicomachean Ethics*, focusing on the detachment of *logos* from experience, on the way in which *logos* may become alienated from the meaningful, orienting structures of the practical, of the realm of action. At stake in the emptiness of the propositions of those who argue against the principle is a kind of ethical failure. It is as though, in speaking in such a way, one would fail to contact oneself, to reach and catch up with oneself. One would speak in such a way only contentiously, with no experience fulfilling one's own statements, without those statements being filled, made complete, by the content that is one's own living. In the final analysis, the problem of incontinence, *akrasia*, indicates not simply a lack of power, but rather a specific inability: the inability to contain – to contain oneself, that is, to contain and hold together one's *logos* (reason, judgment) and one's emotions and drives, to gather and integrate them, mixing them, as it were, in the same *kratēr*. Incontinence would precisely bespeak that inability to hold together and harmonize, that disintegration that makes one's *logos* separate from what is the case, and therefore barren, one-sided. For *logos*, unmixed with respect to life, becomes unconditional, at once overpowering (or even omnipotent) in its claim and impotent in its reach. In this sense, we notice the concomitance of the features of impotence and absoluteness – of being *akratēs* (impotent, uncontrolled, or immoderate; from *krateō*, "to enjoy strength and power") and *akratos* (pure, unmixed, or absolute; from *kerannumi*, "to mix," and hence "to temper").[2]

Ultimately, the principle of non-contradiction is intrinsically related to the ethics of discourse. To be concerned with the truth, that is to say, having been educated, having had a certain upbringing, having cultivated a "healthy" attitude toward the truth (1008b31) – this is what it means to speak from experience or from belief. This is what it means to speak in a way that is not estranged, that adheres to life and responds to the necessity of what is. Such a speaking from experience or belief, that is, a speaking integrated with life, is a manner of *legein* through which the

[2] The problem of *logos* alienated from experience is addressed only partially by the awareness of *logos* as that which should be filled with content, as the containing. This is certainly what marks the transition from incontinence to continence. Continence (*enkrateia*), however, is not yet excellence (*aretē*). As content, experience should not only be contained (forcefully, effectively controlled), but also should affect the container and the manner of containment. Experience (more broadly, the motility of life) and *logos* should be aligned, harmonized, mutually attuned. In the terms of the present discussion, *logos* should be not only the mixing bowl within which life is poured, but itself mixed with life. The way things are is not only contemplated by *logos*, but in fact restricts the possibilities of *logos*, draws its confines.

principle of non-contradiction shines: a speaking that makes such a principle perspicuous in its enactment and performance. But such a *logos* at one with *nous*, with its non-logical inception, with what is, signals the accomplishment of human self-actualization. Such a *logos* signals the attainment of happiness or the good. We may therefore conclude that, in its operation, the principle of non-contradiction (the unity of the ontological and the logical, which shines through the *logos* at one with *nous*) signals or is itself a manifestation of the good, of the good at work, in action. For the principle of non-contradiction, far from merely expressing how *logos* unravels, far from merely being regulative of human thinking and utterance, expresses the unraveling of all that is (acts, moves), the non-indifference of the direction according to which anything becomes, the orientation – the sense – of what is.

This concomitance of the first axiom (the principle of being) and the good should not strike us as altogether surprising. After all, we already took notice of the convergence of first philosophy (the science of being, of first principles) and the inquiry regarding the "highest good in the whole of nature," "that for the sake of which each thing must be done" (982b5–7). In its pursuit of the good (first principle and final cause, the divine itself), first philosophy is the science of god – the science investigating god and belonging to god, investigating the divine and itself divine (983a5–11).

2.4. Principle as the Good

Thus, the principle of non-contradiction, this principle at once of being and *logos*, ontological and logical, sustaining and articulating the phenomenal flow of what is, would itself coincide with the good – or, at least, constitute one of its guises. Such a principle would reveal itself in and through the belonging of *logos* in being. It would be divined in and through a certain speaking – not so much speaking focused on a certain theme, but rather speaking in a certain way, in a way that is necessitated by what is and lets what is come forth and shine. This manner of speaking rooted in the ground (indeed, in the soil) of experience, at one with living, reveals itself in its paradigmatic excellence and, hence, as an operation of the good: a guarding of language within the compass of lived experience and, more broadly, the harmonization of rational and other-than-rational dimensions of the human *psukhē*. In this sense, we find no discontinuity among the various strands of the discussion in the

Metaphysics. On the contrary, we come to glimpse the profound unity of the logical, ontological, and properly theological dimensions of this inquiry, all disclosed through the ethical analysis.

In Book Gamma, at length and vigorously, Aristotle insists on the refutation of his antagonists based on the examination of their comportment. The following remarks sound quite familiar at this stage: "But if one says that all speak alike falsely and truly, then such a person can neither utter nor say anything; for one says that this is so and not so at the same time. If one has no belief of anything, but is equally thinking and not thinking, how would one differ from a plant?" (1008b7–12). Denying the principle of non-contradiction means destroying the very possibility and operation of *logos*, thus annihilating what distinguishes the human being from other living beings. Aristotle continues by reinforcing the connection between judgment regarding ethical questions (the good course of action or, at least, the better and worse) and judgment *tout court* (whether this here is or is not, e.g., a human being). Referring to those who deny the principle, he states:

> It is most evident that no one of those who speak this *logos*, or anyone else, is disposed [διάκειται] in this way. For why does one walk to Megara and not stay where one is with the thought that one is walking to Megara? And why does one not walk straight into a well or over a precipice, if such happens to be in the way, but appear to guard oneself against it, with the thought that it is not equally good and not good to fall in? Clearly, then, one believes one course of action to be better and the opposite not better. And if this is so, then one must also believe one thing to be a human being and another not a human being, one thing to be sweet and another not to be sweet. For when one thinks that it is better to drink water and see a human being and then makes inquiries about them, one does not equally seek and believe everything; yet one should, if the same thing were alike a human being and not a human being. But, as we said, there is no one who does not appear to guard him- or herself against some things and not against others. Thus, as it seems, all people have beliefs in an unqualified way, if not about all things, at least about what is better and what is worse. And if it is not knowledge but opinion that they have, they should be all the more concerned about the truth, just as those who are sick are more concerned to be healthy than those who are healthy; for compared with someone with knowledge, someone with opinion, too, is not healthily disposed toward the truth [οὐχ ὑγιεινῶς διάκειται πρὸς τὴν ἀλήθειαν]. (1008b12–31)

Against those who hold that anything and its contrary may be the case and that any position and its contrary may be defended with equal legitimacy, Aristotle then states that not even the lack of certainty would grant such a conclusion. The knowledge we gather may well be qualified, but it does not follow from this that all theses are alike plausible and truthful. The claim is quite extreme: even if there were no absolute standard of truth by which to evaluate the relative worth of various statements, even if our knowledge were ultimately qualified, still, the fact remains that things can be thoughtfully encountered in such a way as to become manifest with a degree of clarity, of determinacy. Such a determinacy, however qualified, is not nothing, so much so that we exhibit an immediate ability to discern degrees of accuracy, that is, of the adherence of *logos* to what is. Thus, the "unmixed" (unqualified and absolute) *logos* of those who proclaim the impossibility of determining what is somehow turns out to be untenable:

> Again, however much things may be so and not so, at least the more and the less are still present in the nature of beings [ἐν τῇ φύσει τῶν ὄντων]; for we should not say that both two and three are alike even, nor that both one who regards four to be five and one who regards one thousand to be five are alike mistaken. And if they are not alike mistaken, it is clear that the former is less mistaken and so considers more truly [μᾶλλον ἀληθεύει]. Accordingly, if that which has more of something is nearer to it, there should be a truth to which the more true is nearer. And even if there is not, still there is at least something which is more certain and more true, and this would free us from the unconditional doctrine [τοῦ λόγου... τοῦ ἀκράτου] which prevents a thing from being made definite by thought [τι τῇ διανοίᾳ ὁρίσαι]. (1008b31–1009a5)

Besides the emphatically ethical tenor of this overall discussion, we should notice what we could almost call an anti-Cartesian strand in Aristotle's line of argumentation. As though in order to counter hyperbolical doubt, Aristotle aims at showing that thinking and its logical structures are not separable from experience and, more broadly, from the involvement in action. Rather, ethical involvement always already makes a difference, always already determines the perspective according to which we are, think, know, and speak. Formulating the thought of walking to Megara presupposes the experience of having walked to some place or other and the ability to discern Megara as a place one can possibly walk to. Furthermore, such a formulation manifests a thrust toward its own practical fulfillment, toward action. Also, we are not indifferent to possible obstacles or dangers on our way – so much so that we avoid them, change our course if needed, thus practically demonstrating our recognition of better or worse options, our ability both to distinguish and to evaluate determinate alternatives. These facts, evident (if unthematized) in the way we live, act, and are, carry the utmost consequence with respect to what and how we think. In fact, they draw beforehand the horizon and confines within which our thinking develops. They crucially reveal its unspoken structures. Ignoring them makes sterile contention possible – as is the case, for instance, of those who believe they can meaningfully reject the principle of non-contradiction.

With the last remarks, about being more or less intimate with the truth, more or less close to it, Aristotle seems to be decisively pointing beyond the facile polarity of relativism and objective truth, of absolute indeterminacy and absolute determination. He is pointing toward a determination that is neither absolute nor doubtful, for absoluteness, the quest for certainty, and hence the irrepressible specter of skepticism, are scientific projections and issue from the logic of demonstration.

It might be fruitful to connect this other-than-scientific determination with the reflection on infinite regress in Alpha Elatton. Here, once again, the good is associated with the ultimate principle and, hence, with the possibility of determinacy – not the determinacy yielded by a demonstrative process of determination, but rather the determinacy prior to all demonstration, the determinacy making all demonstration possible. The good would be connected with that determinacy without process of determination, that determinacy somehow giving itself without mediation. It is, therefore, both remarkable and far from accidental that the good and intellect, *nous*, should be implicated in the same considerations. Aristotle observes:

> Moreover, the final cause is an end, and as such it is not for the sake of something else but others are for its sake. Thus, if there is to be such one which is last, the process will not be infinite; but if there is no such, there will be no final cause. But those who introduce an infinite series are unaware [λανθάνουσιν] of the fact that they are eliminating the nature of the good [ἀγαθοῦ φύσιν] (although no one would try to do anything if he or she did not intend to come to a limit). Nor would there be intellect in the world [νοῦς ἐν τοῖς οὖσιν]; for, at any rate, one who has an intellect always acts for the sake of something, and this is a limit, for the end is a limit [τὸ γὰρ τέλος πέρας ἐστίν]. (994b9–16)

Final cause is limit: beginning and end, that which delimits the series of demonstrations. Without final cause or first principle, the demonstrative chain would go on infinitely, ever referring back to further proofs. That there is indeed final cause or first principle is evident from the bare fact that human beings undertake all manners of enterprise, that is, are always projected toward a limit or end. Such a limit, that for the sake of which anything is undertaken, is itself first principle and final cause. The discussion of it is essentially intertwined with that of the good and of *nous*, since denying it would amount to "eliminating" both.

Aristotle adds that knowing, too, would thereby be eliminated. Thus, it becomes evident that the delimitation provided by the first and last has everything to do with the intuition or intellection of matter, that is, with the capacity to put an end to the demand for demonstration by coming to rest in the necessity of what is, as it gives itself in experience:

> But the what-it-was-to-be [τὸ τί ἦν εἶναι], too, cannot always be referred back to another definition [λόγῳ] longer than the preceding one. First, if this were possible, each definition in the resulting series would be a definition to a higher degree than the one which precedes it; but if there is no [final definition] which is first, neither will any of the others be such as stated. Second, those who speak in this manner eliminate knowing; for it is not possible for us to understand [εἰδέναι] unless we come to know the indivisibles. Nor is it possible to know [γιγνώσκειν] anything; for how can we think [νοεῖν] of an infinite number of parts in this sense? For the situation here is not similar to that with the line which, being divisible without a stop [οὐχ ἵσταται], cannot be thought [νοῆσαι] unless we stop [στήσαντα] (for here, one who is to traverse the infinite line will not count the sections). But the matter [ὕλην] in a moving object must also be thought [νοεῖν]. Moreover, no object can be infinite; and if it is, at least the being of the infinite [ἀπείρῳ εἶναι] is not infinite. Again, if the kinds of causes were infinitely many, knowing [γιγνώσκειν] would still be impossible; for we think we have understanding [εἰδέναι] when we know [γνωρίσωμεν] the causes, but the infinite by addition cannot be gone through in a finite time. (994b16–31)

Thus, either, by admitting infinite regress, we renounce the possibility of knowing or we preserve such a possibility, but recognize that it is not a matter of scientific or apodictic knowledge. Rather, the knowing at stake would have to be understood in intellectual or intuitive terms. In order to admit first principle and final cause, that is, in order to preserve the possibility of determination, meaningful inquiry, and, subsequently, scientific knowledge, we must learn to recognize that which is irreducible to our syllogistical constructions. We must learn to recognize and rely on that underived knowing implicit in what is, in us, in our experiences and practices. What is at stake here is learning to acknowledge and trust that which can only be trusted, for it can be neither controlled nor proved – learning to trust it as ground and rest on it. Of course, in this movement "ground" comes to signify something quite other than the unassailable ground of Cartesian conception, which coincides with absolute certainty. The ground that can only be trusted is no conceptual ground. It is the ground we live on, and that must suffice. It is the emergence and reception of what is, in its unity, integrity, and determinacy, prior to and beyond the perception of its infinite divisibility. That, Aristotle insists, must not be doubted. Doubting it, that is, requiring proofs of it, would be like asking for a demonstration of the indemonstrable, and this is the mark of the uneducated.

The hypothesis of an infinite series, Aristotle surmises, would entail the simultaneous elimination of the good, of the intellect, and of knowing. However, the regress is brought to an end and the first/final cause discerned when we acknowledge an evidence, a knowledge other than discursive and demonstrative. The discussion of infinite regress in Alpha Elatton and the discussion of other-than-scientific determination and knowledge in Gamma intersect in a revealing manner. In both cases, at stake is the possibility, indeed, the affirmation of an orientation to and by the good. It is such a directionality, or teleology, that allows for meaning, for knowing, and for determinacy. Without such an orientation, we would be exposed to the threat of nonsense and aimless, chaotic, undirected motion – which means motion endless and indifferent. However, this turns out to be a merely alleged threat: Aristotle insists that our lives, our experiences, in deed show that the possibility of nonsensicality is an abstract concern and that, in one way or another, we are always sustained, directed – however multilayered the experience of direction and polysemic the language of directedness may be.

2.5. Teleology and Life

It is in recognizing as sufficient the evidence provided by experience that Aristotle proceeds to *assume* a first and last principle that would bring the demonstrative series to a halt. The ultimate principle, thus, transpires from the acknowledgment of the dignity of what life shows.[3] The acknowledgment of life should be enough to compel the opponents to accept the principle and "to believe that of beings there is a certain other substance to which neither motion nor destruction nor generation belong at all" (1009a36–8). Rather paradoxically, then, from the practice of trust vis-à-vis becoming stems the indication of a principle somewhat irreducible, if not to becoming as a whole, to anything that becomes. It would seem that life itself necessitates the contemplation of a transcendent, excessive principle. Such a transcendent principle may be understood in terms of life, each time singular and concrete, pointing beyond itself, in order to embrace itself in its wholeness. At stake would be life's own movement of self-transcendence and self-comprehension.

[3] In this connection, see Giovanni Reale's meditations on "the loss of the sense [meaning] of end" in *Saggezza antica: terapia per il mali dell'uomo d'oggi* (Milan: Cortina, 1995), 171–97.

In this perspective, teleology of the good (ultimate orientation to the good) would signify developmental directionality, that which guides being in its becoming, becoming in its being. In other words, teleology would come to indicate the course, determinacy, and non-indifference of life.

Those who deny such a logical/ontological principle do so either because they disdain experiential evidence or because they make their limited experience absolute and fail to situate it within that which surrounds, the whole. Aristotle dismissively diagnoses their predicament:

> those who have such beliefs deserve criticism also in view of the fact that from their observation of sensible things, small in number, they have expressed themselves similarly about the entire heaven. For it is only in the place of sensible beings around us that destructions and generations constantly occur, but this place is, in a manner of speaking, not even a part of the whole; so that it would be more just to reject the sensible beings in virtue of the rest than to condemn the latter in virtue of the former. Moreover, it is clear that our reply to them, too, will be the same as that made earlier to the others; for we shall have to show and convince them that there is a certain unmoved nature [ἀκίνητός τις φύσις]. (1010a25–35)

What is fascinating in the overall thrust of this discussion is the tension between the precedence accorded to the eternal beings (the heaven in its wholeness and, in the final analysis, the immutable principles) and the emphasis on human situatedness. Two lines of argumentation intersect in Aristotle's analysis here. On the one hand, Aristotle wishes to show that all manners of inquiry, including investigations into ultimate principles such as the one here at stake, are situated within a human environment and depend on practical configurations, ways of constructing the human, and hence ethical considerations. On the other hand, and precisely on the ground of his heightened attention to human experience, Aristotle underlines the priority of the eternal beings over against the beings most proximate to us and affirms the necessity of an ultimate principle as the beginning and end, the origin and direction, of all becoming. The ambitiousness of this discourse lies in the attempt at amalgamating these apparently heterogeneous, if not altogether divergent, lines of inquiry. The intimation is that, precisely in its orientation, sense, and non-indifference, life (and most notably human life) demands to be situated in an environment exceeding the human. It implies a context neither merely human-made nor merely based on the arbitrariness of human self-assertion. Of their own accord, the meaning and direction found in life necessitate and reveal a plot in which the human is implicated, while being neither the author nor the source of it. The task, then, involves acknowledging the broader fabric of sense into which the human is woven, which provides the limits and direction orienting human life.

The so-called principle of non-contradiction speaks at once of the way beings (including us) are and of the way we perceive what is. Beings cannot be *and* not be such-and-such at the same and in the same respect. Nor can we believe that they are *and* are not such-and-such at the same time and in the same respect. To the extent that we adhere to what is, what is dictates our perception, and hence our thinking and speaking. Thus, this is a principle gathering all that is, precisely in its differentiation and determinacy – a principle of interconnectedness. Interestingly enough, then, the reference to a principle (indicated as the sky, the all) immovable, ungenerated, and indestructible points to the interweaving of all that is, to the fabric of becoming. The formulation of such a principle constitutes the acknowledgement of belonging in the broader organization and articulation of being. It is within such a global articulation that meaning is granted. In this sense, here we have suggested that, in speaking of the principle of non-contradiction, Aristotle is speaking of the principle of and as the good – the indemonstrable condition and guidance of being, thinking, and speaking.

The inadmissibility of contradiction (at the same time, in the same respect) both in elocution and in being; the noetic ground halting infinite regress and making it finite; and the teleology of the good, that is, the orientation to a final cause that is at once first, may all be seen as aspects of the same principle. Such a manifold principle both grants and explicates the way being takes place, that is, occurs as beings. By the same token, the structures of sense, signification, and thinking are illuminated.

2.6. Anti-Cartesianism

We already underscored the punctual, if anachronistic, anti-Cartesian strand in Book Gamma. This is evident in the whole discussion, but most notable in the passage considered below (1010b1–1011b7). In this long segment we notice, among other things, considerations that could be brought to bear on the question of time left somewhat suspended in *Physics* Delta ("whether time would be or not if no soul would be" [223a23]) and, in general, on the question of sensible beings as subsisting aside from sensing, that is, aside from the perception of them carried out in and by the soul. Also articulated here is a rejection of the view according to which, based on the undeniable fluctuation and inconstancy of appearance (*phantasia*), the possibility of an insight into the truth and of more or less accurate statements should be altogether relinquished. Once more, at stake is the trustworthiness, however qualified, of phenomena. The passage deserves to be considered at length:

Concerning the truth regarding the fact that not every phenomenon is true, first, it is a fact that no sensation of its proper sensible is false; but appearance [φαντασία] is not the same as sensation. Then we are fairly surprised if these thinkers raise the question whether the size of the magnitudes and the kinds of colors are such as they appear [φαίνεται] to those at a distance or to those who are near, whether things are such as they appear to the sick or the healthy, whether those things are heavy which so appear to the weak or to the strong, and whether those things are true which appear to those who are asleep or to those who are awake. For it is evident that they themselves do not think so; at least no one in Libya, believing at night that he or she is in Athens, starts walking to the Odeum. Again, with regard to the future, as Plato too says, the opinion of a doctor and that of an ignorant person are indeed not equally reliable, that is, as to whether the sick will become healthy or not. Again, with regard to the powers of sensation themselves, the power of the non-proper object is not so reliable as the power of the proper object, or, that of the object nearby is not so reliable as that of its own object; but in the case of colors it is sight that judges and not taste, and in the case of flavors it is taste and not sight. And no power of sensation ever says about its proper object that it is so and not so at the same time. But not even at another time does it doubt about that affection [πάθος], but it may doubt about the thing to which the affection belongs. For example, the same wine, either due to its own change or due to a change of one's body, might seem sweet at one time but not at another; but at least sweetness, such as it is when it is, never changes, and one always thinks truly [ἀληθεύει] of it as such, and that which will be sweet will of necessity be of this kind. (1010b1–26)

While "no sensation of its proper sensible" may be mistaken, appearances may be evaluated, interpreted differently, and such evaluations admit of varying degrees of falsity. Yet not all sources of a given evaluation indifferently carry the same authoritativeness. Opinions are in fact discerned as more or less likely, according to the conditions in which they were formed and the reliability or expertise of their source. At any rate, aside from the undeniable fluctuation of the sensible, the features sensed by each power of sensation are unvarying. The "proper sensibles," such as tastes (e.g., sweetness) for the sense of taste or the visible (e.g., colors) for the sense of vision, may be erroneously attributed to this or that being, but, as such, abide in their definition and definiteness. "Yet," Aristotle laments in turning to his opponents, "all these doctrines [λόγοι] do away with this; and just as they deny the being of a substance of anything, so they deny that anything is of necessity; for the necessary cannot be now this and now that, and so if something is of necessity, it will not be so and not so" (1010b26–30).

Pursuing this line of thinking further, Aristotle insists on the non-derivative character of sensible beings, on their being somehow autonomous from, or even prior to, their being sensed and the organs sensing them. The primordiality of the sensible is thus made prominent, in a formulation whose laboriousness is in and of itself noteworthy:

In general, if indeed only the sensible is, nothing would be if those with a soul were not, for then there would be no sensation. On the one hand, it is equally true that the sensible beings [αἰσθητά] and the sensations thereof [αἰσθήματα] would not be (for the latter are affections [πάθος] of that which senses), but for another, it is impossible that the underlying subjects which cause sensation [ποιεῖ τὴν αἴσθησιν] should not be, even if there is no sensation of them. For a sensation is surely not a sensation of itself, but there is also something else besides the sensation which must be prior to the sensation; for that which moves is by nature prior to that which is moved. And even if the two are spoken of in relation to each other, this is no less true. (1010b30–1011a2)

Aristotle, then, turns once more to consider the continuing (incontinent, we may say) demand for demonstration, for *logos* alone. The inappropriate quest for omni-demonstrability is here considered in connection with the attempt to establish ultimate authorities or judges. Regarding his opponents, Aristotle notes:

There are some, among both those who are convinced of these doctrines [λόγους] and those who only utter them, who raise the problem by asking who is to be the judge of the healthy person, and, in general, who is to judge correctly any thing. But raising such problems is like raising the problem whether we are now sleeping or awake. All such problems amount to the same thing, for they demand a *logos* for everything; they ask for a principle but they demand a demonstration of it, although from their actions it is obvious that they are not convinced. But as we just said, their trouble [πάθος] is this: they seek a *logos* for that which has no *logos*; for the origin [ἀρχή] of a demonstration is not a demonstration. Now the former may be easily convinced of this fact (for it is not difficult to grasp). But those who seek cogency in the *logos* alone [ἐν τῷ λόγῳ τὴν βίαν μόνον ζητοῦντες] are seeking the impossible; for they claim the right of stating the contraries, and so they state them right away. (1011a3–17)

Those who deny the so-called principle of non-contradiction demand demonstrations of everything and, failing to satisfy the criterion of absolute certainty, fall into unmitigated skepticism. They quickly relinquish all possibility of asserting anything truthfully and hold that everything is relative, every view of it equally viable and legitimate. Aristotle sustains the controversy against them without transcending phenomenality – in fact, by resorting to an even closer, and hence more nuanced, approach to the sensible. It is certainly not the case that all appearances (the sensible and the perception thereof) are indifferently true (and, by the same token, false). The claim that all appearances are "alike false and true" must be qualified: an appearance may be true or false to someone, at a particular time, in a particular circumstance, from a particular vantage point, and according to a particular sense organ.

This qualification carries three crucial consequences. In the first place, it allows one to discern between relatively more or less reliable perceptions, according to their circumstances. Second, however, the fact *that* an appearance has been perceived unmistakably signals *that* something has come to pass – something and not nothing. Regardless of the degree of accuracy or distortion in perceiving, beings are neither constituted nor brought forth through the perception of them. Third, a perception, regardless of its truthfulness, is determinate: it is such and such, not everything and nothing. Above all, it is not true *and* false. For a given person, or for a person's given organ of perception, at a given time, in a given circumstance, the appearance is exactly what it is, and not anything else, let alone its contrary. In Aristotle's words:

> Now if not all things are relative, but there are some things which are according to themselves, not every phenomenon would be true; for a phenomenon is a phenomenon to someone, so one who says that all phenomena are true makes all beings relative. For this reason we should guard ourselves against those who seek cogency in arguments [τὴν βίαν ἐν τῷ λόγῳ ζητοῦσιν] and who at the same time claim to be defending their argument [λόγον], by requiring them to say, not that a phenomenon just is, but that a phenomenon is for the one to whom it appears [φαίνεται], and when it appears, and in the respect in which it appears, and in the manner in which it appears. And if they are giving a defense of their argument [λόγον], but not in this manner, they will soon turn out to be making contrary statements. For it is possible for the same thing to appear to be honey to sight but not to the sense of taste, and for the same thing to appear unlike to the sight of each of two eyes, if these are unlike. So against at least those who say that that which appears is true, for the reasons stated formerly, and that because of this everything is alike false and true (for things do not appear the same to all, nor always the same to the same person, but often contrary at the same time [κατὰ τὸν αὐτὸν χρόνον]; for the sense of touch says that there are two objects when the fingers are crossed, but sight says that there is one), we reply "yes, but not to the same power of sensation and according to the same aspect of it and in the same manner and at the same time [ἐν τῷ αὐτῷ χρόνῳ]"; so that it is with these qualifications that the phenomenon is true. But perhaps it is because of this that those who speak not because of the difficulty but for the sake of *logos* are compelled to say, not that what appears is true, but that it is true to whomever it so appears. And as we said before, they are also compelled to

make everything relative and resting on opinion and sensation, so that nothing has occurred and nothing will be unless someone has first formed an opinion about it. But if something did occur or will be, it is clear that not everything will be relative to opinion. (1011a17–b7)

Appearances are neither unqualifiedly true nor unqualifiedly false. They are what they are, for the one to whom they appear, and at the time and in the manner in which they do appear. In this highly qualified sense, they are true. However, not only is it possible, at times even immediately, to assess the relative worth of various opinions, but, moreover, what takes place in the domain of appearing enjoys a certain emancipation from the opinions formed about it. What happens is not merely projected or constituted through being perceived. Opinions are not of nothing; if they are formed, something must have given itself in some guise. Something must have happened; something and not, simultaneously, anything and its contrary – something definite and definable, albeit in a qualified way. These considerations reveal the questionable character of the unconditional claim that, because what appears gives rise to interpretive uncertainty, all is relative to opinion, any opinion.

Aristotle emphasizes with great insistence that coming to know implies living in a certain way, behaving in line with what one comprehends, and in turn, comprehending in line with the basic features of comportment and what these features reveal, if carefully attended to. The strands of the inquiries regarding being, axioms, and ethical matters are indissolubly intertwined. The so-called principle of non-contradiction and the good come to be superimposed as different aspects of the granting of meaning or finality. If one were to speak in a way consistent with one's comportment or experience, one would be forced to admit that, much as appearances may present interpretive difficulties and insidious possibilities of error, still, living in the midst of appearances does not thereby mean living in an altogether nonsensical world, being paralyzed by meaninglessness, by the inability of choosing, deciding, and discerning. On the contrary, even before manifesting itself in and through human thinking and utterance, meaning gives itself precisely in the order and coherence with which beings take place, in the organization of what is. Our comportment shows that, despite all manners of disorder and randomness, we rely on the rhythms of becoming, presuppose its regularities, recurrences, and continuing developments.

We have pointed out that, after an inceptive discussion of the first *aporia*, Book Gamma, almost in its entirety (1005a19–1012b31), constitutes a sustained confrontation with the second *aporia*. To conclude, then, we may also notice the relation between *aporia* and teleology, the way in which the elaboration of *aporia* clarifies and defines teleology. For, indeed, in the course of Book Gamma it becomes increasingly evident that the so-called principle of principles, the axiomatic statement of the impossibility of contradiction, comes to coincide with the very orientation to and teleology of the good.

3. REITERATIONS

As Aristotle's returns to this topic demonstrate, the issues considered thus far are of utmost concern and utterly central in his inquiry. It may be worth considering a few of these repetitions. In *Metaphysics* Kappa, Aristotle exposes the first axiom again as a principle at once ontological and logical, illuminating it in terms of *ēthos*, and above all in terms of always already operative communal structures. It is on the ground of the community always already in place, on the ground of the communication, exchange, and intelligibility always already experienced within the community, that such a principle is non-demonstratively demonstrated to shine forth in its compelling truth and absolute priority. Aristotle opens with a series of by now familiar statements:

> There is a principle in things about which we cannot be mistaken but must always be disposed [ποιεῖν] in the contrary way, that is, to think truly [ἀληθεύειν]; and the principle is this, that the same thing cannot at one and the same time be and not be, or admit of any other opposites in the same manner. And although there is no demonstration of such principles in an unqualified sense, there is a demonstration against anyone who denies them. For it is not possible to make a syllogism of the principle from a more convincing principle, yet if indeed one is to demonstrate it without qualification, one should have at least such a syllogism. But to show the asserter of opposites why they speak falsely, one must obtain from them such a statement which is the same as "it is not possible for the same thing to be and not to be at one and the same time" but which does not seem to be the same; for only thus can a demonstration be given against the one who says that opposite assertions may be truly made of the same thing. (1061b34–1062a11)

As in the previous treatise, Aristotle proceeds to link contradiction at the same time and in the same respect with nonsensicality, indifference, or the inhibition of signification:

> Now those who are to share the *logos* with each other [ἀλλήλοις λόγου κοινωνήσειν] must also understand each other; for if this does not happen, how can they share

the *logos* with each other? Accordingly, each name must be known and signify [γνώριμον καὶ δηλοῦν] something, but only one thing, not many; and if it signifies [σημαίνῃ] many things, it must be made evident to which one of them it applies. So, in saying "it is this" and also "it is not this," that which one says it is one denies that it is, so what a given name signifies [σημαίνει] one denies that it does so signify [σημαίνειν]; and this is impossible. So, if indeed "it is so-and-so" signifies [σημαίνει] something, it is impossible for its contradictory to be true [ἀληθεύειν] of the same thing. (1062a12–20)

Again and analogously, Aristotle links *logos* and being in such a way that the possibility of *logos* is measured, even restricted, by what is. If it is to lay a claim to truth, *logos* should not exceed such bounds: "Again, if the name signifies [σημαίνει] something and this is truly asserted [ἀληθεύεται], it is necessary for that which is asserted to be; and if it is necessary that it be, it cannot at that time not be; hence, it is not possible for opposite assertions to be true [ἀληθεύειν] of that same thing" (1062a20–23). The rootedness of *logos* (of judgment and assertion) in the way of beings (in the way beings are) could hardly be more emphasized.

It is perhaps in accord with this emphasis that, in the final analysis, Aristotle contemplates the possibility of considering Heraclitus as a genuine interlocutor, whose speaking may unfold in the exposure to what is. Unlike the contentious adversaries, who wish to defend their position merely in *logos*, disregarding their own experience and the necessitating force of phenomena, Heraclitus may simply have been inaccurate in speaking, may have spoken without fully realizing the implications of his words:

Now none of the above arguments is an unqualified demonstration of the principle in question, nevertheless they are demonstrations against those who posit contrary opinions. Perhaps Heraclitus himself, if he were questioned in this manner, would have been quickly compelled to agree [ὁμολογεῖν] that contradictory assertions can never be true [ἀληθεύεσθαι] of the same things; but as it is, he adopted this doctrine [δόξαν] without an understanding of what he was saying. On the whole, if his statement is true, neither will it itself be true, namely, the statement "it is possible for the same thing to be and not to be at one and the same time." (1062a30–1062b2)

Besides the unsustainability of a *logos* that is at odds with being, Aristotle is also very meticulous in pointing out the internal inconsistencies of such a *logos*, the way in which it is at odds with itself, even self-destructive: "Further, if nothing can be affirmed truly, this statement itself, namely, 'nothing can be affirmed truly' would also be false. But if there is a true affirmation, this would refute what is said by those who oppose such statements and eliminate discursive exchange [τὸ διαλέγεσθαι] completely" (1062b7–11).

As the thrust of the discussion considered thus far makes abundantly clear, the thought of demonstration receives a quite unusual development. While demonstration as strictly logical procedure is out of the question here, it is still explored it in its qualified, extra-logical, indeed, practical-performative, sense. Practical matters are shown in their cogency, in their power to compel assent and form basic conviction. Such a qualified demonstration points not to what is assessed and finally proved in *logos*, but rather to what is demonstrated by dialogue – by the very fact that dialogue (and, by extension, all manner of involvement in action) is possible and meaningfully takes place. At any given time and in any given circumstance, we say this, do this, and not that, not everything and its opposite. What we say or do may not shine forth in uncontroversial determinacy or immediate transparency. It may need clarification, elucidation, interpretation, that is, the work of judgment. However, it is neither nothing nor indifferently any thing.

As the discussion in Book Kappa continues, Aristotle also underlines that the principle of non-contradiction has to do with a radical delimitation of anthropocentrism. His critical assessment of Protagoras' position is almost Heraclitean in tenor, hinting as it does at a kind of "private" understanding, at the retreat into an idiosyncratic perspective making it impossible to perceive that which is common:

> The saying of Protagoras is almost like the doctrines we have mentioned; for he, too, said that a human being is the measure of all things, and this is saying none other than that what a thing seems to be to each human being is precisely what the thing is. If this happens to be the case, then it follows that the same thing both is and is not, so that it is both good and bad, and likewise with the other so-called opposite assertions; and this is because a thing often appears to be beautiful to some but the contrary to other people, and that which appears to each human being is the measure. This difficulty may be solved if we examine the source of this belief. (1062b12–1062b21)

To confront this difficulty, Aristotle proceeds to contrast sensation to opinion and appearance or imagination, along the lines already considered in Book Gamma. In and of itself, as pertaining to its proper sensible, sensation can never be false. However, the same cannot be said of the opinions and appearances or imaginations (*doxai* and *phantasiai*) that arise from sensory perception. They may indeed be mistaken and, subsequently, not every opinion or imagination carries the same authoritativeness and not everyone may be equally and indifferently reliable in the evaluation one provides:

> Moreover, it is foolish to attend alike to the opinions and imaginations [φαντασίαις] of disputing parties, for clearly those on one side must be mistaken. This is evident from what happens with respect to sensations; for the same thing never appears sweet to some people and the contrary of this to others, unless in the one case the sense organ which judges the said flavor is injured or defective. In such a case, we should believe those on one side to be the measure but not those on the other. My statement applies alike to the good and the bad, the beautiful and the ugly, and all other such. For the claim of our opponents does not differ from that of those who make one thing appear two by pressing below the eye with their finger, and say that there are two things, because two things appear, and again that there is one, for one thing appears as one to those who do not press the finger. (1062b33–1063a10)

In this way, Aristotle asserts once again the self-evidence of what is the case and, at the same time, maintains that not all views and perceptions are equally authoritative. Just as there may be disagreements regarding a sensory perception, in which case the health and integrity of the sense organ will be decisive, so there may be disagreements regarding the perception of the good or the beautiful. In the latter case, decisive will be the health and integrity of that "organ" that is the soul itself, in its configuration and enactment. As Aristotle notes in the *Nicomachean Ethics*, there are many disagreements among human beings concerning what happiness might be, for instance, and this seems to be due to "their ways of living" (1095b17). However, the wise tend to agree on such matters, and their perception, far from being mere opinion, can provide an access to what is "by nature" (1099a12–15). Nonetheless, it should still be underlined that the point is not so much selecting the most truthful perception as the unique paradigm, but rather realizing the varying degrees of truth in the various views, and even the fact that diverse views may illuminate different aspects of the matter and be simultaneously truthful. Truth reveals itself chorally. Thus, considering numerous opinions about something, "it is reasonable that none of them should be altogether mistaken but should be right at least in one and even in most respects" (1098b28–9). This is most notably the case with perceptions such as that of the good and bad.

Despite the variations in perception and the inevitability of divergences, inadequacies, or diverse abilities, we experience sharing, having in common. At a most basic level, what is the case imposes itself on us, compels us to assent, beyond discourse and demonstration:

> A solution of the difficulties mentioned is not easy for those who possess them from discussion [ἐκ λόγου], unless they posit something for which they no longer demand a reason [λόγον], for this is how all discussions [πᾶς λόγος] and all demonstrations take place; for if they posit nothing, they eliminate dialogue [διαλέγεσθαι] and any discourse whatever [ὅλως λόγον]. Hence, there is no argument [λόγος] against such people. But it is easy to answer those who are perplexed by the difficulties as handed down and to put an end to the causes of their perplexity. This is evident from what has been said. (1063b7–15)

Here Aristotle's formulation is remarkable in its incisiveness. Positing a beginning without and beyond *logos* (a beginning "for which they no longer demand *logos*") constitutes the condition for the possibility of *logos.* Indeed, "if they posit nothing, they eliminate . . . any *logos* whatever." The secondariness of *logos* could not be more peremptorily diagnosed.

Echoing Book Gamma, the discussion in Book Kappa proposes once more the turn from the sensible beings surrounding us in our worldly circumstances to the celestial bodies in the sky, delimiting the environment within which humankind is situated and constituting that which is most common to all. Still sensible but eternal and immutable, the heavenly bodies are contemplated as the first principle(s) in their radiant phenomenality (as we saw, they are *ta phanerōtata,* the most shining). Shared by all in their enduring clarity, they constitute the visible evidence of the impossibility of contradiction. They are, as Aristotle observes, the condition of truth, of what is and what is said:

> In general it is absurd to form our judgment of the truth from the fact that the things about us appear to change and never to stay the same. For, in seeking the truth, we should start from things which are always the same and suffer no change. Such are the heavenly bodies [τὰ κατὰ τὸν κόσμον], for these do not appear to be now of one kind and now of another but are always the same and share in no change. (1063a10–16)

It is from these beings that are sensible yet abide in and as themselves that Aristotle understands the motility and mutability of the sensible. Again, contemplating that which dwells immutable means *sensing* the impossibility of contradiction – sensing it in its in(de)finite primacy, in its non-logical and non-historical priority. Neither severed from nor antithetical to the experience of phenomena, such a contemplation shelters the experience of phenomena in its very possibility. The contemplation of the abiding grants the temporal unraveling of difference, that is, determinacy in and as becoming:

> Again, if there is motion there is also something which is in motion, and every thing in motion is moved from something and into something. So, the thing in motion must be in that from which it will be moved and not be in itself, must then be moving into another thing, and must finally become in it; but then two contradictories cannot be true of it in each of these at the same time. (1063a17–21)

From what has been said, it is clear that the contrast between the celestial bodies (and, therefore, the sky) and the sensible beings surrounding us should not be hastily interpreted. In particular, we should tirelessly underscore that, far from referring the sensible to some supersensible domain, the bifurcation between the heavenly bodies and other bodies articulates the domain of the sensible. To be sure, the shining bodies of the firmament constitute a peculiar phenomenon, for they offer unparalleled constancy, consistency, and continuity, at once in themselves and in our experience of them. Yet they constitutively and essentially belong in the sensible. Thus, this contrast internal to the sensible illuminates the self-differing character of the sensible and, more importantly, discloses the intuition of self-sameness (of the intelligible) as a resource of the sensible, enfolded within and intrinsic to it. In this respect, far from indicating logical fixity, self-sameness indicates abidingness, no more and no less than phenomenal endurance and integrity.

We could venture further and surmise that the point here is not even emphasizing that the celestial bodies are a paradigm of truth in virtue of their immutability, in contrast to the other mutable sensible beings. The central concern, rather, may be to underline a certain endurance and stability at the heart of the sensible as such, even in its most fleeting manifestations. Despite the unrest of beings in their becoming, their sensible characteristics, that is, the qualitative features articulating the sensible as such, exhibit a certain permanence. The sweet is sweet regardless of shifting circumstances, regardless of specific beings changing from sweet to some other taste, and also regardless of possible alterations in the perceiver's organ of perception, which may perceive something as sweet at one point and as otherwise tasting at another point. Even in the case of the sensible beings by which we are surrounded, the structures of sensibility remain constant despite the fluctuation of becoming. Let it be underlined that this outcome does not rest on an eidetic sublimation of experience, but rather is dictated by experience and finds in experience its compelling evidence. It is experience that compels us to trust what is perceptually given, to recognize it in its determinate lineaments, to accept its evidence, and to discern with relative safety an accurate assessment from a vitiated or inadequate one.

Thus, at stake seems to be the abidingness of the structures of the sensible – an abidingness not affirmed despite and beyond the fluctuations of becoming, but rather bespeaking such fluctuations, structuring the becoming of beings in their determinacy and uniqueness. Harbored in such an affirmation are beings in their taking place (however fleeting), in their taking and leaving place. In virtue of such an abidingness granting definiteness, what is would come to be, unique each time and in each respect, each time and in each respect discernible.

4. TELEOLOGY, INDEFINABLE AND INDUBITABLE

If, as has been proposed, the discourse on the first axiom encrypts and anticipates the discourse on the good, then a few further remarks are in order. The teleology of the highest good is a desirous teleology where the end is the beloved. It is in the undergoing and pursuit of such a love that beings find in each case their fullest realization. To participate in such a teleology, thus, means to be ensouled, to be alive. As long as cosmic teleology embraces all, the entire cosmos is illuminated as alive. This is pervasively evident in *Metaphysics* Lambda, where the divine is systematically addressed in terms of fully enacted aliveness, life in light of eternity, unmitigated *energeia.* It is also evident in *De Caelo,* where we are told that "the sky is *empsukhos,*" alive, animated, and "has a principle of motion" (285a29–30). From the sky thus understood comes the life, the aliveness of all beings that are alive, as Aristotle suggests:

> The end [τέλος] which circumscribes [περιέχον] the time of the life of every being, and which cannot be exceeded according to nature, they named the *aiōn* of each. According to the same *logos* also the end of the whole sky, the end which circumscribes all time and infinity, is *aiōn,* taking the name from *aei einai,* immortal and divine. From it all other things derive their being and life, some more precisely, others more obscurely. (279a23–30)

The Platonic and pre-Platonic hypothesis of all-encompassing and all-pervasive aliveness may still be discerned in Aristotle, while already in Theophrastus we find a rather pronounced distinction between the animate, understood as desiring, and the inanimate – and this means a distinction between finality and mechanism or mechanical necessity.

The assumption of teleology as all-embracing is for Aristotle a matter of faith, in the sense of *pistis*, trust; it is a pre-demonstrative assumption. We cannot provide an unqualified account of finality in its *whatness*, but must assert *that* finality is. As we read in the *Metaphysics*, "if we cannot say what they are, it is just as necessary that some eternal substances are" (1041a2–3). That they are necessarily follows from our experience of the sense, meaning, and directionality of what is.

We have repeatedly pointed out that first principles or origins cannot, for Aristotle, be demonstratively known. However, their elusiveness deserves a further, if brief, annotation. What is first is eternal, fully at work, and simple, that is, non-composite – most clearly, not a form-matter composite. This holds, a fortiori, for the good. Aristotle draws the contrast as follows: "Thus, we are seeking the cause (and this is the *eidos*) through which the matter is a thing; and this cause is the substance of the thing. Concerning that which is simple, however, it is evident that there is no inquiry and no teaching, but there is another manner of inquiring about such a thing" (1041b7–11). That which is not composite, that is, ultimate and not derived, is discursively unknowable and, hence, strictly a matter of intuition, *noein*: "either one intuits it or one does not" (1051b31–2). The intellectual or intuitive perception, however, does not yield an analytical definition of it: "As for the simple things and the whatness of them, not even in thought [ἐν διανοίᾳ] is there truth or falsity of them" (1027b27–8). That which is eternal, thus, constitutes an intrinsically non-analyzable, if not altogether inscrutable, beginning or teleological principle. This is all the more so because, despite its being most shared, what is first is utterly unique, and "no individual," whether sensible or intelligible, "can be defined" (1040a8). Indeed, "it is impossible to define individuals among eternal beings, especially if each of them is unique, such as the sun or the moon" (1040a28–9).

From these considerations emerges a twofold emphasis on trust: trust in what we perceive and, by the same token, in the oriented order implied by and implicated in all that we perceive – an order that remains folded into all that we perceive, cryptic in its evidence. Ultimately, at issue is trust in the continuity and constancy of the earth beneath us, our ground; trust in what surrounds and envelops us, remaining always the same and unmoved, unchanging though revolving for all eternity. This is a fundamental reliance on the continuity and constancy of what sustains us, even though the many disorderly occurrences in the sublunar realm might make one think that certain domains do not submit to the rule of teleological orientation – that in certain domains things take place blindly and randomly. However, trusting *that* teleology is pervasively at work, albeit not fully knowing its *what* and *how*, involves considering randomness as only apparent, that is, ascribing the phenomenon of randomness to the unintelligibility or inaccessibility of teleological operativity – to its indefiniteness.

Aristotle insists on the question of trust, *pistis*, also in *De Caelo*, and we shall limit ourselves to mentioning two paradigmatic passages from this text, the first in Alpha 3 and the second at the very beginning of Beta. The former underscores the hypothetical/mythical character of discourses on beginnings and the necessary alignment of *logos* to phenomena: "if what we laid down is to be trusted [εἴ τις τοῖς ὑποκειμένοις πιστεύει], the first body of all is eternal, suffers neither growth nor diminution, but is ageless, unalterable, and impassive. It seems also that the *logos* bears witness [μαρτυρεῖν] to the phenomena, and they to it. All human beings have a belief regarding the gods, and all attribute the highest place to the divine, both barbarians and Greeks" (270b1–8).[4] What "all human beings" have sensed and said, that is, what they have seen in common, trusted, and variously shared, ends up providing the confirmation of the hypothesis put forth, regarding things first and divine. Such a confirmation is altogether practical in tenor:

> If, then, as is the case, there is something divine, what we have said about the first substance of bodies is well said. For, it also follows from sensation, sufficiently at least to speak for human *pistis*; for throughout all past time, according to the records handed down from generation to generation, no change appears either according to the whole of the outermost heaven or according to any one of its proper parts. (270b10–16)

Needless to say, the intertwinement of the languages of trust, sensation, and historical-dialectical transmission carries considerable implications.

In this context, Aristotle resorts to the language of *aisthēsis* and *pistis* precisely in order to maintain his presupposition, his positing, of the first body as in perfect and uniform motion. This gesture is repeated in Book Beta, which opens by referring the assumption of the ungenerated and imperishable first body back to the confirmatory function of belief and trust. Aristotle first proposes: "Trusting what was previously said, we may surmise that the heaven as a whole was not generated and cannot be

[4] In *Generation of Animals*, Aristotle goes beyond the suggestion of an alignment between *logos* and sensation, stating that "trust must be given to sensation more than to *logoi*, and to *logoi* too provided that what they show agrees with, *homologein*, phenomena" (760b31–3).

destroyed, as some allege, but is one and eternal [εἷς καὶ ἀΐδιος], having no beginning or end of its whole being [τοῦ παντὸς αἰῶνος], having and circumscribing in itself infinite time" (283b26–30). He, then, turns again to the ancestors' beliefs and doctrines:

> Therefore, we may well be convinced that those archaic discourses are true, especially those inherited from our forefathers, and according to which there is something immortal and divine among the beings that have motion, but whose motion is such that there is no limit to it, rather it is itself the limit of other motions. For being a limit [πέρας] belongs to that which circumscribes [τῶν περιεχόντων], and the circular motion [κυκλοφορία] at issue, being complete, circumscribes [περιέχει] those [motions] that are incomplete and have limit and pause. Itself without beginning or end, continuing without pause for infinite time, it causes the beginning of some [motions], and receives the pause of others. The ancients [ἀρχαῖοι] assigned the sky and place above to the gods, holding it alone as imperishable; and our present discourse bears witness [μαρτυρεῖ λόγος] that it is indestructible and ungenerated. (284a2–14)

What is transparent here is the search for a pre-ontological confirmation of the thesis laid out in the treatise – which is, then, properly speaking, a hypothesis. First principles and ultimate movers, matters physical and divine, are established prior to and aside from the order of the thetic and the properly ontological. This reliance on circulating beliefs, not necessarily enjoying the authoritativeness of what is ancient, also transpires from an earlier passage: "In the ordinary philosophical works [ἐγκυκλίοις φιλοσοφήμασι] regarding divinity it is often made evident by the discourses that the first and highest divinity must be entirely immutable, which bears testimony [μαρτυρεῖ] to what we have been saying" (279a30–3).

Let us mention, in passing, that this mode of inquiry is reminiscent of a certain strand in the Platonic meditation. In *Republic* VI, during the elaboration of the so-called divided line, Plato has Socrates point out that trust, *pistis,* is the affection of the soul corresponding to sensible beings, the beings that surround us. In other words, the proper attitude toward the sensible is trust. All subsequent knowledge on the higher segments of the line (most notably on the level of *dianoia*) rests upon it. Here, again, at stake is trust as pertaining precisely to that which is sensibly perceived, that which must be assumed as the prerequisite and springboard for further knowledge – even that knowledge that will allegedly have emancipated itself from the sensible ground.

The thrust of Aristotle's discourse suggests that, whether or not this can be turned into a rational claim, we do rely on a certain order and constancy. Quite simply, the fact is that we do rest on this assumption. We live according to and thanks to this reliance. Aristotle, therefore, retains an ultimately unified view regarding the whole, its structures and origin. He contemplates no duality of principles, that is to say, no duality such as the good and its opposite. Rather, he contemplates a teleological principle consistently ordering all becoming, and even what appears to be random occurrence. The only proviso or qualification is that such a teleology may not be and in fact is not completely intelligible to us. And this has to do with the cryptic character of principles, which exceed human demonstrative procedure: they are phenomenally clear in their self-evidence, yet cannot be conclusively defined, stably brought into *logos*. However, it is only in a qualified way that Aristotle may be said to be a "monist." For his "monism" does not have the status of a scientific discourse in the strict (syllogistic) sense, but rather is discursively developed out of the posture of trust in intuitive evidence. Such evidence is considered sufficient and as such brought to speak, suggesting that the assurance provided by intuition lies even deeper than the scientist's most profound disquietudes and quest for certainty. (In a way, the scientist can only and properly doubt – for, as such, he or she seeks certainty as demonstrated knowledge, while knowing that she cannot control her presuppositions, i.e., employ the criterion of certainty outside the scientific domain.)

Even deeper than the disquietudes of scientific incompleteness lie a reliance on and a sense of trust in what is not scientifically proven but nevertheless experienced beyond doubt. In this sense, Aristotle should again be distinguished from Theophrastus, not only in the way a monist is distinct from a dualist, but also in the way in which the privilege of wisdom as essentially intuitive is distinct from the privilege of reason, and therefore from the posture of a certain intellectualism.

5. THE PHENOMENON OF TRUTH AND THE ACTION OF THINKING

What has been clarified by reference to Book Gamma, and secondarily to Book Kappa, is actually quite exemplary of the broader framework of the treatises known as the *Metaphysics*. In fact, as pointed out earlier in this work, the inceptive discourses of the *Metaphysics* already announce the overall inquiring attitude examined thus far.

From the start, Aristotle makes explicit the two-fold character of the confirmation of a scientific statement. First, we notice the compulsion, the necessitating force, of truth and/or phenomena and/or things themselves. Here I am referring to three moments in Book Alpha, in which it is said that it is the truth, the *phainomenon*, or *auto to pragma*, that forces and directs the inquiry in a certain way. Considering the studies of his predecessors, Aristotle notes that, as philosophers "progressed in this manner, the facts themselves opened the path for them and contributed in forcing them to inquire" (984a18–19). Again, later thinkers, "forced once more by the truth itself as we said, sought the next principle" (984b9–11). Most notably, Parmenides, exceeding all others in excellence and "being more observant" (μᾶλλον βλέπων), "seems to be saying something" (986b27–8). Aristotle elucidates further: "being forced to conform to phenomena, and believing that these are one according to *logos* but many according to sensation, he in turn posits two causes and two principles, the hot and the cold, as if speaking of fire and earth; and he classifies the hot as the principle with respect to being but the other [the cold] as the principle with respect to non-being" (986b31–987a2).

Thus, it can be said that the difference between "being defeated by an inquiry" (984a30–1) and proceeding correctly lies in being "observant," that is, in looking more attentively, attending to vision more diligently – remaining open to being reached, open to being affected by "other." We need, therefore, to wonder what happens when the *logos* of inquiry obfuscates, hinders the self-manifestation of what is; when it proceeds according to its own logic, alone; when it becomes an obstacle such that the truth can no longer do its work of necessitation, can no longer perform its function of prompting and leading the inquiry.

Second, and just as crucially, the confirmation of a scientific inquiry or discourse comes from the consideration of previous experiences, that is to say, from the confrontation with the past. The following passage underlines the two-fold source of confirmation of scientific outcome, namely, phenomena themselves and other inquirers. Aristotle says:

> All these thinkers, then, being unable to touch upon another cause, seem to bear witness to the fact that we have described the number and kinds of causes rightly. Moreover, it is clear that, if we are to seek the causes, we must either seek all of them in the ways stated or seek them in some of the ways stated. Let us next go over the possible difficulties with regard to the way in which each of these thinkers has spoken and also state what the situation is concerning the principles. (988b16–21)

As we have seen, considerations of this tenor can also be found in *Metaphysics* Alpha Elatton, in which we have the clearest acknowledgment of the communal nature of the pursuit of truth and community is understood both temporally and spatially, in both genealogical and synchronous terms. The source of confirmation, then, is as much a matter of history, discursive transmission, and shared practices as it is a matter of phenomenal necessitation. For, indeed, culture, that is to say, inherited discourses, shapes and complements our reception of and receptivity to what is.

To conclude, let us underline once more, on the ground of the preceding analyses, the priority of ethics in the context of the pursuit of truth, the pursuit that is first philosophy itself. It might seem that ethics, especially in its prescriptive vocation, should start once the good "in the whole of nature" (982b7) has been established in virtue of wisdom. And yet, conversely, we have seen that wisdom itself is irreducible to knowing in the strict rational sense – that, rather, it rests on an intuitive apprehension ethically and phenomenologically determined. To the extent that first principles, and hence the ultimate teleological guidance, remain shrouded from rational cognition, a purely rational ethical discourse, resting on the prior determination of the good as such, is unthinkable. The ethical inquiry is that inquiry working toward an end that, while as such trusted, remains only liminally known. Thus, not only is the ethical inquiry not dependent on an a priori determination of the good, but the inquiry pursuing such a determination, that is, first philosophy, is grounded, clarified, and brought to completion by the examination of ethical structures. Let us recall again Alpha Elatton 3, where Aristotle speaks of the formations of custom, education, and even individual inclination already at work long *before* the scientific pursuit proper begins, in fact, laying the ground for such a pursuit. As we pointed out, this issue will be taken up even later in Books Gamma and Kappa. However, it is important to notice that already at these early stages of the *Metaphysics* we have the statement that, albeit as yet unthematized, ethics frames and determines the discourse of wisdom. The relevant passage may simply be quoted here:

> The way we receive a lecture depends on our customs [ἔθη]; for we expect a lecturer to use the language we are accustomed to, and any other language appears not agreeable but rather unknown and strange because we are not accustomed to it; for the customary is well known [σύνηθες γνώριμον]. The power of custom is clearly seen in the laws, in which the mythical and childish beliefs prevail over

the knowledge [γιγνώσκειν] about them, because of custom. Some people do not accept statements unless they are expressed mathematically; others, unless they are expressed by way of examples; and there are some who demand that a poet be quoted as a witness. Again, some demand accuracy in everything, while others are annoyed by it, either because they are unable to follow connections or because they regard it as petty. For accuracy is sometimes petty, and as in business transactions, so in speech it seems mean to some people. Therefore one should already be trained in how to accept statements, for it is absurd to be seeking science and at the same time the way of acquiring science; and neither of them can be acquired easily. The accuracy that exists in mathematical statements should not be demanded in everything but only in whatever has no matter. Accordingly, the manner of proceeding in such cases is not that of physics; for perhaps all nature has matter. Hence, we should first inquire what nature is; for in this way, too, it will become clear what the objects of physics are, and in addition, whether one science or more than one should contemplate causes and principles. (994b32–995a20)

From the point of view of the primordiality of ethical considerations, the various treatises that will have been gathered under the title of *Metaphysics* exhibit an undeniable consistency.

Thus, we are left with a rather unusual conclusion. On the one hand, this text, the *Metaphysics*, establishes from the beginning a dichotomous differentiation between theory and practical thought, between contemplation and *praxis*. This points to a distinction between that which is for its own sake and that which is for the sake of action. Suffice it to recall the already quoted passage at *Metaphysics* Alpha 982b21, in which we are told that the science of wisdom is free, for it alone is for its own sake, and not for the sake of something else. And yet, on the other hand, we cannot but call into question this very distinction on the ground of the segments of text we have examined. And calling into question the distinction does not mean so much that theoretical and practical thought may be conflated into one, but that their hierarchical organization (*theōria* guiding *praxis* and practical thought) as well as the autonomy of *theōria* may be shown in a problematic light. Again, we are left wondering how to understand *theōrein*, this contemplative endeavor, in the context of the human condition. Such a condition intimates that the objectifying distance, the separation simultaneously constituting the object as such and the subject in its emancipation, may never be attainable simply and without any further qualification.

In the end, I would like to bring to our attention once more a passage from the *Politics*, directly disempowering such an apparently obvious distinction: "But the practical human being is not necessarily one [whose actions are] related to others, as some suppose; and practical thoughts, too, are not only those occurring for the sake of what follows from acting, but much more those which are complete in themselves [αὐτοτελεῖς] and are contemplations [θεωρίας] and [acts of] thinking [διανοήσεις] for their own sake; for a good deed [εὐπραξία] is an end in itself, and so it is a certain action [πρᾶξίς τις]" (1325b17–21).

4

Concluding Section

Ēthikōn Nikomakheiōn Theta to Kappa

Books Theta and Iota of the *Nicomachean Ethics* are devoted to the issue of friendship, *philia.* With regard to length, the discussion on friendship exceeds by far any other thematic elaboration in the treatise. Following this analysis, Book Kappa, which contains a meditation on the good in light of political association, brings the *Ethics* to a close.

Let us, from the outset, highlight the belonging of the phenomenon of friendship in the problematic of the good. Friendship occurs for the sake of and thanks to the good. In other words, the good is what elicits it, what calls for friendship. Friendship, love in the broadest sense, is for and of the good. Adhering to the Aristotelian articulation, what follows aims at illuminating this interpretive hypothesis.

At the very beginning of Book Theta, Aristotle points out that "friendship is a virtue, or something with virtue, and besides, it is most necessary to life, for no one would choose to live without friends, though they would have all the other goods" (1155a4–6). We should underline both the connection of friendship with excellence and the necessity of friendship. Aristotle further underscores this necessity in the lines shortly following the passage just quoted:

> Friends help the young in guarding them from error, and they help the old who, because of their weakness, need care [θεραπείαν] and additional support for their actions, and they help those in their prime of life to do beautiful actions, as in the saying: "And the two are coming together," for with friends human beings are more able [δυνατώτεροι] to think [νοῆσαι] and to act [πρᾶξαι]. (1155a13–16)

As the various forms of friendship make perspicuous, the closeness of friends supports one in every aspect of life, in all manner of practical endeavor, including the practice of thinking. In other words, in virtue of friendship human beings are more able to be fully who they are, to become according to their potentiality. They have the opportunity of being more fully, of fulfilling their own task, which is a certain action illuminated by reason or, more broadly, by the exercise of thinking. Thus, friendship is intimately connected with the possibility of realizing the potential of human beings, precisely as human beings. In this sense, it is elating and empowering. Friendship provides the condition and context for the explication of human *dunamis*.

1. FRIENDSHIP AND JUSTICE: INCEPTIVE REMARKS

The link between friendship and virtue is mentioned in passing. Accordingly, friendship is associated with justice, previously disclosed as excellence in the comprehensive sense. In a key passage, Aristotle states:

> In travels [ἐν ταῖς πλάναις], too, one may observe how close [οἰκεῖον] and dear [φίλον] every human being is to another human being. Friendship seems to hold a *polis* together [συνέχειν], too, and lawgivers seem to pay more attention to friendship than to justice; for concord [ὁμόνοια] seems to be somewhat akin [ὅμοιον] to friendship, and this they aim at most of all and try their utmost to drive out faction, which is enmity. And when human beings are friends, they have no need of justice at all, but when they are just, they still need friendship; and that which is most just is thought to be done in a friendly way [φιλικόν]. (1155a21–9)

In the course of a journey, human beings tend to regard one another with sympathy. Not unlike sailors at sea, conscious of the perils of their worldly transit, they share the same vulnerability to the measureless and nonhuman. Friendship, then, would stem from such an elemental sentiment of solidarity and promote accord within the community. In this way, it encourages likemindedness, a community "of one mind," as it were.

Thus, in the very passage explicitly maintaining that friendship surpasses justice to the point of making justice obsolete, indeed unnecessary (friends "have no need of justice at all"), Aristotle is also developing an understanding of friendship in terms of communal or political cohesion and, hence, of justice. Yet the tension between friendship as irreducible to justice and friendship as equivalent with justice may be only apparent: it may be due to a tension harbored within the language itself of justice no less than to the exuberant semantic proliferation pertaining to friendship. The manifoldness of the phenomenon of friendship, and especially the difficult intersection of friendship as loving intimacy between excellent individuals (*teleia philia*) and friendship as a genuinely political bond, will occupy us in the following pages.

Insofar as both of them grant the harmonious cohesiveness of the *polis,* friendship and justice may be seen as coextensive. Aristotle asserts, "In each kind of government friendship appears to the extent that what is just does" (1161a10–11). Such a relation between friendship and justice may imply either that (1) friendship is understood *lato sensu,* as a vaguely defined bond of solidarity, or that (2) being just will never have meant merely following the laws. Such a view of justice is in line with the previous analysis in Book Epsilon: as "complete virtue," *aretē teleia,* justice indicates excellence with respect to another, that is, in relation, and cannot as such coincide with the mere observance of extrinsic prescriptions. Thus, in its irreducibility to legality, justice is illuminated by the loving solicitude characteristic of friends. It may be said that friendship completes justice, brings justice to its fullest manifestation: that which is most just, just even beyond just laws, carries the mark of friendship. In a certain sense, justice as *teleia aretē* already bespeaks friendship: as we shall see, "complete excellence" with respect to another (i.e., excellence relationally manifested, the complete exercise of excellence by essentially relational beings), not unlike friendship, indicates the harmonious articulation (order) of difference, whether in self-relation or in relation to another.

On the other hand, and perfectly in line with the preceding remarks, Aristotle states that friendship far exceeds justice understood in its narrow, legal sense. As the system of legality that grants stability and protects the *polis* from faction or divisiveness, justice is the necessary condition for the institution, subsistence, and continuation of the *polis.* But friendship (at least friendship for the sake of excellence, as distinct from convenience, expediency, pleasure, or material advantage) surpasses this logic of survival: it is what adorns life in such a way as to turn living into living well. Time and again it becomes apparent that, in this sense, friendship would make juridical measures and the whole legislative effort somewhat unnecessary, or would crucially change their function. In this way, the Aristotelian reflection reveals a twofold convergence: a convergence, on the one hand, of friendship as *teleia philia* and justice as *teleia aretē,* and, on the other hand, of justice as legality and friendship as the basic accord and concord allowing for coexistence.

If friendship in the complete sense would reign, then justice as that to which human beings asymptotically aspire would be fulfilled. Concomitantly, justice as the system of juridical institutions would be superseded, revealed as superfluous. This intimates that politics as juridical institution (let alone in its pre-juridical, pre-normative, auroral stratum), is not coeval with friendship, but rather precedes it. The suggestion is that political constitution in its juridical expression is necessary and called for precisely to the extent that friendship is not the common condition, that is, to the extent that the members of the community are not as a whole gathered together in virtue of a prevailing bond of friendship. As we shall see better, friendship in its achieved sense is a "rare" phenomenon. Its sporadic incidence, nevertheless, may function as a reminder and even a promise, however unreadable and fragmentary, of the justice that is not yet, that is to come: the justice for which human beings keep striving.

That politics (and, hence, legality) may be understood not as contemporary or equiprimordial with friendship, but rather as preceding friendship, entails that politics somehow is the condition of friendship. In a way, politics constitutes the environment, the context, whereby friendship becomes possible – friendship, that is, no longer determined by the need or reasons of survival, but perfected, *teleia philia.*

In turn, however, friendship constitutes the end or destination of politics, in the sense that it indicates the highest manifestation and achievement of politics. Indeed, friendship may even appear to presage the self-overcoming of politics understood as the work of merely extrinsic institution. In this latter sense, friendship would signal the perfection of politics – the politics to come, no longer resting on the institution of external order and institutional self-enforcement. It would illuminate politics as the harmonization of the many, organically gathered beyond legal prescriptions: no longer having to protect their own from the other's projected infringement, but choosing and recognizing each other, wishing each other's good, in an expansive projection of further development.

Such a completion would be announced (if not reached) when the togetherness at first perceived as merely factual, as the de facto "journeying in the company of many" (*Republic* 614c), would occasion the realization of a deeper, more significant sharing. It would be announced if the mere necessity of being together were to allow for a margin of insight revealing the other(s) as partaking in common conditions, and hence for a vantage point engendering compassion, the recognition of shared undergoing, of a common *pathos.* At stake, then, would be the acknowledgment, the conscious taking note of what is always already the case, the (perhaps sudden) becoming remarkable of the primal condition of togetherness, which at first remains altogether unremarkable, indeed, shrouded. In this conscious awakening to interdependence would lie the possibility of the transfiguration of politics into friendship.

It appears, let this be noted only in passing, that nothing would prevent such a transfiguration from entailing destabilization, perhaps even a certain destructiveness, since friendship in the "perfect" sense gestures toward the obsolescence of political structures securing stability. Love or friendship (Aristotle often utilizes the language of *philia* and that of *erōs* interchangeably) may even constitute a threat to civil coexistence as it is known. It may constitute a principle before, beyond, or outside the law.

Once more, we should underline that the friendship at stake in these brief digressive remarks is friendship proper, in the primary sense, and not what Aristotle calls "qualified" friendship, that is, friendship "in virtue of an attribute." The latter includes relationships for the sake of pleasure, appetite, and material advantage or usefulness. To the extent that friendship is seen as ancillary to a political program, as a mere instrument of political cohesiveness, it includes relationships that are highly conventional, ritualized, for the sake of "goods" in a limited sense. Analogously to Plato, Aristotle considers such instrumental interpretation of friendship truncated and impoverished.[1] Conversely, as we shall see, in "complete" friendship he acknowledges an excess both intractable (not lending itself to either conceptual or political control) and carrying extraordinarily far-reaching implications.

1.1. Digression: Friendship and the Problem of Cosmopolitanism

We shall return to the intertwinement of friendship and justice and hence, to the political dimensions of this relational mode. The questions to be addressed in this perspective are numerous and complex. However, we should focus first on friendship as an intimate bond between individuals – which, in this context, does *not* mean friendship as a purely "private" affair. We have already more than once underlined the distance between the philosophical ambiance here examined and the genuinely modern, paradigmatically Kantian, stance. If, with and after Kant, friendship as well as happiness come to be understood as categories pertaining to individual experience, marked by contingency and subsequently relegated

[1] Let us recall Plato's treatment of *erōs* in the early stages of the *Symposium*. Whereas, especially through the figures of Phaedrus and Pausanias, *erōs* is presented as subservient to political functioning, somewhat conducive to optimal political dynamics, the comprehensive framework of the Platonic dialogue clearly exposes the partiality and incompleteness of this view of love.

to the private (indeed, it could be said that the very separation and contraposition of private and public rest on such a construal of friendship and happiness as, in each case, insular, diverse, essentially unrelated, and politically irrelevant pursuits), at this stage of the Greek reflection, and most notably with Aristotle, we consistently find the indication of a certain undecidability between private and public matters. The pursuit of friendship and of self-realization is, to be sure, recognized and magnified in its ever-unique unfolding and unrepeatability, and yet this never leads to a clear-cut severance of this phenomenon from the sphere of political implications and determinations. Conversely, the interaction called friendship as well as the pursuit of happiness as living well are, to be sure, understood also in terms of political teleology, and yet this never means that individual becoming is or should be subjected to, let alone resolved into, the logic of political holism.[2]

It could be said that the Aristotelian reflection provides resources for the systematic overcoming of the opposition of public and private or universality and singularity; that, indeed, far from such a dichotomy, from the hierarchy it entails, and even from the mere reversal thereof, such a reflection allows for the conception of universality precisely in terms of singularity; that, in other words, it makes possible to glimpse at the universality of the singular – at singularity, that is, infinite irreducibility and irreplaceability, as that which is shared in common, and in this sense "universal." We could envision, in sum, a commonality of utter uniqueness, of that which, though elusive, is not nothing: a commonality, then, of *almost* nothing in common (for that which cannot be determinately known, known in its determinacy, is nothing only from the point of view of the determining work of reason). The vision of such a commonality presents a fecund contribution to the meditations on universalism and cosmopolitanism, which have recently obtained renewed impulse (consider thinkers as diverse as Habermas, Derrida, Kristeva, Nancy). Indeed, it may allow us to pursue the Kantian vision beyond the unmitigated privilege of reason: to think the global community of humankind as otherwise than resting solely on rational (inter)subjectivity.

A host of questions arises in the wake of such considerations. Indeed, especially in light of the circumstances in which we find ourselves at

[2] On these issues, see Gianfrancesco Zanetti, *Amicizia, felicità, diritto. Due argomenti sul perfezionismo giuridico* (Rome: Carocci, 1998) and *Ragion pratica e diritto: un percorso aristotelico/Practical Reason and Law: An Aristotelian Itinerary* (Milan: Giuffrè, 2001), parts I and II.

the outset of another millennium, how could it be possible to think the community of human beings as community emancipated from, and yet not oblivious of, tribal/cultural identifications? How can community be thought, if not by reference to the privilege of reason alone (which, as could be witnessed in the last century, has not nearly exhibited the authoritativeness that any rationalistic political thinker would attribute to it)? How could we envision a community in which national and territorial belonging would be recognized as crucial determinations of individual stories, lives, and identities, and yet not as exhausting the infinitely excessive phenomenon of individuals becoming themselves, of individuals individuating themselves in their radically singular becoming? In other words: how is one to acknowledge cultural/material bonds without turning them into bondage, and how, conversely, is one to conceive of freedom without turning it into the predictability and in-difference of dematerialized rational subjects? How could the de-territorialization of the human be thought otherwise than in terms of disembodiment?

Again, how would we think cosmopolitanism without excluding that which is distinctive (that which can be viewed neither as universal nor even as "particular," i.e., as a declension of the universal), that is, body and embodiment, differences in gender, race, culture, religion, history, and experience? How could we think the exclusive trait otherwise than in terms of exclusion and exclusivity, let alone of insularity? How are we to think, on the one hand, distinctiveness as other than individualism, provincialism, nationalism, and, on the other hand, universality as other than the obliteration of differences? How could we heal the wound of this dichotomy? How could we think community also, if not exclusively, starting from *pathos* – not from that which we are, know, and own, but from that which we are not, do not know, do not own?[3] How could we think community not only from identity, but also from that which, inside as well as outside ourselves, remains strange to us and a stranger – extraneous, estranged, perturbing, finally, *unheimlich*? Such would be (if it were ever to be) the community of those who, as has been said, have nothing in common – not in the sense that they do not share anything in common, but in the sense that what they share (which may not be nothing) is neither their own property nor conceptually possessed.

If it were ever to be, this would be the community of singularities sharing in common, in each case, their singularity. It would entail not a denial, demotion, or de-valuation of reason, but the understanding that

[3] Such would be the community of desire, according to *Symp.* 200e.

reason (*logos*) is not all-comprehending but rather itself comprehended, that reason (*logos*) *never* gives itself *as such*, but always as deflected and inflected through and as life – through the life in which it necessarily belongs, through the time-space into which it is necessarily folded (indefinite multiplicity of languages, of reasons, of ways and paths). Such would be the community of singularities inflecting the community of reason, exposing the latter in its incompleteness and aspectival character.

Let us, then, turn to the Aristotelian discourse on the love between friends. It may prove not to be extraneous to the above concerns.

Indeed, in what follows the operative hypothesis is that Aristotle's ethico-political thinking, and especially his discussion of friendship (outstanding in its amplitude vis-à-vis other thematizations in the treatises), may be enormously suggestive in the attempt to address such questions. As we shall see, the examination of friendship between excellent individuals allows Aristotle paradigmatically to outline the figure of the human being exceeding itself, caught in a movement of self-overcoming: the human being as, precisely qua human, a structure of excess, openness, and hospitality. In this sense, the human being properly (paradoxically) finds and recomposes itself only in the thrust outside itself and detour through the other. Even more radically, far from simply bringing the other back to oneself, far from returning to oneself as if the alienating detour were but an obvious diversion, in the mirror of the other the human being sees the trace of an ulterior openness that cannot yield any self-contained identity – the trace of a shared openness to an other that is neither another human being nor (any other) being. In the other that the friend is, one catches a glimpse of the shared openness to (love of) the good. In the loving thrust beyond oneself and the detour through the other, one is disclosed in terms of infinite receptivity. But let us proceed to consider Aristotle's text.

2. PERFECTION OF FRIENDSHIP

According to Aristotle, friendship in its primary sense (i.e., perfect, complete) is based on similarity (*homoiōsis*, 1156b8) and reciprocity (1155b34).[4] Albeit neither determinable nor strictly calculable, these are observed between friends, between the individuals involved in the relationship of friendship. On the ground of the assumption of similarity

4 As Thomas Aquinas observes in his commentary on *Nicomachean Ethics*, friendship exceeds virtue, for it requires reciprocity and, hence, entails a doubling of excellent action.

and reciprocity, it is said that friendship is a kind of love of oneself. (In Plato's *Republic*, on a most basic level, friendship is revealed in terms of inner harmonization, "becoming one's own friend," 443c–e.)

It is relevant to underline that what is common, that is, what is involved in such a similarity and reciprocation, is not some accidental feature, but excellence itself. In other words, what is common is psychological conformation, that is, one's disposition with respect to the good, the very structure in virtue of which one may be good and toward the good. As Aristotle observes, "[p]erfect friendship is between human beings who are good and similar [ὁμοίων] with respect to virtue; for, insofar as they are good, it is in a similar manner that they wish [βούλονται] each other the good [things], and such human beings are good in themselves" (1156b7–10). At stake in friendship primarily understood is the sharing of excellence. It is such a movement toward the good, entailing excellence in psychological formation, which is eminently lovable in the friend.

Thus, the similarity between the friends is not based on something owned in the narrow sense of the term – a property or possession that can be the object of comparison and comparative evaluation. The friends resemble one another in their being similarly turned toward the good, in their pursuing and striving for the good. What they share is nothing possessed but, rather, that which is sought after or loved. As Aristotle puts it in the *Eudemian Ethics*, "for us [human beings] the good [τὸ εὖ] is according to the other [καθ' ἕτερον]" (1245b18) and "each one wishes to live together [with one's friends] in the end that one may be capable of" (1245b8), especially "in the superior good [βελτίονι ἀγαθῷ]" (1245b2), enjoying "more divine pleasures" (1245a39–b1).

The similarity between friends may be a matter of possession only in the strict sense of the having (*ekhein*) of habits, more precisely the having of excellent ones. Excellent habituation, that is, the stabilization of excellent psychological structures, may indeed be considered a property. Yet it is that peculiar property that turns the one who has it toward that which exceeds one, that which is not possessed – that peculiar property that turns the one to whom it properly belongs beyond oneself, that is, beyond the structures themselves of propriety as well as property and ownership, toward a certain self-dispossession. In this sense, excellent habituation signals that the human being in its culminating manifestation cannot be understood in terms of autonomy, self-enclosure, and self-identity, let alone individualism. In its highest accomplishment, the human being bespeaks constitutive permeability and heteronomous determination.

Friends, then, share their disposition toward the good: they are similarly turned toward the good, similarly caught in the love of the good. It is such a thrust, such a love irreducible to their love for each other, which friends share. Similarity as well as reciprocity must be understood in light of such an excess, of such an openness beyond each of the friends involved, beyond even their relatedness, their tending to be at one, to become one. Aristotle recognizes the exuberance and overflowing character of friendship: friendship is *huperbolē*, hyperbolic, inherently marked by excess (1158a12, 1166b1). One loves another in virtue of the other's orientation toward the good, an orientation that one experiences as well. So, in loving the other, each is first of all recognizing him- or herself as other. This is so not only because each recognizes him- or herself through the other, that is, because one comes to oneself essentially thanks to the departure toward the other, in an ecstatic movement outside oneself that can never allow for a simple return without dispersal. More remarkably still, one recognizes oneself as other because one contemplates in the other an infinite openness to radical alterity, to an alterity altogether irreducible to another human being as well as to (any other) being. That one recognizes oneself as other means that one catches a glimpse of oneself as an open structure of receptivity and hospitality, inhabited by, and striving toward, that which is irreducible to oneself. Friendship would entail sharing in common that which is not owned, but desired – sharing (experiencing, sustaining, finally being) in common the open structure of incompleteness, the longing thereby implied, and the unique orientation toward not just any expedient or surrogate manner of filling the void.

Thus, in loving the other, each is at the same time projected beyond him- or herself, beyond the other, and beyond their relationship as well. Indeed, friendship can neither be reduced to nor be contained within the exchange merely between the friends. For, in loving the other, one is caught in the shared common movement toward the good, that is to say, in the movement of living well, of life in its plenitude (in a plenitude that coincides with a yearning for fulfillment). This is, of course, what is named by happiness. The love of the friend is *at once* a thrust beyond the friend. Indeed, such a thrust beyond is essentially involved in the inception as well as the abiding of friendship.

2.1. Similarity and Reciprocity beyond Measure

Again, we must emphasize that similarity and reciprocity thus understood can hardly be considered a calculable matter. So it is certainly the case, as Aristotle points out, that friendship is among equals, is a matter of equality (*philotēs isotēs*, 1158a1).[5] However, *isotēs* here seems to name the togetherness of two people who are equal in that each of them enacts him- or herself as a strange oneness entailing openness. In the privileged and paradigmatically conducive space that friendship offers, each of them can more fully unfold, more excellently take up the task of becoming oneself – the task of living. They are equal in sharing the same aspiration, the same propulsion, the same longing orienting them toward a certain kind of life. Aristotle observes: "Equality in what is just does not appear to be similar to equality in friendship; for the equal in what is just is primarily according to merit but secondarily according to quantity, while in friendship the equal according to quantity is primary but that according to merit is secondary" (1158b29–33). In other words, at stake in "perfect" friendship is not so much proportional equality, based on the evaluation of worth, but rather numerical equality. In such a friendship, the friends are one before the other one, together in sharing a common desire, and each one of them is one precisely in virtue of such an orientation, of such a movement that is simultaneously transgressive (movement beyond oneself) and relational (movement toward another).

And yet, pursuing the same desire will not possibly have meant becoming the same. On the contrary, taking up the task of living well will have entailed confronting the ever unique question regarding oneself, one's utterly singular circumstances and conditions, and hence developing the traits and actualizing the genuinely distinctive potentiality each one bears. Pursuing the same desire, thus, will have meant becoming oneself.[6] In

5 Aristotle is here reporting a saying ("*legetai gar* . . ."). Already, Timaeus referred the assonant equivalence *philotēs-isotēs*, friendship-equality, to Pythagoras (Diogenes Laertius, *Vitae Philosophorum* VIII.10). To Pythagoras is also attributed the formulation *koina ta tōn philōn*, the pronouncement dear to Plato stating that friends share everything in common. Both sayings on friendship enjoyed lasting authoritativeness as expressions of ancient wisdom. See, e.g., Plato's *Lysis* 207c and *De legibus* 757a, Aristotle's *Nicomachean Ethics* Iota 1168b8, and Cicero's *De officiis* I.51.

6 The friendship among philosophers (those who, in turn, are friends of wisdom) makes this especially perspicuous: pursuing wisdom together, as friends, will not have meant coming to the same results, but rather cultivating together a certain *ēthos*, sharing a life of (self-)examination. Consider the passage in *Nicomachean Ethics* Alpha in which Aristotle prepares to undertake a critique of the Platonists' (if not Plato's) view of the good: "such an inquiry is made with great reluctance," warns Aristotle, "because the men, *andras*, who introduced the *eidē* are friends. Yet, it would perhaps be thought better, and also a duty, to forsake, *anairein*, even what is close in order to save the truth, especially as we are philosophers; for while both are dear, it is pious to honor truth" (1096a12–16). If, prima facie, it appears as though friendship and the pursuit of the truth are dissociated

the thrust of friendship lies the possibility of the individuation of each, the phenomenon of each pursuing his or her most unique development. Individuation, the becoming of each according to one's potential, is not individualism: unbridgeable singularity takes shape in and as relatedness, relationality, interconnectedness.

Thus – and this is of paramount importance, although seldom observed – the similarity and equality at stake in this discourse cannot be resolved into matters of custom, communal conventions, status and reputation. The relationship here explored may no more be viewed merely as the bond of convenience and conformity uniting those enjoying the same political visibility than the community of those striving after the good (the community of the best) may be mistaken for aristocracy as the class endowed with material advantage, power, automatically inherited rights. Indeed, one could even say that relatedness in the mode of friendship discloses the possibility for the dawning of the individual as such, beyond

and the latter is chosen over against the former, it should nonetheless be recalled that the alleged privilege of truth is affirmed by turning to and quoting the friend. Aristotle is here echoing Plato, who, again, attributes this posture to Socrates: we should pursue the truth despite the rifts and differences this may bring about between us and those we love, our friends (*Phaed.* 91c, *Resp.* X 595b–c). In his commentary on the *Nicomachean Ethics*, with his usual equanimity, Thomas underlines the closeness between the friends (Aristotle, Plato) precisely there where the pursuit of the truth seems to be contrasted to friendship and shown as incompatible with it: "Along the same lines is also the judgment of Plato who, in rejecting the opinion of his teacher Socrates, says that it is necessary to care more for truth than for anything else. Somewhere else he affirms that Socrates is certainly a friend, but truth is even more so (*amicus quidem Socrates, sed magis amica veritas*). In yet another place he says that one should certainly care little for Socrates but a lot for truth" (I.6.5). Thus, no sooner is the friendship with "men" set aside, for the sake of companionship with the truth, than it is taken up again. Indeed, the friendship among "men" is reasserted in a privileged sense, as the friendship among the friends of wisdom: for "we," Aristotle emphatically affirms, "are philosophers." The philosophers are revealed, thus, as those exemplary friends who share the same compulsion toward wisdom, even as the manner in which each comports himself in his pursuit may be quite unique, even at odds with others. The friendship among philosophers casts light on the many ways in which the same may be shared. In this sense, friendship appears to be not a matter of agreement (of saying the same) in any straightforward sense, but a matter of undergoing the same experience (*pathos*), of being exposed to the same claim, of sharing a certain thrust, a certain searching relation to the truth: to the truth not owned, known, and mastered but, once again, searched – even more precisely, loved. Thus understood, friendship can be no alternative to the love of truth, but appears to rest on the sharing of such a love. The philosophical impulse discloses friendship as the sharing of a desire to understand, a desire that prescribes an unrelenting exploration, the tracing of one's own path of inquiry and not the acquiescence to friends and teachers – a desire that, therefore, not only may but almost inevitably does lead to trajectories in tension with each other, when not altogether incompatible. Yet these paths that may not agree and, at the limit, not even intersect, are drawn in response to a shared, common compulsion.

functional relationships, satisfaction of conventional requirements, and fulfillment of given roles – beyond the highly codified civic-political interactions.

In this way, the Aristotelian reflection cannot simply be interpreted and expounded in terms of the historical/cultural context it reflects and out of which it develops. Aristotle's understanding of friendship cannot be said purely to pertain to relationships between and among free male adults or, more precisely, between and among citizens belonging to the dominant class – the only ones living a life of political engagement and leisure. While, to be sure, in the context Aristotle lived in only free men, emancipated from the strictures of necessity, would be in the position of experiencing the bond of friendship in its accomplished sense, Aristotle's thinking is not merely delimited by such a framework. Irreducible to the historically determined relational/communal shapes whose mark it nevertheless bears, Aristotle's thinking envisions friendship as the terrain most conducive to human growth and development, as the relational engagement above all and most fully promoting the unfolding of human possibility and, hence, displaying the human being in its structural openness, caught in the in(de)finite task of becoming toward the good. Far from being a matter of self-identity or sameness, of identification with and belonging in a certain class or clan, friendship, precisely in casting light on the experience of excess, calls identity into question in its very possibility, whether at the level of conceptual determinacy, categorial stability, or socio-cultural taxonomy. Friendship rests on sameness (of desire) not defined in its whatness, on a sameness that cannot be resolved into conformity. It is in this perspective that Aristotle's analysis remains alive and vibrant, well beyond considerations of historiographic, archeological, or antiquarian tenor.

Similarly, it should be pointed out that, in the reading here proposed, friendship cannot be understood in terms of competition, as if it were a matter of noble rivalry.[7] Sharing the love of the good can by no means signify competing for the exclusive favors of a beloved, engaging in the *agōn* whose prize would be the conquest of the desired one to the detriment of the other contender: the good, in the sense of living well and striving toward self-realization, can hardly be a matter of scarcity and hence of exclusion, of an attainment necessarily restricted to one or few. Rather, the good names the task of excellent self-accomplishment that pertains

7 See Gilles Deleuze and Felix Guattari, *Qu'est-ce que la philosophie?* (Paris: Les éditions de Minuit, 1991), Introduction.

to each being in its becoming – a task for which friendship provides élan and inspiration. For friendship indicates encountering and interacting with another, catching sight of the good in and as the other, being drawn and open to the other in his or her openness to the good, and finding oneself in such an undergoing and attraction.

2.2. The First Friend

As was anticipated, in loving a friend one loves oneself. In this sense, Aristotle states that "being disposed toward a friend is like being disposed to oneself (for a friend is another self)" (1166a31–2).[8] This echoes the Platonic intimations both in the *Phaedrus* and in the *Republic.* In accord with oneself and harboring the love elicited by happiness (the love of the good), as if overflowing, one loves outside oneself, wishing the good of another and actively pursuing it (1166a1–14). Indeed, because the traits of such a bearing belong to "someone good [ἐπιεικεῖ] in relation to him- or herself . . . friendship too seems to be some of these features, and friends seem to be those who have them" (1166a30–3). Friendship is thought to originate from one's disposition toward oneself (1166a1–2), and hence to reflect and resemble it: "the excess of friendship [ὑπερβολὴ τῆς φιλίας] is similar [ὁμοιοῦται] to that [sentiment] toward oneself" (1166b1).

Thus, being one's own friend by no means signifies being a self-enclosed harmony, but rather points to the harmonious movement of a love that overflows, connects, and attunes. Again, friendship with oneself hardly bespeaks self-identity: it rather indicates the love and pursuit of that which exceeds. In turn, friendship with another cannot be reduced to a process of appropriation assimilating the friend (the other) to structures of identity. The friend as "another self" cannot signify that I bring the other back to myself, but that I am toward the other and the other pervades me *ab origine*; that I am thus deprived of (self-)possession and control; that alterity, not even anthropologically reducible, is constitutive of me and I am always already late with respect to such constitution.

Experiencing oneself in such a relation to oneself that cannot be a matter of self-possession or self-knowledge unqualified, one is in the condition of loving, outside oneself, those who are similarly harboring and enacting the good – those similarly living toward the good or longing for

[8] Porphyry attributes to Pythagoras the view of the friend as an alter ego (*Vita Pythagorae* 33).

an attunement to it.[9] It is in this sense that, as we said in the beginning, friendship occurs for the sake of and thanks to the good. It is in this sense that, as we have suggested, the good elicits friendship and, therefore, that friendship or love is of and for the good. The love of another is folded into the shared love of the altogether other designated as the good. Taking it with utmost caution, we may in this regard recall Plato's understanding of the good, in the *Lysis*, as *prōton philon*, "the first friend," or friend in the primary sense.

Of course we should also, concomitantly, recall that the highest good is perceived by a power that exceeds *logos*, as we have seen especially in Aristotle's remarks on *nous* and *sophia*. The good, indeed, is perceived by a power that exceeds discourse, demonstration, and argument, let alone contention. Aristotle, as we read in *Nicomachean Ethics* Alpha, suggests that ethics-politics, the "most architectonic" discourse, is not geometry: the construction that ethics-politics is takes place with no knowledge of the principle (the good, happiness) guiding it. The construction of ethics-politics is architecture without geometry. Even in the *Metaphysics*, at the culmination of the discourse of first philosophy, the highest good (god, *nous*) is not an object of knowledge but the *erōmenos*, beloved. In the Platonic texts themselves (most notably the *Republic*, *Timaeus*, and *Philebus*), the good is consistently highlighted in its excess vis-à-vis the order of being and, hence, of knowledge. Strictly speaking, there is no *logos*, no proper discourse of the good or the god, and, hence, no theology: only a

9 In *L'anima alle soglie del pensiero nella filosofia greca* (Naples: Bibliopolis, 1988), Hans Georg Gadamer focuses on the connection between friendship and self-knowledge (93–109) and, most notably, on the question of *philautia* in Aristotle. The Platonic legacy can be discerned in the view that friendship with another requires friendship with oneself (101). Yet, Gadamer maintains, such a condition of friendship entails neither the priority nor the autarchy of the contemplative moment, whether knowledge or self-knowledge (103). This is evident from the determination of the human being obtained through the contrast to the gods, a contrast putting human limits and finitude into relief. According to Aristotle, Gadamer argues, humans may not know themselves without qualification, let alone know themselves prior to and aside from their involvement with others. Indeed, precisely because they are not gods, humans may know (and hence be friends with) others to a higher degree than they know themselves; most notably, they may know, find access to themselves, only thanks to the detour through others (103–9). Aristotle recognizes the prescription of self-knowledge (*Magna moralia* 1213a13–26). Yet while the god cannot think the other than itself (its simplicity and completeness prevent that), the human can elucidate itself to itself only through the exposure to and elucidation of the other. The very capacity of the human for realizing difference and effecting integration is distinctive of the human vis-à-vis the divine. That one mirrors oneself in the friend (*Phaedrus* 255d) means that one comes to oneself through the other, thanks to "being-with" (*suzēn*). Gadamer's argumentation is also supported by *Eudemian Ethics* 1245b16–19.

"likely discourse" (*eikos logos*) or *muthos.* Thus, in Plato as well as Aristotle, the centrality and encompassing character of the good cannot be seen in the perspective of a *reductio ad bonum,* as a subordination of friendship (of practical matters broadly) to the good as an over-arching metaphysical principle, that is, a principle both intelligible and granting intelligibility. Far from performing such an operation, the Platonic-Aristotelian discourses reveal the good in its radical elusiveness and the investigations of first philosophy as resting on the *pathos* of love.

Thus, the good seems to elude knowledge, the most representative virtue of *logos,* of reason in the strict sense. Indeed, it may be only in virtue of wisdom, *sophia,* that the human being gains an insight into the good, if not knowledge understood in the narrow sense. And it is wisdom that holds *logos* in check, restraining this both remarkable and dangerous "possession" of human beings, this potentially destructive ability of discourse to alienate itself from its living evidence. It is wisdom that articulates the desire for the good and recognizes an orientation to it, while keeping such longing thrust rooted in life. On the one hand, as we saw, wisdom situates the human in the beyond-human, explicating the human by reference to what envelops, pervades, and exceeds it. On the other hand, precisely in this infinite thrust, wisdom maintains a vital link with intuitive understanding and nourishes awareness with experience. In this sense, we can glimpse at the connection between wisdom and friendship, contemplation and relatedness, insight and love – we can glimpse at friendship, paradigmatically exposing the human being in its shared search for the good, as the privileged space for the exercise and cultivation of wisdom. The discussion of friendship seems to be vitally linked to first philosophy and the contemplative enactment no less than to politics.

2.3. Finite Conditions of an Infinite Thrust

Insisting on the measurelessness (indeterminability) characterizing the similarity as well as reciprocity of friends aims at underlining the critique, implicit in the Aristotelian discussion, of identity structures. If we neglect such imperviousness to measurement (to determination), we can hardly avoid interpreting similarity in terms of equal political-economic status and reciprocity in terms of any marketplace transaction. Aristotle's entire line of thinking would wither into conventionalism, mere celebration of the political-cultural formations of its time. This much is at stake in the interpretation of similarity and reciprocity.

In light of such measurelessness and incommensurability, friendship cannot exhaust itself in an enclosed relationship between two (or among few). Rather, it always involves the sense of belonging together in that which exceeds both, in that which exceeds the human as such and can, thus, be designated as inhuman. I am attracted to another because in him or her I perceive the same propulsion toward a common end: because we love the same, which is beyond (not "the" beyond).

And yet Aristotle is also acutely aware that such an infinite movement beyond rests on altogether finite conditions: that the experience of such a driving relatedness cannot be lived with infinitely and indifferently many others; that, on the contrary, friendship in this sense is a rare occurrence. It is at this juncture that the connection is drawn between friendship as the relation that can be experienced only with a few others and friendship gathering human beings as such, in the *polis* and beyond. As we shall see, Aristotle's remarks on *eunoia*, the attitude of benevolence that remains latent, not actualized in a relationship, provide a *trait d'union* between friendship in its irreducible uniqueness and friendship in its political valence (*homonoia*). However, to begin with, let us consider the finitude characterizing the occurrence of "perfect" friendship – a finitude that cannot be explained simply by reference to the rarity of excellent human beings.

In friendship, in the kinds of friendship one experiences, it is possible to seize the manifestation of the *psukhē*. One reveals oneself in one's relations: relationships image inner relations. Whether at stake are individual human beings or communities, an isomorphism holds between inside and outside, between implicit, implicated, intra-psychic dynamics and explicit, outward, worldly relationships. Let us consider the following passage, in which Aristotle examines friendship in the complete sense:

> Such friendships are likely to be rare indeed, for few can be such friends. Further, such friendships require time and familiarity [συνηθείας]; for, as the proverb says, it is impossible for human beings to know each other well until "they have consumed together much salt," nor can they accept each other and be friends until each has shown him- or herself dear [φιλητός] and trustworthy to the other. Those who quickly show the marks of friendship [τὰ φιλικά] toward each other wish to be friends indeed but are not, unless both are dear to each other and also have come to know this; for while a wish for friendship may arise quickly, friendship does not come to be quickly. (1156b25–33)

Aristotle emphasizes the importance of actually sharing experiences and of time lived together. We will shortly turn to this and to the broader considerations on the temporality of friendship. However, let us first note how the relationship of friendship is said to make manifest the character of the friends. Friendship lays one bare, shows in action the psychological structures of the human beings involved. A further passage is illuminating in this regard:

> It is evident that only good human beings can be friends because of what they are in themselves, for bad human beings do not enjoy each other's company unless some benefit is exchanged. Again, only the friendship of good human beings cannot be harmed by slander; for it is not easy for a good person to trust what anyone says about his or her good friend who has stood the test of time. And it is among the good that trust and unwillingness to act unjustly and whatever else belongs to true friendship are expected without question, while in the other kinds of friendship nothing prevents those things from taking place. (1157a18–26)

It becomes evident that friendship not only reveals character, but also, in its perfection, unfailingly indicates and further encourages excellence. Only in the context of this relationship does the expectation arise concerning the most beautiful way of living and acting, the fullest way of being human.

When discussing friendship without qualification, Aristotle also emphasizes the factor of stability. Friendship, we are told, is not easily shaken. It tends to the radiant endurance it loves:

> Now those who wish the good [things] of their friends for the sake of their friends are friends in the highest degree; for they comport themselves thus in virtue of themselves and not according to an attribute. Accordingly, their friendship lasts as long as they are good, and virtue is something abiding. And each friend is good without qualification and also good to his or her friends; for good human beings are good without qualification as well as beneficial to each other. And they are similarly pleasant, since good human beings are pleasant without qualification and also pleasant to each other; for one's own actions and the actions which are similar to them are pleasant to oneself, and the actions of good human beings are the same or similar [αὗται ἢ ὅμοιαι]. (1156b10–17)

The element of stability is granted precisely by reference to the ground of virtue, of excellence in habituation. Likewise, as anticipated, Aristotle underscores the importance of shared time. Spending time together is essential to the coming to be of friendship in its most accomplished enactment. As Aristotle repeats shortly thereafter, "distances [places] do not break up a friendship entirely but only the exercise [ἐνέργειαν] of it. But if friends are apart from each other for a long time, this seems to make them forget [λήθην ποιεῖν] their friendship; hence the saying 'lack of conversation has broken many a friendship'" (1157b10–13).

At the same time, however, in the passages just considered Aristotle intimates that temporality poses limits on the number of friendships that one can form in one's allotted time. One may cultivate a kind disposition or benevolence (*eunoia*) toward others: the *pathos* of *eunoia* may be manifest or latent (*lanthanō*) to the one to whom it is directed, may or may not be reciprocated, and may be undergone with respect to indefinitely many others held to be good, whether known or unknown (1155b32–1156a5). However, friendships in the sense of lived relationship, intimate frequentation, and shared experience are as numerically limited as human life and scope are finite.[10] While, through friendship, human life crucially opens itself up to infinity, human beings' finitude in space, time, and resources quantitatively delimits the realization or actualization (*energeia*) of friendship. Humans possess neither the endurance nor the energy to sustain love toward indifferently many others:

> It is impossible to be a friend to many in a perfect friendship, just as it is impossible to love [ἐρᾶν] many persons at the same time (for love is like an excess [ὑπερβολή], and such excess is by nature felt toward one), and it is not easy for many people to satisfy very much the same person at the same time, or perhaps for many to be good at the same time. (1158a10–14)

Here Aristotle's reflection is twofold. In the first place, because of the intensity characteristic of friendship as well as love, one can envision only a limited number of such experiences. The hyperbolic character of friendship can be sustained only according to a certain measure. Sharing widely and indiscriminately with many such a condition seems to be out of the question: "the actual community of sensibility" (*energeia tēs sunaisthēseōs*), Aristotle affirms, "is necessarily in a small group" (*Eudemian Ethics* 1245b23–4). Second, because of the structure of what is, of communities as we know them, it may indeed be impossible for many to be good, and therefore this would automatically limit the possibility of perfect friendship. Again, this is apparent to the extent that friendship is understood as a concrete, lived practice.[11]

[10] Unlike the Stoics, Aristotle emphasizes friendship as "loving exchange," as a matter of *pathos*, of affection in the broadest sense of the term. Luigi Pizzolato draws the contrast between, on the one hand, the friendship that is shared and reciprocated virtue and, on the other hand, the "cold" disposition of benevolence, which is non-affective, unidirectional, not reciprocated (*L'idea di amicizia nel mondo antico classico e cristiano* [Turin: Einaudi, 1993], 53).

[11] In this connection, consider also *Politics* 1328a36–b2, displaying the tension between goodness as that which can be shared in varying degrees ("by some but not others or only a little") and goodness as that which can be pursued "in different ways."

However, there seem to be further concerns that Aristotle is attempting to articulate in this regard. In particular, the question stands out regarding what is proper and proportionate to the human condition. Connected with this is the problematic non-coincidence of what is possible in principle, abstractly, and what is practicable, actually realizable. Broadly speaking, at stake are the issues of measure and sustainability.[12] The question thus broached regards the *metron* properly defining the human, letting the human become definite and manifest as such, in its integrity and distinctive outline, at its best. Aristotle wonders:

> In the case of virtuous human beings, should there be as many friends as possible, or is there, as in the case of a city, a certain limit [μέτρον] of them? For neither would ten human beings make a city, nor will it remain a city if increased to one hundred thousand human beings. Perhaps a plurality has no unity unless it falls between certain limits [ὡρισμένων]. So in the case of friends, too, there is a limited plurality, and perhaps there is an upper limit of those with whom one could live together; for, as we remarked, this is thought to be friendship at its best [φιλικώτατον]. It is clear, then, that one cannot live together with many friends and attend to all of them in turn. (1170b30–1171a4)

We cannot fail to notice Aristotle's tentativeness in drawing these conclusions (his repeated "perhaps," his appeal to what "is thought"). And yet, experience provides compelling evidence: "It is difficult, too, to share the joys and sorrows in an intimate way with a great number of friends; for it is quite likely that at the same time one will be sharing pleasures with one of them but grieving with another" (1171a6–8). There seems to be an insurmountable difficulty concerning the indeterminate extension and extendibility of actually lived friendship. As was observed above, the cause of this is the finite (or, we could say, aspectival) character of the human being, of each discrete human venture. Such is the restraining condition of a being whose power, potency, or potentiality, if not unqualifiedly determinate, remains far from all-encompassing, infinite, and absolute. The experience of friendship in the perfect sense entails thrusting oneself to and being traversed by the incalculable or measureless. In being thus projected and traversed, the human being *as such* undergoes measure: it undergoes measure as its own, indeed, obtains the measure it requires in order to be. The human being is itself the phenomenon of such a measure taking place. This becomes most perspicuous in the experience

[12] As Aristotle points out, the question of the measure, *metron*, of the human may be framed by reference to the excellent human being (1166a13).

of friendship, for it is in such a *pathos* of excess that the human being is disclosed as structurally incapable of infinite undergoing.

The thrust beyond and the being traversed (which define friendship) imply the limit they transgress; in transgressing such a limit or measure they also, at once, reinstate it. This means: one will experience the *huperbolē* of friendship perhaps once, twice, at most very few times in one's life. Again, these remarks on friendship reveal Aristotle's clear distinction between, on the one hand, a posture or sentiment of benevolence, *eunoia*, possibly toward each and every other, and, on the other hand, friendship in its actuality and embodiment. The former feeling is no mere formality. It is not nothing. However, the emphasis here is on friendship in its embodied being at work.

The following passage elaborates this point further, differentiating friendship in its practical unfolding from the not necessarily enacted inclination toward someone. The latter may be seen as the incipit of friendship, incipient friendship:

> Benevolence, then, is like the beginning [ἀρχή] of friendship, just like the pleasure of being in love with another by sight; for no one is in love if he or she has not first been pleased by the look [ἰδέᾳ] [of the beloved], and the one who enjoys the form of a person is not by this alone in love, unless he or she also longs for that person when absent and desires that person's presence. So, too, people cannot be friends unless they have first become well disposed [εὔνους] toward each other, but those who are well disposed are not by this alone friends; for they only wish what is good for those toward whom they are well disposed but would neither participate in any actions with them nor trouble themselves for them. Thus one might say, metaphorically, that benevolence is untilled [ἀργήν] friendship; and it is when benevolence is prolonged and reaches the point of familiarity [συνήθειαν] that it becomes friendship, not the friendship for the sake of usefulness or pleasure, for no benevolence arises in these. (1167a3–14)

Thus, the posture of kindness toward others is seen as the precursor of friendship, indeed, as the condition for its possibility. However, if not temporally developing and resulting in practical community, it remains uncultivated friendship, friendship suffering from *argia* (*a-ergia*), that is, not working, inoperative. Action constitutes the cultivation, the setting-to-work (*energeia*), even the refinement of friendship. As we shall see, the enactment distinctive of friendship is driven and sustained by love.

2.4. Loving

Such a friendship as the friendship for the sake of the good does not exclude, but rather encompasses, pleasure and usefulness. On the contrary, pleasure and usefulness narrowly construed do exclude the good without qualification, for they fall short of it. Along with the inclusiveness and completeness of the good as the principle motivating friendship in the perfect sense, Aristotle also greatly emphasizes the priority and dignity of loving over being loved. This is an issue he repeatedly returns to, but let it suffice to mention the following passage:

> Since friendship depends more on loving [φιλεῖν] [than being loved], and since it is those who love their friends [φιλοφίλων] who are praised, loving [φιλεῖν] [rather than being loved] seems to be the virtue of a friend [φίλων], and so it is those displaying this [feeling or disposition] according to merit who endure as friends and who have an enduring friendship. And such is the manner in which unequals can be friends in the highest degree, for in this way they are made equal. Friendship [φιλότης] is equality [ἰσότης] and similarity [ὁμοιότης], and especially similarity in virtue. For the virtuous, being steadfast in themselves [in view of their virtue], remain steadfast toward each other also, and they neither ask others to do what is bad nor do they themselves do such things for others, but one might say that they even prevent such things from being done; for good human beings as such neither err nor allow their friends to fall into error. Wicked human beings, on the other hand, have nothing to be certain about, for they do not even remain alike [in their feelings and actions]; they become friends but for a short time, enjoying each other's evil habits. (1159a33–1159b11)

Here, again, the association should be noted between wickedness and instability or uncertainty. In contrast, perfect friendship is outlined in terms of the stability afforded by excellence. But what crucially emerges is the privileged status accorded to loving, to the actuality of love. Loving a friend means enacting and actively demanding a certain *ēthos*. However, such an activity as loving can hardly be understood as the act carried out by a self-determining agent, aside from the moment of passivity and receptivity. For loving means being taken, being enraptured by the other, undergoing a motion that is neither rationally nor autonomously determined (desire, *orexis*, remains a crucial feature of friendship proper). As we saw above, "being enraptured by the other" means both that the lover is drawn to the friend in virtue of their sharing the same longing (the same disposition toward the good) and that the lover is carried away by the good itself. A two-fold rapture is at stake here, a rapture irreducible to being drawn toward another human being. For this reciprocated being drawn to the other, this being drawn one to another, is in turn enraptured by the good, which, in fact, envelops this relationship and calls forth the friends involved.

According to Aristotle, what is revealing about one is not the fact of being loved, but the ability to love and the condition of loving. The ability to love constitutes the site of one's dignity and superiority. Thus, here we have a certain reversal of the logic well known to us, according to which being loved would be more desirable – indeed, desirable even to the point of obscuring the beauty of loving. Following that logic, in fact, receiving love would be preferable, for this would provide a confirmation of one's worth, desirability, and so on. But loving responds to an inner exigency and makes manifest who one is, discloses one in one's complete and genuinely singular activation: in this way, it is easy to perceive its fundamental character. Compelled and responsive, the lover responds to that which enlivens him or her, giving him- or herself over to the infinite task of living most fully, of completion. Such a task is taken up through the exercise of solicitude and care for the beloved (*euergein*, 1167b17ff.).

The superior worth of enacting love over against being the recipient thereof is also decisive in addressing the *vexata quaestio* of the autonomy, or even the autarchy, of the good human being. Are friends necessary to such a being (1169b3ff.)? Let us simply note, at this juncture, that the superiority of loving may not simply be a matter of comparative worth vis-à-vis being loved. The experience of overflowing characteristic of friendship, of the superabundance taking one beyond oneself, may at once be distinctive of the excellent human being as such. The desire to share, to (give) love, to enact love toward an other may constitute the cipher of goodness itself. In *Magna moralia* we read that someone "having [ἔχων] all good things" would need a friend "most of all" (*malista*). For, the author wonders, "to whom will one do good [εὖ ποιήσει]?" (1212b31). The mark of human excellence will have been not so much a matter of "having" but a thrust to giving.[13]

3. AGAIN ON FRIENDSHIP AND JUSTICE

A few considerations are in order regarding the elaboration of friendship analyzed thus far. As we have seen, benevolence (*eunoia*), albeit not friendship in its accomplished sense, is said to be the origin, *arkhē*, of friendship. Benevolence is *teleia philia* without shared time and experience, neither enacted, exercised, nor cultivated: it is "perfect" friendship

[13] In this regard, see, e.g., J. C. Fraisse, *"Philía": la notion d'amitié dans la philosophie antique* (Paris: J. Vrin, 1974). Fraisse emphasizes the essential contribution of friendship to the attainment of happiness, to the extent that the latter is a matter of activation and activity, and friendship supports and encourages the active exercise of being (238–46, 275).

but *argē*, deprived of its manifestation in *ergon* and of the condition of *energeia*. It could be said that benevolence is friendship not taking place, friendship in principle. In the other I intuit a possibility, a possible opening, the development of a possible interaction – though I may not (do not, will not) act on it.

In the *Nicomachean Ethics* (1166b30–1167b16) and *Eudemian Ethics* (1241a1–34) alike, the phenomena of benevolence, *eunoia*, and concord, or like-mindedness, *homonoia*, are treated concomitantly and never sharply separated. We encountered the latter already at the very outset of the discussion of friendship (1155a21ff.), where Aristotle employed it to describe the sense of accord among voyagers. At that juncture we pointed out that *homonoia*, even before granting the unity and coherence of a political organism, thus being functionally equivalent with justice, indicates the elementary feeling of bonding, solidarity, and recognition – a feeling characterizing less the political aggregation in contraposition to other *poleis* than the human community as such.

In the later elaborations, *homonoia* is said to designate community of intent, shared vision regarding practical and political matters. It is what Aristotle calls "political friendship," *politikē philia* (1167b2, 1241a33). While *eunoia* and *homonoia* do not exactly overlap, they similarly refer to a bond that can potentially be extended indefinitely, even to people far and unknown. Benevolence, *eunoia*, the friendship that remains "in principle," seems to provide the middle term between "perfect" friendship, of which it constitutes the origin, and the political bond, *homonoia*. In fact, *eunoia*, the basic awareness that there are others with whom I belong and, consequently, a common good with which I am concerned, casts light on the fact that the experience of friendship, which cannot be lived indefinitely many times, can nevertheless be universalized – transposed into the experience of shared finality and political accord, *homonoia*. It can be universalized without thereby turning into mere abstraction, for it rests on the primordial *pathos* of commonality and attraction. In this sense, the phenomenon of *homonoia*, like-mindedness regarding political deliberation, remains significantly bound to the matrix (the *arkhē*) of friendship as each time unique, lived, and hyperbolic.

While refusing the conflation of "perfect" and "political" friendship, Aristotle no less resists the simple disjunction thereof. Divining the contiguity and continuity of these phenomena and the importance of thinking them jointly, he explores the *continuum* of friendship, ultimately referring the political relation back to the experience of friendship between excellent human beings (the infinite thrust through finite conditions). Such an experience remains for Aristotle the root and "measure" of the manifold phenomenology of friendship.

To corroborate this point further, we should underline that *homonoia* is itself conceived of by reference to excellence. Indeed,

> [s]uch concord is in good human beings [ἐν τοῖς ἐπιεικέσιν], for these have the same thoughts [ὁμονοοῦσι] in themselves as well as in relation to one another, resting upon the same [ground], so to speak; for the things wished by such human beings are constant and do not ebb and flow like the water in the straight of Euripus, and they also wish things just and conducive, and these are the things they aim at in common. Bad human beings, on the other hand, cannot have the same thoughts except to a small extent, just as they cannot be friends. (1167b5–11)

In the *Eudemian Ethics*, Aristotle is even more decisive in capturing the dependence of *homonoia* on excellence or goodness: "Concord," he states, "occurs in the case of good human beings [ἐπὶ τῶν ἀγαθῶν]" (1241a22). Furthermore, because "it seems that, like friendship, concord cannot be said simply," it follows that "the primary and natural [πρώτη καὶ φύσει] manifestation of it is good [σπουδαία], so that it is not the case that those who are bad can concur [ὁμονοεῖν] in that way" (1241a23–6). Not only, then, does Aristotle not oppose "perfect" friendship, understood as a private affair, and "political" friendship, understood as the alliance through dogmatic or ideological identification for the sake of public prosperity. Quite outstandingly, Aristotle is intimating that political friendship should be disclosed by reference to the basic phenomenon of individual friendship – to that relationship in the context of which most of all individuals can become themselves and exercise, magnify, and further cultivate excellence or goodness. Political aggregation should be disclosed by reference to this basic experience – even as, in its hyperbolic character, such an experience can hardly provide a calculable paradigm for the erection of ideological programs.[14]

[14] The view of the political as resting on the elementary experience of friendship, albeit in its minimalistic version as solidarity, is at odds with Carl Schmitt's theorization of radical enmity as the condition for the possibility of the political, motivating the constitution of the political as such. It is equally at odds with his treatment of friendship as a mere factor of political cohesion, somehow derivative vis-à-vis the primordiality of conflict. While this exceeds the scope of the present work, it would be relevant to disallow the Schmittian claims to a Greek ancestry and retrieve, most evidently in the Platonic-Aristotelian lineage, a quite different perspective on the question of the origin of the political. Such an inquiry would call into question the construal of political friendship as purely ancillary to programmatic politics and separate from the loving relation. At the inception of the founding discourse in Plato's *Republic*, the *arkhē* of the *polis* is not

The question of communal togetherness is approached on the ground of the lived, radically singular experience of friendship. The embodied uniqueness of each friendship can provide no pattern, no principle on which to structure political interaction, and yet the political seems to rest on the universality of such a radically unique vicissitude. It presupposes that the experience of friendship, if in each case different, is precisely as such shared in common, available to human beings as such. It presupposes, furthermore, that the feeling of sympathy and affection, if not possibly enacted ad infinitum, is in principle infinitely extendible.

Thus, political friendship should not be construed merely in terms of computation and strategic alignment. First and foremost, political friendship refers to and reveals the possibility, in principle, of being together and sharing kindness and projects in common. We have already pointed out that friendship, even in its political sense, does and does not coincide with justice: to the extent that justice is understood as legality, friendship clearly exceeds its scope; however, to the extent that justice is understood as excessive vis-à-vis the texts of the law, it indicates in a certain sense

said to be the establishment of a common identity over against the enemy outside – i.e., the establishment of the bond of friendship among those akin and identical, committed to one another and to the defense of their own. In this context, the bond of friendship for the sake of self-defense against the common enemy comes into play only later: war is secondary to political founding, not equiprimordial with it. Rather, what is constitutive of the political is the fact that, as Plato has Socrates say, each one is in need of much and is not self-sufficient (369b). Human beings come together out of need, on the ground of the implicit recognition of a shared condition, and with the awareness, however nebulous, that they may grow together. One of the tasks taken up in the conversation is indeed bringing the "community of pleasures and pains" more incisively to consciousness (464a). An articulate consideration of this dialogue in light of the present concerns would have to take into account the progression from Book II to Book V: the peaceful city, peacefully interacting with other cities, is superseded, and war is introduced, because the growth of appetites in the city requires more resources and they must be acquired by conquering neighboring land (373d–e); the city/soul is established in its threefold structure, according to the logic of friendship/identity inside and war against the enemy/other outside (Books II–V); all the while, the disruption and devaluation of the institution of the family/clan in the city tends to take the issue of identification on a level other than tribal/conventional, a psychological/biological level whose workings will not be mastered in the end (Book VIII); ultimately, the logic on which this city rests is overcome: the citizens of other *poleis* are not for the most part enemies: those "men, women, and children" are "friendly," only a few among them are to be held responsible, and therefore destruction of war must be avoided (471a–b). The community in which one belongs becomes increasingly inclusive. This broadening of the political organism culminates in the "cosmopolitan dream" of the ending myth: the figure of Er points to a human being so unique as to be *pamphulos*, "of all tribes," irreducible to any political, tribal, territorial identification (614b). See my *Of Myth, Life, and War in Plato's* Republic (Bloomington: Indiana UP, 2002).

friendship itself. Whether elaborated in terms of friendship or of justice, ultimately *homonoia* indicates a togetherness that cannot simply be brought back to prescriptive regulations, codification of duty, the economy of quantifiable giving and taking. An element of excess, even in terms of gratuitous generosity, is the mark not only of "perfect" friendship (consider the enactment of loving beneficence, *euergein*, characteristic of friendship, or the impulse to *eu poiein* in *Magna moralia* 1212b31), but, as was observed earlier on, also of justice itself. Itself irreducible to the obligation "to return a service to one who has shown grace," justice may in principle involve the excessive giving that is the "proper mark of grace": the initiative "to show grace" to begin with, in a gesture of unsolicited giving (1133a3–5).

Thus, when affirming that, if human beings were friends, justice (as juridical normativity) would be superfluous, Aristotle is envisioning friendship as the end or destination of politics: as the highest conceivable accomplishment of politics, or even politics' own self-overcoming. In this sense, friendship would mark the overcoming of politics as mere policy, as the work of instituting extrinsic rules of coexistence. It would mark the perfection of politics to come – the harmonization of the many, gathered beyond legal prescriptions. The vision of such an open teleology discloses the domain of becoming as the possibility of formation, growth, and evolution. The orientation to such a completion and accomplishment would be announced precisely in friendship (in politics) as *homonoia*: the proximity with others and awareness of belonging together (as in the course of a voyage), of common circumstances, of mutual implication and dependence.

In the folds of such a vision of the possible lies the insight that the end of politics is neither mere expediency nor the structuring, ordering, and coordination of civil coexistence. As is the case with friendship, rather, politics aims at happiness, at living well, at the flowering of life in its manifold potential. In the strand of his analysis confronting the issue of friendship between unequals (vertical relationships), Aristotle touches on these issues with further suggestions.

3.1. Beyond Perfection and Imperfection

In its secondary or imperfect sense, friendship is for the sake of usefulness or pleasures – bodily, worldly, material. Such a friendship entails inequality, lack of reciprocity, asymmetry, as in the case of the bond between lover and beloved, or the agreement contracted by rich and poor. Yet we should point out that inequality and asymmetry are not necessarily symptomatic of friendship as incomplete, imperfect, or derivative, that is, merely driven by appetite or self-interest. As we saw, Aristotle suggests that, in the broadest sense, friendship informs every relation, every gathering of human beings. In this perspective, friendship is akin to justice, if irreducible to legality. Both friendship and justice name those proportionate and harmonious bonds, those harmonized and equalizing exchanges that keep the *polis* together. Friendship understood along these lines may not be the same as friendship unqualified and perfect. However, although entailing inequality and asymmetry, friendship as justice is just as much irreducible to friendship "in virtue of an attribute," that is, the friendship promoting trivial advantages, the "fallen" or minor version of the perfect bond. As the articulation of community, friendship demands to be viewed beyond the polarity of perfection and imperfection.

Thus far, we severally pointed out Aristotle's oscillation regarding whether or not friendship and justice may coincide. The ambiguity regarding this point signals, yet again, Aristotle's responsiveness to the motility of signification, to the many ways in which *dikaiosunē* no less than *philia* can be said. The following passage provides an elaboration of friendship as an expression of justice and should be considered at length. It begins with a compendium of issues by now familiar to us:

> In every association there seems to be both something which is just and also friendship. At least, human beings address their fellow-voyagers and fellow-soldiers as friends also, and similarly with those in any of the other associations. Friendship goes as far as the members associate with each other; for what is just goes as far also. And it has been rightly said, "to friends all things are common"; for friendship is in association. Now brothers [ἀδελφοῖς] and comrades [ἑταίροις] have all things in common, but others have only certain things in common, some more, some fewer; for of friendships, too, some are to a higher degree but others to a lower degree. Just things, too, differ; for the things that are just for parents toward their children are not the same as those between brothers, nor are those between comrades the same as those between citizens, and similarly with the other [kinds of] friendships. Accordingly, unjust things toward human beings are different also; and they become increasingly unjust by being directed toward the more friendly, e.g., it is more terrible [δεινότερον] to defraud a comrade than a citizen, or to refuse help to a brother than to a stranger, or to strike a father than anyone else. What is just, too, increases by nature simultaneously with friendship, since they are in the same beings and extend equally. (1159b27–1160a8)

In this strand of the Aristotelian discourse, friendship comes to be indiscernible from the dynamics of political coexistence and, by the same token, of familial bonds. Friendship and justice are viewed as concomitant ingredients of every association and seem to carry the same meaning and implications. Of course, saying that every association, every communal gathering, is structured not without the essential element of friendship implies that *polis* and *philia* similarly aim at happiness. Just like friendship, the political association aims at the highest good as well as at the proper positioning of the human good with respect to the non-human (such would be the work of wisdom, first philosophy). It is essential to underline that the end of the *polis* itself is irreducible to expediency.

In this discussion we come to appreciate the tension due to a shift in emphasis from friendship as based on similarity and equality to friendship as a relation between beings of unequal stature. In the former case, inequality bespeaks imperfection, the derivative character of friendships for the sake of partial ends. In the latter case, the unequal is that which friendship (as justice) at once preserves as such and amalgamates. The second half of Book Theta is devoted to a treatment of friendship especially in terms of verticality – as the vertical relation holding beings together that are heterogeneous and infinitely uneven in their power and worth.

As we shall see, what comes to be illuminated in this way is the relation between humans (mortals) and gods (immortals) and, at the same time, the relation between humans and nature as such. Again, at stake here is the disclosure of the end of the *polis*, the end of community or communal gathering, as exceeding mere convenience. The good, which is incommensurably beyond utility, is the end of the political organism as well. In this perspective, friendship is taken to be essential to communal constitution, to lie at the very heart of the phenomenon of politics. Aristotle addresses this cluster of issues in the following reflection:

> Now all associations are like parts of the political association [τῆς πολιτικῆς]; for people come together for the sake of something expedient [συμφέροντι] and bring along something which contributes to life. The political association itself seems to have originated and to continue to exist for the sake of expediency; for the law-givers, too, are aiming at this and say that what is commonly expedient is just. The other associations, then, are aiming at some part of what is expedient; e.g., sailors undertake a voyage for the sake of making money or some other such thing, fellow-soldiers go to war for the sake of spoils or victory or [capturing] a city, and similarly for the members of a tribe or of a town. (1160a8–19)

At first, Aristotle seems to understand political finality in terms of conduciveness to common advantage. However, he immediately adds that advantage must be conceived in the most encompassing sense, as transcending partial, ephemeral, or myopic preoccupations:

> Again, some associations seem to be formed for the sake of pleasure, e.g., confraternities [θιασωτῶν] and social circles [ἐρανιστῶν], for these are formed for the sake of sacrifice and being together, respectively. All these, however, seem to come under the political association, for the aim of the political association seems not to be limited to the expediency of the moment but to extend to life as a whole. (1160a19–23)

We should note the overflowing richness with which the theme of political association is laid out. The prominence initially accorded to expediency may not be altogether dropped or set aside. Nevertheless, and perhaps more significantly, the language of the advantageous, while preserved, undergoes a semantic reconfiguration, even a transfiguration. Extended to "life as a whole," contemplating the human venture in the long term, advantage may no longer signify immediate gratification, let alone the privilege of narrow-minded or one-sided pursuits. Thus understood, advantage comes to embrace the highest, in the sense of most inclusive, finality. The trajectory of this discourse illuminates political association as that network of relationships and relational structures in virtue of which the whole of life may be contemplated in its scansion and significance.

Such a position is exposed even more incisively in the *Politics*, where Aristotle repeatedly states that political aggregation is ultimately oriented to living well (*eu zēn, zōē teleia, zēn eudaimonōs kai kalōs, zōē aristē*) and subsists for the sake of this (1280a32, 1280b34, 1281a2, 1281a3, 1328a37), whereas exchanges, shared place, and defense against aggression by others cannot alone account for the coming to be of the *polis* (1280a32–9, 1280b30–5). Of particular interest in the development of the passage presently under consideration, however, is the powerful synthetic gesture with which Aristotle connects the issue of political finality to matters regarding the divine and nature. The various associations "coming under" the comprehensive political organism, Aristotle continues,

> make sacrifices and arrange gatherings for these, pay honors to the gods, and provide pleasant relaxations for their members. For the ancient sacrifices and gatherings appear to have occurred after the harvest as a sort of first-fruits, since it is at that time that human beings had most leisure. (1160a23–8)

The practice of the sacrifices to the gods, that is, the bond between the human sphere and the divine, is aligned with the bond between humans and nature. This meditation draws together the rhythms of nature as well as those of human beings, the cycles of fruit-bearing and barren seasons as well as the cycles of human effort and leisure. It presents nature as the theater of divine manifestation as well as dictating the times of human gathering, celebration, and ritual. Intimated here is the convergence, if not simplistically the identity, of the relation to the natural and the relation to the divine.[15]

3.2. Friendship with the Gods

It is in the context of these observations that we should situate Aristotle's hierarchy of relational forms and corresponding forms of government. In the *Nicomachean Ethics*, this discussion takes place at 1160a30–1161a9, but can be rendered here only most schematically. Let us simply recall, in order of rank, the relational and political typologies. First, Aristotle mentions the relation of father to children, corresponding to the form of government of kingdom. Second, the relation of husband to wife, corresponding to aristocracy. Third, the relation among brothers, corresponding to timocracy. Fourth, *dēmokratia* (occasionally translated as "mob rule," but meaning no more and no less than "democracy," albeit in its degeneracy), representing a corruption of the relation among brothers and hence of timocracy.[16] Fifth, oligarchy, representing a corruption of the husband-wife relation and hence of aristocracy. Finally, the relation between master and slave, corresponding to tyranny and representing a perversion of the father-children relation and of kingdom. The tension should be noticed between the previous emphasis on the highest friendship as occurring between equals and the positive devaluation, in this passage, of such a friendship (the relation between or among brothers). Indeed, brotherhood, the fraternal, horizontal relation among peers, whether timocratic or democratic, does not enjoy any privilege in this context.

[15] A moment in the *Protreptic*, addressing the question of contemplation, actually suggests the identity of nature and the divine as that from which humankind is generated: "The most noble animal down here is the human being, hence it is clear that it was generated by nature and in conformity with nature. What could, then, be the end in view of which nature and god generated us? Questioned about this, Pythagoras answered: 'looking at the sky,' and he used to say that he was one who speculates on nature and that in view of this end he was born" (fr.11 Ross). See also *Eudemian Ethics* 1216a11–16.

[16] Regarding the four forms of democracy, see *Politics* 1291b30–1292a17.

It seems important to highlight the significance of this transition. The hypothesis pursued here is that, in such a move, Aristotle is attempting to cast light on the limits of the brotherly relation as a paradigm of human community. Such a configuration, based on the equal standing, if not the identity, of its members, may involve a certain severance from otherness and its asperity – a remoteness from the radically and irreducibly heterogeneous. It may induce a perception of human togetherness both as relatively homogeneous in composition and, most importantly, as a self-contained and self-referential domain, marked by the oblivion of its own non-human conditions, severed from the higher and the lower, from that which precedes and that which follows, source and offshoot. The humanity solely resolving itself into horizontality, after the figure of the brotherly bond, may be disinclined to interrogate itself concerning its own origin and end – incapable of wonder vis-à-vis the past, ancestry in the broadest sense, and the future, the openness of the present thrust. At this juncture, Aristotle's emphasis on unequal, indeed, asymmetrical relations may function as a reminder of the human procession from and dependence on the inhuman – nature or god. It may remind us of the human as natural/divine *child.*

The discussion of these relations in the *Eudemian Ethics* confirms, from the outset, this hypothesis. The introduction of the theme of friendship between unequals, whether political (ruler/ruled) or familial (parent/child), at once evokes relations exceeding the human domain (god/human being). Here Aristotle resorts again to the language of excess, *huperbolē*, but the issue in this case is not so much the rapture characterizing "perfect" friendship, but rather the exceeding unevenness of the relationships under consideration. In these cases the heterogeneity of those involved and of their respective ways of loving is so unbridgeable that reciprocity becomes unthinkable, not only incalculable (as was the case with "perfect" friendship). Paradigmatically illuminated by reference to the love "of god for human being," such friendships take place "according to excess," *kath'huperbolēn*: they cross utter discontinuity, establish a bond between the radically foreign (1238b18–23).

But let us follow the development of this analysis in the *Nicomachean Ethics.* While considering the relation between sovereign and subjects, Aristotle notes:

Such, too, is the friendship of a father toward his children (although it differs in the magnitude of good services [ἐυεργετημάτων]; for he is the cause of their being, which seems to be the greatest [good], and also of their nurture and education; these things apply to ancestors also); for the relation of a father to his sons or of ancestors to descendants or of a king to his subjects is by nature that of a ruler [to those ruled]. And these are friendships by virtue of superiority; hence parents are also honored. Accordingly, also what is just in those friendships is not the same for the two parties but is according to merit; for friendship, too, is in this manner. (1161a16–22)

Underlined here is the archic character of the parent or, broadly speaking, of the ancestors with regard to their children and subsequent lineages. The father and the ancestor are rulers precisely because they are the causes of the coming into being of what follows – because they engender and inform. The community of brothers should be referred back to such a primal scene: in this perspective alone can it be adequately understood and understand itself. Thus, the development, in Book Theta, from friendship requiring equality to friendship entailing radical asymmetry can be seen as Aristotle's attempt at a critique of the strictures of the horizontal relation.[17]

The relationship among brothers, in its relatively self-enclosed character, tends to be forgetful of its links to the other: of all manners of non-conformity and of its own involvement with it. Above all, the bond among peers tends to be oblivious of vertical relationality, thus confining such friends to the condition of orphans, of parentless children. The brothers' oblivion, their absorption in the brotherly bond, reveals human beings uprooted from nature, cut off from the gods, deprived of source and orientation. It reveals humanity unable even to sustain the question regarding its own parents and offspring, endowment and fruits – the beginning and destination of humankind as such, that is, the situation and belonging of the human in the inhuman (nature or divinity). In intimating this limit in the love between equals, Aristotle is encouraging a disruption of horizontality: a love opening up to the infinite, opening up to that which cannot be horizontally embraced, which abides

[17] The relation between adults and children (as well as, more broadly, vertical friendship) paradigmatically reveals friendship as a bond extending beyond the community of those who "have" reason, who humanly share in reason – extending to living beings not yet human or not even on the way to becoming human, not tending to the human because unfolding otherwise. In his fascinating study *Il coltello e lo stilo* (Milan: Il Saggiatore, 1979), Mario Vegetti discusses the philosopher and the sovereign, the child and the slave, as figures exceeding the political-anthropological range (whether in the direction of divinity or of animality), marking (or confusing) its confines (177). Of particular interest is the reflection on the child and on that peculiar kind of child that is the slave (186–94).

vertiginously excessive and impervious to reciprocation. Eventually, the figure of asymmetrical relationships is strategically conducive to a vision surpassing the relations among human beings as such and, by the same token, the relations exclusively involving thinking male adults – thus exposing the irreducibility of humankind as such to the community of the same (brothers, peers, equally privileged citizens). Aristotle seems to point to the relation between the human and the non-human, at once in the direction of the gods or nature.[18]

At this point, friendship comes to signify a bond of cosmic unity, very much in line with pre-Socratic insights from various sources, Pythagorean as well as Empedoclean. In the context of such a vision of the *kosmos* should be situated the considerations concerning *polis* as well as *anthrōpos*. As Aristotle makes explicit, the insistence on human genealogy is ultimately meant to puncture the exclusively human horizon: "The friendship of children toward parents, and of human beings toward gods, is one toward the good and superior [ἀγαθὸν καὶ ὑπερέχον]; for parents have done the greatest of goods [εὖ γὰρ πεποιήκασι τὰ μέγιστα], since they are the causes of the being and nurture of their children and then of their education" (1162a4–7). At stake is not only the birth of children, but also that of humankind as such; not only the verticality of physiological procreation, but also the verticality of the fabric into which the human is woven; not only origin understood as beginning, but also origin understood as continuing sustenance and guidance, as informing principle at work in its propulsion. The focus on the figures of the parents, forefathers, kings, and gods signals the urgency of the interrogation regarding human provenance and ambiance.

Love on the part of the higher being takes on the form of granting, protecting, and furthering. In turn, love on the part of the more vulnerable being takes on the form of desiring the other, stretching beyond oneself in order to become more comprehensive, to embrace and be traversed, to let the other in and be opened by it. This structure of love on the part of the more vulnerable being illustrates the condition of human beings with regard to what transcends them, to what constitutes their own condition – most notably, to the divine that comes to be identified with the good (*Eudemian Ethics* 1249b14–15). This love entails

18 Again, the question of *sophia*, of human beings looking at the sky, lifting their gaze beyond their most immediate and exiguous preoccupations, finding attunement and insight in this contact with radiant nature/divinity. It would be fruitful to pursue this Aristotelian motif along with analogous Platonic formulations, most notably in the *Timaeus*, *Philebus*, and, once more, in the myth concluding the *Republic*.

the desire that takes one outside oneself, in a movement of striving and receptivity.

3.3. Interdependence

What comes to be delineated through these various (and not always easily cohabiting) discussions of friendship is the figure of interdependence. Indeed, such a figure emerges both horizontally, in intrahuman (whether intra- or inter-communal) relations, and vertically, in the human exchanges with the non-human. In the context of intra-human relations and interactions, whether within a *polis* or among *poleis*, the prominence of the dialectical practice highlights the salience of dialogue: of communing and communication, of the unending work of negotiation and transmission animating togetherness. Certainly, dialogue may be understood here not as a rhetorical, let alone contentious, competition, but rather as the conversation whose premise and condition is the attitude of friendship. However, since the phenomenon of interdependence is not confined to the human horizon, we are compelled to consider the issue of communication further, beyond strictly human conversation and language(s). More broadly, we are encouraged to focus on the patient work of mediation, engagement, and exchange with the other-than-human domains – the work of communing and communication exceeding human dialectic and always already taking place, albeit for the most part unconsciously. How can we begin to hear and practice the many languages of friendship – the languages, manners of communication and of living, which may do justice to the fact of interdependence? In what way, other than ordering, disposing, plundering, objectifying, can we interact with the surroundings (the forms of life all around us, above and below)? How can we take in that which surrounds us and act responsively, that is, adequately, out of such a reception?

Aristotle does not offer a compilation of precepts to this end. As we have variously noted from the outset, he restlessly underlines the importance of evaluations adhering to the unique traits of each circumstance, responding most perceptively to the singular demands each time in play. Far from signaling the limit of ethico-political reflection (ethics being bound, as is often said, to contingent details and falling short of geometrical/conceptual clarity), this way of proceeding reveals supreme precision, subtlety, and refinement. The architecture without geometry that ethics/politics names displays a sensitivity to proliferating difference, a capacity to work with all that "admits of being otherwise," which is altogether inaccessible to conceptual modes of inquiry. Again, this marks less the shortcoming of ethics than the coarseness of the concept, impoverished in its unmoving abstractness and in its interpretation of clarity as simplicity/simplification. There is indeed a crucial difference between geometrical precision and precision as wakeful adhesion to infinite variability.

Thus, for Aristotle particular dispositions or comportments may or may not be desirable, depending on the particular configuration of space and time – not absolutely.[19] The good and the privation thereof may not be fixed, inherent properties of any separate being or typology of comportment, but rather emerge out of a comprehensive, fluctuating relational environment. What is affirmed in an absolute sense is the meta-disposition or, if you like, the over-arching disposition enabling one, in each case, to reckon with circumstances in a balanced and healthy way, in a way that furthers well-being as inclusively as possible. However, reckoning with circumstances in such a way as to be guided by the encompassing finality of well-being entails always keeping in mind the complexity of interaction, holding it in care and attention, remaining mindful of the whole context of interrelation, intersection, and mutual implication. Implied in such a posture is the discernment and acceptance, at some level, of a rule of harmony and proportion governing togetherness, governing the manifold of all that belongs together. Responding and corresponding to such a rule is perhaps what lies at the heart of friendship, broadly understood as harmonizing relatedness (horizontal as well as vertical, among humans as well as gathering the human and non-human): friendship grants fluidity in the exchanges among (the) many, balanced interspersion of the differing. It is only in lack of friendship that one resorts to justice – or, more precisely, to its various ministers and administrators, judges *et al.*

4. ON HAPPINESS OR THE GOOD

We conclude with a brief reflection on the discussion in Book Kappa, concerning happiness or the good. This discussion is a prelude to the *Politics*. It is a prelude to politics understood as the continuation and

[19] In *The Therapy of Desire: Theory and Practice in Hellenistic Ethics*, Martha Nussbaum proposes: "we may say that excellent ethical choice cannot be captured completely in general rules because – like medicine – it is a matter of fitting one's choice to the complex requirements of a concrete situation, taking all of its contextual features into account." "In the context of love and friendship," she adds, "it is possible that Aristotle may recognize particularity in a yet stronger sense, recognizing that some valuable forms of ethical attention and care are not even in principle universalizable" (67).

highest accomplishment of ethics. Happiness and politics: once again we must underline their conjunction. Indeed, as Aristotle said in Book Alpha concerning the pursuit of the good, "even if this end be the same for an individual as for the *polis*, nevertheless the end of the *polis* appears to be greater and more complete to attain and to preserve; for though this end is dear also to a single individual, it appears to be more beautiful and more divine to a race [ἔθνει] or to a *polis*" (1094b8–11). Moreover, as pointed out during the discussion on friendship, though the human being may experience the compulsion and urgency of biological reproduction as the most primordial condition, prior even to political life *stricto sensu*, the political dimension of life appears most choice-worthy – both because of the honor and beauty inherent in public involvement and because even the activities that are theoretical in character are made possible by the leisure only political coexistence affords. Says Aristotle:

> The friendship between husband and wife seems to be by nature; for human beings by nature tend to form couples more than to be political, and they do this to the extent that a household is prior and more necessary than a *polis* and that reproduction [τεκνοποιία] is more common to animals. Accordingly, associations in the other animals exist only to that extent, but human beings live together not only for the sake of reproduction but for other things in life as well. (1162a16–22)

As observed already, it is in and through life in the *polis* that the human being can develop into what it is to be – that the human being can realize its inherent potential, including the capacity for contemplation. Contemplation, let it be repeated again, is an activity, in the sense of actualization, activation, being-at-work; Aristotle views it as the worthiest, most distinctive mode of human enactment. Moreover, we noted already that such an activity, *energeia*, should be understood in terms of action: thinking as such, with no further "practical application," is a matter of *praxis* (*Politics* 1325b16–24). Book Kappa corroborates this crucial point on numerous occasions, as we shall see.

4.1. Pleasure

It could be said that the discussion in Book Kappa casts light on the intimacy between a soul that knows (a soul absorbed in contemplative endeavors) and a *polis* that thrives. In this Book, which lies at the conjunction of the ethical treatise proper and the *Politics*, we catch a glimpse of the closeness of (1) the psychological involvement in *theōrein*, said to be the highest good, and (2) a *polis* constituted in such a way as to excel.

The Book progresses from a discussion of pleasure to the examination of contemplation, to the issue of political *poiēsis.* Again, the discussion of contemplation appears to be a preface, indeed *the* preface, to political study and, even more importantly, to political activity.

With this in mind, let us turn to examine Aristotle's treatment of pleasure at this juncture.[20] It would seem that, in its fullest achievement, activity is always accompanied by pleasure. Of course, asserting the concomitance of pleasure and the most accomplished enactment, actualization, or being-at-work, means asserting the concomitance of pleasure and happiness or the good itself. The passages pointing in this direction are numerous, but let us examine the following exemplary statement:

> Now, since living itself is good and pleasant (and this seems to be the case since all desire it, and especially those who are good [ἐπιεικεῖς] and blessed; for it is to these that life [βίος] is most choice-worthy, and the most blessed life [ζωή] belongs to them), and since one who sees senses [αἰσθάνεται] that he or she sees, one who hears senses that he or she hears, one who walks senses that he or she walks, and similarly in the other cases, there is something in us which senses that we are in activity, and so we would be sensing that we are sensing and we would be thinking that we are thinking. But [to be aware] that we are sensing or thinking [is to be aware] that we are (for to be [for human beings] was stated to be sensing or thinking), and sensing that one lives is in itself one of the things which are pleasant (for life is by nature good, and *to sense that the good belongs to oneself is pleasant*). Now living is choice-worthy, and especially by those who are good, since being to them is good and pleasant (for they are *pleased by sensing that which is in itself good*). (1170a27–1170b5; emphasis added)

Here, besides the repeatedly mentioned concurrence of pleasure and happiness or the good, we should note the intertwinement of the motifs of the good and aliveness. Aliveness, being alive, signifies self-enactment, the proper domain of self-realization and accomplishment. Accordingly, perceiving the good is a matter of perceiving oneself live.[21] Above all, however, we are struck by the Aristotelian terminology at this point: perceiving the good, that is, perceiving oneself in one's aliveness is, more precisely, a matter of sensing, *aisthanesthai,* of feeling oneself be or become. At stake in the awareness of the good is the capacity for sensing oneself in act, in activity, in the course of being.[22] In other words, being aware of the good

[20] See A. J. Festugière's analysis of the discussions of pleasure in Book Eta 11–14 and Book Kappa 1–5, in *Aristote: le plaisir* (Paris: J. Vrin, 1936).

[21] In the earlier discussion of friendship, see the pertinent remarks at 1166a11–29.

[22] On the inseparability of sensing and the sensed (of actual sensing and what enacts itself), i.e., on the concomitance of affection and activity, see *De anima* 425b26–426a12.

means sensing that one is alive, the felt awareness that one is at work, in deed: that one is, is there, in action.

Aristotle sharpens his remarks on the pleasure accompanying such a sensing, such a being aware of the good, of the aliveness that is said to be good and seems to coincide with the good. Indeed, he notes, "living and pleasure appear to go together and not to admit separation; for there can be no pleasure without activity, and pleasure perfects every activity" (1175a19–21). Pleasure is presented as the genuine culmination of any activity, as the crowning moment in which an activity is fulfilled, that is to say, perfected and completed. Any such fulfillment would by definition be marked by pleasure. But Aristotle takes the issue even further, pointing to pleasure as a kind of surplus, as an excess of the activity or, indeed, as an excess to the activity – as that which would bring the activity beyond itself. This gesture indicates a different kind of completion, a different sense of perfection of an activity:

> (It is clear that pleasure arises with respect to each [faculty of] sensation, for we speak of sights and of things heard as being pleasant. It is also clear that these activities are most pleasant whenever both the sensation is at its best and its activity is directed toward its best corresponding object; and if both the object sensed and the one who senses it are such, there will always be pleasure provided both the one acting [ποιήσοντος] and that which is acted upon [πεισομένου] are present.) But pleasure perfects the activity not as a habit inhering in the one acting but as an end which supervenes like the bloom of youth to those in their prime of life. (1174b27–34)

Pleasure is developed as that completion that supervenes despite oneself, in a way – as that completion taking over the being-at-work in its unfolding, drawing it further. Pleasure supervenes, dawns on one, taking one beyond, in delight. Thus, pleasure comes to name the beauty and elation experienced in the unmasterable fulfillment of activity, even of self-activation and self-realization (1177a22–7).

Again, regarding the overall strategy of Book Kappa, we should emphasize the coincidence of the themes of action (most notably, political) and contemplation. As we anticipated, the Book undertakes to address the contemplative posture as the highest human enactment and highest good, in human terms and beyond. However, it is fascinating that Aristotle should never leave action (let alone the world in which it unfolds) behind. Even in its culminating moment, *theōrein* does not appear to bespeak emancipation from the world. Aristotle seems to be very careful in his insistence that, on the one hand, this world provides the condition for the possibility of contemplation, while, on the other hand, contemplation may optimally guide the worldly course of a human being and community alike. Contemplation and living well, that is, attaining a certain harmony in action, are far from separate.[23]

To the extent that living well is, above all, the finality of the *polis* (that which the *polis* infinitely strives for and to a finite extent makes possible) (again, see also *Politics* 1280a7–1281a10, 1328a22–b23), we may not assume the respective autonomy of politics and contemplation. Political action infused with a longing for the good and cultivation of human insight into the good seem to be mutually implicating.

4.2. Contemplation

In the wake of these minimal remarks on pleasure and related matters, let us consider the discussion of contemplation as the highest attainment of human enactment. In the meditation on the most excellent activity attributed to human beings, we should underline a terminological slippage with respect to Book Zeta: a shift from the language of *logos* to the language of *nous, theōrein,* and *sophia* (intellect or intuition, contemplation, and wisdom). Let us read a couple of passages that frame this discussion. Aristotle proposes:

> Since happiness is an activity according to virtue, it is reasonable that it should be an activity according to the highest virtue; and this would be an activity of the best [part of a human being]. So whether this be intellect or something else which seems to rule and guide us by nature and to have comprehension [ἔννοιαν ἔχειν] of beautiful and divine beings, being itself divine or else the most divine part in us, its activity according to its proper virtue would be perfect happiness. That this activity is contemplative [θεωρετική] has already been mentioned; and this would seem to be in agreement both with our previous remarks and with the truth. (1177a12–20)

Aristotle seems to be distancing himself from the previous emphasis on *logos* and is now identifying the most outstanding of human activities, and perhaps the highest activity *tout court,* with *nous,* intellect or intuition. Of course, the "comprehension of beautiful and divine beings" recalls those beings which in Book Zeta were said to be most phenomenal, most shining, *ta phanerōtata,* and related to the virtue of *sophia,* wisdom. It should also be noticed that the "comprehension of beautiful and divine

[23] John L. Ackrill (*Aristotle the Philosopher* [Oxford: Oxford UP, 1981]) comes to a similar position, articulating the continuity of ethics and the contemplative activity, and viewing the exercise of excellence (action, political and otherwise) as promoting and cultivating the contemplative moment.

beings" is itself divine, or else that in us which is "most divine." Aristotle is oscillating between announcing the highest good attainable for human beings and speaking of the highest good without qualification. A few lines down, he continues:

> We think that pleasure should be intermingled with happiness; and it is agreed that the most pleasant of our virtuous activities is the one in accordance with wisdom. Indeed, philosophy seems to possess pleasures which are wonderful in purity as well as in certainty, and it is reasonable for those who have understanding [τοῖς εἰδόσι] to pass their time more pleasantly than those who [merely] inquire. (1177a23–7)

Once more, the best activity is intrinsically marked by pleasure. As full deployment of potentiality, as flourishing and stretching out toward fulfillment, happiness would imply pleasure genuinely understood. Such would be the expanse and expansiveness of the good.

Aristotle elaborates further on what is at stake in contemplation and, in so doing, recalls the teleology of the good with which the *Nicomachean Ethics* began. Such a comprehensive teleology is predicated on a hierarchical arrangement of human activities:

> If, among virtuous actions, those pertaining to the *polis* and to war stand out in beauty and greatness and, being toilsome, are aimed at some other end but are not chosen for their own sake, whereas the activity of the intellect, being theoretical, seems to be superior in seriousness and to aim at no other end besides itself but to have its own pleasure [ἡδονὴν οἰκείαν] (which increases that activity), then also self-sufficiency and leisure and freedom from weariness, as much as are possible for a human being, and all the other things which are attributed to a blessed human being appear to be in this activity. This, then, would be the perfect happiness for a human being, if extended to the full length of life, for none of the attributes of happiness is incomplete. (1177b16–26)

The most complete enactment of the human being involves a certain overcoming of toil and fatigue. Indeed, no one would choose an exhausting activity for its own sake, but only for the sake of further, more desirable ends. Thus, perfect human enactment is characterized by leisure, by the luxury of "having" time, by that condition in which necessary matters become less pressing and one can enjoy the possibility of passing time without being pushed by the urgent worries of survival. In this way, one enjoys the possibility of becoming aware of time as such, of realizing time. We can see in such a condition an originary discovery of time, time disclosed in light of freedom from immediate need: time in its spaciousness and possibility. Such a thrust beyond necessity is experienced as a privilege, indeed, as that condition sufficient onto itself, projected toward no other end, marked by its own "characteristic" (*oikeia*) pleasure. Once again, we are told that pleasure supervenes so as to crown and complete activity, in fact, that pleasure "augments" (*sunauxei*) the activity. Of course, the privilege of such a pleasure can be tasted only thanks to the protected condition afforded by the political bond of solidarity.

Indeed, within the structure of the *polis* the human being may find not only a more expedient manner of survival, but also the possibility of life's fullest unfolding. Within the *polis* the human being may thrust itself beyond necessary cares: find its measure as a being in(de)finitely open to the measureless and excessive. Communal life (friendship as "the deliberate choice of living together," *Politics* 1280b39) is necessary to the human being as such (even the most insular, autarchic one), to the human pursuit of excellent self-articulation. It is necessary to a certain overcoming of necessity, so that the possibility of freedom may be even marginally glimpsed.

As observed more than once, Aristotle consistently confirms that political action is the condition for contemplation opening beyond the political and that, in turn, contemplation (the divine insight into the divine) nourishes political action. At issue in such a mutual implication is the dialectic of *polis* and *kosmos*: of human and divine, measure and excess, institution and transgression of conventions, order and disruption – of human order and an order altogether other. In the *Politics*, Aristotle contrasts human and divine law or order (*nomos, taxis*): while, in human affairs, beauty and order can be brought to bear only on a "limited magnitude," it is imaginable that the "work" of "divine power," which "holds all together," is bringing "an excessive number" (*huperballōn arithmos*) to "partake of order" (1326a30–4). And yet, even though for human beings the work of ordering entails delimiting, bringing into an outline, the glimpse of the divine caught through contemplation constantly exposes human delimiting to an excess both perturbing and demanding endless revision, transformation, reconstitution. However intermittent, the intuition of excess destabilizes human finitude and compels reconfiguration.

4.3. Self-Transcendence

Returning to Book Kappa, we need to consider yet again how the (self-) transcendence, or (self-) overcoming of the human, is implied, enfolded, in the activity of *nous*. Aristotle develops the issue of contemplative enactment in terms of a movement beyond: beyond the human as merely human, beyond the limits of mortality and its concerns. Contemplation articulates the irreducibility of the human to itself, to a structure of self-enclosed determinacy, and raises the question of divine pervasiveness. As we noted, in this context belong the questions concerning freedom, emancipation from toil, the irreducibility of human life to necessity, its bonds, and its mechanisms. The contemplative involvement ultimately procures the respite and regeneration that are the marks of a life no longer completely absorbed in the task of survival:

> Such a life, of course, would be above [κρείττων] that of a human being, for a human being will live in this manner not insofar as one is human, but insofar as one has something divine in oneself; and the activity of this divine part of the soul is as much superior to that of the other kind of virtue as that divine part is superior to the composite soul of a human being. So since the intellect is divine relative to a human being, the life according to this intellect, too, will be divine relative to human life. Thus, we should not follow the recommendation of thinkers who say that those who are human beings should think only of human things and that mortals should think only of mortal things, but we should try as far as possible to partake of immortality and to make every effort to live according to the best [κράτιστον] [part of the soul] in us; for even if this part be of small measure, it surpasses all the others by far in power and worth. It would seem, too, that each human being is this part, if indeed this is the dominant part and is better [ἄμεινον] than the other parts; so it would be absurd if one did not choose one's own life but that of another. And what was stated earlier is appropriate here also: that which is by nature proper [οἰκεῖον] to each being is the best [κράτιστον] and most pleasant for that being. So for a human being, too, the life according to the intellect is the best and most pleasant, if indeed a human being in the highest sense is this intellect. Hence this life, too, is the happiest. (1177b26–1178a8)

This passage, addressing the question of human self-transcendence, could also be taken as a further development of friendship understood as asymmetrical relationship. Human self-transcendence would designate the friendship of human and divine, articulating the togetherness of the human and that which is not human – of the human and that which pervades and encompasses the human while remaining incommensurate, excessive to it. In this sense, friendship would name that bond situating the human within that which is irreducible to the human, the bond in virtue of which the human may acknowledge itself as belonging in the irreducible. Of course, our emphasis on such a relation between the human and the non-human or beyond-human is due to the fact that, on Aristotle's own terms, the other-than-human *is in* the human and *is* the human: both "is in" the human as one of its parts and "is" the human in its distinctiveness. Interestingly, the Aristotelian indication of the distinctive feature of the human being amounts neither to a simple definition of human nature nor to an emphasis on the centrality of the human. In a decidedly non-anthropocentric gesture, Aristotle points out that what is decisively at the heart of the human being is other-than-human, non-human, or inhuman. In this sense, friendship bespeaks harmonization within and without oneself, inside and outside: the open articulation of radical alterity, the gathering of that which cannot be brought under the same measure. The genuinely human trait would precisely reside in the hospitality with respect to the wholly other.

Thus, the Aristotelian discourse regarding contemplation withstands a crucial tension. On the one hand, the intellect at work in human beings is considered as not human, indeed, divine. A human being lives the supremely joyous life of intellectual activity not insofar as he or she is a human being, but insofar as he or she has something divine in him- or herself (1177b27). On the other hand, the human being *is* such an activity, *is* the divine, and should therefore be identified with that "part." Not only, then, is *nous* the most excellent, divine "part" of the human soul, not only is living according to *nous* the most desirable and unqualified good for a human being, but, furthermore, "each" human being "in the highest sense" is *nous* (1178a2, 1178a8). The human lets the divine dwell to the point of becoming (one with) it. Precisely as not self-same, as indeterminately open (hospitable) to ultimate alterity, the human being *is divine.*

Again, surmising that "each" human being *is* this "part" makes it difficult to conceive of *nous* as separable (i.e., separable from the phenomenal and worldly matters) – unless, as suggested during the examination of Book Zeta on the intellectual virtues, by "separability" one would mean, here, the separability from singular individuals. In this case, *nous* would indeed be separable, but in the sense of separable from "me," from any one, because common and most shared.

Let us elaborate on this further. Human self-overcoming points to the question of the divine, to the question of the other-than-human that resides in the human: the other-than-human in and as the human. In this connection, we should emphasize the paradoxical "propriety of alterity," the propriety and opportunity of the other in and as the human. Indeed, the human being is defined by such a self-transcendence, a self-transcendence in virtue of which the human, in fact each human being, may distance him- or herself from him- or herself in order to transpire otherwise, in order to enact him- or herself on a plane where individuality narrowly understood is superseded, transmuted. We could say that what distinctively characterizes the human is precisely the capacity for such a self-distancing, the opening of such a space, the spacing within and as oneself.

Understanding the separation of *nous* in terms of separation from oneself, thus, may point to the phenomenon of becoming more spacious, more comprehensive – of distancing oneself from oneself so as to experience one's own irreducibility to one's own narrowly confined identity. In this sense, separation from oneself may mean finding oneself well beyond individual bounds: finding oneself, but otherwise, on another plane – as *nous,* at one with *nous.* It may mean discovering in oneself a vastness coinciding with the starry sky. Separation, distance, non-coincidence vis-à-vis oneself, thus, may come to signify self-recovery, joining oneself (again), (re)turning to oneself in a more genuine way, connecting with one's more comprehensive (utterly unique and yet widely shared) self.

Here we seize an almost proto-Kantian thought of disinterestedness, the self-overcoming characteristic of the good soul spontaneously interested in nature, drawn to a contemplation of nature in its most shining, divine manifestations. Along these lines, once more, we should insist on the connection between the Aristotelian ethico-political discourses and the so-called metaphysical treatises. For even the relation to the highest good, treated in *Metaphysics* Lambda as a matter of pursuing the beloved, seems to corroborate this understanding of the subject caught in the rapture of contemplation, carried away, beyond itself, by the vision allowed by *sophia,* taken over by the intuition, absorbed in the contemplation of divine bliss. Such a contemplation or intuition, qua erotic in character, has everything to do with genuine lived involvement, with the engagement in the matters of life. Thus, not even the pursuit of the unqualified would be presented as theoretically aloof from living, from the practical and experiential dimensions thereof. As Aristotle proposes in *Metaphysics* Lambda, that which is supremely desirable and that which is supremely intelligible are one (1072a26ff.).[24]

[24] In this regard, Pierre Hadot observes: "Yet again, the theoretical way of life reveals its ethical dimension. If the philosopher delights in coming to know other beings, this is because he only desires that which leads him to the supremely desirable." He also speaks of "that detachment from oneself in virtue of which the individual reaches to the level of spirit, of intellect, which is one's true self, thus becoming conscious of the attraction that the supreme principle exerts on him or her, supreme desirable and supreme intelligible." Finally, referring to a moment in *Metaphysics* 1075a5ff. (also echoed by Theophrastus in *Metaphysics* 9b15ff.), Hadot underlines that the highest manner of intellectual

But what, then, is at stake in self-transcendence, in the transcendence of the self narrowly understood and its transmutation into a self at once more genuine and shared? At stake seems to be the commonality of the divine, the divine belonging to this human being and to every other human being. This does not make the divine absolutely heterogeneous. Because the conjunction of human and divine is a togetherness of incommensurables, it could be said that the divine remains the same in each case, but incommensurably: the same inflected through a human articulation each time unique. The divinity of the human, in the human, as the human, may be glimpsed as the shining of "the same" through infinite and irreducible singularity: a sameness to be acknowledged but not possibly reckoned. The human being is illuminated as incalculable sameness and shared singularity.

Qua common, not identified with "me," not simply individual let alone personal, *nous* cannot be altered by accidents or contingent particulars. Rather, it seizes them, makes them light up and become perspicuous. It seizes them, yet remains impassive, "the same" – as though always already comprehending them all, as a kind of collective repository of all experience conscious and unconscious, as collective consciousness and unconsciousness.

5. AGAIN ON *LOGOS* AND *PRAXIS*

Toward the end of Book Kappa, Aristotle returns to a point that he has emphasized with great care already numerous times: the dissociation of reason and speech, *logos*, from action and experience, in particular as this dissociation is exemplified by the sophists. Aristotle states:

> As for those of the sophists who profess to know politics, they appear to be very far from teaching it; for, in general, they do not even know what kind of thing it is or what it is concerned with, otherwise they would not have posited it as being the same as rhetoric, or even inferior to it, nor would they have thought it easy to legislate by collecting the laws which are well thought of. Thus, they say that it is possible to select the best laws, as if (a) that selection did not require intelligence [συνέσεως] and (b) right judgment [κρῖναι ὀρθῶς] [in making the selection] were not the greatest thing, as in the case of music; for while those who

perception, for Aristotle, is a matter not of knowledge but of coincidence (however ephemeral) with the divine, with thought thinking itself for eternity: "It would really seem that the bliss of human intellect reaches its culmination when, at times, it thinks, with indivisible intuition, the indivisibility of divine bliss." "Nothing," he concludes, "is farther removed from the theory of the theoretical, that is, of contemplation" (84).

are experienced [ἔμπειροι] judge rightly the works in their field and understand by what means and in what manner [they are achieved], and also what harmonizes with what, those who are inexperienced should be content if they do not fail to notice [διαλανθάνειν] whether the work is well or badly made, as in painting. (1181a12–23)

In the lines that follow this passage (esp. 1181b5–12), Aristotle is very clear in associating and in fact binding together *theōria* and politics, the speculative posture of contemplation and political involvement. The capacity for judgment alone can be of assistance in assessing political action and institution, *politikē* (1181b1) – but such a capacity necessarily rests on habituation. Says Aristotle:

So perhaps the collection of laws or constitutions, too, would be helpful to those who can contemplate and judge [θεωρῆσαι καὶ κρῖναι] what is beautifully stated or the contrary and what kinds of laws or constitutions harmonize with a given situation; but those who go over such collection without the habit of contemplation or judgment cannot judge beautifully, except by accident, although they might gain more intelligence concerning them. (1181b7–12)

Invoked here are a political practice (or making) infused with intellectual insight and a speculative posture involved in ethico-political matters. Once more, at the very end of this treatise we find prescribed the unity of *logos* and ethical excellence, that is to say, practical orientation to the good. Without such a union, *logos* would be but rational cleverness, allowing one indifferently to play each and every part, without solicitude for the true and good. Again, the prescription here is doing as one says or as one reasons and, conversely, speaking or reasoning according to one's own doing, experience, and vicissitudes. Only through such rootedness can *logos* gain the depth and resonance of genuine wisdom. Now as well as then, this thought may strike many as naïve. Yet it may be not quite so.

Indeed, such a call for the unity of *logos* and *praxis* must have struck even Greek listeners or readers as rather impractical or unrealistic. The requirement of exercise, experience, and habituation forces *logos* to proceed too close to phenomena in their infinite complexity. Plato himself stages this impatience vis-à-vis that which may slow *logos* down, veil its swiftness, agility, and brilliance. In *Republic* I (343d), Thrasymachus the sophist scornfully calls Socrates "most simple" (*euēthestatos*). *Euēthēs* would literally signify one of harmonious comportment, showing integrity in his or her behavior. However, it is telling that in common usage, which the sophist is here following, *euēthēs* means "simple" in the sense of "simple-minded," not especially sophisticated or intellectually endowed. Already in his own context and time, Aristotle is working against the grain of this entrenched trope that dictates the secondary status of "merely acting well" – and precisely suggests the utmost relevance of the unity, whether simple or not, of language and deed.

5

Kolophon

This excursus began with a reading of segments from the *Metaphysics* and *Posterior Analytics*. Through these texts, first philosophy, that is, the investigation of conditions, emerges as essentially informed by considerations regarding at once sensibility and action (*aisthēsis* and *praxis*). In this context, Aristotle delineates the intertwinement of perceptual and practical motifs in its phenomenal or even phenomenological character.

The Main Section is devoted to an analysis of *Nicomachean Ethics* Alpha to Zeta and related texts. Aristotle's discussion of *ēthos*, far from a circumscribed and secondary discipline, is progressively disclosed as involved in casting light on primordial structures – of nature, human nature, first origins, final causality. The ethical treatises interrogate those altogether embodied and practical matters in which any human inquiry, including the "science of wisdom," is rooted. In this way, they make explicit and articulate the awareness of the non-scientific ground of science.

The Interlude returns to the *Metaphysics*, most notably to the discussion of the so-called principle of non-contradiction in Book Gamma. It aims to show at work what was previously observed regarding the intellectual virtues (particularly, intellect and wisdom) in their inseparability from the virtues pertaining to character and action. Far from being a "metaphysical" law, the principle of non-contradiction is shown in its genuinely physical traits, as that which informs what is – as that which informs being in its becoming and acting.

The Concluding Section focuses on *Nicomachean Ethics* Theta to Kappa, the discussions of friendship and the good. It draws together the ethico-political motifs and the study of the most comprehensive teleology. In other words, it shows how, on Aristotelian terms, politics and final causality, engagement in action as well as the contemplative activity, imply each other.

To be sure, the variety and magnitude of the themes here intersecting may have allowed only a rather preliminary and schematic approach. However, the attempt at a reconfiguration of our reception of Greek thought, paradigmatically of Aristotle, seems to be relevant for reasons exceeding the study of ancient philosophy (I shall not say: of the "classics") narrowly understood. To make just an example, let us consider the very contemporary question raised in various domains of the so-called human sciences, regarding the anthropological relativity of Western culture. The contrast between what is recognized as the Greek legacy and cultures not European, not Greek, not even Judeo-Greek-Christian, is now customary and has come to concern even domains such as the scientific-mathematical ones, until recently held (no doubt, in an arrogant, hasty gesture) to have neither parallel nor strictly comparable developments in non-Western cultures. In ethnomathematics and similar fields of study the contrast, for example, between logic as a quintessentially Greek expression (principle of non-contradiction, etc.) and radically other ways of thinking, ordering, and organizing may present itself as a self-evident assumption. However, contrasts of such a tenor may also turn out to be rather facile, questionable, particularly if we activate an understanding of Greek matters that is more nuanced, problematic, less caricatured.

The attempts to break through Eurocentric prejudice of colonial matrix and open to alterity, cultural and otherwise, may be most urgently needed. However, at times they rest on rhetorical devices and tropes that, if not altogether fictitious, still deserve close examination. For instance, they may resort to an exceedingly simplified, homogenous construction of what is called "Western," its origin, and its development. In so doing, they may end up with accounts as violently blind toward the irreducibility, plurality, and alterity of origin (said to be Greek, in our instance) as they are eager to found a respectful acknowledgment of the presently designated "other." But whether a direct line connects "us" to those who are claimed as "our" Greek "forefathers," whether "the Greeks" are closer to "us here" (to the scientific as well as political practices current in Europe and North America today) than other cultures are – this, in a serious sense, remains to be seen.

There are, of course, other intersecting preoccupations that may call for this kind of investigation of the complexity of origins. Last but not least, there is the desire to instill a sense of unease vis-à-vis both the anxiety of the "post-" (the need to have overcome and disposed of, a need not all that distant from the rhetoric of new beginnings and of the unqualifiedly new) and the repressiveness of the "back to" (the nostalgic call claiming to save us from ever-decadent times). Beyond the patricidal quest for survival (always a quest for the new) as well as filial piety, beyond Hesiod's archaic fathers swallowing their children (pushing time back under) as well as the ineffable father forever withdrawing, here I attempted an engagement with Aristotle.

Selected Bibliography

Abed, Shukri. *Aristotelian Logic and the Arabic Language in Alfarabi.* Albany: SUNY Press, 1991.

Achtenberg, Deborah. *Cognition of Value in Aristotle's* Ethics: *Promise of Enrichment, Threat of Destruction.* Albany: SUNY Press, 2002.

Ackrill, John L. *Aristotle: Categories and* De interpretatione. Oxford: Clarendon Press, 1963.

______. "Aristotle's Definitions of *psuchē.*" *Proceedings of the Aristotelian Society* 73 (1972–3): 119–34.

______. *Aristotle the Philosopher.* Oxford: Oxford UP, 1981.

______. *Essays on Plato and Aristotle.* Oxford: Clarendon Press, 1997.

Adams, Don. "Virtue without Morality." *Contemporary Philosophy* 22, nos. 3–4 (2000): 38–44.

Addis, L. "Aristotle and the Independence of Substances." *Philosophy and Phenomenological Research* 54 (1972): 699–708.

Alberti, Antonina, and Robert Sharples, eds. *Aspasius: The Earliest Extant Commentary on Aristotle's Ethics.* Berlin: W. de Gruyter, 1999.

Alexander of Aphrodisias. *In Aristotelis Metaphysica commentaria.* Ed. Michael Hayduck. Vol. 1. Berlin: Reimer, 1891.

______. *On Aristotle's Metaphysics 1.* Trans. William E. Dooley. London and Ithaca, N.Y.: Cornell UP, 1989.

______. *Ethical Problems.* Trans. R. W. Sharples. Ithaca, N.Y.: Cornell UP, 1990.

______. *On Aristotle's Metaphysics 2 and 3.* Trans. William E. Dooley and Arthur Madigan. London and Ithaca, N.Y.: Cornell UP, 1992.

______. *Quaestiones 1.1–2.15.* Trans. R. W. Sharples. Ithaca, N.Y.: Cornell UP, 1992.

______. *On Aristotle's Metaphysics 4.* Trans. Arthur Madigan. London and Ithaca, N.Y.: Cornell UP, 1993.

______. *On Aristotle's Metaphysics 5.* Trans. William E. Dooley. Ithaca, N.Y.: Cornell UP, 1993.

———. *Quaestiones 2.16–3.15.* Trans. R. W. Sharples. Ithaca, N.Y.: Cornell UP, 1994.

———. *Supplement to* On the Soul. Trans. R. W. Sharples. Ithaca, N.Y.: Cornell UP, 2004.

Alexander of Aphrodisias and Themistius. *Two Greek Aristotelian Commentators on the Intellect.* Trans. Frederic M. Schroeder and Robert B. Todd. Toronto: Pontifical Institute of Medieval Studies, 1990.

Al-Farabi. *Alfarabi's Philosophy of Plato and Aristotle.* Trans. Muhsin Mahdi. Ithaca, N.Y.: Cornell UP, 1969.

———. *Book of Letters.* Ed. M. Mahdi. Beirut: Dar el-Mashreq, 1969.

———. *On the Perfect State.* Trans. Richard Walzer. Oxford: Oxford UP, 1985.

———. *The Political Writings.* Trans. Charles E. Butterworth. Ithaca, N.Y.: Cornell UP, 2001.

Algra, Keimpe. "Aristotle and Hellenistic Philosophy." *Phronesis* 46, no. 1 (2001): 93–104.

Anagnostopoulos, Georgios. *Aristotle on the Goals and Exactness of Ethics.* Berkeley: University of California Press, 1994.

Annas, Julia. "Aristotle on Memory and the Self." *Oxford Studies in Ancient Philosophy* 4 (1986): 99–117.

———. *The Morality of Happiness.* New York: Oxford UP, 1993.

Anscombe, G. E. M. "The Principle of Individuation." *Proceedings of the Aristotelian Society,* supp. vol. 27 (1953): 83–96.

Anton, J. P., and A. Preus, eds. *Aristotle's Ethics: Essays in Ancient Greek Philosophy.* Vol. 4. Albany: SUNY Press, 1991.

Aquinas, Saint Thomas. *Commentary on Aristotle's* Nicomachean Ethics. Trans. C. I. Litzinger. Notre Dame, Ind.: Dumb Ox, 1993.

———. *Commentary on Aristotle's* Metaphysics. Trans. John P. Rowan. Notre Dame, Ind.: Dumb Ox, 1995.

———. *Commentary on Aristotle's* De Anima. Trans. Kenelm Foster and Silvester Humphries. Notre Dame, Ind.: Dumb Ox, 1999.

Arendt, Hannah. *The Human Condition.* Chicago: University of Chicago, 1958.

Arnim, Hans von. "Das Ethische in Aristoteles *Topik.*" *Sitzungsberichte der Akademie der Wissenschaften in Wien* 205, no. 4 (1927): 76–94.

Aspasius, Anonymous, and Michael of Ephesus. *On Aristotle* Nicomachean Ethics *8–9.* Trans. D. Konstan. Ithaca, N.Y.: Cornell UP, 2001.

Aubenque, Pierre. *Le problème de l'être chez Aristote: essai sur la problématique aristotélicienne.* Paris: PUF, 1962.

———. *La prudence chez Aristote.* Paris: PUF, 1963.

———. "Sense et structure de la métaphysique aristotélicienne." *Bulletin de la Société Française de Philosophie* 57 (1964): 1–56.

———. "La loi selon Aristote." *Archives de philosophie du droit* XXV. Paris (1980), 147–57.

———. "Politique et éthique chez Aristote." *Ktema* 5 (1980): 211–21.

———. "La matière de l'intelligible." *Revue Philosophique de la France et de l'Etranger* 172 (1982): 307–20.

———. "The Origins of the Doctrine of the Analogy of Being." *Graduate Faculty Philosophy Journal* 11, no. 1 (1986): 35–45.

______. "Aristote et la démocratie." *Actes du Colloque sur l'influence d'Aristote dans le monde méditerranéen, Istanbul, janvier 1986*, 31–38. Istanbul: Institut Français d'Études Anatoliennes, 1988.
______. "La philosophie aristotélicienne et nous." In Mohamed A. Sinaceur, ed., *Aristote aujourd'hui*, 320–25. Paris and Toulouse: Unesco/Erès, 1988.
______. "The Twofold Natural Foundation of Justice According to Aristotle." In Robert Heinaman, ed., *Aristotle and Moral Realism*, 35–47. Boulder: Westview, 1995.
Aubenque, Pierre, et al. *Études aristotéliciennes: métaphysique et théologie.* Paris: Vrin, 1985.
Aubenque, Pierre, and Pierre Rodrigo. *Aristote et les choses humaines, suivi de "la politique stoïcienne."* Paris: Didier, 1998.
Aubenque, Pierre, and Alonso Tordesillas. *Aristote politique.* Paris: PUF, 1993.
Averroes. *Averroes on Plato's* Republic. Trans. Ralph Lerner. Ithaca, N.Y.: Cornell UP, 1974.
______. *Averroes' Middle Commentaries on Aristotle's Categories and De interpretatione.* Trans. Charles Butterworth. Princeton: Princeton UP, 1983.
______. *Ibn Rushd's Metaphysics: A Translation with an Introduction of Ibn Rushd's Commentary on Aristotle's Metaphysics, Book Lam.* Trans. Charles Genequand. Leiden: Brill, 1984.
______. *Averroes' Middle Commentary on Aristotle's* Poetics. Trans. Charles Butterworth. Princeton: Princeton UP, 1986.
______. *Talkhis kitab al-Akhlaq* [Averroes' Commentary on the *Nicomachean Ethics*]. Trans. Samuel ben Judah. Jerusalem: *ha-Akademyah ha-Le'umit ha-Yisre'elit le-Mada'im*, 1999.
Avicenna. *Avicenna's Treatise on Logic.* Trans. Farhang Zabeeh. The Hague: Nijhoff, 1971.
______. *Metaphysica of Avicenna.* Trans. Parviz Morewedge. New York: Columbia UP, 1973.
______. *Avicenna's Commentary on the Poetics of Aristotle.* Trans. Ismail M. Dahiyat. Leiden: Brill, 1974.
______. *The Life of Ibn Sina.* Trans. William E. Gohlman. Albany: SUNY Press, 1974.
______. *La métaphysique du Shifa'.* Trans. G. Anawati. 2 vols. Paris: Vrin, 1978.
______. *Remarks and Admonitions.* Trans. Shams Constantine Inati. Toronto: Pontifical Institute of Medieval Studies, 1984.
Badawi, Abdurrahman. *La transmission de la philosophie grecque au monde arabe.* Paris: Vrin, 1968.
Baracchi, Claudia. *Of Myth, Life, and War in Plato's* Republic. Bloomington: Indiana UP, 2002.
______. "The Nature of Reason and the Sublimity of First Philosophy: Toward a Reconfiguration of Aristotelian Interpretation." *Epoché* 7, no. 2 (Spring 2003): 223–49.
______. "On Heidegger, the Greeks, and Us: Once More on the Relation of *Praxis* and *Theoria.*" *Philosophy Today* 50 (Supplement 2006):162–9.
______. "Ethics as First Philosophy: Aristotelian Reflections on Intelligence, Sensibility, and Transcendence." In Silvia Benso and Brian Schroeder, eds., *Levinas and the Ancients.* Bloomington: Indiana UP, 2007.

Barker, A. "Aristotle on Perception and Ratios." *Phronesis* 26 (1981): 248–66.

Barker, Ernest. *The Political Thought of Plato and Aristotle.* New York: Dover, 1959.

Barnes, Jonathan. "Aristotle's Concept of Mind." *Proceedings of the Aristotelian Society* 72 (1971–2): 101–14.

———. "Aristotle and the Methods of Ethics." *Revue Internationale de la Philosophie* 34 (1981): 490–511.

Barnes, Jonathan, Malcolm Schofield, and Richard Sorabji, eds. *Articles on Aristotle.* 4 vols. London: Duckworth, 1979.

Bartlett, Robert, and Susan Collins. *Action and Contemplation: Studies in the Moral and Political Thought of Aristotle.* Albany: SUNY Press, 1999.

Belfiore, Elizabeth. "Family Friendship in Aristotle's *Ethics.*" *Ancient Philosophy* 21, no. 1 (Spring 2001): 113–32.

Benardete, Seth. "Aristotle, *De anima* III. 3–5." *Review of Metaphysics* 28 (1975): 611–22.

Berryman, Sylvia. "Aristotle on *Pneuma* and Animal Self-Motion." *Oxford Studies in Ancient Philosophy* 23 (2002): 85–97.

Berti, Enrico. *Studi Aristotelici. L'Aquila: Methodos* 7, 1975.

———. "The Intellection of Indivisibles According to Aristotle." In G. E. R. Lloyd and G. E. L. Owen, eds., *Aristotle on Mind and the Senses: Proceedings of the Seventh Symposium Aristotelicum,* 141–64. Cambridge: Cambridge UP, 1978.

———. *Aristotele nel Novecento.* Rome: Laterza, 1992.

———. *Nuovi Studi Aristotelici.* Vol. 2. Brescia: Morcelliana, 2005.

Berti, Enrico, ed. *Tradizione e attualità della filosofia pratica.* Genova: Marietti, 1988.

Bien, Günther. *Die Grundlegung der politischen Philosophie bei Aristoteles.* Freiburg: Alber, 1973.

Birondo, Noell. "Aristotle on Illusory Perception: *Phantasia* without *Phantasmata.*" *Ancient Philosophy* 21 (2001): 57–71.

Block, Irving. "Aristotle and the Physical Object." *Philosophy and Phenomenological Research* 21 (1960): 93–101.

———. "Truth and Error in Aristotle's Theory of Sense Perception." *Philosophical Quarterly* 11 (1961): 1–9.

———. "On the Commonness of the Common Sensibles." *Australasian Journal of Philosophy* 43 (1965): 189–95.

———. "Substance in Aristotle." In G. C. Simmons, ed., *Paideia*: Special Aristotle Issue, 59–64. Brockport, N.Y., 1978.

———. "Aristotle on Common Sense: A Reply to Kahn and Others." *Ancient Philosophy* 8 (1988): 235–49.

Blumenthal, H., and H. Robinson, eds., *Aristotle and the Later Tradition.* Oxford: Oxford UP, 1991.

Bodéüs, Richard. *Le philosophe et la cité: recherches sur les rapports entre morale et politique dans la pensée d'Aristote.* Paris: Belles Lettres, 1982.

———. *Aristote: la justice et la cité.* Paris: PUF, 1996.

———. *Aristotle and the Theology of the Living Immortals.* Trans. Ian Edward Garrett. Albany: SUNY Press, 2000.

Bolton, R. "Aristotle's Definitions of the Soul: *De Anima* II, 1–3." *Phronesis* 23 (1978): 258–78.

Booth, Edward. *Aristotelian Aporetic Ontology in Islamic and Christian Thinkers.* Cambridge: Cambridge UP, 1983.

Bos, Abraham P. *The Soul and Its Instrumental Body: A Reinterpretation of Aristotle's Psychology of Living Nature.* Leiden: Brill, 2003.

Bosley, Richard, Roger A. Shiner, and Janet D. Sisson, eds. *Aristotle, Virtue and the Mean.* Edmonton, Canada: Academic Printing & Publishing, 1995.

Bostock, David. *Aristotle's Ethics.* Oxford: Oxford UP, 2000.

Bottin, Francesco. *La scienza degli occamisti. La scienza tardo-medievale dalle origini del paradigma nominalista alla rivoluzione scientifica.* Rimini: Maggioli, 1982.

Bradshaw, D. "Aristotle on Perception: The Dual-Logos Theory." *Apeiron* 30 (1997): 143–61.

Brague, Rémi. *Du temps chez Platon et Aristote: quatre études.* Paris: PUF, 1982.

______. *Aristote et la question du monde: essai sur le contexte cosmologique et anthropologique de l'ontologie.* Paris: PUF, 1988.

______. "Aristotle's Definition of Motion and Its Ontological Implications." *Graduate Faculty Philosophy Journal* 13, no. 2 (1990): 1–22.

______. *La sagesse du monde: histoire de l'expérience humaine de l'univers.* Paris: LGF, 2002.

Brentano, Franz. *The Psychology of Aristotle: In Particular His Doctrine of the Active Intellect, with an Appendix Concerning the Activity of Aristotle's God.* Trans. Rolf George. Berkeley: University of California Press, 1977.

Brickhouse, Thomas C. "Does Aristotle Have a Consistent Account of Vice?" *Review of Metaphysics* 57 (2003): 3–23.

Broackes, Justin. "Aristotle, Objectivity and Perception." *Oxford Studies in Ancient Philosophy* 17 (1999): 57–113.

Broadie, Sarah. *Ethics with Aristotle.* New York: Oxford UP, 1991.

______. "*Nous* and Nature in Aristotle's *De Anima* III." *Proceedings of the Boston Area Colloquium in Ancient Philosophy* 12 (1996): 163–76.

______. "Interpreting Aristotle's Directions." In Jyl Gentzler, ed., *Method in Ancient Philosophy,* 291–306. Oxford: Oxford UP, 1998.

Brown, Lesley. "What Is the Mean Relative to Us in Aristotle's *Ethics*?" *Phronesis* 42 (1997): 77–93.

Brunschwig, Jacques. "The Aristotelian Theory of Equity." In Michael Frede and Gisela Striker, eds., *Rationality in Greek Thought,* 115–55. Oxford: Clarendon Press, 1996.

Burnet, J. *The Ethics of Aristotle.* London: Methuen, 1900.

Burns, Tony. "Aristotle and Natural Law." *History of Political Thought* 19, no. 2 (1998): 142–66.

Burnyeat, Myles. *A Map of Metaphysics Zeta.* Pittsburgh, Pa.: Mathesis, 2001.

Bynum, T. W. "A New Look at Aristotle's Theory of Perception." *History of Philosophy Quarterly* 4 (1987): 163–78.

Bywater, Ingram. *Aristotle, Ethica Nicomachea.* Oxford: Oxford UP, 1891.

______. *Contributions to the Textual Criticism of Aristotle's Nicomachean Ethics.* New York: Arno, 1973.

Cassin, Barbara. *Aristote et le logos: contes de la phénoménologie ordinaire.* Paris: PUF, 1997.

Cassin, Barbara, and Michel Narcy. *La décision du sens: le livre Gamma de la* Métaphysique *d'Aristote.* Paris: Vrin, 1989.

Caston, Victor. "Aristotle and the Problem of Intentionality." *Philosophy and Phenomenological Research* 58 (1998): 249–98.

———. "Aristotle's Two Intellects: A Modest Proposal." *Phronesis* 44 (1999): 199–227.

Chappell, T. D. J. *Aristotle and Augustine on Freedom: Two Theories of Freedom, Voluntary Action, and Akrasia.* New York: St. Martin's, 1995.

Chappell, V. "Aristotle's Conception of Matter." *Journal of Philosophy* 70 (1973): 679–96.

Charles, David. *Aristotle's Philosophy of Action.* Ithaca, N.Y.: Cornell UP, 1984.

———. "Aristotle on Well-Being and Intellectual Contemplation." *Aristotelian Society*, supp. vol. 73 (1999): 205–23.

Charlton, W. "Aristotle and the Principle of Individuation." *Phronesis* 17 (1972): 239–49.

———. "Aristotle and the *harmonia* Theory." In Allan Gotthelf, ed., *Aristotle on Nature and Living Things: Philosophical and Historical Studies*, 131–50. Pittsburgh, Pa.: Mathesis, 1985.

———. "Aristotle on the Place of the Mind in Nature." In A. Gotthelf and J. G. Lennox, eds., *Philosophical Issues in Aristotle's Biology*, 408–23. Cambridge: Cambridge UP, 1987.

Chiodi, Giulio Maria. *Equità: la categoria regolativa del diritto.* Naples: Guida, 1989.

Code, Alan. "On the Origins of Some Aristotelian Theses about Predication." In J. Bogen and J. E. McGuire, eds., *How Things Are: Studies in Predication and the History of Philosophy*, 101–31. Dordrecht: Reidel, 1985.

———. "Soul as Efficient Cause in Aristotle's Embryology." *Philosophical Topics* 15 (1987): 51–9.

———. "Aristotle's Metaphysics as a Science of Principles." *Revue Internationale de Philosophie* 51 (1997): 357–78.

Code, Alan, and Julius Moravcsik. "Explaining Various Forms of Living." In M. C. Nussbaum and A. Oksenberg Rorty, eds., *Essays on Aristotle's* De anima, 129–45. Oxford: Clarendon Press, 1992.

Cooper, John M. *Reason and Human Good in Aristotle.* Indianapolis: Hackett, 1986.

———. "Metaphysics in Aristotle's Embryology." *Proceedings of the Cambridge Philological Society* 214 (1988): 14–41. Reprinted in D. Devereux and P. Pellegrin, eds., *Biologie, logique et métaphysique chez Aristote*, 55–84. Paris: CNRS, 1990.

———. *Reason and Emotion: Essays on Ancient Moral Psychology and Ethical Theory.* Princeton: Princeton UP, 1999.

———. *Knowledge, Nature, and the Good.* Princeton: Princeton UP, 2004.

Cooper, Neil. "Aristotle's Crowning Virtue." *Apeiron* 22 (1989): 191–205.

Corbin, Henry. *Avicenna and the Visionary Recital.* Trans. Willard R. Trask. Princeton: Princeton UP, 1990.

Cottingham, John. *Philosophy and the Good Life: Reason and the Passions in Greek, Cartesian and Psychoanalytic Ethics.* Cambridge: Cambridge UP, 1998.

Croissant, Jeanne. *Aristote et les mystères.* Liége: Fac. de Philosophie et Lettres, 1933.

Curzer, Howard J. "A Great Philosopher's Not So Great Account of Great Virtue: Aristotle's Treatment of 'Greatness of Soul.'" *Canadian Journal of Philosophy* 20 (1990): 517–37.

______. "The Supremely Happy Life in Aristotle's *Nicomachean Ethics.*" *Apeiron* 24 (1991): 47–69.

______. "Aristotle's Account of the Virtue of Justice." *Apeiron* 28 (1995): 207–38.

______. "A Defense of Aristotle's Doctrine of the Mean." *Ancient Philosophy* 16 (1996): 129–38.

______. "Aristotle's Account of the Virtue of Temperance in *Nicomachean Ethics* III 10–11." *Journal of the History of Philosophy* 35 (1997): 5–25.

Dahl, Norman. *Practical Reason, Aristotle and the Weakness of the Will.* Minneapolis: University of Minnesota Press, 1984.

Davidson, Herbert A. *Alfarabi, Avicenna, and Averroes on Intellect: Their Cosmologies, Theories of the Active Intellect, and Theories of Human Intellect.* New York: Oxford UP, 1992.

Delebecque, Edouard. "Sur un sens oublié du mot ΠΡΑΓΜΑ." *Revue des Études Grecques* 92, no. 436–7 (1979): 67–76.

Deleuze, Gilles, and Felix Guattari. *Qu'est-ce que la philosophie?* Paris: Les éditions de Minuit, 1991.

Dempf, Alois. *Der Wertgedanke in der Aristotelischen* Ethik *und* Politik. Wien: VWGÖ, 1989.

Depew, David J. "Humans and Other Political Animals in Aristotle's *History of Animals.*" *Phronesis* 40 (1995): 156–81.

Destrée, Pierre. "Aristote et la question du droit naturel (*Eth. Nic.*, V, 10, 1134b18–1135a5)." *Phronesis* 45, no. 3 (August 2000): 220–39.

Diels, Hermann, et al., eds. *Commentaria in Aristotelem Graeca.* 23 vols. Berlin: Reimer, 1882–1909.

Dobbs-Weinstein, Idit. *Maimonides and St. Thomas on the Limits of Reason.* Albany: SUNY Press, 1995.

Dodds, E. R. *The Greeks and the Irrational.* Berkeley: University of California Press, 1964.

Driscoll, J. "*Eidê* in Aristotle's Earlier and Later Theories of Substance." In D. J. O'Meara, ed., *Studies in Aristotle,* 129–59. Washington: Catholic UP, 1981.

Dumont, Jean-Paul. *Introduction à la méthode d'Aristote.* Paris: Vrin, 1986.

Dumoulin, Bertrand. *Recherches sur le premier Aristote: Eudème, De la philosophie, Protreptique.* Paris: Vrin, 1981.

Düring, Ingemar. *Aristoteles: Darstellung und Interpretation seines Denkens.* Heidelberg: Winter, 1966.

Easterling, H. J. "A Note on *De anima* 414a4–14." *Phronesis* 11 (1966): 159–62.

Ebert, T. "Aristotle on What Is Done in Perceiving." *Zeitschrift für philosophische Forschung* 37 (1983): 181–98.

Endress, Gerhard, and Jan A. Aertsen, eds. *Averroes and the Aristotelian Tradition: Sources, Constitution and Reception of the Philosophy of Ibn Rushd (1126–1198). Proceedings of the Fourth Symposium Averroicum, Cologne, 1996.* Leiden and Boston: Brill, 1999.

Engberg-Pedersen, Troels. *Aristotle's Theory of Moral Insight.* Oxford: Clarendon Press, 1983.

Engmann, Joyce. "Aristotle's Distinction between Substance and Universal." *Phronesis* 18 (1973): 139–55.

———. "Imagination and Truth in Aristotle." *Journal of the History of Philosophy* 14 (1976): 259–65.

Everson, Stephan. *Aristotle on Perception.* Oxford: Clarendon Press, 1997.

Festugière, A. J. "Notes aristotéliciennes. I. Les méthodes de la définition de l'âme. II. La théorie du Premier Moteur." *Revue des Sciences Philosophiques et Théologiques* 20 (1931): 83–94.

———. *Aristote: le plaisir.* Paris: J. Vrin, 1936.

Findler, Richard S. "Memory and Forgetfulness in Aristotle's *Ethics*: A Nietzschean Reading." *New Nietzsche Studies* 2, nos. 3–4 (Summer 1998): 27–39.

Fortenbaugh, W. W. *Aristotle on Emotion.* London: Duckworth, 1975.

Fraisse, J. C. *"Philía": la notion d'amitié dans la philosophie antique.* Paris: J. Vrin, 1974.

Frede, Michael. *Essays in Ancient Philosophy.* Minneapolis: University of Minnesota Press, 1987.

Freeland, Cynthia. "Aristotle on the Sense of Touch." In M. C. Nussbaum and A. Oksenberg Rorty, eds., *Essays on Aristotle's De anima*, 226–48. Oxford: Clarendon Press, 1992.

———. "Aristotle on Perception, Appetition, and Self-Motion." In M. L. Gill and James Lennox, eds., *Self Motion*, 35–63. Princeton: Princeton UP, 1994.

Freeland, Cynthia, ed. *Feminist Interpretations of Aristotle.* University Park: Penn State UP, 1998.

Fritz, Kurt von. *Beiträge zu Aristoteles.* Berlin: W. de Gruyter, 1984.

Furth, Montgomery. *Substance, Form, and Psyche: An Aristotelian Metaphysics.* Cambridge: Cambridge UP, 1988.

Gadamer, Hans Georg. *The Idea of the Good in Platonic-Aristotelian Philosophy.* Trans. P. Christopher Smith. New Haven: Yale UP, 1986.

———. *L'anima alle soglie del pensiero nella filosofia greca.* Naples: Bibliopolis, 1988.

———. *Truth and Method.* Trans. Joel Weinsheimer and Donald G. Marshall. New York: Continuum, 1995.

Gallop, David. "Aristotle on Sleep, Dreams, and Final Causes." *Proceedings of the Boston Area Colloquium in Ancient Philosophy* 4 (1988): 257–90.

Gauthier, René Antoine. *La morale d'Aristote.* Paris: PUF, 1958.

Gauthier, R. A., and Jean Yves Jolif. *Aristote: L'Ethique à Nicomaque.* 3 vols. Louvain: Publications Universitaires, 1958–9.

Gauthier-Muzellec, Marie-Hélène. *Aristote et la juste mesure.* Paris: PUF, 1998.

Gerson, Lloyd P. *Aristotle and Other Platonists.* Ithaca, N.Y.: Cornell UP, 2005.

Gill, Mary Louise. *Aristotle on Substance: The Paradox of Unity.* Princeton: Princeton UP, 1989.

Gill, M. L., and James Lennox, eds. *Self-Motion: From Aristotle to Newton.* Princeton: Princeton UP, 1994.

Gohlke, Paul. *Die Entstehung der Aristotelischen Prinzipienlehre.* Tübingen: Mohr, 1954.

Gomez-Lobo, Alfonso. "The *Ergon* Inference." *Phronesis* 34 (1989): 170–84.

Gosling, J. C. B. and C. C. W. Taylor. *The Greeks on Pleasure.* Oxford: Clarendon Press, 1982.

Gotthelf, Alan. "A Biological Provenance." *Philosophical Studies* 94 (1999): 35–56.

Gotthelf, Alan, ed. *Aristotle on Nature and Living Things: Philosophical and Historical Studies.* Pittsburgh, Pa.: Mathesis, 1985.

Gottlieb, Paula. "Aristotle and Protagoras: The Good Human Being as the Measure of Goods." *Apeiron* 24 (1991): 25–45.

______. "Aristotle's Measure Doctrine and Pleasure." *Archiv für Geschichte der Philosophie* 75 (1993): 31–46.

______. "Aristotle on Dividing the Soul and Uniting the Virtues." *Phronesis* 39 (1994): 275–90.

______. "Aristotle's 'Nameless' Virtues." *Apeiron* 27 (1994): 1–15.

Graham, D. W. "The Paradox of Prime Matter." *Journal of the History of Philosophy* 25 (1987): 475–90.

Grice, H. P. "Aristotle on the Multiplicity of Being." *Pacific Philosophical Quarterly* 69 (1988): 175–200.

Granger, Herbert. *Aristotle's Idea of the Soul.* Dordrecht: Kluwer, 1996.

Guidi, L. "Sulla giustizia distributiva." *Studium* (1940): 349–99.

Gutas, Dimitri. *Avicenna and the Aristotelian Tradition.* Leiden: Brill, 1988.

Guthrie, W. *A History of Greek Philosophy, VI. Aristotle: An Encounter.* Cambridge: Cambridge UP, 1990.

Haddad, Fuad Said. *Alfarabi's Theory of Communication.* Beirut: American University of Beirut, 1989.

Hadot, Pierre. "Sur divers sens du mot *pragma* dans la tradition philosophique grecque." In P. Aubenque, ed. *Concepts et catégories dans la pensée antique,* 309–19. Paris: Vrin, 1980.

______. *Philosophy as a Way of Life: Spiritual Exercises from Socrates to Foucault.* Ed. Arnold Davidson, trans. Michael Chase. Oxford: Blackwell, 1995.

______. *Che cos'è la filosofia antica?* Trans. Elena Giovanelli. Turin: Einaudi, 1998.

______. *Exercises spirituels et philosophie antique.* Paris: Albin Michel, 2002.

Hamlyn, D. W. "Aristotle's Account of *aisthēsis* in the *De Anima.*" *Classical Quarterly* 9 (1959): 6–16.

______. *Aristotle's De anima II-III.* Oxford: Clarendon Press, 1968.

Happ, Heinz. *Hyle: Studien zur aristotelischen Materie-Begriff.* Berlin: W. de Gruyter, 1971.

Hardie, W. F. R. *Aristotle's Ethical Theory.* Oxford: Clarendon Press, 1980.

Hartman, Edwin. *Substance, Body, and Soul: Aristotelian Investigations.* Princeton: Princeton UP, 1977.

Havelock, Eric A. *The Greek Concept of Justice from Its Shadow in Homer to Its Substance in Plato.* Cambridge, Mass.: Harvard UP, 1978.

Heidegger, Martin. *Die Grundprobleme der Phänomenologie. Gesamtausgabe 24.* Frankfurt: Klostermann, 1975.

______. *Wegmarken. Gesamtausgabe 9.* Frankfurt: Klostermann, 1976.

______. *Metaphysische Anfangsgründe der Logik im Ausgang von Leibniz. Gesamtausgabe 26.* Frankfurt: Klostermann, 1978.

———. *Aristoteles: Metaphysik IX, 1–3: Von Wesen und Wirklichkeit der Kraft.* Gesamtausgabe 33. Frankfurt: Klostermann, 1981.
———. *Phänomenologische Interpretationen zu Aristoteles: Einführung in die phänomenologische Forschung.* Gesamtausgabe 61. Frankfurt: Klostermann, 1985.
———. *Platon Sophistes. Gesamtausgabe 19.* Frankfurt: Klostermann, 1992.
———. *Grundbegriffe der aristotelischen Philosophie.* Gesamtausgabe 18. Frankfurt: Klostermann, 2002.
Heinaman, Robert, ed. *Aristotle and Moral Realism.* Boulder: Westview Press, 1995.
Heller, Agnes. *A Philosophy of Morals.* Oxford: Blackwell, 1990.
Höffe, Otfried. *Politische Gerechtigkeit. Grundlegung einer kritischen Philosophie von Recht und Staat.* Frankfurt: Suhrkamp, 1987.
Hutchinson, D. E. *The Virtues of Aristotle.* London and New York: Routledge & Kegan Paul, 1986.
Hyland, Drew. "Self-Reflection and Knowing in Aristotle." *Giornale di Metafisica* 23, no. 1 (1968): 49–61.
Irwin, T. H. "Homonymy in Aristotle." *Review of Metaphysics* 34 (1981): 523–44.
———. *Aristotle, Nicomachean Ethics.* Indianapolis: Hackett, 1985.
———. *Aristotle's First Principles.* Oxford: Clarendon Press, 1988.
———. "Disunity in the Aristotelian Virtues." *Oxford Studies in Ancient Philosophy,* supp. vol. (1988): 61–78.
Jaeger, Werner. *Studien zur Entstehungsgeschichte der Metaphysik des Aristoteles.* Berlin: Weidmann, 1912.
———. *Aristotle: Fundamentals of the History of His Development.* Trans. Richard Robinson. Oxford: Clarendon Press, 1948.
Joachim, Harold H. *Aristotle. The Nicomachean Ethics. A Commentary.* Oxford: Clarendon Press, 1951.
Johansen, T. K. *Aristotle on the Sense-Organs.* Cambridge: Cambridge UP, 1997.
Jordan, Mark. *The Alleged Aristotelianism of Thomas Aquinas.* Toronto: Pontifical Institute of Medieval Studies, 1992.
Kahn, Charles H. "Sensation and Consciousness in Aristotle's Psychology." *Archiv für Geschichte der Philosophie* 48 (1966): 43–81.
———. "The Role of *Nous* in the Cognition of First Principles in *Posterior Analytics* ii 19." In Enrico Berti, ed., *Aristotle on Science: The* Posterior Analytics, *385–414.* Padova: Antenore, 1981.
———. "Aristotle on Thinking." In M. C. Nussbaum and A. Oksenberg Rorty, eds., *Essays on Aristotle's De anima,* 359–80. Oxford: Clarendon Press, 1992.
Kalimtzis, Kostas. *Aristotle on Political Enmity and Disease: An Inquiry into Stasis.* Albany: SUNY Press, 2000.
Kenny, Anthony. *The Aristotelian Ethics: A Study of the Relationship between the Eudemian and Nicomachean Ethics of Aristotle.* Oxford: Clarendon Press, 1978.
———. *Aristotle's Theory of the Will.* New Haven: Yale UP, 1979.
———. *Aristotle on the Perfect Life.* Oxford: Clarendon Press, 1992.
Keyt, David. "Intellectualism in Aristotle." *Paideia* 7 (1978): 138–57.
———. "Distributive Justice in Aristotle's *Ethics* and *Politics.*" *Topoi* 4 (1985): 23–45.
———. "Aristotle's Theory of Distributive Justice." In D. Keyt and Fred D. Miller, Jr., eds., *A Companion to Aristotle's Politics,* 238–78. Oxford: Blackwell, 1991.
———. "Aristotle and the Ancient Roots of Anarchism." *Topoi* 15 (1996): 129–42.

Kirwan, C. A. *Aristotle: Metaphysics Books Gamma, Delta, and Epsilon.* Oxford: Clarendon Press, 1971.

Klein, Jacob. *Greek Mathematical Thought and the Origin of Algebra.* New York: Dover, 1992.

Korsgaard, Christine. "Aristotle on Function and Virtue." *History of Philosophy Quarterly* 3 (1986): 259–79.

______. "Aristotle and Kant on the Source of Value." *Ethics* 96 (1986): 486–505.

Kosman, Aryeh. "Aristotle's Definition of Motion." *Phronesis* 14 (1969): 40–62.

______. "Understanding, Explanation, and Insight in the *Posterior Analytics.*" In E. N. Lee, A. P. D. Mourelatos, and R. M. Rorty, eds., *Exegesis and Argument,* 374–92. Assen: Van Gorcum, 1973.

______. "Perceiving That We Perceive: *On the Soul* III, 2." *Philosophical Review* 84 (1975): 499–519.

______. "Being Properly Affected: Virtues and Feelings in Aristotle's Ethics." In A. Rorty, ed., *Essays on Aristotle's Ethics,* 103–16. Berkeley: University of California Press, 1980.

______. "Substance, Being, and *Energeia.*" *Oxford Studies in Ancient Philosophy* 2 (1984): 121–49.

______. "Divine Being and Divine Thinking in *Metaphysics* Lambda." In John J. Cleary, ed., *Proceedings of the Boston Area Colloquium in Ancient Philosophy* 3, 165–201. Lanham, Md.: University Press of America, 1987.

______. "Animals and Other Beings in Aristotle." In Allan Gotthelf and James G. Lennox, eds., *Philosophical Issues in Aristotle's Biology,* 360–91. Cambridge: Cambridge UP, 1987.

______. "What Does the Maker Mind Make?" In M. C. Nussbaum and A. Oksenberg Rorty, eds., *Essays on Aristotle's* De anima, *343–58.* Oxford: Clarendon Press, 1992.

______. "Aristotelian Metaphysics and Biology: Furth's *Substance, Form and Psyche.*" *Philosophical Studies* 94 (1999): 57–68.

Koumakis, G. "Die 'korrigierende' Gerechtigkeit bei Aristoteles." *Dodone* 14, no. 3 (1985): 21–31.

Krämer, Hans Joachim. Arete *bei Platon und Aristoteles. Zum Wesen und zur Geschichte der platonischen Ontologie.* Heidelberg: Winter, 1959.

Kraut, Richard. "The Peculiar Function of Human Beings." *Canadian Journal of Philosophy* 9 (1979): 53–62.

______. "Two Conceptions of Happiness." *Philosophical Review* 88 (1979): 167–97.

______. *Aristotle on the Human Good.* Princeton: Princeton UP, 1989.

______. *Aristotle: Political Philosophy.* New York: Oxford UP, 2002.

Kraut, Richard, ed. *The Blackwell Guide to Aristotle's Ethics.* Oxford: Blackwell, 2005.

Kristeller, P. O. *The Classics and Renaissance Thought.* Cambridge, Mass.: Harvard UP, 1955.

Kung, Joan. "Aristotle on 'Being Is Said in Many Ways.'" *History of Philosophy Quarterly* 3 (1986): 3–18.

Lacey, A. R. "*Ousia* and Form in Aristotle." *Phronesis* 10 (1965): 54–69.

Lameer, Joep. *Al-Farabi and Aristotelian Syllogistics: Greek Theory and Islamic Practice.* Leiden: Brill, 1994.

Lang, Helen. "On Memory: Aristotle's Corrections of Plato." *Journal of the History of Philosophy* 18 (1980): 379–93.

Lear, Jonathan. *Aristotle: The Desire to Understand.* Cambridge: Cambridge UP, 1988.

———. *Happiness, Death, and the Remainder of Life.* Cambridge, Mass.: Harvard UP, 2000.

Lewis, Frank A. "Self-Knowledge in Aristotle." *Topoi* 15 (1996): 39–58.

Lloyd, A. C. *Form and Universal in Aristotle.* Liverpool: F. Cairns, 1981.

Lloyd, G. E. R. *Aristotelian Explorations.* Cambridge: Cambridge UP, 1996.

Lloyd, G. E. R., and G. E. L. Owen, eds. *Aristotle on Mind and the Senses: Proceedings of the Seventh Symposium Aristotelicum.* Cambridge: Cambridge UP, 1978.

Long, Christopher. "The Ontological Reappropriation of *Phronēsis.*" *Continental Philosophy Review* 35 (2002): 35–60.

———. "The Ethical Culmination of Aristotle's *Metaphysics.*" *Epoché* 8, no. 1 (Fall 2003), 53–72.

———. *The Ethics of Ontology: Rethinking an Aristotelian Legacy.* Albany: SUNY Press, 2004.

Lotito, Gianfranco. "Aristotele su moneta scambio bisogni (*Eth. Nic.* 5)." *Materiali e discussioni per l'analisi dei testi classici* 4, 5, and 6 (1980–1): 125–80, 27–85, and 9–69.

Loux, Michael. "Symposium on Aristotle's *Metaphysics.*" *Ancient Philosophy* 15 (1995): 495–510.

Lowe, Malcolm. "Aristotle on Kinds of Thinking." *Phronesis* 28 (1983): 17–30.

Lycos, K. "Aristotle and Plato on 'Appearing.'" *Mind* 73 (1964): 496–514.

MacDonald, Scott. "Aristotle and the Homonymy of the Good." *Archiv für Geschichte der Philosophie* 71 (1989): 150–74.

MacIntyre, A. *After Virtue.* Notre Dame: Notre Dame UP, 1988.

MacKinnon, D. M. "Aristotle's Conception of Substance." In R. Bambrough, ed., *New Essays on Plato and Aristotle,* 97–119. London: Routledge, 1965.

Malcolm, John. "On the Endangered Species of the *Metaphysics.*" *Ancient Philosophy* 13 (1993): 79–93.

———. "On the Duality of *Eidos* in Aristotle's *Metaphysics.*" *Archiv für Geschichte der Philosophie* 78 (1996): 1–10.

Mansion, Suzanne. "Soul and Life in the *De anima.*" In G. E. R. Lloyd and G. E. L. Owen, eds., *Aristotle on Mind and the Senses: Proceedings of the Seventh Symposium Aristotelicum,* 1–20. Cambridge: Cambridge UP, 1978.

Marx, Werner. *Einführung in Aristoteles' Theorie vom Seienden.* Freiburg: Rombach, 1972.

Massie, Pascal. "The Irony of Chance: On Aristotle's *Physics* B, 4–6." *International Philosophical Quarterly* 43, no. 1 (2003): 15–28.

Massignon, L., D. Remondon, and G. Vajda. *Miscellanea.* Cairo: Institut Français D'Archéologie Orientale, 1954.

Mathie, William. "Justice and the Question of Regimes in Ancient and Modern Political Philosophy." *Canadian Journal of Political Science* 9 (1976): 449–63.

———. "Political and Distributive Justice in the Political Science of Aristotle." *Review of Politics* 49 (1987): 59–84.

Matthen, Mohan, ed. *Aristotle Today: Essays on Aristotle's Ideal of Science.* Edmonton, Canada: Academic Printing and Publishing, 1987.

Matthews, Gareth B. "Gender and Essence in Aristotle." In J. L. Thompson, ed., *Women and Philosophy. Supplement to Australasian Journal of Philosophy* 64 (1986): 16–25.

Matthews, Gareth B., and S. Marc Cohen. "The One and the Many." *Review of Metaphysics* 21 (1968): 630–55.

Maudlin, T. "*De anima* 3.1: Is Any Sense Missing?" *Phronesis* 31 (1986): 51–67.

McDowell, John. "Some Issues in Aristotle's Moral Psychology." In *Mind, Value, and Reality*, 23–49. Cambridge, Mass.: Harvard UP, 2001.

McKerlie, Dennis. "Aristotle's Theory of Justice." *Southern Journal of Philosophy* 39 (2001): 119–41.

McKinney, Ronald H. "Aristotle and the Comic Hero: Uses of the Moral Imagination." *Philosophy Today* 42, no. 4 (1998): 386–92.

Merlan, Philip. *Monopsychism, Mysticism, Metaconsciousness: Problems of the Soul in the Neoaristotelian and Neoplatonic Tradition.* The Hague: Nijhoff, 1963.

______. "Aristoteles, Averroes, und die beiden Eckharts." In *Kleine Philosophische Schriften.* Hildescheim and New York: Olms, 1976.

Miller, Fred D. "Aristotle's Philosophy of Perception." *Proceedings of the Boston Area Colloquium in Ancient Philosophy* 15 (1999): 177–213.

Milo, Ronald D. *Aristotle on Practical Knowledge and Weakness of Will.* The Hague: Mouton, 1966.

Minio-Paluello, Lorenzo. *Opuscula: The Latin Aristotle.* Amsterdam: Hakkert, 1972.

Mirus, Christopher V. "Homonymy and the Matter of a Living Body." *Ancient Philosophy* 21 (2001): 357–73.

Modrak, Deborah K. "An Aristotelian Theory of Consciousness?" *Ancient Philosophy* 1 (1981): 160–70.

______. "*Koinē Aisthēsis* and the Discrimination of Sensible Difference in *De anima* iii.2." *Canadian Journal of Philosophy* 11 (1981): 404–23.

______. *Aristotle: The Power of Perception.* Chicago: University of Chicago Press, 1987.

______. "Aristotle on Thinking." In John J. Cleary, ed., *Proceedings of the Boston Area Colloquium in Ancient Philosophy* 3, 209–36. Lanham, Md.: University Press of America, 1987.

______. "Aristotle on the Difference between Mathematics and Physics and First Philosophy." *Apeiron* 22 (1989): 121–39.

______. "Aristotle: Women, Deliberation, and Nature." In Bat-Ami Bar On, ed., *Engendering Origins: Critical Feminist Readings in Plato and Aristotle*, 207–22. Albany: SUNY, Press, 1994.

Moraux, Paul. *Les listes anciennes des ouvrages d'Aristote.* Louvain: Éditions Universitaires, 1951.

______. *Á la recherche de l'Aristote perdu. Le dialogue sur la justice.* Louvain and Paris: Nauwelaerts, 1957.

______. "Le *De anima* dans la tradition grecque. Quelques aspects de l'interprétation du traité, de Théophraste à Themistius." In G. E. R. Lloyd and G. E. L. Owen, eds., *Aristotle on Mind and the Senses: Proceedings of the Seventh Symposium Aristotelicum*, 281–324. Cambridge: Cambridge UP, 1978.

Moraux, Paul, and Jürgen Wiesner, eds. *Zweifelhaftes im Corpus Aristotelicum, Studien zu einigen Dubia. Aktes des 9. Symposium Aristotelicum, Berlin, 7–16. September 1981.* Berlin: W. de Gruyter, 1983.

Moreau, J. "L'idée d'univers dans la pensée antique." *Biblioteca del Giornale di Metafisica* 10 (1953).

Morrison, D. "The Place of Unity in Aristotle's Metaphysical Project." *Proceedings of the Boston Area Colloquium in Ancient Philosophy* 9 (1993): 131–56.

Natali, Carlo. *The Wisdom of Aristotle.* Trans. Gerald Parks. Albany: SUNY Press, 2001.

Nussbaum, Martha C. "Aristotle on Teleological Explanation." In M. C. Nussbaum, ed. and trans., *Aristotle's De motu animalium*, 59–106. Princeton: Princeton UP, 1978.

———. "The *Sumphuton Pneuma* and the *De motu animalium*'s Account of Soul and Body." In M. C. Nussbaum, ed. and trans., *Aristotle's De motu animalium*, 143–64. Princeton: Princeton UP, 1978.

———. "Aristotelian Dualism: Reply to Howard Robinson." *Oxford Studies in Ancient Philosophy* 2 (1984): 197–207.

———. *The Fragility of Goodness: Luck and Ethics in Greek Tragedy and Philosophy.* Cambridge: Cambridge UP, 1986.

———. *Love's Knowledge: Essays on Philosophy and Literature.* New York: Oxford UP, 1990.

———. *The Therapy of Desire: Theory and Practice in Hellenistic Ethics.* Princeton: Princeton UP, 1994.

———. "Patriotism and Cosmopolitanism." In Joshua Cohen, ed., *For Love of Country?*, 3–17. Boston: Beacon Press, 1996.

Nussbaum, Martha C., and Hilary Putnam. "Changing Aristotle's Mind." In Nussbaum and Amélie Oksenberg Rorty, eds., *Essays on Aristotle's De anima*, 27–56.

Nussbaum, Martha C., and Amélie Oksenberg Rorty, eds. *Essays on Aristotle's De anima.* Oxford: Clarendon Press, 1992.

O'Meara, Dominic J., ed. *Studies in Aristotle.* Washington: Catholic UP, 1981.

Osborne, C. "Aristotle, *De anima* 3, 2: How Do We Perceive That We See and Hear?" *Classical Quarterly* 33 (1983): 401–11.

Ott, Walter. "A Troublesome Passage in Aristotle's *Nicomachean Ethics* iii 5." *Ancient Philosophy* 20, no. 1 (2000): 99–107.

Owen, G. E. L. "*Tithenai ta phainomena.*" *Aristote et le problèmes de méthode*, 83–103. Louvain: Éditions de l'Institut Supérieur de Philosophie, 1961.

———. "The Platonism of Aristotle." *Proceedings of the British Academy* 50 (1965): 125–50.

Owens, J. "Teleology of Nature in Aristotle." *Monist* 52 (1968): 159–73.

———. "Aristotle: Cognition a Way of Being." *Canadian Journal of Philosophy* 6 (1976), 1–11. Reprinted in John R. Catan, ed., *Aristotle: The Collected Papers of Joseph Owens*, 74–80. Albany: SUNY Press, 1981.

———. *The Doctrine of Being in the Aristotelian Metaphysics: A Study in the Greek Background of Mediaeval Thought.* Toronto: Pontifical Institute of Medieval Studies, 1978.

———. "Aristotle on Common Sensibles and Incidental Perception." *Phoenix* 36 (1982): 215–36.

Page, C. "Predicating Forms of Matter in Aristotle's Metaphysics." *Review of Metaphysics* 39 (1985): 57–82.

Pakaluk, Michael. *Aristotle: Nicomachean Ethics Books VIII and IX.* Oxford: Clarendon Press, 1998.

Panayides, Christos. "Aristotle on the Priority of Actuality in Substance." *Ancient Philosophy* 19 (1999): 327–44.

Pangle, Lorraine Smith. *Aristotle and the Philosophy of Friendship.* Cambridge: Cambridge UP, 2003.

Payne, Andrew. "Character and the Forms of Friendship in Aristotle." *Apeiron* 33, no. 1 (2000): 53–74.

Pépin, Jean. *Idées grecques sur l'homme et sur dieu.* Paris: Les Belles-Lettres, 1971.

Perricone, Christopher. "The Body and Aristotle's Idea of Moral Virtue." *Dialogos* 35, no. 75 (2000): 111–22.

Peters, F. E. *Aristoteles Arabus: The Oriental Translations and Commentaries on the Aristotelian Corpus.* Leiden: Brill, 1968.

______. *Aristotle and the Arabs. The Aristotelian Tradition in Islam.* New York: NYU Press, 1968.

Peterson, Sandra. "'Horos' (Limit) in Aristotle's *Nicomachean Ethics,*" *Phronesis* 33 (1988): 233–50.

Philoponus, John. *On Aristotle on the Intellect (De anima 3.4–8).* Trans. W. Charlton. Ithaca, N.Y.: Cornell UP, 1991.

______. *On Aristotle on the Soul 3.1–8.* Trans. W. Charlton. Ithaca, N.Y.: Cornell UP, 2000.

______. *On Aristotle on the Soul 3.9–13.* Trans. W. Charlton. Ithaca, N.Y.: Cornell UP, 2000.

______. *On Aristotle on the Soul 2.1–6.* Trans. W. Charlton. Ithaca, N.Y.: Cornell UP, 2005.

______. *On Aristotle on the Soul 2.7–12.* Trans. W. Charlton. Ithaca, N.Y.: Cornell University Press, 2005.

______. *On Aristotle on the Soul 1.3–5.* Trans. Philip van der Eijk. London: Duckworth, 2006.

Pizzolato, Luigi. *L'idea di amicizia nel mondo antico classico e cristiano.* Turin: Einaudi, 1993.

Politis, Vasilis. "Aristotle's Advocacy of Non-Productive Action." *Ancient Philosophy* 18 (1998): 353–79.

______. "Aristotle's Account of the Intellect as Pure Capacity." *Ancient Philosophy* 21 (2001): 375–402.

Price, A. W. *Love and Friendship in Plato and Aristotle.* New York: Oxford UP, 1989.

Radice, Roberto. *La Metafisica di Aristotele nel XX secolo.* Milan: Vita e Pensiero, 1996.

Rasmussen, Douglas B., and Douglas J. Den Uyl. *Liberty and Nature: An Aristotelian Defense of Liberal Order.* La Salle, Ill.: Open Court, 1991.

Reale, Giovanni. *Il concetto di filosofia prima e l'unità della Metafisica di Aristotele.* Milan: Vita e Pensiero, 1961.

______. *Saggezza antica. Terapia per il mali dell'uomo d'oggi.* Milan: Cortina, 1995.

Reeve, C. D. C. *Practices of Reason: Aristotle's Nicomachean Ethics.* Oxford: Oxford UP, 1992.

Rese, Friederike. *Praxis und Logos bei Aristoteles. Handlung, Vernunft und Rede in* Nikomachischer Ethik, Rhetorik *und* Politik. Tübingen: Mohr Siebeck, 2003.

Richardson Lear, Gabriel. *Happy Lives and the Highest Good: An Essay on Aristotle's* Nicomachean Ethics. Princeton: Princeton UP, 2004.

Ricoeur, Paul. "À la gloire de la *phronèsis.*" In Jean-Yves Chateau, ed., *La vérité pratique: Éthique à Nicomaque Livre VI,* 13–22. Paris: Vrin, 1997.

Rist, John. "Notes on *De anima* 3.5." *Classical Philology* 61 (1966): 8–20.

Roche, Timothy. "*Ergon* and *Eudaimonia* in *Nicomachean Ethics* I: Reconsidering the Intellectualist Interpretation." *Journal of the History of Philosophy* 26 (1988): 175–94.

———. "On the Alleged Metaphysical Foundation of Aristotle's *Ethics.*" *Ancient Philosophy* 8 (1988): 49–62.

———. "In Defense of an Alternative View of the Foundation of Aristotle's Moral Theory." *Phronesis* 37 (1992): 46–84.

Roche, Timothy, ed. *Aristotle's Ethics: The Southern Journal of Philosophy, Spindel Conference,* Supp. 27 (1988).

Rodrigo, Pierre. *Aristote. Une philosophie pratique: praxis, politique at bonheur.* Paris: Vrin, 2006.

Rorty, Amélie Oksenberg. "The Place of Pleasure in Aristotle's *Ethics.*" *Mind* 83 (1974): 481–93.

Rorty, Amélie Oksenberg, ed. *Essays on Aristotle's Ethics.* Berkeley: University of California Press, 1980.

Rosen, Stanley. "Thought and Touch: A Note on Aristotle's *De anima.*" *Phronesis* 6 (1961): 127–37.

Ross, W. D. *Aristotle's Metaphysics.* Oxford: Clarendon Press, 1924.

———. *Aristotelis fragmenta selecta.* Oxford: Clarendon Press, 1955.

———. *Aristotle, De anima.* Oxford: Clarendon Press, 1961.

Rowe, C. J. *The* Eudemian *and* Nicomachean Ethics*: A Study in the Development of Aristotle's Thought.* Cambridge: Cambridge Philological Society, 1971.

Salkever, Stephen G. *Finding the Mean: Theory and Practice in Aristotelian Political Philosophy.* Princeton: Princeton UP, 1994.

Sallis, John. *Platonic Legacies.* Albany: SUNY Press, 2004.

Salomon, Max. *Der Begriff der Gerechtigkeit bei Aristoteles.* Leiden: Sijthoff, 1937. Reprint, New York: Arno, 1979.

———. "Le droit naturel chez Aristote." *Archives de Philosophie du Droit et de Sociologie Juridique* 7, nos. 3–4 (1937): 120–7.

———. "Der Begriff des Naturrechts in der *Grossen Ethik.*" *Archiv für Rechts- und Sozialphilosophie* 41 (1954–5): 422–35.

Santas, Gerasimos X. *Goodness and Justice: Plato, Aristotle, and the Moderns.* Oxford: Blackwell, 2001.

Sauvé-Meyer, Susan. *Aristotle on Moral Responsibility: Character and Cause.* Oxford: Blackwell, 1993.

Scaltsas, Theodore. "Reciprocal Justice in Aristotle's *Nicomachean Ethics.*" *Archiv für Geschichte der Philosophie* 77 (1995): 248–62.

Schiller, J. "Aristotle and the Concept of Awareness in Sense-Perception." *Journal of the History of Philosophy* 13 (1975): 283–96.

Schmitt, Charles B. *A Critical Survey and Bibliography of Studies on Renaissance Aristotelianism.* Padova: Antenore, 1971.

______. *Aristotle and the Renaissance.* Cambridge, Mass.: Harvard UP, 1983.
______. *The Aristotelian Tradition and Renaissance Universities.* London: Variorum Reprints, 1984.
Schollmeier, Paul. *Other Selves: Aristotle on Personal and Political Friendship.* Albany: SUNY Press, 1994.
Schütrumpf, Eckart. *Die Bedeutung des Wortes ethos in der Poetik des Aristoteles.* München: Beck, 1970.
______. *Die Analyse der polis durch Aristoteles.* Amsterdam: Grüner, 1980.
______. "Magnanimity, *Megalopsuchia,* and the System of Aristotle's *Nicomachean Ethics.*" *Archiv für Geschichte der Philosophie* 71 (1989): 10–22.
Scott, Dominic. "Aristotle on Well-Being and Intellectual Contemplation: Primary and Secondary *Eudaimonia.*" *Aristotelian Society,* supp. vol. 73 (1999): 225–42.
Sellars, Wilfrid. "Substance and Form in Aristotle." *Journal of Philosophy* 54 (1957): 688–99.
Severino, Emanuele. *Aristotele. Il principio di non contraddizione. Libro quarto della Metafisica.* Brescia: La Scuola, 1959.
Sharpels, R., ed. *Whose Aristotle? Whose Aristotelianism?* Burlington: Ashgate, 2001.
Sherman, Nancy. *The Fabric of Character: Aristotle's Theory of Virtue.* Oxford: Clarendon Press, 1989.
______. *Making a Virtue of Necessity: Aristotle and Kant on Virtue.* Cambridge: Cambridge UP, 1997.
______. "Is the Ghost of Aristotle Haunting Freud's House?" *Proceedings of the Boston Area Colloquium in Ancient Philosophy* 16 (2000): 63–81.
Sherman, Nancy, ed. *Aristotle's Ethics: Critical Essays.* Lanham, Md: Rowman and Littlefield, 1999.
Shields, C. "The Generation of Form in Aristotle." *History of Philosophy Quarterly* 7 (1990): 367–90.
______. "The Homonymy of the Body in Aristotle." *Archiv für Geschiche der Philosophie* 75 (1993): 1–30.
Sim, May. *The Crossroads of Norm and Nature: Essays on Aristotle's Ethics and Metaphysics.* Lanham, Md.: Rowman and Littlefield, 1995.
Simplicius. *On Aristotle On the Soul 1.1–2.4.* Trans. J. O. Urmson and Peter Lautner. Ithaca, N.Y.: Cornell UP, 1995.
______. *On Aristotle On the Soul 2.5–12.* Trans. C. Steel. Ithaca, N.Y.: Cornell UP, 1997.
______. *On Aristotle On the Soul 3.1–5.* Trans. H. J. Blumenthal. Ithaca, N.Y.: Cornell UP, 2000.
Sisko, John. "Space, Time, and Phantasms in Aristotle, *De memoria* 2, 452b7–25." *Classical Quarterly* 47 (1997): 167–75.
______. "On Separating the Intellect from the Body: Aristotle's *De anima* iii.4, 429a10–b5." *Archiv für Geschichte der Philosophie* 81 (1999): 249–67.
______. "Aristotle's *Nous* and the Modern Mind." *Proceedings of the Boston Area Colloquium in Ancient Philosophy* 16 (2000): 177–98.
Smith, J. A. "*Tode ti* in Aristotle." *Classical Review* 35 (1921): 19.
Sorabji, Richard. "Aristotle, Mathematics, and Colour." *Classical Quarterly* 22 (1972): 293–308.
______. *Aristotle on Memory.* Providence: Brown UP, 1972.

———. "From Aristotle to Brentano: The Development of the Concept of Intentionality." In Henry Blumenthal and Howard Robinson, eds., *Aristotle and the Later Tradition. Oxford Studies in Ancient Philosophy*, supp. vol., 227–59. Oxford: Oxford UP, 1991.

Sorabji, Richard, ed. *Aristotle Transformed: The Ancient Commentators and Their Influence.* Ithaca, N.Y.: Cornell UP, 1990.

Sparshott, Francis. *Taking Life Seriously: A Study of the Argument of the* Nicomachean Ethics. Toronto: University of Toronto Press, 1994.

Steenberghen, F. van. *Aristote en Occident: les origines de l'aristotélisme parisien.* Louvain: Éditions de l'Institut Supérieur de Philosophie, 1946.

Stenzel, Julius. *Studien zur Entwicklung der Platonischen Dialektik von Sokrates zu Aristoteles.* Darmstadt: Wissenschaftliche Buchgesellschaft, 1974.

Stern-Gillet, Suzanne. *Aristotle's Philosophy of Friendship.* Albany: SUNY Press, 1995.

Strauss, Leo. *Persecution and the Art of Writing.* Chicago: University of Chicago Press, 1988.

Suits, Bernard. "Aristotle on the Function of Man." *Canadian Journal of Philosophy* 4 (1974): 23–40.

Taylor, C. C. W. "Pleasure: Aristotle's Response to Plato." In Robert Heinaman, ed., *Plato and Aristotle's Ethics*, 1–20. Aldershot: Ashgate, 2003.

Telfer, Elizabeth. "The Unity of Moral Virtues in Aristotle's *Nicomachean Ethics.*" *Proceedings of the Aristotelian Society* 91 (1989–90): 35–48.

Tessitore, Aristide. *Reading Aristotle's Ethics: Virtue, Rhetoric, and Political Philosophy.* Albany: SUNY Press, 1996.

Theiler, Willy. *Zur Geschichte der teleologischen Naturbetrachtung bis auf Aristoteles.* Zürich: Hoenn, 1924.

———. *De anima: Über die Seele.* Berlin: Akademie-Verlag, 1959.

Tracy, Theodore. "The Soul/Boatman Analogy in Aristotle's *De anima.*" *Classical Philology* 77 (1982): 97–112.

Tugendhat, Ernst. Ti kata tinos: *Eine Untersuchung zu Struktur und Ursprung aristotelischer Grundbegriffe.* Freiburg: Alber, 1982.

Tuozzo, Thomas. "Contemplation, the Noble, and the Mean: The Standard of Moral Virtue in Aristotle's *Ethics.*" R. Bosley, In R. Shiner, and J. Sisson, eds., *Aristotle, Virtue and the Mean,* 129–54. Edmonton, Canada: Academic Printing and Publishing, 1995.

Turnbull, Robert G. "The Role of the Special Sensibles in the Perception Theories of Plato and Aristotle." In P. K. Machamer and R. G. Turnbull, eds., *Studies in Perception: Interrelations in the History of Philosophy and Science,* 3–26. Columbus: Ohio State UP, 1978.

Urmson, J. O. "Aristotle on Pleasure." In J. M. E. Moravcsik, ed., *Aristotle: A Collection of Critical Essays,* 323–33. Garden City, N.Y.: Anchor Books, 1967.

———. *Aristotle's Ethics.* Oxford: Blackwell, 1988.

Vegetti, Mario. *Il coltello e lo stilo.* Milan: Il Saggiatore, 1979.

Verbeke, G. "Aristotle's Metaphysics Viewed by the Ancient Greek Commentators." In D. J. O'Meara, ed., *Studies in Aristotle,* 107–27. Washington: Catholic UP, 1981.

Vergnières, Solange. *Éthique et politique chez Aristote.* Paris: PUF, 1995.

Volpi, Franco. "Che cosa significa neoaristotelismo? La riabilitazione della filosofia pratica e il suo senso nella crisi della modernità." In Enrico Berti, ed., *Tradizione e attualità della filosofia pratica*, 111–35. Genova: Marietti, 1988.

Vuillemin, Jules. *De la logique à la théologie. Cinq études sur Aristote.* Paris: Flammarion, 1967.

Walsh, James. *Aristotle's Conception of Moral Weakness.* New York: Columbia UP, 1963.

______. *Aristotle's Ethics: Issues and Interpretations.* Belmont, Calif.: Wadsworth, 1967.

Walzer, Richard. *Greek into Arabic.* Cambridge, Mass.: Harvard UP, 1962.

Ward, Julie K., ed. *Feminism and Ancient Philosophy.* New York: Routledge, 1996.

Wartelle, André. *Inventaire des manuscrits grecs d'Aristote et de ses commentateurs.* Paris: Les Belles-Lettres, 1963.

Watson, G. "*Phantasia* in Aristotle, *De anima* 3.3." *Classical Quarterly* 32 (1982): 100–13.

Webb, P. "Bodily Structure and Psychic Faculties in Aristotle's Theory of Perception." *Hermes* 110 (1982): 25–50.

Wedin, Michael V. "Keeping the Matter in Mind: Aristotle on the Passions and the Soul." *Pacific Philosophical Quarterly* 76 (1995): 183–221.

______. "Aristotle on How to Define a Psychological State." *Topoi* 15 (1996): 11–24.

______. *Mind and Imagination in Aristotle.* New Haven: Yale UP, 1998.

______. "The Scope of Non-Contradiction: A Note on Aristotle's 'Elenctic' Proof in *Metaphysics* Gamma 4." *Apeiron* 32 (1999): 231–42.

White, Kevin. "The Meaning of *Phantasia* in Aristotle's *De anima*, III, 3–8." *Dialogue* 24 (1985): 483–505.

White, Nicholas. *Individual and Conflict in Greek Ethics.* Oxford: Oxford UP, 2002.

White, Stephen A. *Sovereign Virtue: Aristotle on the Relation between Happiness and Prosperity.* Stanford, Calif.: Stanford UP, 1992.

Whiting, Jennifer. "Form and Individuation in Aristotle." *History of Philosophy Quarterly* 3 (1986): 359–77.

______. "Human Nature and Intellectualism in Aristotle." *Archiv für Geschichte der Philosophie* 68 (1986): 70–95.

______. "Aristotle's Function Argument: A Defense." *Ancient Philosophy* 8 (1988): 33–48.

______. "Impersonal Friends." *Monist* 75 (1991): 3–29.

______. "Self-Love and Authoritative Virtue: Prolegomenon to a Kantian Reading of *Eudemian Ethics* viii.3." In S. Engstrom and J. Whiting, eds., *Aristotle, Kant, and the Stoics: Rethinking Happiness and Duty*, 162–99. New York: Cambridge UP, 1996.

Williams, Bernard. *Ethics and the Limits of Philosophy.* Cambridge, Mass: Harvard UP, 1985.

______. "Hylomorphism." *Oxford Studies in Ancient Philosophy* 4 (1986): 189–99.

Witt, Charlotte. "Aristotelian Perceptions." *Proceedings of the Boston Area Colloquium in Ancient Philosophy* 12 (1996): 310–16.

Yack, Bernard. "Natural Right and Aristotle's Understanding of Justice." *Political Theory* 18, no. 2 (May 1990): 216–37.

———. *The Problems of a Political Animal: Community, Justice, and Conflict in Aristotelian Political Thought.* Berkeley: University of California Press, 1993.

Young, Charles. "Aristotle on Temperance." *Philosophical Review* 97 (1988): 521–42.

Zanetti, Gianfrancesco. *La nozione di giustizia in Aristotele.* Bologna: Il Mulino, 1993.

———. *Amicizia, felicità, diritto. Due argomenti sul perfezionismo giuridico.* Rome: Carocci, 1998.

———. *Ragion pratica e diritto: un percorso aristotelico/Practical Reason and Law: An Aristotelian Itinerary.* Milan: Giuffrè, 2001.

Index of Passages

Index of Subjects and Names

CPSIA information can be obtained
at www.ICGtesting.com
Printed in the USA
LVHW112126120821
695175LV00004B/30

9 781107 400511